Dreyfus Protests His Innocence at the Second Court-Martial at Rennes (*Petit Journal*, August 20, 1899)

The Dreyfus Case

A Documentary History

The Dreyfus Case

A Documentary History

Louis L. Snyder

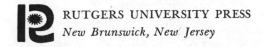

RUTGERS UNIVERSITY PRESS
New Brunswick, New Jersey

I wish to express my appreciation not only to the scores of librarians who helped me in the search for germane material but especially to my wife, who carefully watched over the entire project and contributed many original ideas.

L. L. S.

Library of Congress Cataloging in Publication Data

Snyder, Louis Leo, 1907–
    The Dreyfus case: a documentary history.

    1. Dreyfus, Alfred, 1859–1935. I. Title.
DC354.S6   944.081′092′4 [B]   72–4200
ISBN 0–8135–0741–3

This Book Is Dedicated to
Alfred A. Knopf
Gentleman, Scholar, Doyen of American
Publishers, and Friend
to the Entire Brotherhood of Historians

"The lie was dead
And damned, and truth stood up instead."
Robert Browning

Contents

Chapter XI. Finale: Vindication and Rehabilitation   345

Chapter XII. The Dreyfus Case in History   387

Index   395

Illustrations

Chronology of the Dreyfus Case

1847

December 16   Marie-Charles-Ferdinand Walsin-Esterhazy born in Paris.

1859

October 9   Alfred Dreyfus born at Mulhouse in Alsace.

1893

January 1   Dreyfus assigned as Probationer-Officer to the General Staff in Paris.

December 3   General Auguste Mercier appointed Minister of War.

1894

March 14   New Field Artillery Manual issued.

May 17   General Staff Probationer-Officers excluded from participation in maneuvers.

May 20–25   Esterhazy attends Artillery Brigade Cadre Training course.

July 20   Esterhazy appears for the first time at the German Embassy and offers Military Attaché Maximilian von Schwartzkoppen his services.

July 21   Letter from Esterhazy reaches Schwartzkoppen; it concerned a forthcoming journey and information about Russia.

July 27   Esterhazy visits Schwartzkoppen again and asks 2,000 francs a month for his services.

August 5–12   Esterhazy attends artillery exercises near Châlons.

August 13   Esterhazy's third visit to the German Embassy.

August 15   Schwartzkoppen pays Esterhazy 1,000 francs for plans on the mobilization of the artillery.

September 1   The *bordereau* arrives at the German Embassy.

September 6   Esterhazy leaves at the German Embassy papers concerning the planned expedition to Madagascar.

Mid-September   The *bordereau* is stolen and delivered to the Fourth
                    Bureau.
October 6   The name of Dreyfus is mentioned for the first time
                    as the possible writer of the *bordereau*.
October 11   Mercier informs the Minister President, the Minister
                    for Foreign Affairs, and the Chief of the General
                    Staff that he is on the trail of the traitor.
October 13   Alfred Gobert, handwriting expert of the Bank of
                    France, refuses to ascribe the *bordereau* to Dreyfus.
                    Mercier invites Dreyfus to the Ministry of War for an
                    interview the following Monday.
                    Alphonse Bertillon, Chief of the Judicial Identifica-
                    tion Department of the Paris Police Prefecture,
                    names Dreyfus as the writer of the *bordereau*.
October 14   Mercier signs order for arrest of Dreyfus.
                    Lieutenant-Colonel du Paty de Clam conducts the first
                    investigation of Dreyfus.
                    Major Ferdinand Forzinetti, Director of Military Pris-
                    ons, is given special orders for handling the prisoner.
October 15   Dreyfus is arrested.
October 29   *La Libre Parole,* anti-Semitic newspaper, tipped off by
                    Major Henry, hints at investigation of treason.
October 31   Du Paty de Clam ends his interrogation of Dreyfus.
                    The Havas Agency announces that an officer has been
                    arrested for high treason.
November 1   *La Libre Parole* mentions Dreyfus as the traitor.
November 2   Major Panizzardi, Italian Military Attaché in Paris,
                    sends telegram to Rome denying any relations with
                    Dreyfus.
November 3   Major d'Ormescheville begins preliminary inquiry.
December 3   Major d'Ormescheville submits his report.
December 4   Military court-martial is ordered.
                    Dreyfus permitted to communicate with his family for
                    the first time since his arrest.
December 19–22   The court-martial of Dreyfus is held in secret in Paris.
December 22   Dreyfus is condemned by unanimous vote and sen-
                    tenced to transportation for life.
December 31   Denial of appeal against the verdict.
                    Du Paty de Clam visits Dreyfus.

1895

January 5   Military degradation of Dreyfus.
January 15   M. Casimir-Périer, President of the Republic, resigns.

January 18   Dreyfus is brought to the *Île de Ré.*

February 21   Dreyfus sails for Devil's Island.

April 13   Dreyfus is placed in specially constructed prison camp on Devil's Island.

July 1   Major Picquart is named Chief of the Intelligence Bureau.

1896

March   Picquart discovers the *petit bleu.*

March 19   Schwartzkoppen waives Esterhazy's service.

April 6   Picquart promoted to Lieutenant-Colonel.

August 5   Picquart reports Esterhazy to General Raoul-François-Charles Le Mouton de Boisdeffre, Chief of the General Staff.

End of August   Picquart discovers Esterhazy as author of the *bordereau.*

September   False report of Dreyfus's escape from Devil's Island.

Picquart informs General Charles-Arthur Gonse, Acting Chief of Staff, about Esterhazy and submits to him a written report.

September 8   Colonial Minister André Lebon orders Dreyfus placed in chains (until October 20).

September 15   Revelations in *L'Éclair:* article on "The Traitor."

September 18   Mme. Dreyfus petitions for a revision of the trial of her husband.

October 26   Picquart ordered to duty in North Africa.

November 2   Henry's falsification reaches the War Ministry.

November 6   Bernard-Lazare publishes his pamphlet, "A Judicial Error," in Brussels.

November 10   *Le Matin* publishes the *bordereau* in facsimile.

November 14   Picquart leaves the Intelligence Bureau and two days later departs for "detached service" in Africa, a tour of duty lasting two months.

December   Henry adds further forged documents to Picquart's *dossier.*

1897

January 6   Picquart is attached to the 4th Algerian regiment of *tirailleurs.*

April 2   Picquart draws up a testament to be added to his will: addressed to the President of the Republic, it was a memorandum on the matter of Dreyfus-Esterhazy and was to be delivered in the event of his death.

May 18   Picquart writes a letter of protest to Major Henry.

May 31   Henry replies with a threatening letter.

June 29   Picquart hands his material to the lawyer Maître
                Leblois.

July 13   Leblois discloses Picquart's material to M. Auguste
                Scheurer-Kestner, Vice President of the Senate.

July 14   Scheurer-Kestner informs his colleagues that he be-
                lieves Dreyfus innocent.

August 17   Picquart is retired from the Army.

October 18   Esterhazy called back to Paris by General Staff.

October 20 on   Esterhazy and General Staff in collusion to avoid his
                conviction.

October 23   Esterhazy visits Schwartzkoppen for the last time.

October 29   Esterhazy's first letter to the President of the Republic.

October 31   Esterhazy's second letter to the President of the Re-
                public.

November 2   Schwartzkoppen recalled.

November 5   Esterhazy's third letter to the President of the Re-
                public.

November 7   Esterhazy sends a threatening letter to Picquart.

November 10   Forged telegrams "Speranza" and "Blanche" sent to
                Picquart.

November 15   Mathieu Dreyfus denounces Esterhazy in an open let-
                ter to the President of the Republic.

                Esterhazy requests an inquiry to be made by General
                de Pellieux.

                Schwartzkoppen leaves Paris.

November 19   Picquart recalled to Paris.

November 26   Picquart returns to Paris.

November 28   *Le Figaro* publishes Esterhazy's private letters to Mme.
                de Boulancy.

                Publication of the "Uhlan Letter."

December 2   Esterhazy demands a court-martial.

December 13   Zola publishes his "Letter to Youth."

December 24   Experts Belhomme, Couard, and Varinard declare
                that Esterhazy did not write the *bordereau*.

December 31   Major Ravary completes his investigation of Esterhazy
                and finds no grounds for prosecution.

                              1898

January 2   General Felix-Gaston Saussier, Governor of Paris, or-
                ders court-martial for Esterhazy.

January 7   *Le Siècle* publishes the report by Major d'Ormesche-
                 ville.

January 10   First session of the Esterhazy court-martial, only par-
                 tially public.

January 11   Esterhazy is acquitted; greeted by cries: "Long Live
                 the Army!" "Down with the Jews!"

January 13   Letter from Émile Zola, "J'Accuse," to the President
                 of the Republic published in *L'Aurore*.
                 Picquart is arrested and sent to fortress of Mont-
                 Valérien.

January 18   The Minister of War brings suit against Zola and
                 L'Aurore.

January 19   *Le Siècle* begins publication of Dreyfus's *Letters of an
                 Innocent*.

January 22   Interpellation by M. Cavaignac in the Chamber of
                 Deputies.

January 24   Bülow states before the Reichstag that the German
                 Embassy never had relations with Dreyfus.

February 1   Officers' Board of Inquiry recommends that Picquart
                 be prepared for resignation "because of severe fail-
                 ures in duty."

February 7   Zola's trial begins before the *Cour d'Assises*.

February 17   General de Pellieux as witness designates the Henry
                 forgery as "absolute proof" of Dreyfus's guilt.

February 18   General de Boisdeffre substantiates de Pellieux's testi-
                 mony.

February 20   Founding of the League of the Rights of Man.

February 23   Zola sentenced to one year in prison and 3,000 francs
                 fine; Perrenx, editor of *L'Aurore*, receives four
                 months imprisonment and 3,000 francs fine.

February 24   Minister President Méline threatens special laws
                 against the Dreyfusards.
                 Debate in the Chamber of Deputies.

February 26   Picquart is dismissed from the Army.
                 Duel between Clemenceau and Drumont.

February 28   Mme. Dreyfus is refused permission to visit her hus-
                 band.

March 5   Duel between Picquart and Henry.

April 2   The Court of Cassation annuls decision condemning
                 Zola.

April 8   The court-martial charges Zola and Perrenx.

April 11   Zola and *L'Aurore* are re-summoned.

April 12 and 15   Esterhazy does not prosecute either *Le Siècle* or other newspapers.

May 15   Rumors that General Staff possesses a photograph of Picquart in conversation with Schwartzkoppen.

May 23   Zola is prosecuted at Versailles; he applies for suspension of trial.

June 4   First meeting of the League of the Rights of Man.

June 15   Fall of the Méline ministry.

June 16   Zola's appeal is rejected.

June 18 and 22   Ministerial crisis.

June 28   Beginning of Brisson ministry; Cavaignac becomes War Minister.

July 8   Cavaignac speaks to the Chamber of Deputies, reads the forged Henry document, and bases his conviction of Dreyfus's guilt on it.

July 9   Picquart protests to Cavaignac that he has used a forged document.

July 12   Esterhazy is placed under arrest.

July 13   Picquart is arrested and prosecuted for facts brought against him in February.

July 18   Versailles court finds Zola guilty.

July 19   Zola flees to England.

July 23   Zola's name is stricken from the rolls of the Legion of Honor.

August 13   Henry's forgery discovered.

August 24   Esterhazy appears before the Court of Inquiry.

August 30   Henry is arrested and placed in the fortress at Mont-Valérien.

August 31   Suicide of Henry.
Esterhazy is cashiered.
General Boisdeffre resigns.

September 1   Esterhazy flees from France.

September 3   War Minister Cavaignac resigns.
Mme. Dreyfus petitions for an appeal.

September 5   General Zurlinden becomes Minister of War.

September 12   Du Paty de Clam is removed from active service and retires on half pay.

September 17   General Zurlinden resigns.
Chanoine becomes Minister of War.

September 20   The new Minister of War brings charges against Picquart.

September 25	Esterhazy states for first time that he had written the *bordereau* on command of Colonel Sandherr.
October 31	Dupuy forms a new cabinet.
November 7	Reinach accuses Henry of being Esterhazy's accomplice.
November 24	Picquart is brought before a court-martial.
November 25	Minister of War Chanoine resigns.
December 2	Picquart demands a change of venue.

1899

January 8	M. Quesnay de Beaurepaire, President of the Civil Chamber of the Court of Cassation, resigns and is succeeded by Ballot-Beaupre.
January 15	The subscription for Henry's widow is closed. *La Libre Parole* announces that it has received 131,-000 francs for Henry's widow to use in her battle against Reinach.
January 27	Prosecution of Reinach by Mme. Henry for defamation of her husband's memory.
January 30	Justice Minister Lebret lays before the Chamber a proposal of an act of disqualification.
February 10	The proposal is passed in the Chamber by a vote of 324 to 207.
February 16	Death of President of the Republic Félix Faure.
February 18	Émile Loubet is elected President of the Republic.
March 1	The "Law of Disqualification" considered by the Senate.
March 3	The Court of Cassation admits the assignment demanded by Picquart.
March 21	The full bench of the Court of Cassation begins investigation of the secret *dossier*.
March 31	Publication of the inquiry made by the Criminal Court.
May 5	War Minister de Freycinet resigns; Kranze becomes his successor.
May 29	Beginning of deliberations of Court of Cassation.
June 3	The Court of Cassation sets aside the 1894 decision condemning Dreyfus and refers the matter to a new court-martial at Rennes.
June 5	Zola returns to France.
June 9	Dreyfus leaves Guiana for France on the cruiser *Sfax*. Picquart is freed.

June 12   The Deputy cabinet resigns.

June 22   New cabinet is formed with Waldeck-Rousseau as Premier and General de Galliffet as Minister of War.

June 30   Dreyfus lands at Port-Houliguen and during the night of July 1 is taken to the military prison at Rennes.

August 9–11   The court sits in secret session.

August 12   Second public session: General Mercier confronted by Dreyfus.

August 14   Attempt to assassinate Maître Labori.

                 Clash between Mercier and former President Casimir-Périer at Rennes court-martial.

August 16   Story of Dreyfus's sufferings on Devil's Island; testimony of M. Lebon, former Minister of Colonies.

August 17–18   Picquart supports Dreyfus in testimony as witness.

August 19   Three enemies of Dreyfus, Major Cuignet, General de Boisdeffre, and General Gonse testify.

August 21   Dreyfus replies to his accusers.

August 22   M. Labori resumes his defense of Dreyfus.

August 23   General Gonse grilled by M. Labori.

August 24   Lawyers attack testimony of the generals.

August 25   "Expert" Bertillon attacks Dreyfus.

August 26   General Mercier on the stand.

August 28   The evidence of M. Bertillon is ridiculed by witnesses.

August 29   Testimony by former Minister of War M. de Freycinet.

August 30   Esterhazy accused by four witnesses.

August 31   Dreyfus breaks down under the strain.

September 1–2   Additional testimony for Dreyfus.

September 4   Conflicting testimony in the courtroom.

September 5   Appeals to Emperor William II and King Humbert.

September 6   M. Labori threatens to withdraw from the case.

September 7   President Jouaust refuses to take evidence of the German and Italian Military Attachés.

September 8   Summations by counsel.

September 9   Dreyfus re-condemned by vote of five to two "with extenuating circumstances."

September 15   Dreyfus decides not to appeal the verdict.

September 19   Dreyfus is pardoned.

September 21   De Galliffet's Order of the Day: "The incident is closed."

November 17   The Government proposes a general amnesty on the case.

1900

January 28	General Mercier is elected to the Senate.
May 5	In the Parisian elections the Nationalists win a majority.
May 22	The Chamber of Deputies demands that the Government energetically oppose any revival of the case.
May 28	Resignation of War Minister de Galliffett. André succeeds him.
December 27	Amnesty Bill, stopping all suits and prosecutions arising out of the Dreyfus case, comes into effect.

1901

May 1	Dreyfus publishes his book, *Five Years of My Life*.

1902

June 10	The Combes Ministry takes office.
September 30	Death of Zola in a tragic home accident.

1903

April 6	Jean Jaurés demands in the Chamber of Deputies an investigation of the "annotated *bordereau*."
May–October	Inquiry by André's cabinet.
October 19	Andre's report on the results of his inquiry.
November 26	Dreyfus petitions for a revision.
December 24	The Committee on Appeal of the Ministry of Justice unanimously favors appeal.
	The case is laid before the Court of Cassation.

1904

March 3	Proceedings begin before the Criminal Division of the Court of Cassation.
March 5	The Criminal Court orders a new inquiry.
November 15	Resignation of André.

1906

June 18	Deliberations of the Court of Cassation.
July 12	By unanimous vote the Court of Cassation sets aside the Rennes court-martial judgment and orders rehabilitation of Dreyfus.

July 13   Act passed to reinstate Dreyfus and Picquart.
                    Dreyfus promoted to Major; Picquart to General.
July 20   Dreyfus is restored to Army in ceremony at the *École Militaire*.
                    Dreyfus made Chevalier of the Legion of Honor.

1907

July 26   Dreyfus applies for retirement from the Army.

1908

June 4   Zola's ashes transferred to the Panthéon.
                    Dreyfus wounded by Gregori, a journalist.

1914

January 19   Death of General Picquart after fall from horse.
August 2   Dreyfus returned to active service.
September 26   Dreyfus promoted to Lieutenant-Colonel.

1923

May 21   Death of Esterhazy in London.

1935

July 11, 1935   Death of Dreyfus in Paris.

Introduction

"I wish that he were innocent," said the fashionable lady to a group of admirers in a Paris *salon*. "Then he would suffer more."

That was the atmosphere of hatred in which the drama of the Dreyfus case unrolled. "The tragic affair," wrote Georges Bernanos, "reveals an inhuman character, preserving amidst the welter of unbridled passions and the flames of hate an inconceivably cold and callous heart."

There was nothing quite like it since the world began. For more than five years the attention of the world was riveted upon an obscure French artillery officer who was stubbornly fighting his way to innocence. How the villain, whose name was Bigotry, was unmasked makes one of the most sensational detective stories of history.

It began near the end of the year 1894. Alfred Dreyfus, a captain attached to the General Staff in Paris, was arrested and accused, on the basis of the handwriting in a document stolen by French agents from the German Embassy in Paris, of selling important military secrets to Germany. Tried *in camera* by court-martial, he was found guilty, sentenced to public degradation, and condemned to solitary confinement on Devil's Island, the notorious convict settlement off the coast of French Guiana. The verdict was, in reality, a sentence to a lingering death.

The complicating factors were that Dreyfus was innocent and he was a Jew. Following the humiliating defeat of 1871, French nationalists sought a scapegoat for the country's troubles. One of the results was the beginning of a vigorous anti-Semitic campaign which became the setting for the Dreyfus Affair.

The case might have been forgotten altogether had not Colonel Georges Picquart, head of the Intelligence Department of the General Staff, become convinced of Dreyfus's innocence and the guilt of another officer. In late 1897 there began a struggle for re-examination of the case. Émile Zola, the distinguished novelist, joined the Dreyfus side with the publication in January 1898 of his famous *J'Accuse* letter. Meanwhile Picquart, who had been exiled to a post in Tunisia, was arrested. When Colonel Hubert Henry, central figure of the cabal against Dreyfus, confessed forgeries of key documents, and then committed suicide, the Court of Appeal ordered an investigation.

xxi

The original sentence was annulled in June 1899. After his years on Devil's Island, the prematurely grey and physically emaciated Dreyfus was brought to Rennes for a second court-martial, again found guilty, and sentenced to ten years' imprisonment due to "extenuating circumstances." But a week later he was pardoned. Eventually, in July 1906, he was acquitted of all charges. He was rehabilitated in a public ceremony at the *École Militaire,* near the scene of his original degradation.

So much for the bare facts. They give little indication of the passions that stirred the hearts of Frenchmen in this their hour of trial. More than the innocence of Alfred Dreyfus was involved. The Affair became a matter of life and death for the Third French Republic. The Jewish captain was caught in the subterranean socio-political forces of his time. Those who seized the cudgel against Dreyfus were not only anti-Semitic but also anti-democratic. Even after it became certain that Dreyfus was not guilty, the military refused to make amends and maintained with all the obstinacy of a monolithic mind that the "honor" of the Army made it necessary that the verdict stand.

Men have been known to oppose the most powerful kings. But few have had the courage to stand up to the multitude, the mob howling for revenge. There was baseness here, but also heroism of a high order. The Dreyfus Affair demonstrated how a small group of honorable men seeking to achieve justice for one individual could triumph over a majority shrieking for vengeance. Frenchmen who were sensitive to the conscience of mankind successfully withstood hostile public opinion. The novelists Émile Zola and Anatole France, the journalist Georges Clemenceau, the statesman Jean Jaurès, the scholar Joseph Reinach, above all the officer Colonel Georges Picquart—these were the heroes who faced the lynchers, stared them down, and helped preserve the institutions of an open society.

For an unhappy France the Dreyfus Affair was a judgment day come before its time. Throughout the case the French people, from the highest elected officials to the men and women on the streets, saw the case pass like a magic mirror reflecting their own souls. Driven apart by hostility and hatred, Frenchmen eventually recovered their sanity and smashed the evil in their midst. The country was rescued almost miraculously from the kind of bestial epidemic that was to engulf the Germans under Adolf Hitler.

If Dreyfus had been merely racked on Devil's Island, he would have been a small wonder to a disinterested world. Here he was, the Little Man, Captain Nobody, catapulted before mankind as a suffering unit of humanity. Just an ordinary man, perhaps a bit too ambitious, intelligent, vain, set apart by his mediocrity. Hannah Arendt calls him a *"parvenu."*

Struck down by catastrophe, by the most serious charge affecting the honor of a military man, he could only cry out his innocence. Tormented and tortured by resentment against unknown foes, he could only scream for justice. And then, incredibly enough, a miracle emerged out of nothingness.

Because there already exists a vast literature on Dreyfus and his ordeal by hate, another book is indicated only if the approach is new and different. An attempt is made here to present the Affair exclusively in terms of documents, using the word in its broader sense, woven together with before-and-after notes. Included are the stenographic reports of the various trials, testimony at investigations, official governmental documents, genuine and falsified pieces in Dreyfus's *dossier*, extracts from autobiographies, letters, and diaries of the principal characters, selections from the hate literature, pamphlets, the enormous newspaper coverage, and editorial commentaries. Students, scholars, and the detective-story aficionados alike can find here the impact of immediacy in such entries as the critical *bordereau*, the *petit bleu*, the complete version of Zola's *J'Accuse* letter, the official German reports in *Die Grosse Politik* with William II's revealing marginal notations, and scores of other pertinent contemporary documents. The reader will find here the story of the individual crushed—without understanding why or how—between the jaws of a relentless governmental power and mass hysteria.

LOUIS L. SNYDER

Princeton, New Jersey
April 1973.

The
Dreyfus
Case

A Documentary
History

I

The First Act: Captain Dreyfus
Walks into Tragedy

The milieu was utterly depressing. France, mighty home of *la gloire*, had been dozing for two decades in the fitful sleep of the badly wounded. Her colors had been trampled in 1870–1871 by the "barbarians from across the Rhine." There was only one way to express that humiliation: "We were betrayed!" Was there any other explanation?

France would one day have her *revanche*. But a close watch must be kept on traitors, especially in the Army and the diplomatic service. It was even more necessary to observe all Germans and Italians in Paris, especially the Military Attachés of those two allied countries. The reckoning with Germany would come one day, but meanwhile keep an eye on all possible traitors.

The country was nearly torn apart by financial scandals connected with the construction of the Panama Canal. In May 1879 an international Congress composed of 135 delegates from various nations convened in Paris under leadership of Ferdinand de Lesseps, to consider plans for the piercing of the isthmus of Panama. The Panama Canal Company was organized with de Lesseps as President. Efforts were made during the next two years to float the company financially. Many Frenchmen invested their hard-earned savings in the project. The work went on for five years, but an extravagant and corrupt management led to bankruptcy. Subsequent investigations disclosed that high public officials were involved in shady operations connected with the project. Even Ministers and members of Parliament were implicated in the scandal. Royalists charged that the

3

Republic had fallen under control of "Panamists" and "grafters."

A wave of anti-Semitism swept through the country when it was revealed that several prominent Jewish politicians were involved in the Panama scandal. Édouard Drumont and his anti-Semitic followers looked upon the Panama scandal as presenting an opportunity for driving the Jews out of French life.

In this atmosphere, superheated by humiliation in defeat, fear of treason, disgust with financial scandals, and revived anti-Semitism, was born the Dreyfus case. The affair turned out to be a reactionary nationalist movement directed outwardly against Germany, inwardly against French Jews—"agents of foreigners," and the socialist "creators of disorder." In the words of Rudolph A. Winnacker, "The Dreyfus Affair merely speeded up a movement in French politics which had been gathering force since the beginning of the last decade of the nineteenth century."

The Beginning: The Incriminating *Bordereau*

". . . I am sending you, Monsieur, some interesting information."

L'Affaire Dreyfus: La revision du procès de Rennes: Débats de la Cour de Cassation, June 15–July 12, 1906, 2 vols. (Paris: Ligue Française pour la défense des droits de l'homme et du citoyen, 1906), vol. I, pp. 22–23. Translated by the editor. Hereafter cited as L'Affaire Dreyfus: La revision du procès de Rennes.

The Dreyfus case began with the *bordereau*, a name given to the official form or covering note for documents enclosed with it. It was supposed to have been addressed to Lieutenant-Colonel Maximilian von Schwartzkoppen, the German Military Attaché in Paris, whose job it was to accumulate as much information as he could on French military matters. The *bordereau*, which was torn across, was unsigned and undated, and was written in ink on thin, transparent paper. There was no envelope.

It was never clearly established how the *bordereau* came into possession of the French authorities. One version had it that Mme. Bastion, a charwoman employed in the German Embassy, had found it in a wastepaper basket in Schwartzkoppen's office and turned it over to a French agent. Another rumor had it that an agent named Brücker purloined the *bordereau* from the loge of the concierge in the Embassy. Schwartzkoppen later stated: "It is evident that the *bordereau* was not found in the wastepaper basket for the simple reason that I never received it. Mme. Bastion or some secret agent must have found it in my letter box in the porter's loge, and, in order to make it appear that it had come out of my wastepaper basket, must have torn it into shreds."

No matter—it was a most important find indicating that someone was supplying military secrets to the Germans.

Although I have no news that you wish to see me, nevertheless I am sending you, *Monsieur,* some interesting information:

1. A note on the hydraulic brake of the 120 mm. gun and the way in which this gun has behaved;

2. A note on the covering troops (some modifications will be made under the new plan);

3. A note on a modification in artillery formations;

4. A note concerning Madagascar;

5. The projected Field Artillery Firing Manual (14 March, 1894).

This last document is extremely difficult to obtain and I can only have it at my disposal for a very few days. The Ministry of War has sent out a fixed number to the various corps concerned, and the corps are responsible for them. Each officer holding one must return it after maneuvers. If, therefore, you wish to take from it whatever is of interest to you, and then keep the original for me, I will take it back, unless you would prefer that I should have it copied *in extenso* and send you the copy.

I am just about to leave for maneuvers.

The *bordereau* turned up in the Statistical Section of the War Ministry offices in the Rue Saint-Dominique on the morning of September 27, 1894. There were only five officers serving in this small office, among them Major Hubert Henry, a career officer who was the first to see the *bordereau.* Sensing its importance, Henry showed it to his superiors. In the ensuing investigation, Colonel Fabre, Chief of the Fourth Bureau, and his assistant, Lieutenant-Colonel d'Aboville, concluded that the document could only have been written by an artillery officer who was at the same time a probationer on the General Staff. D'Aboville commented that there could not be many officers who were familiar with the work of all four departments of the War Ministry and that the only officers who passed regularly through each of these departments were *stagiaires,* or General Staff probationers on a two-year course with six months in each department.

There were only a few such names, including Captain Souriau,

Captain Putz, and Captain Dreyfus. Colonel Fabre commented that the only one of these officers who had an adverse report was Dreyfus.

How Dreyfus Was Selected as the Culprit
"The name Dreyfus was the only one we could think of. . . ."

Le procès Dreyfus devant le Conseil de Guerre de Rennes (August 7–September 9, 1899), *3 vols. (Paris: Stock, 1900), vol. 1, p. 318. Translated by the editor. Hereafter cited as* Rennes: Le procès Dreyfus.

How Dreyfus was designated as the writer of the *bordereau* was described later (August 21, 1899), before the court-martial at Rennes by General Pierre-Elie Fabre, former Chief of the Fourth Bureau of the General Staff (Major Fabre had been promoted to General) in the following testimony. Because of the superficial resemblance between Dreyfus's handwriting and that in the *bordereau,* Fabre's explanation must be taken *cum grano salis.*

On October 6 [1894] Lieutenant-Colonel d'Aboville [Deputy Chief of the Fourth Bureau] returned from his leave. I brought him up-to-date on the matter that had taken place during his absence by showing him the *bordereau* and asking him if he recognized the handwriting. The Lieutenant-Colonel read the *bordereau,* but the writing reminded him of no one. During the reading and discussion of the various details we came to the conclusion that because of the mentioned technical questions on artillery the document could have come only from an artillery officer who was at that time in the Fourth Bureau, that is, an officer assigned to the General Staff. We attempted to remember all the names of artillery officers assigned to the bureau. The name Dreyfus was the only one we could think of who had not made a good impression and who had received a bad report. That did not mean at all that we regarded him as a traitor. We were moved only by curiosity to compare his handwriting with that of the *bordereau.* I took out of my drawer a report of 1893 that he had filled out. We were struck by the fact that there was a similarity in the word *"artillerie"* in this report and in the *bordereau.* In both cases the middle "i" fell well below the other letters.

It is possible but not probable that General Fabre's story was correct. The handwriting of the *bordereau* and that of Dreyfus were quite different. The decision made by the two officers must have been based on other grounds. Apparently, they were quite ready to point at one who seemed to be the perfect scapegoat.

Dreyfus Sketches His Early Life

"Everything in life seemed to smile on me."

Alfred Dreyfus, Five Years of My Life, 1894–1899 (*New York: McClure, 1901*), pp. 1–3. Hereafter cited as Dreyfus, Five Years.

The central figure in the celebrated case was until then an unknown Army officer. Shy and retiring, he was an introvert who was so anxious to perform his duties in a superior manner that he was resented by colleagues. Later he was to be accused of abnormal inquisitiveness; the inference was that he was seeking information for sale to the Germans. Neither by temperament nor disposition was he disposed to ease his way to promotion by drinking bouts and gambling with his superior officers.

In the following sketch of his early life, Dreyfus did not mention that he was a Jew, a vital fact in the course of his career.

I was born at Mulhouse, in Alsace, October 9, 1859. My childhood passed happily amid the gentle influences of mother and sisters, a kind father devoted to his children, and the companionship of older brothers.

My first sorrow was the Franco-Prussian War. It has never faded from my memory. When peace was concluded my father chose the French nationality, and we had to leave Alsace. I went to Paris to continue my studies.

In 1878 I was received at the *École Polytechnique*, which in the usual order of things I left in 1880, to enter, as cadet of artillery, the *École d'Application* of Fontainebleau, where I spent the regulation two years. After graduating, on the 1st of October, 1882, I was breveted lieutenant in the Thirty-first Regiment of Artillery in the garrison at Le Mans. At the end of the year 1883, I was transferred to the Horse Batteries of the First Independent Cavalry Division, at Paris. On the 12th of September, 1889, I received my commission of captain in the Twenty-first Regiment of Artillery, and was appointed on special service at the *École Centrale de Pyrotechnie Militaire* at Bourges. It was in the course of the following winter that I became engaged to Mlle. Lucie Hadamard, my devoted and heroic wife.

During my engagement I prepared myself for the *École Supérieure de Guerre* (School for Staff Officers), where I was received the 20th of April, 1890; the next day, April 21, I was married. I left the *École Supérieure de Guerre* in 1892 with the degree "very good," and the brevet of Staff Officer. My rank number on leaving the *École* entitled me to be detailed as *stagiaire* (probationer) on the General Staff of the Army. I took service in the Second Bureau of the General Staff (the Intelligence Bureau) on the 1st of January, 1893.

A brilliant and easy career was open to me; the future appeared under the most promising auspices. After my day's work I found rest and delight at home. Every manifestation of the human mind was of profound interested to me. I found pleasure in reading aloud during the long evenings passed at my wife's side. We were perfectly happy, and our first child, a boy, brightened our home; I had no material cares, and the same deep affection united me to the family of my wife as to the members of my own family. Everything in life seemed to smile on me.

Military Performance Reports on the Officer Dreyfus
"Will make a good General Staff officer."

L'Affaire Dreyfus: La revision du procès de Rennes, *vol. I, pp. 36–37. Translated by the editor.*

Dreyfus entered the *École Polytechnique* in 1878 before he reached his eighteenth birthday, and became a sub-lieutenant in the artillery in 1880. Reports on his career as a lieutenant were uniformly good: "intelligent" (1883); "conscientious" (1884); "very energetic" (1885); "very courageous" (1886) ; "good commander" (1887) ; "excellent memory" (1888); "commands without blustering" (1889).

In 1890 Dreyfus was admitted to the *École de Guerre,* where he spent two years and where his superiors continued to make good reports, including "well qualified for staff duty." He was graduated ninth among eighty-one candidates and was admitted to the General Staff.

Following are four military performance reports on Dreyfus after he began his work in Paris on the General Staff. They cover the years 1893 and 1894 until he was charged with treason. Only the second report was unfavorable.

FIRST SEMESTER 1893: BY COLONEL DE GERMINY,
CHIEF OF THE FIRST BUREAU

A very intelligent officer, writes very well, already possesses an extensive knowledge, can treat questions with originality: can and should be successful.

(Signed) de Germiny

SECOND SEMESTER 1893: BY COLONEL FABRE, CHIEF OF THE FOURTH BUREAU

Officer of uneven ability. Very intelligent and highly gifted, but a bit conceited, and from the point of view of character, conscientiousness, and manner of work, does not fulfill the requirements for employment on the General Staff.

(Signed) Fabre

FIRST SEMESTER 1894: BY COLONEL DE SANCY, CHIEF OF THE SECOND BUREAU

A very intelligent officer, quick to grasp affairs, works easily, perhaps a bit too sure of himself. Knows German very well and has worked conscientiously with the Second Bureau.

(Signed) de Sancy

SECOND SEMESTER 1894: BY GENERAL DE BOISDEFFRE, FOURTH BUREAU

A good officer. Alert mind, comprehends quickly, zealous, a worker, made a favorable impression wherever he went. Will make a good General Staff officer.

(Signed) de Boisdeffre

Summons from the Office of the Chief of General Staff
"Civilian dress."

Calm and unsuspecting, Dreyfus spent the evening of October 14–15, 1894, at home. He had received the following summons, the last two words of which puzzled him a bit. Why was he asked to appear at the office of the Chief of the General Staff—not in uniform but in mufti?

Paris, October 13, 1894. Summons.
The Divisional General, Chief of General Staff, will hold an examination of probationary officers during the evening of Monday, October 15.
Captain Dreyfus, currently attached to the 39th Infantry Regiment in Paris, is asked to present himself on that date at nine o'clock in the morning at the office of the Chief of General Staff.
Civilian dress.

[Translated by the editor.]

The Preliminary Examination by Commandant du Paty de Clam
"Pay attention; it is a grave matter."

Dreyfus, Five Years, *pp. 6–13.*

There could not have been a worse choice for the preliminary interrogation of Dreyfus than Major Armand-Auguste-Ferdinand-Marie Mercier du Paty de Clam, an officer attached to the War Office who turned out to be the melodramatic villain of the piece. The titles "Major" and "Commandant" were used interchangeably; du Paty de Clam was later promoted to Lieutenant-Colonel. A Marquis, and a cousin of General Le Mouton de Boisdeffre, the Chief of Staff, du Paty was a blundering and erratic busybody who felt himself honored by the assignment. A man of fertile and cruel imagination, he had the soul of a medieval inquisitor. He was a violent anti-Semite.

For three days du Paty left Dreyfus in his prison cell. Then he began a long series of examinations. After the first interrogation leading to the arrest, du Paty continued his inquiry for another seventeen days. He always came late in the evenings. He would cut up facsimile photographs of letters by Dreyfus and the *bordereau,* mix them together in his cap, and then order the prisoner to select fragments for interrogation. Meanwhile, he refused to inform Dreyfus about the reasons for his arrest. Each evening he withdrew with a theatrical flourish, leaving the prisoner perplexed and despairing. "That my brain did not give way during these endless days and nights," wrote Dreyfus, "was not the fault of Commandant du Paty." Finally, on the fifteenth day after the arrest, du Paty showed Dreyfus a photograph of the *bordereau.*

Following is Dreyfus's own account of the ordeal.

On Monday morning I left my family. My son Pierre, who was then three and a half years old and was accustomed to accompany me to the door when I went out, came with me that morning as usual. That was one of my keenest remembrances through all my misfortunes. Very often in my nights of sorrow and despair I lived over the moment when I held my child in my arms for the last time. In this recollection I always found renewed strength of purpose.

The morning was bright and cool, the rising sun driving away the thin mist; everything foretold a beautiful day. As I was a little ahead of time, I walked back and forth before the Ministry Building for a few minutes, then went upstairs. On entering the office I was received by Commandant Picquart, who seemed to be waiting for me, and who took me at once into his room. I was somewhat surprised at finding none of my comrades, as officers are always called in groups to the general inspection. After a few minutes of commonplace conversation Commandant Picquart conducted me to the private office of the Chief of General Staff. I was greatly amazed to find myself received, not by the Chief of General Staff, but by Commandant du Paty de Clam, who was in uniform. Three persons in civilian dress, who were utterly unknown to me, were also there. These three persons were M. Cochefert, *Chef de la Sûreté* (the head of the secret police), his secretary, and the Keeper of the Records, M. Gribelin.

Commandant du Paty de Clam came directly toward me and said in a choking voice: "The General is coming. While waiting, I have a letter to write, and as my finger is sore, will you write it for me?" Strange as the request was under the circumstances, I at once complied. I sat down at a little table, while Commandant du Paty placed himself at my side and very near me, following my hand with his eye. After first requiring me to fill up an inspection form, he dictated to me a letter of which certain passages recalled the accusing letter that I knew afterward, and which was called the *bordereau*. In the course of his dictation the Commandant interrupted me sharply, saying: "You tremble." (I was not trembling. At the court-martial of 1894, he explained his brusque interruption by saying that he had perceived I was not trembling under the dictation; believing therefore that he had to do with one who was simulating, he had tried in this way to shake my assurance.) This vehement remark surprised me greatly, as did the hostile attitude of Commandant du Paty. But as all suspicion was far from my mind, I thought only that he was displeased at my writing it badly. My fingers were cold, for the temperature outside was chilly, and I had been only a few minutes in the warm room. So I answered, "My fingers are cold."

As I continued writing without any sign of perturbation, Commandant du Paty tried a new interruption and said violently: "Pay attention; it is a grave matter." Whatever may have been my surprise at a procedure as rude as it was uncommon, I said nothing and simply applied myself to writing more carefully. Thereupon Commandant du Paty, as he explained to the court-martial of 1894, concluded that, my self-possession being unshakable, it was useless to push the experiment further. The scene of the dictation had been prepared in every detail; but it had not answered the expectations of those who had arranged it.

As soon as the dictation was over, Commandant du Paty arose and, placing his hand on my shoulder, cried out in a loud voice: "In the name of the law, I arrest you; you are accused of the crime of high treason." A thunderbolt falling at my feet would not have produced in me a more violent emotion; I blurted out disconnected sentences, protesting against so infamous an accusation, which nothing in my life could have given rise to.

Next, M. Cochefert and his secretary threw themselves on me and searched me. I did not offer the slightest resistance, but cried to them: "Take my keys, open everything in my house; I am innocent." Then I added, "Show me at least the proofs of the infamous act you pretend I have committed." They answered that the accusations were overwhelming, but refused to state what they were or who had made them.

I was then taken to the military prison on the rue du Cherche-Midi by Commandant Henry, accompanied by one of the detectives. On the way, Commandant Henry, who knew perfectly well what had passed, for he was hidden behind a curtain during the whole scene, asked me of what I was accused. My reply was made the substance of a report by Commandant Henry,—a report whose falsity was evident from the very questioning to which I had been subjected and which I was again to undergo in a few days.

On my arrival in the prison I was incarcerated in a cell whose solitary grated window looked on the convicts' yard. I was placed in the strictest solitary confinement and all communication with my people was forbidden me. I had at my disposal neither paper, pen and ink, nor pencil. During the first days I was subjected to the *régime* of the convicts, but this illegal measure was afterward done away with.

The men who brought me my food were always accompanied by the sergeant on guard and the chief guard, who had the only key of my cell constantly in his possession. To speak to me was absolutely forbidden to anyone but the Director of the Prison.

When I found myself in that gloomy cell, still under the terrific influence of the scene I had just gone through and of the monstrous accusation brought against me, when I thought of all those whom I had left at home but a few hours before in the fullness of happiness, I fell into a state of fearful excitement and raved from grief.

I walked back and forth in the narrow space, knocking my head against the walls. Commandant Forzinetti, Director of the Prison, came to see me, accompanied by the chief guard, and calmed me for a little while.

I am happy to be able to give here expression to my deep gratitude to Commandant Forzinetti, who found means to unite with his strict duty as a soldier the highest sentiments of humanity.

During the seventeen days which followed, I was subjected to frequent cross-examination by Commandant du Paty, who acted as officer of judicial police. He always came in very late in the evening, accompanied by Gribelin, who was acting as his clerk. He dictated to me bits of sentences taken from the incriminating letter, or passed rapidly under my eyes, in the light, words or fragments of words taken from the same letter, asking me whether or not I recognized the handwriting. Besides all that has been recorded of these examinations, he made all sorts of veiled, mysterious allusions to facts unknown to me, and would finally go away theatrically, leaving my brain bewildered by the tangle of insoluble riddles. During all this time I was ignorant of the basis of the accusation, and in spite of most urgent demands I could obtain no light on the monstrous charge brought against me. I was fighting the empty air.

That my brain did not give way during these endless days and nights, was not the fault of Commandant du Paty. I had neither paper nor ink with which to fix my ideas; I was every moment turning over in my head fragments of sentences which I had drawn from him and which only led me further astray. But no matter what my tortures may have been, my conscience was awake and unerringly dictated my duty to me. "If you die," it said to me, "they will believe you guilty; whatever happens, you must live to cry aloud your innocence in the face of the world."

It was only on the fifteenth day after my arrest that Commandant du Paty showed me a photograph of the accusing letter since called the *bordereau*.

I did not write this letter, NOR WAS I IN ANY WAY RESPONSIBLE FOR IT.

Commandant Forzinetti on Dreyfus at the Cherche-Midi Prison
"You are off the track; this officer is not guilty."

Dreyfus, Five Years, *pp. 40–48.*

Following his retirement, Commandant Ferdinand Forzinetti, Ex-Governor of the Paris Military Prisons and at the time of Dreyfus's conviction the head of the Cherche-Midi Prison, wrote an account of his prisoner's behavior during the first three months of incarceration. This remarkable report reveals how Dreyfus, utterly bewildered by the charges against him, gave way to waves of hysteria. From the beginning Forzinetti had the "intuition" that the imprisoned officer was innocent.

On October 14, 1894, I received a secret message from the Minister of War informing me that on the morrow, at 7 P.M., a superior officer would arrive at the prison to make a confidential communication. Lieutenant Colonel d'Aboville arrived in the morning and handed me a message dated the 14th, informing me that Captain Dreyfus of the Fourteenth Artillery, probationer on the General Staff, would be incarcerated in the morning, charged with the crime of high treason, and that I was to be held responsible for him. Colonel d'Aboville asked me to give him my word of honor to execute the orders, both verbal and written, of the Minister. One of the communications ordered me to place the prisoner in the most complete secrecy, and not to allow him to have by him either paper, ink, pens, penknife, or pencil. He was likewise to be fed like an ordinary criminal; but this measure was annulled later on, as I pointed out that it was irregular. The Colonel ordered me to take whatever precautions I might think necessary for keeping the fact of Captain Dreyfus's presence there secret. He asked me to visit the apartments destined for officers at the prison, and select the room to be occupied by Captain Dreyfus. He put me on my guard against the probable efforts of the "upper Jewdom" as soon as they should hear of the imprisonment. I saw no one, and no such efforts were made, in my case, at all events. I may add that all the time the prisoner was in the Cherche-Midi Prison I never entered or remained in his cell without being accompanied by the chief military police officer at the prison, who alone had the key in his possession.

Toward noon, Captain Dreyfus arrived, in civilian clothes, accompanied by Commandant Henry and an agent of the secret police. Commandant Henry gave the order of imprisonment, which was signed by the Minister himself, and the fact that it was dated the 14th proves that the arrest had been decided upon before the Captain had been called to the Ministry of War and charged with the crime of high treason.

The chief military police officer of the prison, to whom I had given my instructions, took the Captain to the cell which had been selected for him.

From that moment Dreyfus was entombed alive between its four walls, —no one could see him. The door of his cell could be opened only in my presence during the entire length of his stay in the Cherche-Midi Prison.

Shortly afterward I went to see Captain Dreyfus. He was in a state of extraordinary excitement. He looked like a madman; his eyes were bloodshot, and the things in his room had been upset. I had great difficulty in calming him. I had then the intuition that this officer was innocent. He begged me to give him writing materials, or to write myself, to ask the Minister of War for an audience, either of him or of one of the Staff officers.

He told me the details of his arrest, which were neither dignified nor military.

Between the 18th and the 24th of October, Major du Paty de Clam, who had arrested Dreyfus at the War Office, came twice with a special authorization from the Minister to examine him. Before seeing Dreyfus he asked me if he could not enter his cell softly, carrying a lamp powerful enough to throw a blaze of light on the face of the prisoner, whom he wished to surprise and embarrass. I said this was impossible. He had two sittings with him, and each time dictated to him passages from the incriminating document, with the object of comparing the handwriting.

Captain Dreyfus was still frightfully excited. From the corridor he was heard to groan, to talk in loud tones, and to protest his innocence. He struck against the furniture and the walls, and appeared not to know when he had injured himself. He had not a moment's rest, for when, overcome by his sufferings, he flung himself, dressed, upon the bed, his sleep was haunted by horrible nightmares. In fact, he struggled so in his sleep that he often fell out of bed. During these nine days of agony he took nothing but beef-tea and sweetened wine. On the morning of the 24th his mental state, bordering on madness, appeared to me so grave that, anxious as to my own responsibility, I made a report to the Minister as well as to the Governor of Paris. In the afternoon I went to see General de Boisdeffre, having been ordered to do so, and accompanied him to the Minister. In response to the General's question I replied unhesitatingly: "You are off the track; this officer is not guilty." This was my conviction then, and it has only been confirmed since.

The General went in alone to see the Minister, but came out shortly afterward, looking much annoyed, and said: "The Minister is off to his niece's wedding, and leaves me *carte blanche*. Try to manage with Dreyfus until he gets back; then he will deal with the question himself." I was inclined to think that General de Boisdeffre had nothing to do with the arrest, or that he did not approve of it. The General, nevertheless, ordered me to have the Captain secretly visited by the prison doctor, who prescribed calming potions and recommended that constant watch be kept over him.

From the 27th on, Major du Paty de Clam came almost daily to examine him and to obtain copies of his handwriting, his one object now being to obtain from Dreyfus a confession, a procedure against which Dreyfus constantly protested. Up to the day when the poor man was handed over to the Judge Reporter of the court-martial, he knew that he was accused of high treason, but had no idea of the specific nature of the charge. The preparation of the indictment was long and minute, and all the while Dreyfus so little believed that he would be sent up for trial, much less condemned, that more than once he said:—

"What redress shall I ask for? I shall solicit a decoration, and resign. This is what I said to Major du Paty, who put it into his report. He could not find a single proof against me, for there can be none, any more than could the Reporter, who proceeds by inductions and suppositions, without saying anything precise or definite."

A few moments before appearing in court he said, "I hope that finally my martyrdom is to end, and that I shall soon be back in the bosom of my family."

Unfortunately this was not to be. After the verdict, Dreyfus was taken back, at about midnight, to his room, where I awaited him. On seeing me he exclaimed: "My only crime is to have been born a Jew. To this a life of work and toil has brought me. Great heavens! Why did I enter the War School? Why didn't I resign, as my people wished?" Such was his despair that, fearing a fatal ending, I had to redouble my vigilance.

On the morrow his counsel came to see him. On entering the room, Maître Demange opened his arms and, in tears, embracing him, said, "My poor boy, your condemnation is the greatest infamy of the century." I was quite upset. From this day on, Dreyfus, who had heard nothing from his family, was authorized to correspond with them, but under the supervision of the Judge Advocate. I was present at the only two interviews which he had with his wife, and at that with his mother-in-law; they were affecting.

After Dreyfus's appeal, Major du Paty came back with a special authorization from the Minister allowing him free communication with Dreyfus. After having inquired as to the prisoner's *"état d'âme,"* he went into his room, ordering the chief policeman of the prison service to remain within call, in case of necessity. In this last interview, as is shown by a letter written immediately by Dreyfus to the Minister of War, Major du Paty sought to obtain a confession of guilt, or at least of an imprudent act, of laying a trap. Dreyfus replied that never had he made any such attempt, and that he was innocent.

On the 4th of January, 1895, I was relieved of the heavy responsibility that had been laid upon me. After having shaken hands with Captain Dreyfus, I handed him over to the gendarmes, who led him away, handcuffed, to the Military School, where he underwent, while proclaiming his innocence, the degradation,—a torture more terrible than death or exile. I have had to fulfil a mission that was extremely painful, having lived, so to speak, for nearly three months the very existence of this poor man, for I had received formal orders to be present at all his meals, which I was to watch over most carefully, lest any writing reach him from outside hidden in his food.

During the years that I have spent as the head of various military prisons, I have acquired a great experience of prisoners, and I do not fear to say, and to say deliberately, that a terrible mistake has been made. I have never regarded Captain Dreyfus as a traitor to his country and uniform.

From the very first my immediate chiefs and others knew my opinion. I affirmed it in the presence of high officials and political personages, as well as of numerous officers of every rank, of journalists, and of men of letters.

I will go even further. The Government, as well, knew my opinion, for on the eve of the ceremony of the degradation, the head of one of the departments of the Home Office came to me, sent by his Minister, M. Dupuy, to ask me for information in regard to Dreyfus. I made the same reply. This official certainly repeated it to his chiefs. Now, I assert that up to the 5th of last November, never did I receive from any of my chiefs the slightest intimation or order to keep silent, and that I have always continued to proclaim the innocence of Dreyfus, who is the victim either of an inexplicable fatality, or of a machination concocted wittingly and impossible to unravel.

I must say also that if Dreyfus did not commit suicide, it was not from cowardice, but because he was so placed as to be absolutely incapable of doing so, and because he yielded to my exhortations and the supplications of his despairing family. . . .

All convictions are worthy of respect when they are disinterested and sincere, and it will be admitted that if there are people convinced of the guilt, there are also, as I can affirm, a very great number, in the upper civil and military circles, who, like me,—and to the same extent, —are convinced of the innocence of Dreyfus. But fear of consequences has prevented them from saying so publicly. I have not cared to be of the number.

An eminent politician, still a member of Parliament, whom I must not name, said to me:—

"The Dreyfus trial is an anti-Semite trial, grafted upon a political trial!"

This is my opinion.

God grant that the poor man, who is wearing out his life in agony on a rocky isle, may one day be rehabilitated, for the honor of his family, of his children, and also for the honor of our Army!

FORZINETTI
Commandant (Retired), Ex-Governor
of the Paris Military Prisons

Major Henry Informs the Anti-Semitic Press
"All Israel is in a state of agitation."

La revision du procès de Rennes, *vol. I, p. 49. Translated by the editor.*

Aware of Major du Paty's uncertainty, Major Henry decided to precipitate matters by informing the anti-Semitic press of what was going on. On October 28, 1894, the editor of the anti-Semitic paper, *La Libre Parole*, received the following letter from Major Henry.

DEAR FRIEND:
I have already told you that it is Captain Dreyfus, the one who lives at 6, Avenue de Trocadéro, who was arrested on the 15th on a charge of espionage and who is in the Cherche-Midi prison. It is stated that he is traveling, but this is a lie because they want to hush the matter up. All Israel is in a state of agitation.

Yours,
(Signed) HENRY

Follow up inquiry as quickly as possible.

Delighted, but wary, the editor published this paragraph the next day:

Is it true that an extremely important arrest was carried out recently by order of the military authorities? The person arrested is said to be accused of espionage. If this be true why have the military authorities maintained complete silence? An explanation seems to be in order.

Within a few hours, every newspaper in Paris reprinted the news. Reporters began to besiege the offices of the General Staff.

Parisian Newspapers Report a Case of Treason
"He has, through venality, betrayed his country."

L'Éclair, *November 1, 1894. Translated by the editor.*

Three days later, on October 31, 1894, the Havas Agency informed its newspapers that an officer, suspected of conveying several important documents to a foreign power, had been arrested. The papers were urged to handle with discretion any information which followed.

The next day more details appeared in *L'Éclair,* but the name of the officer concerned was carefully omitted.

A number of journals have published a note in several lines asking about an important secret arrest which had been made for the crime of high treason.

Unfortunately, the facts are correct and much more grave than one might believe from the question posed.

An officer, not however a superior officer, is at this moment in the Cherche-Midi prison.

He has committed the most abominable crime that an officer could commit.

He has, through venality, betrayed his country.

The inquiry, held *in camera,* is ended, the *dossier* established, the proof existent.

That officer, guilty of high treason, will shortly be tried before a court-martial sitting in Paris.

At that time one will have the pain of seeing that crime exposed in broad daylight.

It is necessary that the mystery surrounding that painful affair be clarified.

M. Cochefert arrested the criminal. The latter denied it at first, and then overpowered by the evidence, confessed. . . .

"High Treason: Arrest of the Jewish Officer, A. Dreyfus"

"He has made a full confession. . . ."

La Libre Parole, *November 1, 1894. Translated by the editor.*

The next day, November 1, 1894, *La Libre Parole* had no compunctions about naming the officer concerned. It published a special number with a sensational heading: "High Treason: Arrest of the Jewish Officer, A. Dreyfus." The paper stated that it had received the news from an anonymous informer.

The French officer arrested on the charge of treason is attached to the staff of the Ministry of War. . . .

It is said that he is absent on duty.

The affair will be hushed up because this officer is a Jew. One can look for him among the Dreyfus's, the Meyers, or the Lévis and he will be found among them!

He was arrested two weeks ago. He has made a full confession. There is *absolute proof* that he sold our military secrets to Germany.

No matter what is said, this man is in Cherche-Midi prison, but not under his own name. It is believed that he hopes to escape to Mulhouse, where his family lives. . . .

General Mercier Feels that He Cannot Ask the Death Penalty

"If he is condemned, it will be to deportation in a fortified prison."

Le Matin, *November 8, 1894. Translated by the editor.*

The charge of treason was enough to stir public opinion against the accused officer. Public opinion called for "Death to Traitors!" But the law did not permit it in this case, as indicated by the response of Minister of War General Auguste Mercier to a reporter for *Le Matin* on November 8, 1894.

—"If he is guilty, *Monsieur le Ministre,* what will be the punishment?"

—"I think that Articles 76 and 80 are designed to apply to the crime of which he will be accused."

—"That will be the death penalty?"

—"No, that was abolished by a decree of 1848. If he is condemned, it will be to deportation in a fortified prison."

The Act of Accusation, 1894

"Captain Dreyfus was therefore well fitted for the shameful mission that he had mapped out for himself. . . .

G. W. Steevens, The Tragedy of Dreyfus (*New York: Harper & Brothers, 1899*), *pp. 210–220.*

On November 3, 1894, the Cabinet ordered an inquiry to be made concerning Dreyfus. The examination was entrusted to Major Bexon d'Ormescheville. For exactly one month d'Ormescheville pursued this second examination of Dreyfus, who was never allowed to communicate with his wife or with an attorney. On December 3, d'Ormescheville, who was to become *rapporteur* of the first court-martial, submitted the following report, which became the Act of Accusation.

In this document d'Ormescheville reached the same conclusions as du Paty de Clam. Later, at the Rennes court-martial, Colonel Picquart testified:

> It seems to me to be necessary that I tell you something else, namely, that during the investigation when Major d'Ormescheville interviewed Dreyfus, du Paty always was concerned in the matter. I know that he often saw Major d'Ormescheville. I myself saw Major d'Ormescheville come into the Ministry in order to visit du Paty and to ask his advice on this or that question. I am as convinced as I can possibly be, having lived through the episode, that the report of Major d'Ormescheville at least in part came from du Paty. Certain places in the report agree exactly with the ideas that du Paty then expressed, so much so that I have no doubts about the matter.
>
> Rennes: Le procès Dreyfus, vol. 1, p. 318.
[Translated by the editor.]

In his report d'Ormescheville assumed allegations of guilt to be guilt. He based his accusation on the *bordereau.* He quoted as valuable and conclusive evidence the opinion of "handwriting experts." He quoted contradictions in the interrogation of Dreyfus, spoke of his gambling propensities, and concluded that Dreyfus spoke several languages, notably German, and was "a supple character, even obsequious, which is very useful in the relation of a spy with foreign agents." It was a weak, shaky statement, but on its basis the General Staff ordered a court-martial *in camera* as essential "in the interests of France."

December 3, 1894

Captain Dreyfus, of the 14th Artillery, *stagiaire* to the staff-major of the Army, is accused of having, in 1894, given information to several agents of foreign powers, with the object of giving them the means of committing hostilities or undertaking a war against France, and of having delivered to them secret documents on which was based the order given by M. General Military Governor of Paris, Nov. 3, 1894.

Dreyfus is accused of having, in 1894, had dealings with several agents of foreign powers, giving them information which would enable them to commit hostilities or undertake a war with France.

The basis of the accusation against Dreyfus is a letter, not signed and not dated, which is in the *dossier,* proving that these military confidential documents were delivered to an agent of a foreign power.

General Gonse, sub-chief of the staff-major general of the Army, into whose hands the documents fell, gave them, after their seizure, October 15th, to du Paty de Clam, Chief of the Battalion of Infantry *hors cadre*, ordered October 14th, 1894, by the Minister of War, as officer of the police judiciary, to institute proceedings against Captain Dreyfus.

From the seizure of this letter, General Gonse has declared and affirmed to the officer of police commissioned to investigate, that he had some documents addressed to a foreign power, which had come into his possession, but that after the formal order of the Minister of War he could not state by what means the documents had come into his possession.

The exact details of the inquiry which took place in the offices of the staff-major of the Army are found contained in the report which du Paty de Clam addressed to the Minister of War, October 31 last, and which was a part of the *dossier*. An examination of this report shows that it was done without any haste and especially without any person having signed it *a priori*, and it is on this the inquiry has been conducted.

This inquiry is divided into two parts, one preliminary inquiry in order to arrive at the discovery of the culprit, if possible, then the regulation inquiry by the officer of police.

The very nature of the documents addressed to the agent of a foreign power at the same time with the criminal letter, established the fact that it was an officer who was the author of the letter and who had sent it and the documents; moreover, that this officer belonged to the artillery, three of the notes or documents sent concerning this branch of the Army. After a careful examination of all the handwriting of the officers employed in the offices of the staff-major, it was decided that the writing of Dreyfus presented a remarkable similarity to that of the criminal letter. The Minister of War, upon the report which was made to him, ordered that the writing of the letter should be studied and compared with the writing of Dreyfus. M. Gobert, expert of the Bank of France and of the Court of Appeal, was commissioned by General Gonse to make the examination, and for this purpose received from him some documents, October 4th, 1894. Some days after the receipt of these documents M. Gobert asked M. Gonse, who went to see him, the name of the guilty person; naturally the latter refused to give it to him.

A few days afterward M. Gobert was asked to submit his conclusions and the documents which had been confided to him, he having shown his desire for more time in the matter.

October 13th, in the morning, M. Gobert submitted his conclusions in the form of a letter to the Minister. They are worded as follows:—

"The criminal letter might be that of another person than the one suspected."

M. Gobert's manner having displayed a certain defiance, the Minister of War asked the Prefect of Police for the opinion of M. Bertillon.

Some specimens of writing and a photograph of the criminal letter were then submitted to him, and he proceeded to their examination while awaiting the return of the documents confided to M. Gobert. After the return of these documents by M. Gobert, they were sent to M. Bertillon, who, on the evening of October 13th, drew up his conclusions, which are worded as follows:—"If one goes on the hypothesis that the document is forged, it appears manifest that it is the same person who has written the letter and the documents in question."

In compliance with the order of the Minister of War, dated October 14th, 1894, du Paty de Clam proceeded to the arrest of Captain Dreyfus on October 15th.

Before the actual arrest, and in order that Dreyfus might know the accusation against him, and prove his innocence if possible, du Paty de Clam submitted him to the following test:—He made him write a letter in which were enumerated the documents figuring in the criminal letter.

As soon as Dreyfus perceived the object of this letter, his writing, which was up to that point regular, became irregular, and he showed signs of uneasiness. Questioned about this, he declared that his fingers were cold. Now the temperature in the office of the Minister was medium; Dreyfus had been there for a quarter of an hour, and the first four lines written presented no signs of trembling.

After having arrested and interrogated Dreyfus, du Paty de Clam, the same day, Oct. 15, made a search in Dreyfus's house. This superior officer having heard no witness, the duty fell upon us, and by reason of the necessary secrecy, the inquiry in which we heard twenty-three witnesses was as laborious as it was delicate.

It appears, from the testimony of witnesses, that during the two years that Dreyfus spent as *stagiaire* to the General Staff, he was seen in different offices, that his actions were suspicious, that he was found alone at late hours in other offices than his own and where there was no excuse for his presence. In this way he was able to look up matters which might interest him. He was also able, without being seen by anyone, to go into offices other than his for the same motive. It was remarked by the Chief of the section that during his stay in the 4th *Bureau* Dreyfus was specially interested in the study of *dossiers* of mobilization, so that in leaving this *Bureau* he possessed all the mysteries of the concentration upon the network of the East in time of war.

The examination, as well as the conclusions formed on the subject of the criminal letter, belong more particularly to the experts in writing. However, at first sight, and afterwards, we must say that the writing of this document presents a great similarity to the different documents found in the *dossier,* notably in the slanting of the writing, the omission of dates and the cutting of words in two at the end of lines, which are the features of the letters written by Dreyfus (see his letter to the *Procureur* of the Republic of Versailles and the letters or cards to his *fiancée* which are in the *dossier*). In regard to the signature the comparison fails because it ought to fail. Colonel Fabre, chief of the 4th *Bureau* of the staff-major of the Army, in his deposition said that he had been struck by the similarity of the writing of the criminal documents and the writing of Dreyfus when he was in *Bureau* No. 4.

Lieutenant-Colonel d'Aboville, sub-chief of the same *Bureau,* said in his deposition, that the resemblance of the writing of the criminal documents to the writing of the documents of comparison, was very striking.

As regards the experts who reported to us the first phase of the inquiry, that is to say in the commencement of the month of October last, we find first the hurried letter of M. Gobert, which is very vague. The wording of the conclusion of this expert shows that the anonymous letter that he examined could be or might not be from the person accused. It is to be observed that M. Gobert received, among the documents for comparison written by the hands of Dreyfus, a work entitled "Studies upon measures in times of war." This document which contains a detailed *exposé* of the resources of the Bank of France, in case of war, attracted the attention of M. Gobert, who is employed by the Bank of France, and is to-day an expert on writing there.

Captain Dreyfus having had, in the course of his work, to consult the principal officers of that bank, he was quite well-known by a number of its *employés*. It was without doubt this fact which led M. Gobert to tell us that he had surmised the name of the person suspected, but that no one had any knowledge of it. Be that as it may, M. Gobert, as we have said, for some unknown reason had asked General Gonse, sub-chief of the General Staff, the name of the guilty person. What reason had he for doing so? Many hypotheses can be advanced. We can say that such a demand, in contradiction to the professional attitude of an expert in handwriting, warrants the supposition that the account rendered by M. Gobert to the Minister (which, not being certified under oath, was merely in the way of information) was written under the influence of bias, contrary to the invariable practice of professional experts in such matters.

In consequence, this account seems to us suspicious, to say the least. Its dubiousness of tone has no value from the standpoint of law. It does not contain any technical discussion which would allow one to understand on what facts M. Gobert has based his judgment.

We will add that M. Gobert, when asked to add technical explanation to his report, refused; that moreover, before taking the oath, he declared to us that if we should call him in view of making a second expert investigation, a regular one this time, in the Dreyfus affair, he would refuse to do so.

As we have said before, the task of examination given to M. Gobert by the Minister of War, was also entrusted to M. Bertillon, who formulated, October 13th, 1894, his conclusion as follows:—

"If one puts aside the hypothesis of a forged document with the greatest care, it appears manifest that it is one and the same person who has written the letter and the documents in question."

In his report of Oct. 23rd, given after a more thorough examination, bearing upon a larger number of documents, M. Bertillon formulated the following conclusions, which are much more affirmative. "The proof is peremptory. You know what my conviction was in the first place; it is now absolute—complete without any limitation."

The report of M. Charavay, expert in writing near the Tribunal of the Seine, given under oath, contains, first of all, a detailed technical discussion, and the conclusions which resulted from it are given in the following words:—"Based on the statements made in the present report, I, the undersigned expert, conclude that the criminal document No. 1 is written by the same hand as the test documents from 2 to 30."

The report of M. Teyssonnières, expert in handwriting near the Civil Tribunal, given under oath, contains, like the preceding report, a detailed technical discussion of the documents. His conclusions are thus: "Based on the preceding, I declare on my conscience that the writing of the criminal piece No. 1, is by the same hand which has written documents 2 to 30."

The report of M. Pelletier, expert, etc., given under oath, and which bore upon the comparison of the handwriting of the criminal documents with that of two persons, contains, like the preceding reports, a technical discussion of the documents examined. His conclusions are as follows:

"Summing up the whole thing, I do not consider myself warranted in attributing to either one or the other of the persons suspected, the writing of the criminal documents."

It is worthy of note that the experts Charavay, Teyssonnières, and Pelletier, after taking the oath, were put in relation with M. Bertillon, who told them that he was at their disposal to furnish them with certain *pelures,* the photographs of which were not as yet finished, and which were of great importance by reason of the comparisons to be made of the handwritings. Of the three experts above-named, only two returned to see M. Bertillon and receive from him communication of these *pelures;* these two were Charavay and Teyssonnières.

The third, M. Pelletier, did not go again, and did his work, which bore upon the comparison of two handwritings instead of one with the criminal letter, without the help of the documents that M. Bertillon proposed to give him, and which must have had decidedly as much interest for him as for his colleagues.

Dreyfus was subjected to a long interrogatory by M. du Paty de Clam. His answers are full of contradictions, to say the least. Among them some are particularly interesting to note here, notably one at the time of his arrest, October 15th last, when he was searched and said: "Take my keys; open everything in my house, you will find nothing."

The search which was made at his house resulted very nearly as he said; but one is justified in thinking that if any letters, even of the family, except those written to Madame Dreyfus—if even letters from shopkeepers had contained anything compromising they would naturally have been destroyed. The whole of the interrogatory put by M. du Paty de Clam is full of persistent denials by Dreyfus, and also of protestations against the crime of which he is accused. At the beginning of that interrogatory Dreyfus said at first that he thought he recognized in the criminal documents the handwriting of an officer employed in the office of the General Staff of the Army; afterwards, before us, he retracted this allegation, which ought to fall by its own weight, in the face of the complete dissimilarity of the handwriting of the officer he had in mind with that of the criminal document.

Another extraordinary answer made in the course of the first interrogatory is that which related to the insecurity of the official documents which, according to Dreyfus, were not in perfect security at the second *Bureau* of the General Staff of the Army at the time when he was employed in it. This allegation of insecurity has not been confirmed by any of the witnesses heard on this subject; he must therefore have made it with some object in view.

Lastly, there exists, in the first interrogatory, some absolutely incoherent answers, such as these: "The experts are mistaken, the incriminating document is the work of a forger; some one has tried to imitate my handwriting. These documents might have been written with the help of fragments of my handwriting put together with care to form a whole which would resemble this letter. The ensemble of the letter does not resemble my writing; it is not even an attempt to imitate it."

In the interrogatory of Dreyfus, his answers have always been obtained with great difficulty, as one will observe from the many words scratched and underlined in the official report of the interrogatory. When Dreyfus ventured an affirmation, he would hasten to weaken it by vague or mixed-up phrases trying always, in spite of former remarks, to question or to start the conversation without being asked to do so. That system, if

we had allowed it to be adopted, might have had some unfortunate consequences for the form even of the interrogatory, on account of the extreme
cleverness of Captain Dreyfus.

If one compares the answers that Captain Dreyfus has made to us with
the depositions of some of the witnesses heard, they will draw from it the
painful impression that he often veils the truth, and that, whenever he
finds himself hard pressed, he gets out of the trouble without much
difficulty, owing to his mental alertness.

Summing up the depositions of several witnesses, the facts extracted
are these: that Dreyfus had often drawn upon himself the suspicion of his
comrades, that he had asked Captain Boullenger questions about the
secret and confidential affair in his charge, which Boullenger refused to
answer; also that Captain Besse had seen him, September 8th last, working in his office on some unauthorized kind of paper instead of using the
same official papers as the document which he had to bring up to date;
also Captain Maistre said to him that he would give him communication
of the important work which he had in charge, but in his office only. It
appears that Dreyfus indulged in indiscreet conversations, that he made
investigations of matters not in his own department; that he had a habit
of ferreting; that he seemed to be bent on procuring information, either
written or oral, before finishing his term of service as *stagiaire* with the
General Staff of the Army.

His attitude seemed to be one of cross-purposes, and had a suspicious
appearance, like that of one who practices spying. His actions, taken in
connection with the similarity of the handwriting, are a serious factor
against him when the question of his arraignment was brought up.

Although Dreyfus declared to us that he never had gambling propensities, it appears from the information we have been able to gather on the
subject that he frequented several Paris clubs where there is much
gambling. In the course of his interrogatory he acknowledged that he had
gone to the Press Club, but only as a guest to dine, and that he had never
played there. The gambling clubs of Paris, such as the Washington Club,
the Betting Club, the Fencing Club, and the Press Club, have no Club
books, and their frequenters, being a shady class of people, the testimony
of any witnesses we might have called from there would not have been
trustworthy; hence they were not heard.

In regard to his travels, Dreyfus stated that he could go to Alsace in
secret, almost whenever he wanted to, and that the German authorities
would shut their eyes to his presence. This faculty of traveling clandes-
tinely contrasts strongly with the difficulties which our officers experi-

enced at that time, and at all times, in obtaining permission or passports from the German authorities allowing them to return to Alsace. It may be there was a reason for this which the limited time at our disposal will not admit of our fathoming.

In regard to the hints of Dreyfus about the baiting which the Minister of War practised, it appears to us that this accusation was trumped up by Dreyfus in order to defend himself for having any connection with compromising documents, and perhaps this loophole of escape in his mind made him less careful about disguising his handwriting.

On the other hand, the slight alterations which he did make might have had for an object the possible argument of forgery, should the documents after having reached their destination eventually fall into the hands of the Minister of War.

As to the proofs relating to the knowledge Captain Dreyfus had of the notes or documents enumerated in the criminal documents and which have accompanied it, the first interrogatory, as well as the one he has just been submitted to, convinces me, in spite of his denials, that he was in easy position to furnish them. On examining these documents, we find first of all the note upon the hydraulic brake 120.

The allegations of Dreyfus on the subject of this brake, go to show that it was easy for him to procure, either through the artillery, or by conversations with certain officers of the General Staff, the elements necessary to fabricate the note in question.

As to the note upon the *troupes de couverture* with the restriction that some modifications might be brought in by the new plan, to us it seems impossible that Dreyfus did not have knowledge of the modifications bearing on the plan of campaign in the month of April last, which, though confidential, was not altogether secret, being freely discussed by officers of the staff both among themselves and in the presence of Dreyfus.

In that which concerns the note upon certain changes in the artillery staff, an agitation for the suppression of the *pontonniers,* we cannot believe that Dreyfus was not interested in such a transformation, and only knew of it when it became official. About the note on Madagascar which presented the greatest interest for one of the foreign Powers, if as everything suggested, an expedition had been sent at the beginning of 1895, Captain Dreyfus would have easily been able to procure the official note. In fact, last February Corporal Bernillon, then Secretary to Colonel de Sancy, chief of the second *Bureau* of the General Staff, made a copy of a work about twenty-two pages on Madagascar in an antechamber adjoining the office of this superior officer.

The making of that copy took about five days, and during that time original and copy were left in a portfolio on the writing table of the corporal when he left his work. Besides, during office hours this corporal was often absent for a while, leaving his work in full view on the table (consequently easy to read), for he never thought that any officer not belonging to that office, or in fact any officer unknown to him, would be in the room.

This corporal declared to us in his deposition, but without giving any precise date, that Captain Dreyfus, whom he knew, had come four or five times into the room to see Colonel de Sancy, while he was doing service at the German section. This document could also have been read by Dreyfus when he was put back to the English section, which was occupied just then with Madagascar, because these documents had been placed temporarily in an open pasteboard box in that section. In what concerns the project of the *Manuel de tir,* of artillery on March 14, 1894, Dreyfus acknowledged, in his first interrogatory, that he had spoken of it several times with the superior officer of the 2nd *Bureau* of the General Staff.

In conclusion, the elements of the accusation against Dreyfus are of two kinds, moral and material. I have examined the first elements; the second element consists in the criminal letter whose examination by the majority of experts, as well as by us, and by the witnesses who have seen it, has proved, in spite of voluntary dissimilarities, a complete similarity with the writing of Dreyfus.

Besides the preceding, I can say that Dreyfus possesses a very extended knowledge, a remarkable memory; that he speaks several languages, notably German, which he knows thoroughly, and Italian, which he pretends to know very little about now; that he was a supple character, even obsequious, which is very useful in the relation of a spy with foreign agents. Captain Dreyfus was therefore well fitted for the shameful mission that he had mapped out for himself or accepted, but which, happily for France, was put an end to by the discovery of the criminal letter.

In consequence, I am of opinion that Captain Dreyfus, *stagiaire,* etc., be arraigned for having, in 1894, at Paris, delivered to a foreign power a certain number of confidential documents relating to national defense, thus enabling them to undertake a war with France.

A. D'ORMESCHEVILLE

Made at Paris, December 3, 1894   *Reporter*

This was the famous *Acte d'Accusation* which was first made public in *Le Siècle* of Paris on January 8, 1898. Since December 3, 1894, it had been kept secret from the public.

The Times Expresses Grave Doubts

"No doubt the members of the court-martial were honourable men. . . ."

The Times (*London*), *December 24, 1894.*

From the beginning the British press was highly critical of the secrecy surrounding the court-martial. From the English point of view secrecy under such circumstances seemed to be a "vestige of barbarism." The case was sad enough without press exaggerations, which were bound to occur in an atmosphere of secrecy. British commentators could see no safeguard for public liberty if a secret military court exercised such powers. On December 19, 1894, the day after the first hearing, the Paris Correspondent of the *Daily Chronicle* telegraphed to his paper that the doors of the Court had been opened to him by courtesy of the French military authorities but that his mouth "must be closed concerning what he has heard."

On Monday, December 24, the day after the condemnation of Dreyfus, *The Times* made the following remarks in a leading article.

Nevertheless when we come to consider the circumstances of the trial, we cannot refrain from expressing our astonishment at the positive manner in which not only the populace, but the press of Paris appear to have *taken for granted* the criminality of the accused. We are told that public opinion and the newspapers unanimously approve the finding of the court-martial. But, as we have said, the trial was conducted with closed doors, and the Parisian public cannot, therefore, have founded their approval on any knowledge whatever of the facts upon which the conviction was based. At the opening of the proceedings last week the prosecutor, on behalf of the Government, claimed that the inquiry should be secret. The general rule governing courts-martial in France, is that their proceedings are null and void unless conducted in public, but in case publicity is held by the Court to be dangerous to order or morality, secrecy can be enjoined. It was so decided in the case of Captain Dreyfus. His counsel, Maître Demange, entered a protest, and attempted to argue the point, but was summarily cut short by the presiding officer when he ventured to touch even indirectly on the facts, by referring to the single document on which he was understood to assert that the charge really rested. What this is, and why it was deemed necessary to conceal its character and its origin, are questions which have been left by the decision of the court-martial at the mercy of public conjecture. It has been reported that the document or documents abstracted by Captain Dreyfus had passed into the hands of the German Embassy, and that it or they had been won back from its archives by a process of a similar kind. But though the proceedings of the court-martial have been secret, the names of the witnesses for the prosecution and for the defence have been published. It is evident that no persons connected either with the German Embassy, or with any foreign Legation whatever, have been cited on the one side or the other.

We have no wish to criticise the susceptibility of the French people in the case of offences which involve not only the security of a great military Power, but the sanctity of the obligations which are specially binding upon soldiers. Yet we must point out that the more odious and unpopular a crime is, the more necessary is it that its proof and its punishment should be surrounded by all the safeguards of public justice. Of these the most indispensable is publicity. It would be impossible in this country to allow any body of officers to decide with closed doors on a charge involving degrading penalties almost more crushing to a man of honor than death itself. Indeed, if the precedent borrowed from the worst days of the Revolution, and of the Napoleonic despotism, is to prevail, there is no reason why capital sentences should not be determined upon in the same way, with closed doors, and on the pretext, of which the Court itself remains the sole judge, that publicity is dangerous to order. It is intelligible that important military documents, such as that alleged to have been abstracted by Captain Dreyfus, may be of a nature justifying the War Office authorities in declining to permit the public discussion of their contents. But it is quite possible for any tribunal to identify such documents and to deal with the question of their unlawful abstraction or possession without permitting their tenor to be divulged. The objectionable part of the procedure on the trial of Captain Dreyfus was not the suppression of the contents of the papers alleged to have been stolen, but the conviction of the prisoner *without the proof, in open Court and on sworn testimony, of his having stolen them*. No doubt the members of the court-martial were honourable men, whose desire it was to do justice. At the same time, we cannot forget that the very character of the charge against Captain Dreyfus was calculated to create a prejudice against him in the military as well as the popular mind, and that publicity given to the arguments for the defence and to the cross-examination of witnesses is the only effective security against such a bias. It is to be feared also that the anti-Semitic propaganda in France increased the hostility to Captain Dreyfus, who is a member of a well-known Jewish family, and for whom his namesake, the Chief Rabbi of France, was cited as a witness to character. The presumption is, of course, that the verdict of the court-martial was justified by evidence communicated to that tribunal only, *but the conditions of secrecy unfortunately imposed engender doubts, which in the case of so grave an accusation, involving penalties both degrading and severe, ought not to be left undispelled.* It may be important for the French people to preserve the secrets of their War Department, but it is of infinitely greater importance to them to guard their public justice against even the suspicion of unfairness or of subjection to the gusts of popular passion.

Dreyfus's First Statement

"I am that martyr, and I hope the future will prove it to you."

The Letters of Captain Dreyfus to His Wife, *trans. L. G. Moreau (New York: Harper & Brothers, 1899), pp. 232–234.*

On December 31, 1894, Dreyfus sent the following letter to his counsel, Maître Edgar Demange. In it he told of his examination by Commandant du Paty de Clam, during which the latter informed him that since his arrest the leakage at the Ministry had ceased. Dreyfus insisted upon his innocence and asked that every effort be made to unravel the web.

This letter was first made public on July 11, 1898, when it was sent to M. Sarrien, Minister of Justice. In the published version it was deemed best to suppress certain words and phrases.

Commandant du Paty came to-day, Monday, December 31, 1894, at 5:30 P.M., after the rejection of my appeal, to ask me, on behalf of the Minister, whether I had not, perhaps, been the victim of my imprudence, whether I had not meant merely to lay a bait . . . and had then found myself caught fatally in the trap. I replied that I had never had relations with any agent or attaché, . . . that I had undertaken no such process as baiting, and that I was innocent. He then said to me on his own responsibility that he was himself convinced of my guilt, first from an examination of the handwriting of the document brought up against me, and from the nature of the documents enumerated therein; secondly, from information according to which the disappearance of documents corresponded with my presence on the General Staff; that, finally, a secret agent had declared that a Dreyfus was a spy, . . . without, however, affirming that that Dreyfus was an officer. I asked Commandant du Paty to be confronted with this agent. He replied that it was impossible. Commandant du Paty acknowledged that I had never been suspected before the reception of the incriminating document.

I then asked him why there had been no surveillance exercised over the officers from the month of February, since Commandant Henry had affirmed at the court-martial that he had been warned at that date that there was a traitor among the officers. Commandant du Paty replied that he knew nothing about that business, that it was not his affair, but Commandant Henry's; that it was difficult to watch all the officers of the General Staff. . . . Then, perceiving that he had said too much, he added: "We are talking between four walls. If I am questioned on all that I shall deny everything." I preserved entire calmness, for I wished to know his whole idea. To sum up, he said that I had been condemned because there was a clue indicating that the culprit was an officer and the seized letter came to give precision to that clue. He added, also, that since my arrest the leakage at the Ministry had ceased; that, perhaps, . . . had left the letter about expressly to sacrifice me, in order not to satisfy my demands.

He then spoke to me of the remarkable expert testimony of M. Bertillon, according to which I had traced my own handwriting and that of my brother in order to be able in case I should be arrested with the letter on me to protest that it was a conspiracy against me. He further intimated that my wife and family were my accomplices—in short, the whole theory of M. Bertillon. At this point, knowing what I wanted to discover, and not wishing to allow him to insult my family as well, I stopped him, saying, "Enough; I have only one word to say, namely, that I am innocent, and that your duty is to continue your inquiries." "If you are really innocent," he exclaimed, "you are undergoing the most monstrous martyrdom of all time." "I am that martyr," I replied, "and I hope the future will prove it to you."

To sum up, it results from this conversation: 1. That there have been leakages at the Ministry. 2. That . . . must have heard, and must have repeated to Commandant Henry, that there was an officer who was a traitor. I do not think he would have invented it of his own accord. 3. That the incriminating letter was taken at . . . . From all this I draw the following conclusions, the first certain, the two others possible: First, a spy really exists . . . at the French Ministry, for documents have disappeared. Secondly, perhaps that spy slipped in in an officer's uniform, imitating his handwriting in order to divert suspicion. Thirdly (here four lines and a half are blank). This hypothesis does not exclude the fact No. 1, which seems certain. But the tenor of the letter does not render this third hypothesis very probable. It would be connected rather with the first fact and the second hypothesis—that is to say, the presence of a spy at the Ministry and imitation of my handwriting by that spy, or simply resemblance of handwriting.

However this may be, it seems to me that if your agent is clever he should be able to unravel this web by laying his nets as well on the . . . side as on the . . . side. This will not prevent the employment of all the other methods I have indicated, for the truth must be discovered. After the departure of Commandant du Paty I wrote the following letter to the Minister. "I received, by order, the visit of Commandant du Paty, to whom I once more declared that I was innocent, and that I had never even committed an imprudence. I am condemned. I have no favor to ask. But in the name of my honor, which I hope will one day be restored to me, it is my duty to beg you to continue your investigations. When I am gone let the search be kept up; it is the only favor that I solicit."

The Degradation: Three Versions
"I am innocent! Vive la France!"

When he was found guilty, Dreyfus was sentenced to public degradation from his rank and to solitary confinement for life. The first part of this sentence was a concession to the cry of the anti-Semitic press: "Let the people of Paris be summoned to witness it, let the traitor endure this penalty to the accompaniment of public cries of rage and disgust!"

Accordingly, the humiliation prescribed in the first part of the verdict was performed in public ceremony on January 5, 1895, before a large body of troops, civil officials, and press correspondents. Outside, surrounding the square, were 20,000 hooting citizens. The galloons were torn from Dreyfus's *képi,* the trefoils from his sleeves, the numbers from his collar, the buttons from his tunic, and the stripes from his trousers. At the climax his sword was broken and the scabbard thrown contemptuously to the ground. The degraded officer was then forced to march before the men under his command.

Following are three versions of the ceremony of degradation, the first by Dreyfus himself, the second by the newspaper, *L'Autorité,* hostile to Dreyfus, and the third by Jacques St. Cere, the famed correspondent of the New York *Herald.*

1

DREYFUS'S OWN ACCOUNT OF THE DEGRADATION

Dreyfus, Five Years, pp. 49–52.

The degradation took place Saturday, the 5th of January. I underwent the horrible torture without weakness.

Before the ceremony, I waited for an hour in the hall of the garrison adjutant at the *École Militaire,* guarded by the captain of gendarmes, Lebrun-Renault. During these long minutes I gathered up all the forces of my being. The memory of the dreadful months which I had just passed came back to me, and in broken sentences I recalled to the captain the last visit which Commandant du Paty de Clam had made me in my prison. I protested against the vile accusation which had been brought against me; I recalled that I had written again to the Minister to tell him of my innocence. It is by a travesty of these words that Lebrun-Renault, with singular lack of conscience, created or allowed to be created that legend of confession, of which I learned the existence only in January, 1899. If they had spoken to me about it before my departure from France, which did not take place until February, 1895,—that is, more than seven weeks after the degradation,—I should have tried to strangle this calumny in its infancy.

After this I was marched to the center of the square, under a guard of four men and a corporal.

Nine o'clock struck. General Darras, commanding the parade, gave the order to carry arms.

I suffered agonizingly, but held myself erect with all my strength. To sustain me I called up the memory of my wife and children.

As soon as the sentence had been read out, I cried aloud, addressing myself to the troops:

"Soldiers, they are degrading an innocent man. Soldiers, they are dishonoring an innocent man. *Vive la France, vive l'armée!*"

A sergeant of the Republican Guard came up to me. He tore off rapidly buttons, trousers-stripes, the signs of my rank from cap and sleeves, and then broke my sword across his knee. I saw all these material emblems of my honor fall at my feet. Then, my whole being racked by a fearful paroxysm, but with body erect and head high, I shouted again and again to the soldiers and to the assembled crowd the cry of my soul.

"I am innocent!"

The parade continued. I was compelled to make the whole round of the square. I heard the howls of a deluded mob, I felt the thrill which I knew must be running through those people, since they believed that before them was a convicted traitor to France; and I struggled to transmit to their hearts another thrill,—belief in my innocence.

The round of the square made, the torture would be over, I believed.

But the agony of that long day was only beginning.

They tied my hands, and a prison van took me to the *Dépôt* (Central Prison of Paris), passing over the Alma Bridge. On coming to the end of the bridge, I saw through the tiny grating of my compartment in the van the windows of the home where such happy years of my life had been spent, where I was leaving all my happiness behind me. My grief bowed me down.

At the Central Prison, in my torn and stripped uniform, I was dragged from hall to hall, searched, photographed, and measured. At last, toward noon, I was taken to the Santé Prison and shut up in a convict's cell.

2

News Report in "L'Autorité" (Paris)

L'Autorité, *January 6, 1895. Translated by the editor.*

The first stroke of nine sounds from the school clock. General Darras lifts his sword and gives the command, which is repeated at the head of each company:

"Portez les armes!"

The troops obey.

Complete silence ensues.

Hearts stop beating, and all eyes are turned toward the corner of the vast square, where Dreyfus had been shut up in a small building.

Soon a little group appears: it is Alfred Dreyfus who is advancing, between four artillerymen, accompanied by a lieutenant of the Republican Guard and the oldest noncommissioned officer of the regiment. Between the dark dolmans of the gunners we see distinctly the gold of the three stripes and the gold of the cap bands: the sword glitters, and even at this distance we behold the black sword knot on the hilt of the sword.

Dreyfus marches with steady step.

"Look, see how the wretch is carrying himself," someone says.

The group advances toward General Darras, with whom is the clerk of the court-martial, M. Vallecale.

There are cries now in the crowd.

But the group halts.

A sign from the officer in command, the drums beat, and the trumpets blow, and then again all is still; a tragic silence now.

The artillerymen with Dreyfus drop back a few steps, and the condemned man stands well out in full view of us all.

The clerk salutes the general, and turning toward Dreyfus reads distinctly the verdict: "The said Dreyfus is condemned to military degradation and to deportation to a fortress."

The clerk turns to the general and salutes. Dreyfus has listened in silence. The voice of General Darras is then heard, and although it is slightly tremulous with emotion, we catch distinctly this phrase:

"Dreyfus, you are unworthy to wear the uniform. In the name of the French people, we deprive you of your rank."

Thereupon we behold Dreyfus lift his arms in air, and, his head well up, exclaim in a loud voice, in which there is not the slightest tremor:

"I am innocent. I swear that I am innocent. *Vive la France!*"

In reply the immense throng without clamors, "Death to the traitor!"

But the noise is instantly hushed. Already the adjutant whose melancholy duty it is to strip from the prisoner his stripes and arms has begun his work, and they now begin to strew the ground.

Dreyfus makes this the occasion of a fresh protest, and his cries carry distinctly even to the crowd outside:

"In the name of my wife and children, I swear that I am innocent. I swear it. *Vive la France!*"

But the work has been rapid. The adjutant has torn quickly the stripes from the hat, the embroideries from the cuffs, the buttons from the dolman, the numbers from the collar, and ripped off the red stripe worn by the prisoner ever since his entrance into the *École Polytechnique*.

The saber remains: the adjutant draws it from its scabbard and breaks it across his knee. There is a dry click, and the two portions are flung with the insignia upon the ground. Then the belt is detached, and in its turn the scabbard falls.

This is the end. These few seconds have seemed to us ages. Never was there a more terrible sensation of anguish.

And once more, clear and passionless, comes the voice of the prisoner:

"You are degrading an innocent man!"

He must now pass along the line in front of his former comrades and subordinates. For another the torture would have been horrible. Dreyfus does not seem to be affected, however, for he leaps over the insignia of his rank, which two gendarmes are shortly to gather up, and takes his place between the four gunners, who, with drawn swords, have led him before General Darras.

The little group, led by two officers of the Republican Guard, moves toward the band of music in front of the prison van and begins its march along the front of the troops and about three feet distant from them.

Dreyfus holds his head well up. The public cries, "Death to the traitor!" Soon he reaches the great gateway, and the crowd has a better sight of him. The cries increase, thousands of voices demanding the death of the wretch, who still exclaims: "I am innocent! *Vive la France!*"

The crowd has not heard, but it has seen Dreyfus turn toward it and speak.

A formidable burst of hisses replies to him, then an immense shout which rolls like a tempest across the vast courtyard:

"Death to the traitor! Kill him!"

And then outside the mob heaves forward in a murderous surge. Only by a mighty effort can the police restrain the people from breaking through into the yard, to wreak their swift and just vengeance upon Dreyfus for his infamy.

Dreyfus continues his march. He reaches the group made up of the press representatives.

"You will say to the whole of France," he cries, "that I am innocent!"

"Silence, wretch," is the reply. "Coward! Traitor! Judas!"

Under the insult, the abject Dreyfus pulls himself up. He flings at us a glance full of fierce hatred.

"You have no right to insult me!"

A clear voice issues from the group:

"You know well that you are not innocent. *Vive la France!* Dirty Jew!"

Dreyfus continues his route.

His clothing is pitiably disheveled. In the place of his stripes hang long dangling threads, and his cap has no shape.

Dreyfus pulls himself up once more, but the cries of the crowd are beginning to affect him. Though the head of the wretch is still insolently turned toward the troops, his legs are beginning to give way.

The march round the square is ended. Dreyfus is handed over to the two gendarmes, who have gathered up his stripes, and they conduct him to the prison van.

Dreyfus, completely silent now, is placed once more in prison. But there again he protests his innocence.

3

JACQUES ST. CERE, CORRESPONDENT OF THE NEW YORK "HERALD"

Quoted in William Harding, Dreyfus: The Prisoner of Devil's Island *(New York: Associated Publishing Company, 1899), pp. 45–46.*

The degradation of Captain Alfred Dreyfus from his military rank and honors took place this morning (January 5, 1895), on the parade ground of the *École Militaire*.

By order of General Saussier, Military Governor of Paris, no card of admission was issued to the correspondent of any foreign paper. Nevertheless the representative of the *Herald* was present throughout the whole ceremony.

The scene was one that can never be forgotten. When the adjutant tore away the insignia of his rank from his cap, Dreyfus shouted: *"Vive la France!"* and this cry he repeated when his sword was broken. This caused a profound emotion. Then he was led, bareheaded, his uniform stripped of all its gold lace and buttons, along the front of the troops.

When he arrived in front of the group of two hundred journalists and civil officials who were permitted to witness the ceremony, Dreyfus cried out:

"Tell the whole of France that I am an innocent man!"

The way in which this cry was given, and the appearance of the prisoner, who held himself very erect in his mutilated uniform, his red face, his bloodshot but dry eyes, produced a profound impression even on those who were the most thoroughly convinced of his guilt. Dreyfus had in every respect the appearance of a man protesting against a great injustice.

There certainly is a great deal of mystery about this case. On the one hand the officials of the Ministry of War affirm that Captain Dreyfus is guilty, while on the other hand Maître Demange, whose position as a leading member of the French bar is above question, solemnly asserts that his client is innocent, something which, now that the case is at an end, there is no reason for his doing unless he is convinced that such is the fact.

At the end of the ceremony of degradation the prisoner, with handcuffs on his wrists, was placed in a prison van, and removed to the police *dépôt*. His name was struck from the Army rolls, and he was henceforth treated like any ordinary criminal.

The degradation of Dreyfus caused a profound excitement among the Parisian public. Not less than twenty thousand persons, who were kept at a distance from the scene, surrounded the square and hooted at the prisoner throughout the ceremony, shouting:

"Death to the traitor!" "Death to the Jews!"

Such days are bad for the people and bad for the Government, which is now being driven into making a cleaning away of persons prominent in journalistic and political circles, who are suspected simply because of the race to which they are supposed to belong.

"Casimir wants to clean up," is a favorite expression just now among those who belong to the *"entourage"* of the President of the French Republic.

Public opinion is passionately worked up over the Dreyfus case. Here is some information in regard to it which comes to me from a very good source. There is no doubt as to the prisoner's guilt. His arrest was decided on the unanimous vote of the eleven ministers, who at the same time pledged themselves not to reveal anything contained in the report demanding the prosecution of Dreyfus, which was signed by General Mercier, Minister of War; General de Boisdeffre, Chief of the General Staff, and General Gonse, the Assistant Chief of the General Staff.

The secrets betrayed by Dreyfus are of such importance that the Government will ask the chamber to pass a law providing for the imprisonment of Dreyfus, not at Noumea, from which an escape is possible, but on an island of French Guiana, where he will be strictly watched.

It is believed that Dreyfus was the center of the German espionage system in France, and it is asserted that no less than twenty-seven attempts were made by German diplomacy, both at the Ministry of Foreign Affairs and at the Ministry of the Interior, to get the affair hushed up.

These facts, which I have upon the best authority, force me, in spite of the way in which Dreyfus faced the ordeal, to believe in his guilt.

The newspaper reports indicated accurately the temper of the day. The unknown French newspaperman for *L'Autorité* was an unfriendly witness, even if between the lines of his story there appear shadows of doubt as to the condemned man's guilt. Jacques St. Cere, the Parisian correspondent of the New York *Herald,* was impressed by the way in which Dreyfus had faced his ordeal, but he, too, wrote of his belief in the captain's guilt. All reports indicate that Dreyfus went through the degradation with high emotion but with dignity and firmness, although to some observers his bearing seemed almost mechanical. He had spoken loudly to that France that had vilified him in a cruel ceremony.

Note from Dreyfus to His Wife on the Day of His Humiliation
"There is a traitor, but it is not I!"

The Letters of Captain Dreyfus to His Wife, *trans. L. G. Moreau (New York: Harper & Brothers, 1899), pp. 30–33. Hereafter cited as* Letters of an Innocent Man, *from its original title,* Lettres d'un Innocent.

From the prison of La Santé on the day of his degradation, Dreyfus's thoughts turned again and again to his wife. In his agony he wrote three times to her on that tragic day.

5 January, 1895

I will not tell you what I have suffered to-day. Your grief is great enough already. I will not augment it.

In promising you to live, in promising you to resist until my name is rehabilitated, I have made the greatest sacrifice that a man of deep feeling of heart, an upright man, from whom his honor has been taken, can make. My God, let not my physical strength abandon me! My spirit is unshaken; a conscience that has nothing with which to reproach me upholds me, but I am coming to the end of patience and of my physical strength. After having consecrated all my life to honor, never having deserved reproach, to be here, to have borne the most wounding affront that can be inflicted upon a soldier!

Oh, my darling, do everything in the world to find the guilty one; do not relax your efforts for one instant. That is my only hope in the terrible misfortune which pursues me.

If only I may soon be with you there, and if we may soon be united, you will give me back my strength and my courage. I have need of both. This day's emotions have broken my heart; my cell offers me no consolation.

Picture a little room all bare—four yards and a half long, perhaps—closed by a grated garret window; a pallet standing against the wall—no, I will not tear your heart, my poor darling.

I will tell you later, when we are happy again, what I have suffered to-day, in all my wanderings, surrounded by men who are truly guilty, how my heart has bled. I have asked myself why I was there; what I was doing there. I seemed the victim of a hallucination; but alas! my garments, torn, sullied, brought me back roughly to the truth. The looks of scorn they cast on me told me too well why I was there. Oh, why could not my heart have been opened by a surgeon's knife, so that they might have read the truth! All the brave, good people along my way could have read it: *"This is a man of honor!"* But how easy it is to understand them! In their place I could not have contained my contempt for an officer who I had been told was a traitor. But alas! there is the tragedy. There is a traitor, but it is not I!

Write to me soon; do everything in your power so that I may see you, for my strength is giving way. I need to be upheld; come, so that we may be together once again, that I may find in your heart all the strength I need in this awful hour.

I embrace you as I love you.

Saturday afternoon. ALFRED

Saturday, 6 o'clock, 5 January, 1895

In my dark cell, in the tortures of my soul, which refuses to understand why I suffer so, why God so punishes me, it is always to you that I turn, my dear wife, who, in these sad and terrible moments, have shown for me a devotion without boundaries, a love illimitable.

You have been and you are sublime; in my moments of weakness I have been ashamed not to be at the height of your heroism. But this grief must gnaw the best disciplined soul; the grief of seeing so many efforts, so many years of honor, of devotion to one's country, lost because of a machination that seems to belong to the realms of the grotesque, rather than to real life. Sometimes I cannot believe it; but these moments, alas! are rare here, for subjected to the strictest discipline of the prison cell, everything reminds me of the dark reality. Continue to sustain me with your profound love, my darling; aid me in this awful struggle for my honor; let me feel your beautiful soul throbbing close to mine.

When can I see you?

I need affection and consolation in my sorrow.

Alas! I may have the courage of a soldier, but I ask myself have I the heroic soul of the martyr!

A thousand good kisses for you, for our darlings. May these children be your consolation.

A. DREYFUS

Write to me often and at length. Think that I am here alone from morning until evening, and from evening until morning. Not one sympathetic soul comes to lighten my dark sorrow. I long to be there with you, where I can wait in peace and tranquillity, until they rehabilitate me—until they give me back my honor.

7 o'clock, evening, 5 January, 1895

I have just had a moment of terrible weakness; of tears mingled with sobs; all my body shaken by the fever. It was the reaction from the awful tortures of the day. It had to be—I knew it. But alas! instead of being allowed to sob in your arms, to lean my head upon your breast, my sobs have resounded in the emptiness of my prison. It is finished. Be lifted up, my heart; I concentrate all my energy. Strong in my conscience, pure and unstained, I owe myself to my family, I owe myself to my name. I have not the right to desert. While there remains in me a breath of life I will struggle, hoping that light soon may be let in upon the truth. And do you continue your searches. As for me, the only thing that I ask is to leave here as soon as possible; to find you there; to settle down to our life there, while our friends, our families, are busy here searching for the guilty one, so that we may come back to our dear country, martyrs who have borne the most terrible, the most harrowing, of trials.

Headline: "Dreyfus Has Confessed!"

"If I delivered these documents, they were without any value, and it was in order to procure more important ones."

Steevens, The Tragedy of Dreyfus, *pp. 225–227.*

On January 6, 1895, the day after the degradation, there was great excitement in Paris when the news hit the streets that Dreyfus had confessed. The report was soon traced to Captain Charles-Gustave-Nicolas Lebrun-Renault, commander of a squadron of the Republican Guard and responsible for the prisoner at both the *École de Guerre* and on the *Champs de Mars* before and after the degradation. At the *Moulin Rouge* that evening, Captain Lebrun-Renault, an alcoholic, confided to some friends that Dreyfus had confessed his guilt to him about an hour before the ceremony began.

Within hours word of Dreyfus's "confession" reached War Minister General Mercier, who at that time, as he later testified, was concerned about the possibility of war between France and Germany breaking out at any moment. Mercier immediately sent Lebrun-Renault to the President of the Republic to tell his story. By now it was too late to retract it.

Three years later Lieutenant-Colonel Guerin, Assistant Chief of the Military Government of Paris, issued a report on the 1895 declaration of Captain Lebrun-Renault. The purpose at this time was to assemble all the reports that were in circulation about the Dreyfus case which was being discussed in the Chamber of Deputies.

After having been placed, January 5, 1895, by the Military Government of Paris, at the disposition of General Darras, to assist at the military degradation of Captain Dreyfus, I went that day at quarter past five in the morning to the Military School, *cour* Morland. Captain . . . was ordered to verify the cards of representatives of the French Press, reserve and territorial officers, and to place them in the order which was arranged for them.

The prison van, escorted by a squad of the Republican Guard commanded by Captain Lebrun-Renault, entered the Military School at forty-five minutes past seven, and was stopped at the *cour* Morland, before the office of the adjutant of the garrison. Dreyfus stepped out and was conducted to this office and remained there until the moment when all the troops being in position, the captain of the garrison came, about five minutes before nine o'clock, to conduct him at nine o'clock to the place marked for the ceremony.

Meeting Captain Lebrun-Renault at the entrance of the office, he at once told me of his interview with Captain Dreyfus. At the first words, as it did not seem to be advisable that this should be limited to us two, and a group of officers being near us, I begged Captain Lebrun-Renault to relate to them the confidences that Dreyfus had made to him, on account of their importance and interest.

This officer then told us that he had talked of Tahiti with Dreyfus, the place where he would probably be sent. He boasted that the climate would suit him very well and also his wife and children. Captain Dreyfus, showing him the braid on his dolman, told him that it was pride he had lost. He added this declaration, "If I delivered these documents, they were without any value, and it was in order to procure more important ones."

(Signed) Lieutenant-Colonel Guerin

Paris, February 14, 1898.
Copy certified September 16, 1898.

What had happened?

Apparently, Dreyfus had said to Lebrun-Renault something like this: "Du Paty de Clam asked me on behalf of the Minister if I had handed over unimportant documents so that I might receive important ones in exchange." Lebrun-Renault repeated this innocent remark as: "If I delivered these documents, they were without any value, and it was in order to procure more important ones."

In this possible way the truth was perverted from mouth to mouth. Lebrun-Renault's *faux pas* was periodically resurrected during the course of the Affair. Over and over again he attempted to explain how the mistake had been made, but few believed him.

Dreyfus Begins His Journey to Exile

"Throw him overboard!" "Death to the traitor!" "Kill the Jew!"

La Libre Parole, *January 20, 1895. Translated by the editor.*

On January 17, 1895, Dreyfus was awakened in his cell at the Santé Prison in Paris, told to prepare for his departure, and taken to the Orléans railway station in a prison van reserved for convicts on their way to the penal colonies. He was locked in a narrow cell, his wrists handcuffed, with iron chains around his ankles. He was removed from the train at nightfall at La Rochelle, from which the convict ships sailed for the Island of *Ré*.

At La Rochelle a large crowd gathered after an indiscreet warder mentioned the name of Dreyfus. What happened then was described with some relish by E. Cravoisier in *La Libre Parole*.

In order to avoid all attacks against him, it was decided to have him pass not through the entrance but through the exit.

He stepped down from the railway carriage. It was now completely dark.

Outside, the people of La Rochelle, increasing moment by moment in numbers, began a frightful clamor. "Throw him overboard!" "Death to the traitor!" "Kill the Jew!"

Dreyfus was afraid. . . .

Some people lit matches to be able to see the figure of the traitor.

After some jostling, Dreyfus found himself in contact with the crowd. Despite the protection of guards and police, he received hard blows from fists and walking sticks. Finally, he was hoisted into a carriage at the station and he was taken away at a fast gallop. The crowd followed the carriage and picked up stones to hurl at the windows which broke into fragments.

It was an incomplete and slanted report of a disgraceful scene. The precautionary measures were insufficient. As Dreyfus, wrapped in a long coat, descended from the train to cross the platform and enter the waiting carriage, the enraged mob broke through the weak barriers, and attacked the helpless man with sticks, stones, and fists. Dreyfus later described it: "As soon as I appeared, the clamor redoubled and blows fell on and around me. The crowd made sudden and angry rushes. I stood impassive in the midst of this throng, for a moment even alone, ready to deliver my body to the fury of the mob. But my soul was my own, and I understood only too well the outraged feelings of these poor deluded people." Dreyfus was, indeed, close to being lynched.

The Prisoner on the Island of *Ré*

". . . I would rather, a hundred thousand times rather, be dead."

Letters of an Innocent Man, *pp. 56–58.*

Following this miserable episode, Dreyfus was shut up in a cabin on board the *Nénuphar* for the two-mile trip from the mainland of Western France to the Island of *Ré,* the last French station for convicts sentenced to deportation. One newspaper, *La Charente-Inférieure* (January 20, 1895), protested that he was given special treatment: that he was allowed to keep 417 francs in his pockets, that he was served a chicken wing and a cut of frozen ham, and that when he was hungry he was served cold coffee, or if he preferred "a wine of a respectable age." That the prisoner was not altogether happy was indicated by this first letter he sent to his wife from the prison of *Saint-Martin de Ré.*

                                                                    19 January, 1895
MY DARLING:

Thursday evening, toward ten o'clock, they came to wake me to bring me here, where I arrived only last night. I do not want to speak of my journey, it would break your heart. Know only that I have heard the legitimate cries of a brave and generous people against him whom they believe to be a traitor, the lowest of wretches. I am no longer sure if I have a heart.

Oh, what a sacrifice I made the day of my condemnation, when I promised you that I should not kill myself! What a sacrifice I made to the name of my poor, dear, little children, in bearing what I am undergoing! If there is a divine justice, we must hope that I shall be recompensed for this long and fearful torture, for this suffering of every minute and every instant. The other day your father told me that he would have preferred death. And I—I would rather, a hundred thousand times rather, be dead. But this right to die belongs to none of us; the more I suffer the more must it impel your courage and your resolution to find the truth. Look on for the truth, do not waver, do not rest. Let your efforts be in proportion to the sufferings which I have imposed upon myself.

Will you please ask, or have someone ask, at the Ministry for the following authorizations; the Minister alone can accord them:

1. The right to write to all the members of my family—father, mother, brothers, and sisters.

2. The right to write and to work in my cell. At present I have neither *paper,* nor *pen,* nor *ink.* I am given only the sheet of paper on which I write to you; then they take away my pen and ink.

3. Permission to smoke.

I beg you not to come before you are completely cured.

The climate here is very rigorous, and you need all your health, first for our dear children, then for the end for which you are working. *As to my régime here, I am forbidden to speak to you of it.*

And now I must remind you that before you come here you must provide yourself with *all* the authorizations necessary *to see me;* do not forget to ask permission *to kiss me,* etc., etc.

When shall we be reunited, my darling? I live in the hope of that, and in the still greater hope of my restoration to honor. But oh, how my soul suffers! Tell all our family that they must work on without weakening, without resting; for all that comes to us now is appalling, tragic. Write to me soon.

I embrace you as I love you.

II

Golgotha on Devil's Island

On March 12, 1895, after fifteen stormy days aboard the transport *Ville de Saint Nazaire,* Dreyfus reached the *Îles du Salut* (Salvation Islands), the French penal colony on the northeast coast of South America. The archipelago consisted of a group of small islands—the *Île Royale,* where the chief warden had his headquarters, the *Île Saint-Joseph,* and the *Île du Diable,* or Devil's Island. The latter was a miserable barren rock used previously for the isolation of lepers. Fifteen old leper huts were burned to make way for the new prisoner.

After thirty days of confinement on *Île Royale,* Dreyfus was moved to Devil's Island. The stone hut built for him was thirteen feet square, with iron gratings on the windows and the door a latticework of simple iron bars. A guard stationed at the entrance was relieved every two hours. By day the prisoner was allowed to walk only to that part of the island between the landing place and the little valley where the lepers had lived in their camp, a space of about 220 yards. On such walks he was always accompanied by an armed guard, to whom he was forbidden to speak. His rations were those of a soldier in the colonies and he was required to do his own cooking. To make sure that the prisoner could not escape, a large observation tower, about 50 feet high and 100 feet above sea level, was constructed. At the top was a covered platform for the guard on duty. On the platform was a Hotchkiss gun which was to be fired at any suspicious craft in the vicinity.

During the day the weather was suffocatingly hot. During the night Dreyfus was tortured by vermin and poisonous insects. Every two hours he was disturbed by the grinding of locks being unbolted and chains replaced.

The Prisoner Keeps a Diary
"Oh, the hatefulness of man!"

Dreyfus, Five Years, *pp. 103–139.*

For nearly five years Dreyfus was a carefully guarded prisoner in that abominable hellhole. During this time he learned little of what was going on in France concerning his case. For all he knew he had disappeared from the face of the earth and had been forgotten in the rush of events. Two things sustained his spirit: his love for his wife and children and his confidence that one day his innocence would be established.

Dreyfus kept a diary from April 1895 until the autumn of 1896. Intended for his wife, the diary was seized with all his papers and it was never given to Mme. Dreyfus. Dreyfus obtained possession of it only at the Rennes trial in 1899. Following are the entries from April 14 to June 12, 1895, covering the first two months of captivity.

Îles du Salut

MY DIARY

(TO BE HANDED TO MY WIFE)

Sunday, April 14, 1895

To-day I begin the diary of my sad and tragic life. Indeed, only to-day have I paper at my disposal. Each sheet is numbered and signed so that I cannot use it without its being known. I must account for every bit of it. But what could I do with it? Of what use could it be to me? To whom would I give it? What secret have I to confide to paper? Questions and enigmas!

Until now I have worshipped reason, I have believed there was logic in things and events, I have believed in human justice! Anything irrational and extravagant found difficult entrance into my brain. Oh, what a breaking down of all my beliefs and of all sound reason!

What fearful months I have passed, what sad months still await me!

During these first days, when, in the disarray of mind and senses which was the consequence of the iniquitous sentence passed on me, I had resolved to kill myself, my dear wife, with her undaunted devotion and courage, made me realize that it is because I am innocent that I have not the right to abandon her or wilfully to desert my post. I knew she was right, and that this was my duty; but yet I was afraid,—yes, afraid of the atrocious mental sufferings the future had in store for me. Physically I felt myself strong enough; a pure conscience gave me superhuman strength. But the mental and physical tortures have been worse than I feared, and to-day I am broken in body and spirit.

However, I yielded to my wife. I lived! But what a life! I underwent first the worst punishment which can be inflicted on a soldier,—a punishment worse than any death,—then, step by step, I traversed the horrible path which brought me hither, by the *Santé* Prison and the depot of the *Île de Ré,* supporting without flinching the insults and cries, but leaving a fragment of my heart at every turn of the road.

My conscience bore me up; my reason said to me each day: "The truth at last will shine forth triumphant; in a century like ours the light cannot long remain concealed." But, alas! each day brought with it a new deception. The light not only did not shine forth, but everything was done to dim it.

I am still in the closest confinement. All my correspondence is read and checked off at the Ministry, and often not forwarded. They even forbade my writing to my wife about the investigations which I wished to counsel her to have made. It is impossible for me to defend myself.

I thought that, once in my exile, I might find, if not rest,—this I cannot have till my honor is restored,—at least some tranquillity of mind and life, which might help me to wait for the day of rehabilitation. What a new and bitter disappointment!

After a voyage of fifteen days shut up in a cage, I first remained for four days in the roadstead of the *Îles du Salut* without going on deck, in the midst of tropical heat. My brain and my whole being melted away in despair.

When I was landed, I was shut up in a room of the prison, with closed blinds, prohibited from speaking to anyone, alone with my thoughts, with the *régime* of a convict. My correspondence had first to be sent to Cayenne. I do not yet know if it came to hand.

Since I landed a month ago, I have remained locked in my pen without once leaving it, in spite of all the bodily fatigue of my painful journey. Several times I all but went crazy; I had congestion of the brain, and I conceived such a horror of life that the temptation came to me to have no care of myself and so put an end to my martyrdom. This would have been deliverance and the end of my troubles, for I should not have perjured myself, as my death would have been natural.

The remembrance of my wife and of my duty toward my children has given me strength to pull myself together. I am not willing to nullify her efforts and abandon her in her mission of seeking out the truth and the guilty man. For this reason, in spite of my fierce distaste of seeing a new face, which would be sure to be inimical, I asked for the doctor.

At last, after thirty days of this close confinement, they came to fetch me to the *Île du Diable,* where I shall enjoy a semblance of liberty. By day I shall be able to walk about in a space less than half an acre, followed step by step by the guards; at nightfall (between six and half-past six o'clock) I shall be shut up in my hut, thirteen feet square, closed by a door made of iron bars, through which relays of guards will look at me all the night long.

A chief and five guards are exclusively appointed to this service. My rations are half a loaf of bread a day, 300 grammes (.66 of a pound) of meat three times a week, the other days canned pork or canned beef.

For an honorable, an innocent man, what a terrible existence of constant suspicion, of uninterrupted surveillance!

And then I have never any news of my wife and children. Yet I know that since the 29th of March, nearly three weeks ago, there have been letters for me at Cayenne. I have had them telegraph to Cayenne and to France for news of my dear ones. There is no reply.

Oh, how I wish to live until the day of rehabilitation, to cry out my sufferings, and give voice to the pangs of my heart! Shall I last so long? Often I have doubts, my heart is so oppressed and my health so shaken.

Sunday night, April 14 to 15, 1895

It is impossible for me to sleep. This cage before which the guard walks up and down like a phantom appearing in my dreams, the plague of insects which run over my skin, the rage which is smothered in my heart that I should be here, when I have always and everywhere done my duty,—all this over-excites my nerves, which are already shattered, and drives away sleep. When shall I again pass a calm and tranquil night? Perhaps not until I find in the tomb the sleep that is everlasting.

How sweet it will be to have no further concern with human vileness and cowardice!

The sea which I hear murmuring beneath my little window has always for me a strange fascination. It soothes my thoughts, bitter and somber though they be. It recalls dear memories, the happy days I have passed with my wife and darling children.

I have again a violent sensation, which I felt on the boat, of being drawn almost irresistibly toward the sea, whose murmurous waters seem to call me with the voice of a comforter. This tyranny of the sea over me is almost irresistible; on the boat I had to close my eyes and call up the image of my wife not to yield to it.

Where are the beautiful dreams of my youth and the aspirations of my manhood? My heart is dead within me; my brain reels with the turmoil of my thoughts. What is the mystery underlying this tragedy? Even now I understand nothing of what has passed. To be condemned without palpable proofs, on the strength of a bit of handwriting! However clear the soul and conscience of a man may be, is there not more than enough here to enfrenzy him?

The sensitiveness of my nerves, after all this torture, has become so acute that each new impression, even from without, produces on me the effect of a deep wound.

The same night

I have just tried to sleep, but after dozing a few minutes I awoke burning with fever; and it has been so every night for months. How has my body been able to resist such a combination of physical torments added to mental torture? I think that a clear conscience, sure of itself, must give invincible strength.

I open the blind which closes my little window and look again upon the sea. The sky is full of great clouds, but the moonlight filters through, tingeing the sea with silver. The waves break powerless at the foot of the rocks which outline the shape of the island. There is a constant lapping of the water, as it plays on the beach with a rude staccato rhythm that soothes my wounded soul.

And in this night, in the deep calm, there come back to my mind the dear images of my wife and children. How my poor Lucie must suffer from so undeserved a lot, after having had everything to make her happy! And happy she so well deserves to be, for the purity and sweetness of her character, for her tender and devoted heart. Poor, poor little wife! When I think of her and of my children, something within me gives way and my grief finds vent in sobs. . . .

I am going to try to work at my English. Perhaps the task will help me to forget a little.

Monday, April 15, 1895

There was a deluge of rain this morning. For my breakfast I had nothing. The guards took pity on me and gave me a little black coffee and bread.

When the storm lightened, I made the rounds of the little portion of this islet which is reserved to me. It is a sad place, this island. Where I cannot go there are a few banana trees and a few cocoa palms, and the rest is dry soil from which basaltic rocks crop out everywhere.

At ten o'clock they bring me my day's food,—a bit of canned pork, some rice, some coffee berries in filthy condition, and a little moist sugar. I have no means of roasting the coffee, which in bitter derision is given to me raw. I throw it all into the sea. Then I try to make a fire. After several fruitless efforts I succeed. I heat water for my tea. My luncheon is made up of bread and tea.

What agony of my whole being! What a sacrifice I have made in giving my pledge to live! Nothing will be spared me, neither mental torture nor physical suffering.

Oh, that plangent sea which is always muttering and howling at my feet! What an echo to my soul! The foam of the wave which breaks upon the rocks is so softly white that I could throw myself upon it to seek rest, and be lost.

Monday, April 15, evening

Again I had only a bit of bread for my dinner, and I was fainting. The guards, seeing my bodily weakness, passed in to me a bowl of their broth.

Then I smoked,—smoked to calm both my brain and the gnawing of my stomach. I have repeated my request of a fortnight ago to the Governor of Guiana, that I may live at my own expense, getting canned food from Cayenne, as the law allows me to do.

Dear wife, at this very moment does your thought respond to my own? Do you realize what I am undergoing? Yes, I know, I am sure, you feel all that I am suffering.

How this one idea haunts me ceaselessly, that, condemned for a hateful crime, I do not understand anything about it! If there is justice in the world, my untarnished name must be given back to me, and the guilty one, the monster, must suffer the punishment that his crime deserves.

Tuesday, April 16, 1895

Exhausted beyond measure, I have been able to sleep. My first thought as I awoke was for you, my dear and beloved Lucie. I asked myself what you were doing at the same moment. You must have been busy with our children. May they be your comfort if I give way before the end!

Next I go out to cut wood. After two hours of effort, sweating profusely, I succeed in getting together enough for my needs. At eight o'clock they bring me a piece of raw meat and bread. I kindle my fire. The smoke is blown back by the sea breeze and my eyes smart and weep. As soon as there are enough coals I put the meat on some stray scraps of

iron which I have gathered together here and there, and grill it. I breakfast a little better than yesterday, though the meat is tough and dry.
As to my bill of fare for dinner, it is very simple,—bread and water. These
petty exertions have worn me out.

Friday, April 19, 1895

I have not written for some days because the struggle for life has occupied all my activities. No matter what they do, I will resist to the last
drop of my blood.

The diet has not changed: I cannot have my canned goods; they are
always waiting for orders. To-day I boiled my meat with some wild
peppers I had found in the island. This took three hours, during which
my eyes suffered horribly. How miserable!

And never any news from my wife and my dear ones. Have the letters
been intercepted?

Worn out, thinking to calm my nerves by splitting wood for to-morrow,
I go to look for the hatchet in the kitchen. "You cannot enter the
kitchen," calls out the guard. And I go my way, saying nothing, but without lowering my head. Oh, if I could only live in my hut without ever
going out of it!

From time to time I try to do English translations, and to forget myself
in my work. But my brain is so utterly shaken that it will not respond;
after a quarter of an hour I am forced to give it up.

And then, I find that they intercept all my correspondence. I understand that they must take every possible and imaginable precaution to
prevent my escape; it is the right, even the strict duty, of the prison
administration. But that they should bury me alive in a sepulchre, that
they should prevent all communication, even by open letter, with my
family,—this is against all justice. You might think we were thrown back
centuries. For six months I have been in close confinement without being
able to help toward the restoration of my honor.

Saturday, April 20, 1895, 11 o'clock in the morning

I have finished my cooking for the day. This morning I cut my piece
of meat in two: one piece is to boil; the other is for a steak. To cook the
latter, I have contrived a grill from an old piece of sheet iron which I
picked up in the island. For drink, I have water. My food is ill-prepared
in old tin cans. I have nothing with which to clean these properly, and
have no plates. I must pull together all my courage to live under such
conditions, added to all my mental tortures.

Utterly exhausted, I am going to stretch myself out on my bed.

Night from Saturday to Sunday, 2 A.M.

To think that in our century, in a country like France, imbued with ideas of justice and truth, such things, so utterly undeserved, can come to pass. I have written to the President of the Republic, I have written to the Ministers, always asking them to seek out the truth. They have no right thus to allow the honor of an officer and his family to be undermined with no other proof than a bit of handwriting, when the government has the means of investigation necessary to bring out the light. I cry aloud, in the name of my honor, demanding justice.

I was so hungry this afternoon that, to still the gnawings of my stomach, I devoured, raw, ten tomatoes which I found in the island.*

My night was feverish. I dreamed of you, dear Lucie, and of our dear children, as I do every night.

How you must suffer, my poor love!

Happily, our children are still too young to realize, else what an apprenticeship to sorrow would be theirs! As for me, no matter what my martyrdom, my duty is to go to the end of my strength without faltering. I shall go.

I have just written to Commandant du Paty to remind him of the two promises he made me after sentence was pronounced: first, in the name of the Minister to continue the investigations; second, in his own name personally, to warn me as soon as there should be new leakages at the Ministry.

The villain who has committed the crime is on a fatal incline and will not be able to check his descent.

Sunday, April 21, 1895

The commandant of the islands was kind enough to send me this morning, with my meat, two cans of condensed milk. Each can holds about three quarts; by drinking a quart and a half a day, I shall have enough milk for four days.

I have stopped boiling the meat, which I could not make eatable. This morning I have cut it into two slices, and shall grill one of them for the morning meal and one for the evening.

In the intervals of my enforced housework, I continually think of my darling wife and all my dear ones, and of all they must suffer.

May the day of justice soon dawn!

* Raw tomatoes are considered in France as inedible as raw potatoes. The lepers had cultivated the island a little, and there were still traces of their gardening. The tomatoes, which now grow wild, were very numerous.

My days are interminable! Every minute of every hour a long-drawn-out weariness.

I am incapable of any considerable physical exertion; moreover, from ten in the morning until three in the evening the heat makes it impossible for me to go out. I cannot work at my English all day long,—my brain will not stand it,—and I have nothing to read. My only resource is a perpetual companionship with my thoughts! As I was kindling the fire to make my tea, I saw the canoe coming from the *Île Royale*. I was obliged to retire into the hut. It is the order. Do they fear, then, that I shall communicate with the convicts?

Monday, April 22, 1895

I rose at daybreak to wash my linen and to dry my clothing in the sun. Everything moulders here because of the mixture of dampness and heat. Quick showers of rain in torrents alternate with burning heat.

Yesterday I asked the commandant of the islands for one or two plates, of no matter what kind; he answered that he had none. I am forced to exercise my ingenuity and to eat either off paper or old scraps of iron gathered on the island. The dirt I eat in this way is inconceivable.

I hold out in spite of all, for my wife's and my children's sake. I am always alone, in communion with my thoughts. What a martyrdom for an innocent man, as great surely as that of any Christian martyr!

I am still without news from my family, in spite of my repeated demands; for two months I have had no letters.

I have just received some dried vegetables in old preserve cans. In trying to transform these cans into plates, while washing them, I cut my fingers.

I have just been told that I must wash my own linen. I have no soap with which to do it. I have set myself to the task for two hours together, but the result is not encouraging. At all events, the linen will have been soaked in water.

I am utterly worn out. Shall I be able to sleep? I doubt it. I have such a mingling of physical weakness and extreme nervousness that, the moment I am in bed, the nerves get the upper hand, and I am tortured with anxiety about my dear ones.

I wrote to my wife; this is one of my rare moments of calm. I always exhort her to have courage and energy; for our honor must be made to appear to all, without any exception, as it has always been, pure and stainless.

The terrific heat takes away all strength and all physical energy.

Saturday, April 27, 1895

On account of the heat, I am changing my habits. I rise at daybreak (half-past five) and light my fire and make coffee or tea. Then I put the dried vegetables on the fire, and afterward make my bed, clean up my chamber, and perform a summary toilet.

At eight o'clock they bring me the day's rations. I finish cooking the dried vegetables, and on meat days place these rations on the fire. Thus all my cooking is over by ten o'clock, for I eat in the evening what is left over from the morning.

At ten o'clock I lunch. Next I read, work, dream, and, most of all, suffer, until three o'clock. Then I make a thorough toilet. As soon as the heat has diminished, toward five o'clock, I cut my wood, draw water from the well, wash my linen, and so on. At six o'clock I eat the cold remains of my luncheon. Then I am locked up. The night is my longest time. I have not been able to obtain permission to have a lamp in my hut. There is a lantern in the guard post, but the light is too dim to work by long. Nothing is left for me but to lie down, and then my brain begins to work; all my thoughts turn to the frightful drama of which I am the victim, and all my memories center about my wife and children and those who are dear to me. How all of them must suffer with me!

Sunday, April 28, 1895

The wind blows a tempest. The gusts, coming one after the other, buffet the little hut, and everything in it trembles under the shock. How it resembles at times the state of my soul in its passionate storms! Would that I were as strong and powerful as the wind which shakes the trees and uproots them, so that I might sweep aside every obstacle that bars the way to the truth!

I would like to cry aloud all my sufferings, and the revolt of my heart against the ignominy thrust upon an innocent man and his dear ones. Oh, what a punishment is merited by the one who has committed this crime! He has acted like a criminal toward his country, toward an innocent man, and he has driven a whole family to despair. Such a man is certainly an unnatural being, a monster!

To-day I have learned how to clean my kitchen utensils. Until now I simply washed them with hot water, using my handkerchiefs for dishrags. In spite of everything they remained dirty and greasy. Suddenly I thought of the ashes, which contain a large proportion of potash. This combination has succeeded admirably, but in what a state it has put hands and handkerchiefs!

Just now I have been told that, until further order, my linen clothes will be washed at the hospital. This is good luck, for with the constant perspiration they are in need of a thorough scrubbing. I hope this provisional measure will be made permanent.

The same day, 7 o'clock in the evening

I have thought long of you, dear Lucie, and of our children. Because on Sunday we used to spend the whole day together, the time has passed slowly today, very slowly, for me, and my thoughts grow somber as the day draws to an end.

Monday, April 29, 1895, 10 A.M.

Never have I been so tired as this morning, after having drawn water and cut wood. With all that, the luncheon that is waiting for me is made up of dried-up old beans which have been on the fire four hours and will not cook, and some nauseating canned beef. In a debilitating climate, my waning physical strength cannot possibly keep up if this repugnant diet lasts much longer.

Noon

I have tried in vain to sleep. I am worn out with fatigue; but the moment I cease to be active and lie down, the overwhelming consciousness of my sorrows surges in, filling my brain, and I feel the bitterness of my unjustifiable condemnation rise from my heart to my lips. My nerves are so set on edge, so racked that I cannot obtain even a moment of refreshing sleep.

With all this, there is a storm brewing in the air, the sky is overcast, and the heat oppressive, stifling.

I wish for a change that I could hear the rain fall to refresh this eternally furnace-like atmosphere. The sea is pale green, the waves are leaden, massive as if gathering for a great upheaval. How preferable death would be to this slow agony, to this constant martyrdom! But I have no right to think this; for the sake of Lucie and my children I must struggle on.

Wednesday, May 1, 1895

Oh, the horrible nights! Yet I rose yesterday as usual, at half-past five, toiled all day long, took no siesta, and toward evening sawed wood for nearly an hour, until I trembled with fatigue. Yet I could not sleep till long past midnight.

If only I could read or work through the evening! The lantern of the guard post, which is insufficient for my waking pursuits, is still too strong for me when I am in bed.

Thursday, May 2, 11 o'clock

The mail from Cayenne arrived yesterday evening. Does it bring me letters at last, with news of my dear ones? I have been asking myself this question every minute since morning. But I have had so many disappointments during these long months and have heard things so contrary to all ideas of common humanity that I doubt everything and everyone except my own family. I am sure they will get at the truth and will not falter a moment in seeking for it.

I also ask myself if my own letters reach my wife. What a frightful experience for all of us!

. . . So profound is my solitude that often I seem to be lying alive in my tomb.

The same day, 5 o'clock in the afternoon

The boat coming from the *Île Royale* is in sight. My heart beats as though it would burst. Does the boat bring my wife's letters, which have been at Cayenne more than a month? Shall I read her dear thoughts and be comforted by her words of affection?

My joy was boundless on finding there were letters for me at last, but this was soon followed by a cruel disappointment when I saw they were letters addressed to the *Île de Ré* and dated previous to my departure from France. Are they, then, suppressing the letters addressed to me here? Or do they perhaps send them back to France, so that they may be read there first? Could they not at least notify my family that they must send their letters to me through the Ministry?

In spite of all, I have sobbed long over these letters, dated more than two months and a half ago. Could any one possibly imagine such a tragedy? . . .

Nothing of all I had asked for has come from Cayenne, neither cooking utensils nor food.

Saturday, May 4, 1895

The dreary length of these days in maddening isolation and with no news from home! I ask myself repeatedly what my dear ones are doing; what has become of them, how they are, and how far their investigations have gone. My last letter from them was dated February 18.

The mornings pass after a fashion. The struggle for existence gives me something definite, material, to do from half-past five until ten o'clock. But the food I am taking is far from keeping up my strength.

To-day is canned pork day. I lunched on split peas and bread. Bill of fare for dinner: the same.

Why do I so often note the little facts of my daily life? They are but a passing shadow before the ever-present anxiety, that which concerns my good name.

I suffer not only from my tortures, but from those of the dear ones at home. Do they even receive my letters? How anxious they must be about me, quite apart from all their other preoccupations!

The same day, evening

In the eternal silence reigning around me, which is interrupted only by the noise of the waves lapping on the rocks, I recall the letters I wrote to Lucie at the beginning of my stay here, in which I dwelt upon my miseries. What right have I to tear her heart with my lamentations, when she must suffer as much as I do? By sheer force of will I must overcome my anguish, and by my example, give my wife the strength needed to carry out her mission.

Monday, May 6, 1895

Always alone with this poor head of mine, without any news from my beloved ones.

Thus with my sorrows must I live! Yes, I must bear up, worthily inspiring with courage my wife and all my family. No more weakness, then! Accept your lot! You must for your children's sake. Neither the climate nor my own strength permits me to regain full mastery of myself, and I try in vain by hard manual labor to control my nerves.

Tuesday, May 7, 1895

Since yesterday there has been a deluge of rain, and in the intervals the hot, stifling, humid air has been unbearable.

Wednesday, May 8, 1895

I was so wild to-day in this eternal silence, without news of my dear ones for nearly three months, that for two hours I tried to wear down the tension of my nerves by sawing and splitting wood. I also succeed by force of will in working at English again; I am studying it from two to three hours a day.

Thursday, May 9, 1895

This morning, after rising as usual at the break of day and making my coffee, I had a fit of weakness, followed by a copious perspiration. I had to lie down on my bed. I must struggle to support my body; it must not yield until my honor is restored. Then only shall I have the right to give way to weakness.

In spite of all my efforts at self-control, the thought of home brought an uncontrollable outburst of tears. Oh, the truth must surely be revealed. If it is not to be so, I should wish to hear that both my children were dead. What can life have in store for them, if my good name, their name, be not vindicated?

A frightful day. Violent nervous chills. But the soul must master the body.

Friday, May 10, 1895

High fever last night. The medicine chest my wife gave me has not yet been delivered.

Saturday, Sunday, Monday, May 11, 12, 13

Bad days. Fever, stomach trouble, disgust for everything. And what is going on in France all this time? At what point are the investigations?

Sunburn, too, on my feet, because I went out without my shoes for a few seconds.

Thursday, May 16, 1895

Continual fever. A stronger attack yesterday evening, followed by congestion of the brain. I have asked for the doctor, because I am not willing to give up like this.

Friday, May 17, 1895

The doctor came yesterday evening. He ordered heavy doses of quinine, and will send me twelve cans of condensed milk. It is good to be able to live on a milk diet and no longer to eat food, which has become so repulsive to me that I have taken nothing for four days. I would never have believed that the human body had such power of endurance.

Saturday, May 18, 1895

The condensed milk from the hospital was not very good. Still, it is better than nothing. It is a change.

Sunday, May 19, 1895

A gloomy day. A tropical rain pouring without cessation. My temperature has gone down, thanks to the quinine.

I have placed on my table, to have them always before my eyes, the pictures of my wife and my children. I must gather from them all my strength.

Monday, May 27, 1895

The gloomy, monotonous days are hardly distinguishable one from another. I have just written to my wife to say that my courage is unshaken. It must be; I will have the fullest light thrown on this affair.

Oh, my dear children! I am like the animal that interposes its own body between the hunters and its little ones.

Wednesday, May 29, 1895

Constant rains; stifling, heavy, nerve-irritating weather. Oh, my nerves, how they make me suffer! To think that my whole energy of mind and body can only prolong this dying by inches in a wilderness.

But I will have my day yet. The author of the infamous crime will surely be unmasked some day. Oh, if I had hold of him for only five minutes! I would make him undergo some of the torture which he has made me endure; I would tear out his heart without pity!

Saturday, June 1, 1895

The mail boat from Cayenne has just passed before my eyes. Shall I at last have recent news of my wife and children? Since I left France, that is, since the 20th of February, I have had no tidings of my dear ones. What abominable torture!

Sunday, June 2, 1895

Nothing. Nothing. Neither letters nor news of them; always the silence of the grave.

But strong in my conscience and in my right, I will hold out.

Monday, June 3, 1895

I have just seen the mail steamer pass by, sailing for France. My heart beat almost to breaking.

The mail will bring you, dearest Lucie, my last letters, in which I cry to you, Courage and courage again! All France must learn that I am a victim and not a miscreant.

A traitor! At the very word all my blood rushes to my head, everything in me trembles with rage. A traitor! The lowest of the low! Oh, no, I must live; I must master my sufferings, that I may see the day of the full and acknowledged triumph of my innocence.

Wednesday, June 5, 1895

How long the hours are! I have no more paper to write on, in spite of my repeated requests for the past three weeks. Neither have I anything to read, or to help me to escape from my thoughts.

No news from my dear ones for three months and a half!

Friday, June 7, 1895

I have just received some paper and also a few magazines. Torrents of rain today.

Under the tension of my thoughts my brain aches fearfully.

Sunday, June 9, 1895

Still no letters from my dear ones. My heart bleeds. Everything wounds me; death would be a deliverance, yet I have no right to think of it.

Wednesday, June 12, 1895

At last I have received letters from my wife and family. How I can feel between every line the grief and frightful sorrow of all those dear ones! The letters arrived here at the end of March, and must certainly have been sent back to France. So it takes more than three months for mail to reach me! I reproach myself for having written distressing letters to my wife when I first arrived here. I should have known how to bear my cross alone, rather than to inflict a share of my sufferings upon those who have a cruel burden of their own.

There is always this constant, unheard of, incomprehensible suspicion, adding ever to the wounds of my lacerated heart.

When he brought my mail, the commandant of the islands said to me:—

"They ask at Paris whether you or your family have not agreed on a secret correspondence code?"

"Look for it," I said. "What else do they think?"

"Oh," he replied, "they do not appear to believe in your innocence."

"Ah! I hope to live long enough to answer all the infamous calumnies which have sprung from the imaginations of people blinded by hate, passion, and prejudice!"

So, sooner or later, there must come to all the unescapable conviction of the truth, not only concerning my condemnation, but concerning also all that has been said and done since.

I have received my kitchen utensils and, for the first time, canned food from Cayenne. Material life is a matter of indifference to me, but by taking it into account I shall be better able to keep up my strength.

The convicts are to come for a few days to do some work on the island.

So they shut me up in my hut for fear that I shall communicate with them. Oh, the hatefulness of man! . . .

Letters of an Innocent

". . . if you want me to live have my honor given back to me."

The Letters of Captain Dreyfus to His Wife, *trans. L. G. Moreau (New York: Harper & Brothers, 1899), pp. 79–81, 84–87, 138–141.*

While on Devil's Island, Dreyfus's only contact with the outside world came in his correspondence with his wife, Lucie. Mme. Dreyfus was required to deposit her letters at the Colonial Ministry on the 25th day of each month. She was forbidden to write about the case or of events related to it, even if such developments were well known to the public. Her letters passed through many hands and they were read and carefully studied. Dreyfus's communications to his wife were kept by his warders and copies were delivered to her. In an attempt to break the prisoner, he was told that his wife wanted to forget him and desired to marry again.

Dreyfus's letters were written in deep sincerity. Readers can sense his love for his wife, for his children, and for France. He was apparently overcome by the seeming hopelessness of his position. There was no way he could prove his innocence by words in his letters. Throughout the correspondence, however, there were persistent declarations of innocence, repeated and repeated until the cry became almost monotonous. There were no details about the circumstances of the case. Dreyfus wrote regularly until the spring of 1898. In September of that year, overcome with a sense of defeat, he wrote a final *adieu* and declared that he would write no more. The following selections reveal the tone of letters sent from Devil's Island.

Tuesday, 12 March, 1895

MY DEAR LUCIE:

Thursday, the 21st of February, some hours after your departure, I was taken to Rochefort and put on shipboard.

I shall not speak to you of my voyage; I was transported in the manner in which the vile scoundrel whom I represent deserved to be transported. It was only just. They could not accord any pity to a traitor, the lowest of blackguards; and as long as I represent this wretch I can only approve their conduct.

My life here must drag itself out under the same conditions.

But your heart can tell you all that I have suffered—all that I suffer. I live only through the hope in my soul of soon seeing the triumphant light of my rehabilitation. That is the only thing that gives me strength to live. Without honor a man is not worthy of life.

On the day of my departure you assured me that the truth would surely come soon to light. I have lived during that awful voyage, I am living now, only on that word of yours—remember it well. I have been disembarked but a few minutes, and I have obtained permission to send you a cablegram.

I write in haste these few words, which will leave on the 15th by the English mail. It solaces me to have a talk with you, whom I love so profoundly. There are two mails a month for France—the 15th the English, and the 3d the French mail.

And in the same way there are two mails a month for the Isles—the English mail and the French mail. Find out the days of their departure and write to me by both of them.

All that I can tell you more is that if you want me to live have my honor given back to me. Convictions, whatever they may be, do nothing for me; they do not change my lot. What is necessary is a decision which will reinstate me.

I made for your sake the greatest sacrifice a man can make in resigning myself to live after my tragic fate was decided. I did this because you had inculcated in me the conviction that the truth must always come to light. In your turn, my darling, do all that is humanly possible to discover the truth. A wife and a mother yourself, try to move the hearts of wives and mothers, so that they may give up to you the key of this dreadful mystery. I must have my honor if you want me to live. I must have it for our dear children. Do not reason with your heart; that does no good. I have been convicted. Nothing can be changed in our tragic situation until the decision shall have been reversed. Reflect, then, and pursue the solution of this enigma. That will be worth more than coming here to share my horrible life. It will be the best, the only means of saving my life. Say to yourself that it is a question of life or death for me, for our children.

I am incapable of writing to you all. My brain will bear no more; my despair is too great. My nervous system is in a deplorable condition, and it is full time that this horrible tragedy should end.

Now my spirit alone is above water.

Oh, for God's sake, hurry, work with all your might!

Tell them all to write to me.

Embrace them all for me; our poor darlings, too.

And for you a thousand tender kisses from your devoted husband,

ALFRED

When you have some good news to announce to me send me a dispatch. I am waiting for it day by day as for the Messiah.

28 March, 1895

I was hoping to receive news of you at about this time; as yet I have heard nothing. I have already written you two letters.

I know nothing as yet beyond the four walls of my chamber. As for my health, it could not be very brilliant. Aside from my physical miseries, of which I speak only to cite them, the cause of this condition of my health lies chiefly in the disorder of my nervous system, produced by an uninterrupted succession of moral shocks.

You know that no matter how severe they might be at times, physical sufferings never wrung a groan from me, and that I could look death coolly in the face if only my mental sufferings did not darken my thoughts.

My mind cannot extricate itself for an instant from the horrible drama of which I am the victim, a tragedy which has struck a blow not only at my life—that is the least of evils, and truly it would have been better had the wretch who committed the crime killed me instead of wounding me as he has—but at my honor, the honor of my children, the honor of you all.

This piercing thought of my honor torn from me leaves me no rest either by day or by night. My nights, alas! you can imagine what they are! Formerly it was only sleeplessness, now the greater part of the night is passed in such a state of hallucination and of fever that I ask myself each morning how my brain still resists. This is one of the most cruel of all my sufferings. Add to this the long hours of the day passed in solitary communion with my thoughts, in the most absolute isolation.

Is it possible to rise above such preoccupation of the mind? Is it possible to force the mind to turn aside to other subjects of thought? I do not believe it; at least I cannot. When one is in this, the most agitating, the most tragic, plight that can possibly be conceived for a man whose honor has never failed him, nothing can turn the mind from the idea which dominates it.

Then when I think of you, of our dear children, my grief is unutterable; for the weight of the crime which some wretch has committed weighs heavily upon you also. You must, therefore, for our children's sake, pursue without truce, without rest, the work you have undertaken, and you must make my innocence burst forth in such a way that no doubt can be left in the mind of any human being. Whoever may be the persons who are convinced of my innocence, tell yourself that they will change nothing in our position; we often pay ourselves in words and nourish ourselves on illusions; nothing but my rehabilitation can save us.

You see, then, what I cannot cease reiterating to you, that it is a matter of life or of death, not only for me, but for our children. For myself I never will accept life without my honor. To say that an innocent man ought to live, that he always can live, is a commonplace whose triteness drives me to despair.

I used to say it and I used to believe it. Now that I have suffered all this myself, I declare that if a man has any spirit he cannot live under such circumstances. Life is admissible only when he can lift his head and look the world in the face; otherwise, there is nothing left for him but to die. To live for the sake of living is simply low and cowardly.

I am sure that in this you think as I do; any other opinion would be unworthy of us.

The situation, already so tragic, becomes each day more tense. You have not to weep, not to groan, but to face it with all your energy and with all your soul. To make clear this situation, we must not wait for a happy chance, but we must display all-absorbing activity. Knock at all doors. We must employ all means to make the light burst forth. All forms of investigation must be tried; the object we have in view is my life, the life of every one of us.

Here is a very clear bulletin of my state, moral and physical. I will sum it up:

A pitiable nervous and cervical condition, but extreme moral energy, outstretched toward the one object, which, no matter what the price, no matter by what means, we must attain—vindication. I will leave you to judge from this what struggles I am each day forced to make to keep myself from choosing death rather than this slow agony in every fiber of my being, rather than this torture of every instinct, in which physical suffering is added to agony of soul. You see that I am holding to my promise that I made you to struggle to live until the day of my rehabilitation. It remains for you to do the rest if you would have me reach that day.

Then away with weakness. Tell yourself that I am suffering martyrdom, that each day my brain is growing weaker; tell yourself that it is a question of my honor—that is to say, of my life, of the honor of your children. Let these thoughts inspire you, and then act accordingly.

Embrace every one, the children, for me.

A thousand kisses from your husband, who loves you.

ALFRED

How are the children? Give me news of them. I cannot think of you and of them without throbs of pain through my whole being. I would breathe into your soul all the fire that is in my own, to march forward to the assault that is to liberate the truth. I would convince you of the absolute necessity of unmasking the one who is guilty by every means, whatever it may be, and above all without delay.

Send me a few books.

26 March, 1896

MY DEAR LUCIE:

I received the 12th of this month your good letters of January, so impatiently expected every month, also all the letters from the family.

I have seen with happiness that your health and the health of all resist this frightful condition of things, this horrible nightmare, in which we have lived so long. What a trial for you, my good darling, as horrible as it is undeserved—for you who deserve to be so happy! Yes, I have horrible moments, when the heart can bear no longer the blows which open the wound already so deep, when my brain gives way under the weight of thoughts so sad and so deceptive. When, after I have waited for my letters in an agony of anxiety, the mail arrives, and still I do not receive the announcement of the discovery of the truth, or of the author of that infamous and cowardly crime, oh, I have at first a feeling of deep, bitter disappointment. My heart is torn, is broken, under so many sufferings, so long and so undeserved!

I am a little like a sick man who lingers on his bed of torment, suffering anguish, but who lives because his duty demands it, and who keeps asking his doctor, "When will my tortures end?" And as the doctor answers, "Soon, soon," the sick man ends by asking himself, "But when will this 'soon' come?" and he longs to see it come.

It was a long time ago that you announced it to me . . . but be discouraged? Oh, that never! However terrible may be my sufferings, the desire for our honor is far above them!

Neither you, nor any one, will ever have the right to one moment of fatigue, one second of weakness, as long as the goal has not been reached— the absolute honor of our name. As for me, when I feel that I am falling under the united weight of all our suffering, when I feel that my reason is leaving me, then I think of you, of our dear children, of the undeserved dishonor cast upon our name, and I recover my balance by a violent effort of my whole being, and I cry to myself, "No, you shall not bend before the tempest! Your heart may be in bits, your brain may be crushed, but you shall not succumb until you have seen the day when honor shall be given back to your dear children!"

This is why, dear Lucie, I come to cry to you always, to you, as to all,

"Courage!" and more than courage—for will to accomplish! . . . Oh, silently, very silently—for words do not help—but boldly, audaciously to march straight onward to the end—the entire truth, the light upon this awful drama, in one word, all the honor of our name! Means? They must all be employed, of whatever nature they may be—anything that the mind can suggest to obtain the solution of this enigma.

The object is everything; that alone is immutable. I wish our children to enter upon life with heads proudly erect. I wish to animate you with my supreme desire. I wish to see you succeed, and it will be full time, I swear to you!

I hope that you may soon be able to tell me something certain, something positive, oh, for both of us, my dear Lucie! I cannot write to you at greater length, nor speak to you of anything else except my great and deep affection for you. My head is too tired by this bitter discipline, the most terrible, the most cruel that human brain can endure.

Our dear little Pierre asks me to write to him. Ah, I am not strong enough! Each word wrings a sob from my throat and I am obliged to resist with all my strength in order to be with him on the day when they give us back our honor.

Take him in your arms for me, as well as our dear little Jeanne.

Oh, my precious children! . . . Draw from them your invincible courage.

I embrace you with all the forces of my being, as I love you.

ALFRED

Embrace your dear parents, all the family for me; my health is good.

I received from you at the beginning of the month a dozen packages of provisions and some cardigans. I thank you for your touching care for me. I have not yet received any of the reviews and the books you announced in your letters of September, December, and January; not one of them has yet arrived at Cayenne. Please send the things so that they may come by parcel post. Either address them to me directly, care of the Director of the Penitentiary Service at Cayenne, or else have them addressed to me from the Ministry, at your own expense.

From the Condemned Officer to the President of the Republic
"I do not speak of physical sufferings; they are nothing. . . ."

Dreyfus, Five Years, *pp. 170–171.*

For the prisoner on Devil's Island the hours seemed centuries. He suffered from violent palpitations of the heart, from a feeling that he was suffocating, from fearful nightmares. Along with his physical sufferings was a disgust for men and things so deep that "I aspire only to the great rest, to the rest that is eternal." On October 5, 1895, Dreyfus sent the following letter to the President of the Republic.

That I live on, *Monsieur le Président,* is because the sacred duty which I have to fulfil toward my own upholds me; otherwise I should long since have succumbed under a burden too heavy for human shoulders.

In the name of my honor, torn from me by an appalling error, in the name of my wife, in the name of my children,—oh, *Monsieur le Président,* at this last thought alone my father's heart, the heart of a loyal Frenchman and an honorable man, is pierced with grief,—I ask justice from you; and this justice that I beg of you with all my soul, with all the strength of my heart, with hands clasped in prayer, is that you search out the secret of this tragic history, and thus put an end to the martyrdom of a soldier and of a family to whom their honor is their all.

Accused, and then condemned, on the evidence of handwriting, for the most infamous crime which a soldier can commit, I have declared, and I declare once again, that I did not write the letter which was charged against me, and that I have never forfeited my honor.

For a year I have been struggling alone in the consciousness of innocence, against the most terrible fatality which can pursue a man. I do not speak of physical sufferings; they are nothing; the sorrows of the heart are everything. To suffer thus is frightful in itself, but to feel that those who are dear to me are suffering with me is the crowning agony. My whole family writhes under punishment inflicted for an abominable crime which I never committed.

I do not come to beg for grace, or favors, or alleviating assurances; what I ask is that light, revealing and penetrating light, may be thrown upon this cabal of which my family and I are the unhappy victims.

"Dreyfus Escapes!"

". . . the escape was arranged by Mme. Dreyfus. . . ."

L'Agence Havas, *September 3, 1896. Translated by the editor.*

On September 3, 1896, the London *Daily Chronicle* published the sensational news that Dreyfus had escaped from Devil's Island. The London newspaper merely reprinted a report originally in the *South Wales Argus.* Within a few hours *L'Agence Havas* had the following dispatch on the wires. That evening and the next day every newspaper in Paris carried the dramatic report.

The *Daily Chronicle* says that the journal *South Wales Argus* prints a report that a naval captain has made a statement that Captain Dreyfus has escaped from the Salvation Islands on board an American ship.

The *South Wales Argus,* which gave the details, is a journal published in Newport in Monmouthshire. That report is based on declarations made by Captain Hunter of the steamer *Non-Pareil* which had just arrived in Newport.

While taking on a cargo of phosphates at Connétable Island [off the coast of Guiana], Captain Hunter heard that Dreyfus had escaped from Devil's Island. The account is a long one, but it says in substance that the escape was arranged by Mme. Dreyfus immediately after the departure of the French dispatch boat, which, according to the account, visited the Salvation Islands only rarely.

The American schooner, whose name is not mentioned in the report of the *South Wales Argus,* is supposed to have taken on board not only Dreyfus but also his warders.

The news hit Paris with great impact. Every newspaper featured the story. *Le Figaro* on September 4 stated in detail how Mme. Dreyfus had been authorized to rejoin her husband in Cayenne, where she left the French packet boat and helped smuggle her husband and his guards aboard an American schooner. Reporters rushed to interview M. André Lebon, Minister for the Colonies, who could only tell them that he had immediately sent a telegram to Cayenne asking for information. Other journalists hurried to the home of M. Hadamard, Dreyfus's brother-in-law, to seek confirmation or denial, only to find that he was "away on a voyage."

The Times in London (September 4, 1896) was skeptical:

The Colonial Office discredits a report which has been circulated on the escape of ex-Captain Dreyfus, but has telegraphed to Cayenne for information. The answer is not expected until tomorrow night.

The next day, September 5, word came from Cayenne that "no modification has been made in the situation of the deported Dreyfus." *Figaro* reported on that day that the Minister of the Colonies "has taken all measures that *the law permits him to take* to guard the prisoner from an escape which would be dangerous for the country." The *Libre Parole* published an account by a special correspondent who was supposed to have journeyed to Newport and interviewed Captain Hunter and members of his crew. One sailor was said to have commented: "No doubt Dreyfus escaped. He might have been retaken and brought back to Devil's Island, but it is certain that he got away for a time."

The interview was probably invented by the editors of *La Libre Parole*. It was probable that Captain Hunter and his steamer *Non-Pareil* did not exist except in the imagination of Mathieu Dreyfus. It was widely believed that Captain Dreyfus's brother conceived the plan deliberately as a means of keeping his brother's name before the public in the battle to free him.

Apologia: The Minister for the Colonies Explains How He Treated Dreyfus on Devil's Island

". . . a servant of the Republic is not the 'sinister torturer' represented. . . ."

William Harding, Dreyfus: The Prisoner of Devil's Island (*New York: Associated Publishing Company, 1899*), *pp. 103–106.*

André Lebon, the Minister for the Colonies responsible for Dreyfus while on Devil's Island, was a weak bureaucrat beset by fear that his famous prisoner would escape. Although he was aware that Dreyfus had given his guards no cause for complaint, he cabled the Governor of Guiana on September 4, 1896, to keep Dreyfus in his hut with double irons during the night, and to surround his exercise ground with a solid palisade, with a sentinel inside. It was a savage order: confinement during the day and irons that bruised the flesh during the night. "I was put in irons last night," Dreyfus wrote in his diary. "I do not know the reason. . . . Why did I not go mad during that long, atrocious night?"

To maintain a stricter watch on the prisoner, Lebon also sent a new warder, one Deniel, noted for his brutality. The Minister for the Colonies was haunted by the fear that Dreyfus might die in captivity and that reports about his death would not be believed. To guard against any such possibility, Lebon had materials for embalming sent to Devil's Island so that, if it became necessary, Dreyfus's body could be sent back to France.

Lebon was severely criticized in the foreign press as "the torturer of Dreyfus." On July 12, 1899, while no longer a member of the

Ministry, he issued the following statement of his position. It did little to change the opinion widely held about him.

M. Louis Havet having substituted definite charges for the system of vague insults of which I have been the object for two years, and M. Guillian having dispelled some of the legends which there is an attempt to substantiate with reference to the *Île du Diable*, I feel bound to break the silence which I have hitherto imposed upon myself from respect for the work of justice now going on, and to explain myself as clearly as I can as to the measures which I adopted and my reasons for them. I shall say nothing, moreover, which cannot be verified by the records of the Colonial Office, and I declare once for all that I accept entire responsibility for my acts, and that I entirely indorse the action of my old subordinates in the execution of my orders or in the acts which they reported to me, and which I did not blame at the time.

I first recall certain facts outside my own administration. The public degradation of Dreyfus having taken place early in January, 1895, M. Guérin, then Minister of Justice, and M. Delcassé, then Minister for the Colonies, asked Parliament on the 11th of that month to indicate the *Îles du Salut* as a place of transportation in a fortified enclosure, together with the Ducos Peninsula, in order, as the preamble of the bill said, "to increase the guarantee of supervision, and thus render the repression as effective as possible." The bill was promulgated on February 9th, and was countersigned by MM. Trarieux and Chautemps. It was in the spring of the same year, 1895, that general instructions were given for the new transportation service, and I did not become Minister for the Colonies until a year later, at the end of April, 1896. During the first months of my ministry I had no occasion to pay any attention to the system established at the *Île du Diable*. The measures to be taken for the pacification of Madagascar, with the choice of a suitable man to be sent there, occupied my whole time, and I had no inclination to display "fury or hatred or the instinct of an executioner," which M. Louis Havet deigns to admit are totally lacking in me. I will add, in order to reassure him immediately as to the reasons for my action, that I should never have dreamed that I should one day be accused of having yielded to the "fear of journalists." In the mistakes I may have made during my public life it is rather in the contrary direction that I seem to myself to have erred.

What, then, were my motives? And first, how did matters stand in the summer and autumn of 1896, as regards the Dreyfus affair? In the excitement of the past few months this question would appear to have been totally forgotten. No one then publicly defended the innocence, true or supposed, of the prisoner. No one disputed the authority of the *chose jugée*. Everybody, except a few who had special knowledge, was anxious that Dreyfus should not escape, and was eager to discover the accomplices who were almost universally thought to have helped him. It was by no means my duty to listen to outside rumors nor to substitute any personal opinion for the decisions of those who had been qualified to express one. I had in his case, as in that of all transported convicts, merely to insure the execution of the decrees of justice and of the laws. How did I come to think that there might be some doubt of the effectiveness of the system at Devil's Island, and how was I led, a full year before the commencement of the revisionist agitation, and without making the slightest mention of it to the journalists, as can easily be shown, to adopt the measures for which I am now blamed?

Within the space of a few weeks I learned that, one after another, two service telegrams relative to the prisoner had been communicated to the press; that another sent, like the first, by one of my predecessors had never reached its destination; that, finally, a person connected with the penitentiary administration could not be counted upon for the faithful execution of his duties, but that he frequently spoke of the possibility of procuring Dreyfus's escape. It was at this moment, early in September, that the English papers disseminated, broadcast a report that an American ship had carried off Dreyfus, and then for the first time I obtained explanations of the organization of Devil's Island, and easily discovered that such a rescue was physically possible.

Now, I did not wish that Dreyfus should escape, nor was I anxious to have his sentinels obliged to apply the general orders which permit recourse to the most extreme measures in order to prevent a prisoner from escaping. Hence my telegram of September 4th, to the Governor of Guiana. Here is its complete text as regards the point in question:

"You will keep Dreyfus until further orders in hut, double staple at night. You will surround perimeter court round hut with solid palisading, with sentinel inside."

In order thoroughly to indicate the essentially temporary character of this measure of rigor, I telegraphed that the prisoner should be carefully informed that it was a measure of security, not of punishment; and, believing that my orders were already on the point of being fulfilled, I telegraphed again on the 19th, to say that as soon as the palisading was finished the double staple should be removed. Unfortunately, the work was done with less celerity than I had hoped, but neither then nor afterward was I apprised of the slightest disorder in the prisoner's health.

Was I right or wrong in being so anxious as to the possibility of escape? All I can say is that during my two years' tenure of office hardly a month passed in which similar projects were not brought to my attention, either by the Prefecture of Police, by the Detective Department, or by diplomatic or consular agents. The external defense of the island being henceforth assured, none of these projects affected the prisoner's treatment. On the contrary, the work hastily done in September, 1896, having modified the hygienic conditions of his hut, a new building more spacious and healthier was prepared for him early in 1897, at the instance of one of the very agents now being most unjustly attacked.

What is now called the Weyler forgery had nothing whatever to do with all this, though it was contemporaneous with it. It was, however, the cause of other measures which I felt bound to take as regards the prisoner's correspondence. The tenor of that document, and the way in which it reached the Colonial Office, have been sufficiently indicated in the inquiry of the Supreme Court. I will only say that no one then, not even a certain eminent personage in the Intelligence Bureau, affirmed or approved it to be a forgery, and that it gave ground for believing that, apart from the prisoner's regular correspondence, then submitted, like that of all prisoners, to the control of the Penitentiary Department, there existed between Dreyfus and his friends or family other relations which escaped all supervision. This suspicion was confirmed by other facts, either concomitant or subsequent, and gave rise toward the end of 1897 to a very suggestive report by the head of the local service as to the removal at the beginning of 1898 of a suspected sentinel. If I had shown in the affair that blind passion now attributed to me I should, perhaps, have adopted measures other than those which I had definitely adopted. I decided that copies of the letters exchanged between Dreyfus and his family should be transmitted instead of the originals, so that the apparent and known text should alone reach its destination. But as to having attempted by means of subordinates, as is insinuated, to undermine the condemned man's confidence in his family by suppressing, mutilating, or deliberately delaying any of their letters, I affirm that such an idea prevailed neither in Paris nor Guiana.

Such is the strict truth free from all dissimulation or amplification. I am surprised that in facts which have been so long known to the parties concerned, and on which no one ever ventured to present an interpellation, such tardy accusations should be revived. I might, moreover, show by relating either a conversation held or a correspondence exchanged with certain leaders of the sad controversy now witnessed by us, the signal bad faith which has been employed; but having no personal concern in this, and being only anxious to show that a servant of the Republic is not the "sinister torturer" represented, I limit myself to this too long explanation.

Dreyfus Addresses Another Appeal to the President of the Republic, 1896

"I simply declare once more that I am innocent of this abominable crime. . . ."

Dreyfus, Five Years, *pp. 216–217.*

On September 10, 1896, worn in body and soul, Dreyfus decided to stop making entries in his diary and finished it by addressing another appeal to the President of the Republic. It was an agonized call for compassion and justice, in essence repeating the points made in his first letter to the President of the Republic sent eleven months earlier.

Thursday, September 10, 1896

I am so utterly weary, so broken down in body and soul, that to-day I stop my diary, not being able to foresee how long my strength will hold out, or what day my brain will succumb under the weight of so great a burden.

I finish it by addressing to the President of the Republic this supreme appeal, in case strength and sanity fail before the end of this horrible tragedy: —

"Monsieur le Président de la République: —

"I take the liberty of asking you that this diary, written day by day, be handed to my wife.

"There will be found in it, perhaps, *Monsieur le Président,* cries of anger, of affright, at the most awful condemnation that ever befell a human being,—a human being who never forfeited his honor. I no longer feel the courage to re-read it, to retrace the bitter journey.

"To-day I have no recriminations to make against anyone; each one has thought himself acting in the fullness of right and conscience.

"I simply declare once more that I am innocent of this abominable crime, and I ask ever and again for this one thing, always the same thing,—that the search for the culprit who is the real author of this base crime be diligently prosecuted.

"And when he is discovered, I beseech that the compassion which so great a misfortune as mine inspires may be given to my dear wife and my darling children."

End of the Diary

Unfinished Letter to President Faure
"I can endure it no longer."

The Associated Press, *in Harding,* Dreyfus: The Prisoner of Devil's Island, *pp. 108–109.*

Again and again Dreyfus was moved to appeal to the President of the Republic. Not for a single moment during his imprisonment on Devil's Island did he forget the horror of his predicament. Again and again he sat down to write despairing accounts of his torture. The following letter, written on February 14, 1897, but never finished or sent, reveals the extent of his distress.

I venture once more to appeal to your high justice. For more than two years, innocent of an abominable crime the very thought of which revolts my whole being, I have been undergoing the most frightful torture imaginable. I cannot possibly tell you, *Monsieur le Président,* how I have suffered; my heart alone knows. Another pen than mine is needed to describe tortures such as these. And if I have lived, holding down my heart, keeping myself in check, swallowing insults and affronts, it is because I would have wished to be allowed to die tranquil, knowing that I should be leaving to my children a pure and honored name. But, alas! I have been too great a sufferer. I can endure it no longer. Ah! *Monsieur le Président,* I know not how to find words to tell you how I suffer, to describe the horrors of every minute in every hour of the day, horrors against which I succeeded in bearing up only in the supreme hope of beholding once more for my dear children the day when honor will be restored to them. And in this profound distress of my whole being, in this agony of my whole strength, it is to you, *Monsieur le Président,* to the Government of my country, that I throw again this supreme cry of appeal, sure that it will be heard. And this supreme cry of appeal from a Frenchman, a father, who now for more than two years has lain on a bed of torture, is ever the same—namely, for the truth of this terrible drama, for the unmasking of the man or men who committed the infamous crime. . . .

Additional Appeals for Justice
". . . I wished for the light, the complete light. . . ."

The Associated Press, *in Harding,* Dreyfus: The Prisoner of Devil's Island, *pp. 107–108.*

From Devil's Island, in late February and early March 1898, Dreyfus sent final appeals for justice to the Deputies and Senators of the French Parliament and to the Minister of War. These letters were published in the Paris *Figaro* a month after Dreyfus had been landed in France and a week before the opening of the second court-martial at Rennes. However, the letters were not sent on to their addresses by order of Premier Méline. They reveal the persistency with which Dreyfus maintained his innocence.

Letter Addressed to Members of the Chamber of Deputies

Île du Salut, February 28, 1898

On the very morrow of my condemnation, now more than three years ago, when Major du Paty de Clam came to see me on behalf of the Minister of War, to ask me, after I had been condemned for an abominable crime which I had not committed, whether I was innocent or guilty, I declared that not only was I innocent, but that I wished for the light, the complete light, and I asked immediately for the aid of all the customary means of investigation, either through the military attachés or in any other mode at the disposal of the Government. I was told that interests superior to mine, owing to the origin of this lamentable and tragic history and owing to the origin of the incriminating letter, prevented the customary means of investigation, but that the inquiry would be continued. I have waited for three years in the most terrible situation conceivable, suffering continuously and without cause, but these researches never end. If, then, interests superior to mine are to prevent, and must always prevent, the use of the only means of investigation which can finally put an end to this horrible martyrdom of so many human beings and throw complete light on this tragic business, these interests can surely not require that a woman, children, and an innocent man should be sacrificed to them. Otherwise we must go back to the darkest ages of our history, when the truth and the light were stifled. A few months ago I submitted the whole tragic and undeserved horror of this situation to the high equity of the Government. I now do the same to the high equity of *Messieurs les Députés* to ask them for justice for me and mine, the life of my children, and an end to this frightful martyrdom of so many human beings. [Dreyfus addressed a similar letter to the Senators.]

LETTER TO THE MINISTER OF WAR

Île du Salut, March 21, 1898

A few months ago, probably in consequence of a report on the accusation, I was told that this was based—(1) on a charge against my family. [Dreyfus here referred to the theory by M. Bertillon that the *bordereau* was both in Dreyfus's handwriting and that of his brother.] This document was unknown to me. It was never communicated to me, so I could not reply. It is, moreover, as atrocious as it is calumnious. (2) The presumption drawn from the handwriting. I declared that I was not the author of the incriminating letter; I showed from its contents that I could not be. (3) The trembling of the hand. At the court-martial Major du Paty de Clam, in reply to a question, affirmed that it was warm at the time. M. Cochefert, a few moments later, declared with me that it was piercingly cold. (4) The rest of the accusation. Another document. At the court-martial the straightforward protest of Captain Besse against the interpretation given to his deposition, and the explanation given by Major Mercier, forced the Government commissary to abandon this portion of the accusation. Moreover, at the court-martial the oral evidence and the explanations brought out by the defense reduced this entire portion to nothing. (5) Moral causes—gaming, and women. I can only refer to my own declaration, in opposition to which no serious proof was given, no signed deposition. The court upheld none of the atrocious anonymous documents which had been appended to the *dossier*. In a letter to the Minister of Justice a few months ago I asked, in the name of the imprescriptible rights of truth and justice and in the interests of my wife and children, that a serious inquiry should be made to elucidate definitively all the anonymous gossip and reports. To sum up, I appeal, *Monsieur le Ministre,* to General de Boisdeffre's loyalty and to that of those who obtained my condemnation, that it may be made known that at the court-martial, where the minister was represented, the accusation, save for the first document—of which I had no knowledge, and which was communicated therefore solely to the judges—the accusation was reduced by discussion to a presumption as to handwriting.

Dr. Veugmon's Report on the Exiled Officer at Devil's Island
"He was beset by unconquerable sadness. . . ."

Harding, Dreyfus: The Prisoner of Devil's Island, *pp. 56–58.*

In March 1899 Dr. Veugmon, the physician who had Dreyfus under his care while on Devil's Island, was interviewed by a reporter

for the *Associated Press* at Cayenne. The interview was later published by William Harding, cable editor of the *Associated Press,* in
his book on Dreyfus. Harding added to his account a question to
and response by the head keeper of the Cayenne penal settlement.

Dreyfus is a neuropathic subject, and the régime to which he has been
submitted has made him more so; isolation, idleness, boredom, and dis-
couragement irritate his nervous system. His malady displayed itself about
a year after his imprisonment had commenced, and took the form of
cerebral depression. He was beset by unconquerable sadness; he clenched
his teeth; he complained of dyspepsia, exhaustion, and prolonged in-
somnia, caused by moral preoccupations, more particularly by the "fixed
idea" of disculpating himself from the charge of treason. Next came
headaches and pains in the neck, and finally, last year, I was called in to
treat him for fainting fits of considerable duration, which I put a stop to
by subcutaneous injections of morphia. In my presence Dreyfus was
always self-possessed.

Under his strength of will one could detect, however, stormy symptoms,
and his jailers said that often, when first awaking of a morning, he would
break out into furious passion, bursting into tears, gesticulating like a
madman, and shouting unintelligible words. These violent rages usually
resulted in utter exhaustion and general torpor, and sometimes in syn-
cope, when, of course, I was sent for. Unfortunately, I could only put him
through an illusory sort of treatment, prescribing good nourishment,
tonics, work in his little garden, and plenty of walking exercise, to fatigue
his body and distract his mind. But the only palliative remedies for acute
neurasthenia—which I consider incurable—are bracing air, amusement,
active life—a treatment, in short, not to be dreamed of in his case.

The irritability of Dreyfus's character has increased since he has been
told of the application to revise his trial. This proceeding haunts him; he
is a prey to feverish restlessness; a thousand conjectures torment his
fancy, ignorant as he is of the evidence advanced by his defenders to
obtain a new trial.

"Do you believe," the doctor was asked, "that if the application for
revision be rejected, Dreyfus is strong enough to get over his disappointment?"

Dr. Veugmon smiled, hesitated, and then replied:

"I think we had better not consider such an eventuality. Dreyfus has
repeatedly expressed his intention to put an end to his life. His words
have been reported to the authorities, and even M. Deniel, fearing an
attempt at suicide, has ordered Dreyfus's jailers not to lose sight of him

for a second. After carefully searching his habitation they carried off even perfectly harmless objects, such as kitchen utensils."

"Was Dreyfus in earnest?"

"I can mention a characteristic circumstance which took place early in 1898, and justified the belief that he meant what he had said. He sent for me one day, complaining of violent headache, and besought me to give him a quantity of antipyrin, the only drug, he said, that gave him relief. Struck by a sudden suspicion, I acquiesced in his request, but, observing that a portable medicine case did not contain what he wanted, I left him, and soon returned with a dozen perfectly harmless cachets. These I recommended him to use very cautiously, not more than two per diem. Next day I visited him again. His headache had disappeared, and when I asked him to give back the balance of the cachets I had handed to him, he pretended to look for them, and presently told me that he could not remember where he had put them. I dropped the subject, and never thereafter even alluded to the incident, which I consider conclusive. My instructions were to converse with him exclusively about his health, and he never mentioned the offense he was expiating except to protest his innocence.

"At the present time I do not think that Dreyfus will try to kill himself, for the possibility of 'revision' has shed a ray of hope upon his tortured soul. But should he be disappointed, and hurled back into a slough of despond, I should not be surprised were he to carry out his sinister projects and commit an act of desperation."

The head keeper of the Cayenne penal settlement, at about the same time, was questioned confidentially as to whether Dreyfus knew of the efforts being made in France. He said:

"I can positively assert that Dreyfus is ignorant of what has taken place in France since his incarceration, except what has been written to him by members of his family, for every imaginable measure has been taken to preclude indiscretion. Before his arrival here it had been arranged to isolate him completely and cut him off from all external communication. It may be said with truth that a tomb closed upon him as soon as he came hither. In the *bureaux* a special service was organized under the control of a chief inspector to supervise his food and all his appurtenances, of which he himself drew up a list that was handed to a Cayenne storekeeper. They were all minutely examined before being forwarded to the island. All the clothes sent to Dreyfus are unsewn and turned inside out to make sure that no written matter is hidden under the seams or in the lining. His provisions are rigorously searched; meat cans and other tins are opened and resoldered; his cigars—he smokes a good deal—are unrolled and made up again, as they might contain slips of paper. Even the labels on the wine bottles are removed to make certain that nothing is written on them. His letters are read; whatever allusion they contain to his case is pitilessly suppressed, and before delivery to him they are subjected to great heat, in order to detect any sympathetic or other special ink.

"If you take into consideration that Dreyfus is in the custody of incorruptible warders, always in fear of dismissal and punishment at the least infraction of standing rules, you will recognize, as I do, the impossibility that outside rumors should ever reach the former captain. It is not so in the penitentiary, where the convicts enjoy relative freedom; but the situation of Dreyfus and of these common malefactors has absolutely nothing in common."

YOUNG DREYFUS AT THE COLLÈGE SAINTE-BARBE
This was the secondary school where he prepared for entrance to the *École Polytechnique*, School of Higher Mathematics. (*Bibliothèque Nationale*)

ALFRED DREYFUS AT THE TIME OF HIS CONVICTION, 1894 (*Bibliothèque Nationale*)

MME. DREYFUS AND HER CHILDREN
Drawn from life by Paul Renouard. (Associated Press)

Sans nouvelles m'indiquant que vous
désirez me voir, je vous adresse cependant,
Monsieur, quelques renseignements intéressants.

1° Une note sur le frein hydraulique
du 120 et la manière dont s'est conduite
cette pièce;

2° Une note sur les troupes de couverture
(quelques modifications seront apportées par
le nouveau plan.);

3° Une note sur une modification aux
formations de l'artillerie;

4° Une note relative à Madagascar;

5° Le projet de manuel de tir de
l'artillerie de campagne (14 mars 1894.)

Ce dernier document est extrêmement
difficile à se procurer et je ne puis

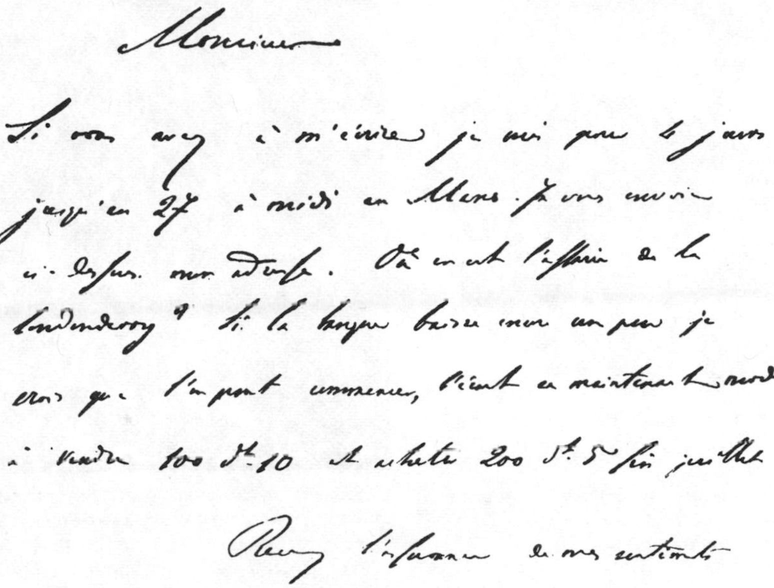
Monsieur

Si vous avez à m'écrire je suis pour le jours jusqu'au 27 à midi au Mans. Je vous envoie ci-dessous mon adresse. Où en est l'affaire de la Londonderry? Si la bourse baisse encore un peu je crois que l'on peut commencer, c'est à dire maintenant à vendre 100 St. 10 et acheter 200 St. 5 fin juillet.

Recevez l'assurance de mes sentiments

ESTERHAZY'S HANDWRITING

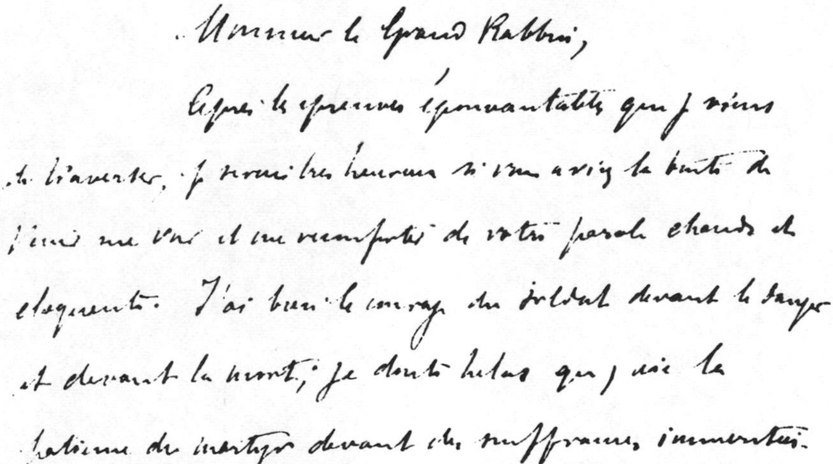
Monsieur le Grand Rabbin,

Après les épreuves épouvantables que je viens de traverser, je serais très heureux si vous aviez la bonté de venir me voir et me réconforter de votre parole chaude et éloquente. J'ai bien le courage du soldat devant le danger et devant la mort; je doute hélas que j'aie la patience du martyr devant des souffrances imméritées.

DREYFUS'S HANDWRITING

LIEUTENANT-COLONEL PANIZZARDI, THE ITALIAN MILITARY ATTACHÉ IN PARIS IN 1894
Panizzardi, victim of Henry's forgeries, protested that he had never known Dreyfus. (Black and White, London)

LIEUTENANT-COLONEL MAX VON SCHWARTZ-KOPPEN, THE MAN WHO KEPT SILENT
German Military Attaché in Paris from 1891 to 1897, Schwartzkoppen employed Esterhazy as a spy. Although he repeatedly denied having had any relations with Dreyfus, he was never able to speak openly and exonerate him. (L'Oeuvre, Paris)

GENERAL AUGUSTE MERCIER, MINISTER OF WAR, 1893–1895, IMPLACABLE FOE OF DREYFUS (Harper's Weekly, August 26, 1899)

MAJOR MERCIER DU PATY DE CLAM
A member of the Third Bureau of the General Staff, he was entrusted with preliminary examination of Dreyfus. (Bibliothèque Nationale)

DU PATY DE CLAM'S PRELIMINARY EXAMINATION OF DREYFUS

Determined to wring a confession of guilt, du Paty de Clam grilled Dreyfus steadily for two weeks, inventing new and insidious ordeals on each occasion. The innocent Dreyfus was bewildered. (*Graphic*, London, August 1899)

GENERAL DE BOISDEFFRE, CHIEF OF
THE GENERAL STAFF FROM 1893 TO
1898, AT THE TIME OF DREYFUS'S
CONVICTION

GENERAL BILLOT, MINISTER OF WAR
FROM 1882 TO 1896
He was certain that the judgment
was correctly given and that Dreyfus was guilty.

GENERAL ROGET, ASSISTANT TO GEN-
ERAL MERCIER
He worked energetically to prove
the guilt of Dreyfus.

GENERAL CHARLES-ARTHUR GONSE
"What business is it of yours if this
Jew is on the *Île du Diable?*"

DREYFUS'S SWORD IS BROKEN

"The saber remains. The adjutant draws it from its scabbard and breaks it across his knee. There is a metallic click, and the two portions are flung with the insignia upon the ground. Then the bolt is detached, and in its turn the scabbard falls." (Drawing by Leon Fauvet)

THE DEGRADATION OF DREYFUS, JANUARY 5, 1895

The march of dishonor as seen by a contemporary artist. (*Illustrated London News*, January 1895)

CAPTAIN LEBRUN-RENAULT (WITH THE MEDALS)

An alcoholic, Lebrun-Renault claimed that Dreyfus had confessed to him, but withdrew the charge. (Gerschel, Paris)

DREYFUS ENTERS A PRISON VAN AFTER HIS
DEGRADATION (*Graphic,* London, September 14, 1899)

DREYFUS DEGRADED
From a photograph taken immediately
after his humiliation. (Romney Studios,
Ltd., London)

DREYFUS IN HIS CELL ON DEVIL'S ISLAND (Associated Press)

DREYFUS'S HUT ON DEVIL'S ISLAND
In a sketch by one of the jailers, it shows, in addition to the hut, the enclosure, the guards' barracks, and the watchtower.

FACSIMILE OF A QUOTATION FROM "HAMLET" WRITTEN BY DREYFUS IN HIS DIARY ON DEVIL'S ISLAND

"Doubt thou the stars are fire,
    Doubt that the sun doth move,
Doubt truth to be a liar,
    But never doubt I love."
                Hamlet, Act 2, Scene 2

III

Nourishing the Secret *Dossier* with Documents*

At the heart of the Dreyfus case was a *dossier secret,* or confidential file, in which all documents connected with the matter were kept. The original case for the prosecution was a weak one because it relied primarily on the *bordereau.* General Mercier and his associates ordered that a search be made for any and all documents that might tend to strengthen the charges against Dreyfus. This was done in the Statistical Section of the General Staff, where there was a large collection of scraps of paper and pieces of information gathered from many sources. The work was entrusted to Colonel Jean Sandherr, Chief of the Intelligence Department at the time when Dreyfus was arrested. The *dossier* became the pivotal point of the entire case.

There were many documents gathered in the *dossier* at the time of the first court-martial. A large proportion came from the correspondence between Lieutenant-Colonel von Schwartzkoppen and Major Panizzardi, close associates particularly because of the cooperation of their countries in the Triple Alliance. Both officers were watched secretly by French intelligence agents; any letters or notes exchanged between them were of utmost importance to the French General Staff. Both used the secret pseudonym "Alexandrine" in their correspondence.

As the officers' cabal in the General Staff became increasingly involved in the embarrassing case, many new documents, including some that were plainly forged, were added to the *dossier.* Those officers convinced of Dreyfus's guilt were inclined to accept any document, no matter how outrageously false, as long as it implicated

* Unless otherwise indicated, the documents in this chapter were translated by the editor.

83

Dreyfus. Rumors were started to the effect that new documents in the *dossier* gave "absolute proof" for the guilt of Dreyfus. In this sorry work Major Henry played the most important role. Major Picquart, who succeeded Sandherr, became convinced, after studying the documents in the *dossier,* that a terrible injustice had been committed against an innocent man.

On December 22, 1894, on the last day of the first court-martial, four major documents were selected by Major du Paty de Clam from the *dossier* and turned over to the judges. Because the proceedings were held in secret, it is not altogether clear exactly which documents were concerned, but it is strongly probable that the first four documents described in the following pages were those passed on to the President of the court-martial in the presence of the Minister of War, the Chief of Staff, and the Chief of the Intelligence Department.

Secret Document No. 1: The "Doubt. Proof" Letter

"Situation dangerous for me with a French officer."

La revision du procès de Rennes, *vol. I, p. 58.*

The first secret document was a set of notes for a memorandum written by Schwartzkoppen in response to a telegram from Berlin. It was sent in January 1894 in response to a telegram from Berlin dated December 29, 1893. Written in German, the order and meaning of the words were uncertain. Apparently Schwartzkoppen seemed to be reporting that a French officer was offering him his services. Schwartzkoppen had certain doubts about the matter, hence the document took on the name of the two words at its beginning: "Doubt. Proof."

Doubt. Proof. Service letter. Situation dangerous for me with a French officer. Cannot personally conduct negotiations. Bring to me what he has. Imperative Ge. . . *Bureau des renseignements* [in French]. No relations with body of troops. Important only as coming from the Ministry. Already somewhere else.

Secret Document No. 2: The *"Canaille de D . . ."* Letter

"Herewith twelve large-scale plans of Nice which that scoundrel D . . . has handed to me for you."

La revision du procès de Rennes, *vol. I, p. 41.*

The so-called *"canaille de D . . ."* letter, undated and sent from Schwartzkoppen to Panizzardi, became one of the most famous documents of the case. The date of April 16, 1894, was falsified. The prosecution, for reasons of its own, attributed the letter to Panizzardi instead of to Schwartzkoppen. Both Military Attachés had received original plans of French fortifications from a certain M. Dubois, a civilian in the Cartographical Section, and both referred to Dubois in their correspondence as "D." The value of this letter for the prosecution lay in the words *"ce canaille de D . . ."* ("that scoundrel D . . ."), who, of course, in its view was Dreyfus.

MY DEAR FRIEND:

I am sorry, indeed, not to have seen you before you left; however, I shall return within a week. Herewith twelve large-scale plans of Nice which that scoundrel D . . . has handed to me for you. I have told him that you have no intention of renewing relations with him. He claims that there has been a misunderstanding and that he will do everything possible in order to satisfy you. He says that he is in the wrong and that you will not be angry with him. I replied to him that he was mad, and that I did not think you would be inclined to resume relations with him.

Do what you like. *Au revoir,* I am in a hurry.

(Signed) ALEXANDRINE

Secret Document No. 3: The Panizzardi Telegram to Rome, November 2, 1894

"If Captain Dreyfus has not had relations with you. . . ."

Joseph Reinach, Histoire de l'affaire Dreyfus *(Paris: Librairie Charpentier et Farquelle, 1907), vol. 3, pp. 647–648.*

On November 2, 1894, Panizzardi telegraphed the following message to Rome in cipher. Apparently he was puzzled by the headlines of *La Libre Parole* of the previous day naming Dreyfus. Neither he nor Schwartzkoppen knew the prisoner.

If Captain Dreyfus has not had relations with you, it would be well in order for the ambassador to publish an official denial, in order to avoid press comment.

Panizzardi's telegram was intercepted by the French Post Office and a copy sent to the Foreign Office. The cipher, a new one, had to be broken down, and in the process the telegram was either garbled or in some way altered. The first part of the text was unraveled, but for the phrase "to avoid press comment" the French version read: "precautions taken." Colonel Sandherr took this altered version to Generals Mercier, Gonse, and Boisdeffre as "another proof of Dreyfus's guilt." At the court-martial of Dreyfus only his name was presented as the certain part of the telegram.

Secret Document No. 4: The Val-Carlos Reports

"You have a wolf, or several wolves, in your fold."

La revision du procès de Rennes, *vol. I, p. 40.*

The fourth secret document used in the court-martial consisted of excerpts from three reports by the Marquis de Val-Carlos, the former Spanish Military Attaché in Paris. The reports were kept together in a folder titled: "Oral Reports by X." Val-Carlos, who had been drawing on the secret funds of the Ministry of War, was a close friend of Major Henry and his reports had every mark of being forgeries. They dated from March, April, and June 1894, and were supposed to point unmistakably to Dreyfus. The first two reports were letters from Val-Carlos to a certain Guénée, an agent of low morals, while the third was supposed to have been reported directly from Val-Carlos to Major Henry.

1. Val-Carlos to Guénée (March 1894)

I must remind you what I have already told you about the relations between Schwartzkoppen and Panizzardi. Tell the gentlemen [of the Intelligence Department] that these relations seem to become closer each day, and anything that one of them does is immediately told to the other. Tell that to Major Henry so that he can inform his Colonel and pass it on to the War Minister. It is advisable to double your vigilance, because out of my last conversation with you it is clear that there is an officer in the General Staff who is keeping them splendidly informed. Follow his tracks, Guénée. If I knew his name, I would mention it.

2. Val-Carlos to Guénée (April 1894)

You have a wolf, or several wolves, in your fold. Look for him! I cannot tell you that often enough. I am wholly certain about this.

3. Val-Carlos to Henry (June 1894)

An officer of Section 2 of the General Staff who came to the bureau in March or April keeps Schwartzkoppen and Panizzardi informed. I know exactly what I am saying, but I do not know the name of the officer. Moreover, even if I did know, I would not tell you.

The Davignon Letter

"It must never be seen that one agent deals with another."

La revision du procès de Rennes, *vol. I, p. 58.*

Still another secret document in Dreyfus's *dossier* was a piece of no importance which may or may not have been shown to the court-martial in 1894. It was a communication from Panizzardi to Schwartzkoppen suggesting that they should adopt a common action over a military matter. If Schwartzkoppen had to speak to his "friend," he was urged to do it privately so that it would not come to the attention of Colonel Davignon. The latter, attached to Section 2, was the officer assigned to supervise foreign Military Attachés, give official answers to their queries, and generally co-operate with them in their legitimate researches. The Davignon letter was intercepted at some time between December 1893 and January 1894.

I have just written again to Colonel Davignon and I beg of you, if you have occasion to speak about the matter to your friend, do it in a private way so that it does not come to Davignon's attention. At any rate, he would not reply. It must never be seen that one agent deals with another.

Henry Falsifies the *"Chemins de Fer"* Document

"I announce to you that I am going to get the organization of the railroads."

Siegfried Thalheimer, Macht und Gerechtigkeit: Ein Beitrag zur Geschichte des Falles Dreyfus *(Munich: Beck'sche Verlagsbuchhandlung, 1969), p. 112.*

French agents continued to obtain copies of the continuing correspondence between the Italian and German Military Attachés. The following document, known as the *"Chemins de fer"* document, was sent by Panizzardi to Schwartzkoppen on March 28, 1895. It ended up in Dreyfus's *dossier.*

Henry, always on the lookout for further evidence against Dreyfus, tore off the correct date from the piece and substituted for it in the lower left column in red ink the date "1894." This was then placed in an envelope which bore the handwriting of General Gonse: "Piece 59, letter of April 1894, concerning the organization of railroads." In this slipshod way General Gonse approved the work of his subordinate.

There was method in Henry's forgery. In the spring of 1894 Dreyfus was working in a bureau of the General Staff and among his tasks was the military organization of the railroads. Witnesses would give evidence that Dreyfus had an astonishing knowledge of transportation matters. General Mercier later testified that the *"chemins de fer"* piece was laid before the judges in the original 1894 court-martial, although no other officer remembered it. At the Rennes court-martial this document was used with devastating effect against Dreyfus.

28 March 1895, 3 P.M.

MY DEAR FRIEND,

I have received it, thanks; you must be good enough to send me what you have copied; because it is necessary that I finish the job, because, on the 31st I must go to Rome, and you must before that date copy the part that I have copied.

I announce to you that I am going to get the organization of the railroads (*l'organization des chemins de fer*).

(Signed) ALEXANDRINE

The *Petit Bleu:* Major Picquart Makes a Key Discovery
"What I want particularly is a more detailed explantion. . . ."

La revision du procès de Rennes, *vol. I, p. 88.*

Toward the end of 1895, Colonel Sandherr, Chief of the Intelligence Department of the General Staff, fell ill. It was decided to replace him and reorganize the entire department. In line as his successor was Major Henry, but superior officers were disturbed by his lack of education, his extreme vulgarity, and especially by his ignorance of foreign languages. He was passed over in favor of Major Georges Picquart, a young, promising officer of high ability and moral standards. The appointment proved to be a critical step in the history of the Dreyfus case.

Picquart quickly learned that documents were still disappearing and that Germany was still receiving secret information from inside the War Office. Apparently there was a traitor at large, even though Dreyfus had been convicted. Picquart instructed his agents to bring to him any incriminating documents collected from the wastepaper baskets of the German Embassy or elsewhere.

In March 1896 Picquart discovered a document that was to become famous. In Paris in the days before the use of the telephone became general, an express letter-card called a *petit bleu* was used to send messages swiftly to any part of the city. The card was taken to the central post office, and sent by compressed air through pneumatic tubes to the office branch nearest the recipient. Then it was delivered by bicycle messenger. The entire procedure took just fifteen minutes.

The *petit bleu* in Picquart's hands consisted of pieces of blue paper that had been torn and then reassembled. It bore no stamp. Apparently it had been dictated by Colonel von Schwartzkoppen—it was not in his handwriting—and was addressed to a Major Esterhazy.

Major Esterhazy,
27, Rue de la Bienfaisance,
Paris.

Sir: What I want particularly is a more detailed explanation than the one you gave me the other day on the matter in question. I would ask you, therefore, to be good enough to give it to me in writing, so that I may be able to decide whether or not I can continue my relations with the firm of R.

(Signed) C.

Picquart was electrified by the contents of the *petit bleu*. His first reaction was that the "Major Esterhazy" concerned was probably another traitor, but he decided to make a careful investigation before referring the matter to his superiors. He ordered his agents to watch Esterhazy. The first reports were damaging: the officer was exceedingly unpopular in his regiment, he was most inquisitive concerning matters of artillery, and he was heavily in debt. Study of the Dreyfus *dossier* aroused Picquart's suspicions: there was an uncomfortable similarity between the writing on the *bordereau* and Esterhazy's handwriting.

Controversy raged around the *petit bleu* throughout the case. General Gabriel de Pellieux, member of the General Staff who was assigned to investigate Esterhazy, was convinced that the *petit bleu* was concocted by Picquart. There were puzzling features: the handwriting was not that of Schwartzkoppen nor was there a stamp on the card. At the Rennes court-martial there was testimony quoting Colonel Schneider, the Austrian Military Attaché, to the effect that, after Schwartzkoppen had broken with Esterhazy, the latter pressed his contact, saying that he was about to enter the War Office. It was in answer to this that Schwartzkoppen dictated the *petit bleu* to a lady friend in his office. Then, thinking the matter over, he decided: "No! One cannot have dealings with a man like that," and tore the letter into fragments.

Another version by Princess Radziwill had it that Schwartzkoppen placed the *petit bleu* in the pocket of his overcoat, and then went to dinner, intending to post it at some distance from the Embassy. While at dinner, the card was stolen from his overcoat and brought to Picquart, who tore it into fragments to conceal that it had been stolen.

Schwartzkoppen himself later said that he believed he had written the *petit bleu* himself and had posted it, that he might have been followed, and the letter seized in transit. Yet, the card was not in his handwriting, nor did it have a stamp on it.

The Weyler Forgery

"Performer ready to act at once."

Jacques Kayser, The Dreyfus Affair, *trans. Nora Bickley (New York: Covici, Friede, 1931), p. 110. Reprinted by permission of Crown Publishers, Inc.*

In late August 1896 an agent of the Intelligence Department at the Ministry of War concocted another forgery to give strength to the argument that the Jews had hired a "ringer" who would confess himself to be the author of the crimes imputed to Dreyfus. The letter was addressed to Dreyfus and later became known as the "Weyler forgery." An attempt was made to disguise the handwriting in sympathetic ink. The idea was to confuse Picquart who would see it. Picquart, indeed, at first believed the letter to be authentic.

Impossible to decode last communication. Resume original procedure in answering. Indicate exactly where documents concerned are to be found . . . and the combination for the safe. Performer ready to act at once.

Document No. 371: A Falsified Letter from Panizzardi to Schwartzkoppen

". . . D . . . has brought me numerous things of interest. . . ."

Thalheimer, Macht und Gerechtigkeit, *p. 111. Translated by the editor.*

In his efforts to prove absolutely the guilt of Dreyfus, Henry proceeded to manufacture evidence by adding forged documents to the secret *dossier*. In August or September 1896 the following letter from Panizzardi to Schwartzkoppen was intercepted by French agents and brought to the attention of Henry. In this note Schwartzkoppen named the person to whom he owed "numerous things of interest." Henry, possibly with the collusion of du Paty de Clam, erased the name of the man, a certain *M. Dubois,* a civilian worker in the Cartographical Section of the General Staff who for years had done a brisk trade in original plans of fortification, and substituted for it the initial "D . . . ." Henry added the date "March 1894" (in September 1896 Dreyfus was on Devil's Island).

Why this letter was not used to a greater extent against Dreyfus is puzzling, because it tended to incriminate him even more than the *"ce canaille de D . . ."* document. On July 7, 1898, War Minister Cavaignac designated this letter as "proof" of Dreyfus's guilt in a grotesque speech before the Chamber of Deputies.

My dear Friend:

Last evening I had to call a doctor, who has forbidden me to go out. Because I cannot see you tomorrow, please drop in on me in the morning, for D . . . has brought me numerous things of interest, and as we have only ten days, we shall have to share the work. Try, therefore, to tell them at the Embassy that you cannot be there. Always yours,

A.

IV

The Role of Anti-Semitism: "The Jews Out of France!"

From the beginning the anti-Semitic press seized the opportunity to intensify its campaign against the Jews. Seldom has so scurrilous an assault been directed against any one individual or against one religion; only in Nazi Germany can one find a similar story. Dreyfus was vilified in the most vulgar prose and in the most hideous cartoons. Anyone who dared defend him was attacked viciously as in the employ of the "Jewish Syndicate."

One cartoon depicted "The House of Alfred Dreyfus, Judas and Company, Selling Military Secrets to the Germans." The cover of *Mon Droit* showed a very Semitic-looking Dreyfus being crucified on a cross in the image of Picquart, while the Jewish God in the background scatters coins to the crowd. The title: "And the Holy Women Always Await the Resurrection of Judas." The cover of *Antijuif* showed M. Brisson, Premier of France, being won over to the Dreyfus side by offers from Rothschild and Reinach of a great future. A little band of *"Youpins"* ("Yids") dance around Brisson and tug at his cloak. Another cover of *Antijuif* showed Picquart as the "Golden Calf" of the Jews pouring gold coins into the hands of surrounding Jews. Still another cover revealed the Grand Rabbi Zadoc-Kahn, assisted by a monkey-like secretary, standing before a huge safe, topped by a golden calf and Moses holding the Torah, as he distributes money bags to Reinach and Clemenceau, the latter in line waiting for "50,000 francs."

The anti-Semitic campaign achieved much popularity during the course of the case. It died down with the pardon and rehabilitation of Dreyfus.

92

Editor Drumont Denounces the Jews

"Never have we had a similar outrage in our fatherland."

La Libre Parole *(weekly and daily editions), November 3, 1894. Translated by the editor.*

For years the publicist Édouard Drumont had warned his country-men that all their troubles were due to Jewish machinations. In *La Libre Parole* he attacked the Jews in such articles as "Jewish France," and "The Testament of an Anti-Semite." Now the Dreyfus case gave him an opportunity to increase his anti-Semitic assaults. On November 3, 1894, he excoriated Dreyfus in two editions of his publications.

"LA LIBRE PAROLE" (WEEKLY ILLUSTRATED EDITION, NOVEMBER 3, 1894)

What a terrible lesson, this disgraceful treason of the Jew Dreyfus! A well-to-do man, the son-in-law of a wealthy merchant, officer in our Army, who holds one of the most sought-after posts, sells our mobilization plans and the names of his comrades entrusted with foreign missions. Never have we had a similar outrage in our fatherland.

Concerning the Judas Dreyfus, Frenchmen, for eight years I have been warning you each day!

"LA LIBRE PAROLE" (DAILY EDITION, NOVEMBER 3, 1894)

The affair of Captain Dreyfus, which has aroused attention even in foreign countries, is only an episode in Jewish history. Judas has sold the compassion and love of God. . . . Captain Dreyfus has sold to Germany our mobilization plans and the names of our officers on foreign duty.

Nationalist Rochefort Joins the Anti-Semitic Campaign

"In this matter Dreyfus is simply a German who has entered our Army. . . ."

L'Intransigeant, *November 4, 1894. Translated by the editor.*

Editor Drumont's anti-Semitic articles attracted the attention of the entire nationalistic press. Among the most fervent nationalists was Count Henri-Victor de Rochefort, who made it a point to attack Dreyfus and the Jews throughout the entire case. He accused the Jews of forcing silence on General Mercier. At one point he wrote that the Jews would refuse to go on "paying the bills of the literary drunkards and swindlers who are making a living out of the Dreyfus Affair." As the Dreyfusards began their battle for vindication, Rochefort predicted that Dreyfus would be "condemned again, degraded again, and execrated again in spite of twelve million skulking Jews." Following is an excerpt from his first assault on Dreyfus, in which he also named Mercier.

The traitor Dreyfus has not hesitated to make a complete confession. He knows that the Germans who rule us have decided to give him a laughable sentence which will be followed promptly by a full pardon.

After Mercier was forced to admit the existence of the crime, which he carefully hoped to keep secret, he allowed it to be said by an agent that a "charge" had been made against a French officer for having sold "several documents of little importance" to a foreign power.

The negligence, the stupidity, and the bad faith of our War Minister really make him a part accomplice of the traitor and explains to us his efforts to give as little importance as possible to the documents.

The Government, which in this business as in others, finds itself choked by lies, allows the rumor to be spread that Captain Dreyfus could not hope for monetary gain because he was rich.

This fraud is typical of the robbers and business louts who tell such stories.

1. Captain Dreyfus is not wealthy. He is a gambler. His not so big fortune is eaten up by often repeated losses running from 2000 to 3000 francs a night.

2. If he were in fact rich, and if he did not have the greed to sell secrets about our national defense, then he acted out of hatred for France engendered by a wish to see our country defeated again.

In this matter Dreyfus is simply a German who has entered our Army in order to disorganize it, and in the War Ministry in order to carry on espionage in favor of William II, his Kaiser.

Mercier is more guilty and knowledgeable than we had believed.

It soon became clear even to the thick-headed Rochefort that General Mercier was to be included in the camp of the anti-Dreyfusards.

Drumont Probes the Soul of Dreyfus

"In order for a man to betray his country, it is necessary first of all that he has a country, and that country cannot be acquired with an act of naturalization."

La Libre Parole, *December 26, 1894. Translated and condensed by the editor.*

Édouard Drumont was primarily a polemicist and only secondarily a newspaperman. For him the Dreyfus case was a gold mine to be worked over again and again. Throughout the course of the case he advocated the "absolute guilt" of Dreyfus and he attacked the Dreyfus "Syndicate" as working for the death of France. He charged that "a gang of traitors" had succumbed to "the Israelitish millions." The whole thing, he said, was a Jewish conspiracy.

Drumont was a fanatic but he was a shrewd one. In his papers he combined varying appeals to find a large audience—a kind of watered-down socialism, a fervent nationalism, an appeal to religious sentiment, a harsh determinism ("The Jews cannot help it!"), and a dose of superstition (he was an amateur palmist). The following story, a typical one, illustrates his technique in stirring up racial tensions.

THE SOUL OF DREYFUS
BY ÉDOUARD DRUMONT

In fact, that man, if one takes into consideration his origins and his type, has done in the Army exactly what he would have done in a bank or in a stable of a race course: he has sold information to a competitor. He has committed an abuse of confidence, but he has not committed a crime against his country. In order for a man to betray his country, it is necessary first of all that he has a country, and that country cannot be acquired by an act of naturalization. That country is the land of one's forefathers. Barrès expressed it in excellent fashion:

> One understands by a nation a group of men united by common legends, with a tradition, with habits fashioned during a more or less long series of ancestors. Naturalization is a legal fiction which is used for the advantage of a nation, but which cannot give it character.

What is needed is a law making it a prerequisite for nationality at least three generations of French descent. In resisting this idea the Jews are preparing for their own destruction.

All the maneuvers of Jewdom are directed against the invincible resistance of the national element, the very soul of France. In insisting impudently upon imposing on us their own conception of equality, the Jews have prepared with their own hands the most frightful catastrophe of their tragic history.

When *Jewish France* was published, Zadoc-Kahn [the Grand Rabbi of France] was told: "It is a pamphlet."

"No," he replied, "it is a prophecy."

Jewish France dates from 1886! That was eight years ago, and that is precious little time for the march of an idea.

Lord, I am not going to boast of that effort! I have always been the most feeble of men, the most sentimental, the most easy to discourage. The courage I have shown in awakening my country you have given to me. Protect me, oh Lord!

All this I shall say to those who have extended congratulations to me and words of encouragement, to those who have hindered me in the past but now recognize that I was right, and especially to those young people of the anti-Semitic committees which have been organized in Paris, in Lyon, in Dijon, in Montpellier.

My books have rendered an immense service to our dear France, in revealing to her the Jewish peril, in preventing her from being delivered bound hand and foot to the enemy, from being ambushed in a moment of war by the Dreyfuses and Reinachs. I am happy to have written those books, but I do not merit praise on the subject, for I could not write them alone. I have merely obeyed the voice of a superior will: "Speak!" I have spoken.

Demonstrations and Attacks upon Jews

"The Rabbi and his family left town this morning."

The Times (*London*), *February 26, 1898.*

The Zola trial set off a series of anti-Semitic demonstrations and riots throughout France. Jews were denounced as devils to be exterminated; they were hooted down in the streets and stones were thrown at their homes. "Boycott the Jews!" Picquart was accused of having sold out to the Jews; Clemenceau was charged with being in the pay of Grand Rabbi Zadoc-Kahn. Children imitated their elders and brutally insulted Jewish pupils. The fever of anti-Semitism was especially strong in Algeria, where there were riots, assaults, and assassinations. In Constantine, in eastern Algeria, Jewish "vermin" were prohibited from entering the schools.

The following report from the London *Times* reveals the atmosphere of the day.

PARIS, Feb. 25. An altercation between a Jewish Rabbi and a hawker selling anti-Semitic songs has led to disturbances. Last night a mob threw stones at the Rabbi's shutters and smashed the windows of shops kept by Jews. The Rabbi and his family left town this morning. The mayor has issued a proclamation urging quiet.

Against this riot must be set the fact that at the Montpellier Assizes today seven Jews of Mosttaganem in Algeria were convicted of a disturbance in May last, which commenced in French cyclists being insulted by Jews, and ended in a general scuffle between Frenchmen and Jews. The case was tried at Montpellier in order to insure a fair trial. The ringleader was sentenced to five years' imprisonment, and the others to terms ranging from ten months to five days.

General de Pellieux Defends Esterhazy and Excoriates the Jews

"This race . . . carries immorality and dishonor to the limit."

Joseph Reinach, Histoire de l'affaire Dreyfus, 6 vols. (Paris: Fasquelle, 1901–1911), vol. IV, p. 576. Translated by the editor.

There were evidences of anti-Semitism throughout the course of the case. General Gabriel de Pellieux, attached to the General Staff, was appointed to conduct the inquiry demanded by Esterhazy. "Esterhazy," he said, "seems to me to be free of all suspicion. He cannot, in my opinion, be accused of the crime of treason. Picquart appears to be guilty."

Pellieux was one of the officers named by Zola in the *J'Accuse* letter:

I accuse General de Pellieux and Major Ravary of having conducted a rascally inquiry. I mean by that a monstrously partial inquiry, of which we have, in the report of the latter, an imperishable monument of naive audacity.

At the Zola trial, Pellieux used the Henry forgery as "absolute proof" of Dreyfus's guilt.

Reactionary, militarist, a declared enemy of the Republic, de Pellieux regarded himself as the servant of a good cause. He was also an anti-Semite, as indicated by this excerpt from a letter he sent his mother on February 11, 1899.

When Dreyfus finally sees that his position has become untenable, he will repeat his confession and name his accomplices. For he has several of them. And that is just what the Jews fear. This race, which introduced us to the cult of the Golden Calf, carries immorality and dishonor to the limit. If you could have seen that abominable Reinach after he insulted the widow of Major Henry, that you would have known that it is impossible to defend these damnable Jews. We fight a good battle, but one without danger, for our enemies are cowards.

V

The German Side of the Affair

From the beginning, responsible German officials were involved in the Dreyfus case. Among them were Lieutenant-Colonel Maximilian von Schwartzkoppen, the Military Attaché in Paris, Count G. H. von Münster-Derneburg, German Ambassador to France, and Emperor William II. A quick official denial from the German side might have saved Dreyfus from his ordeal, but it did not come. As realistic politicians, the German officials felt that they could not very well reveal the secrets of their espionage system without endangering their own security. The game of espionage was a serious one and it was too bad if any innocent individuals were caught in its webs. It is possible that under a reverse situation Frenchmen would have reacted in precisely the same way.

Schwartzkoppen, the chief witness in the case, employed Esterhazy as a spy and knew well that he was the guilty one. During a period of three years, he received from Esterhazy some 162 documents, most of which were in the missing category. From 1894 on, Schwartzkoppen maintained a rigid silence. Although he privately denied ever having had any relations with Dreyfus, he was not able to speak openly.

Schwartzkoppen's widow tells how, in December 1916, as he lay mortally ill in Berlin after his return from the Eastern Front, he raised himself up after a long period of unconsciousness, and cried aloud: "Frenchmen, listen to me! Dreyfus is innocent! There is nothing whatever against him! It was all just intrigue and forgery! Dreyfus is innocent!" His wife took down these words immediately, but not until 1930 was Schwartzkoppen's full story absolving Dreyfus published.

The publication of the files of the Foreign Office, *Die Grosse*

Politik, which began in 1919, brought to light the German side of the case. In an appendix to the thirteenth volume, the files concerning Dreyfus were printed under the title: "The Interrelation of the European Powers between 1897 and 1899." While incomplete and abridged, this section gives a vivid picture of the intense interest and concern with which the German authorities followed every facet of the case. Count Münster again and again telegraphed to Berlin in great excitement about new developments in Paris. For William II, loud and boisterous, the Affair was an incident to be exploited in this careful order—(1) for his own glory and splendor; (2) for the preëminence of the German God; (3) for the German "race"; and (4) for the German Army. To him "Dreyfusism" was a disease from which the French were suffering. As far as he was concerned, it was their problem and they had to find their own solution for their troubles.

The German Ambassador Protests Against the French Press

"But he did not seem to have the courage 'to stir up this wasp's nest.' "

Die Grosse Politik der europäischen Kabinette, 1871–1914 (*Berlin: Deutsche Verlagsgesellschaft für Politik und Geschichte m. b. H., 1924*), *vol. IX, pp. 387– 389. Translated by the editor.*

After Dreyfus was arrested and convicted, Count Münster, the German Ambassador, reported to Berlin that the French press was running adventurous espionage stories and was asking for the abolition of the institution of Military Attachés. Münster reported that he asked not only for protection but also for satisfaction from the French Government. On reading Münster's report, Emperor William II added to it a marginal note: "I agree! Münster must see to it that complete and immediate satisfaction is forthcoming! Otherwise, I shall be forced to be more explicit!"

THE AMBASSADOR IN PARIS COUNT MÜNSTER
TO THE REICHS CHANCELLOR PRINCE VON HOHENLOHE

Paris, November 29, 1894

The shamelessness in the matter of Captain Dreyfus's treason, and the assumption that the arrested former German officers von Kessel and von Schoenbeck both conducted espionage, will once again increase feverishly the disease of the French to smell espionage everywhere. The columns of the newspapers here are once again filled with adventurous spy stories and fantastic assertions about the organization of foreign espionage. A heated campaign against foreigners has been let loose, especially against Germans and Italians. Their organizations, consulates, even their embassies are designated as nests of espionage.

In this connection a long article in yesterday's *Matin* went to unbelievable lengths. It called for the abolition of the entire institution of Military Attachés because they are said to be responsible for military spying. Especially the German military is reproached for conducting espionage, and the German Embassy is described as the center of espionage in France. I said that I could no longer tolerate that.

I sent word at once to the Minister for Foreign Affairs, whom I was not able to see personally because I was not feeling well. I told him that I expected the protection of the French Government against such infamous press attacks, and that I could not remain calm in the face of such evil prevarications in the newspapers. I made it clear that it is the duty of the Government to protect us from such aspersions, and it is up to the Government to find the proper means for this task. When Mohrenheim * was attacked, the Government was quick to find a remedy. I intimated that I should be sorry to be forced to take defensive action myself.

That evening the Minister himself visited me, and I repeated to him my remonstrations with the additional remark that I expected not only protection but also satisfaction. M. Hanotaux was very moved, told me of his lively indignation and his regret, and described the originators of these press attacks as an infamous, obscure gang. But he did not seem to have the courage "to stir up this wasp's nest." Because he was convinced that I regarded the matter as serious, he promised on his side to handle the situation with due seriousness, and requested that you speak with his colleagues.

On the next morning—today—there appeared in the newspapers an official notice that the Government had no intention of initiating a move to abolish the institution of Military Attachés. It was stated further that an article in one newspaper had printed "several errors" about the activities of foreign embassies.

I let it be known immediately in the Ministry for Foreign Affairs—the Minister himself was on a hunting expedition—that this somewhat lame denial was altogether unsatisfactory in dealing with the main point. I demanded a stronger positive declaration satisfactory to the Embassy, and I had to take into consideration whether or not I ought to announce

* Baron von Mohrenheim was the Russian Ambassador in Paris. In 1890 the French police gave secret aid to the Russian police in rounding up Russian terrorists who had taken refuge in Paris. This was a major factor leading to the Franco-Russian alliance.

semi-officially in the German press what the Minister had said about his "indignation and regret" concerning this incident.

I now await a further communication from the Minister.

I am enclosing with respect a copy of the above-mentioned article from *Matin,* the official note, and several other articles of similar content.

MÜNSTER

Diplomatic Incident: Emperor William II Demands Exoneration for the German Embassy

". . . we are authorized to state that the allegations are devoid of all foundation."

L'Agence Havas, *January 9, 1895. Translated by the editor.*

At the time of the degradation of Dreyfus, Emperor William II requested his Ambassador in Paris, Count Münster, to inform the French President, M. Casimir-Périer, that "if it is proven that the German Embassy has never been implicated in the Dreyfus affair, His Majesty hopes that the Government of the Republic will not hesitate to make a statement to that effect." Unless a formal declaration was made, he went on, the rumors the press would continue to spread in regard to the German Embassy would persist and would compromise the position of the Emperor's representative.

The next day Count Münster saw the President, with whom he was on good terms. M. Casimir-Périer informed him orally that the German Embassy was not implicated, that Dreyfus was sentenced for having obtained documents from the General Staff, and that there existed an anonymous letter addressed to the Embassy. The Ambassador said that no one at the German Embassy ever had knowledge of such a letter, and he insisted that the French Government should issue a note to the effect that Germany was not involved in the matter. The President objected that a denial of that kind would add fuel to the controversy. After some discussion, the Premier, Charles Dupuy, was brought into the picture. At this time Chancellor von Hohenlohe telegraphed Count Münster that if he did not obtain a note of denial the Imperial Government might be forced to "grant its Ambassador leave of long duration."

Finally, on January 9, 1894, *L'Agence Havas* published the following report. It was a lame denial, emasculated in form, and exculpating all the foreign embassies and legations. The French public paid no attention to it.

Since, subsequent to the sentencing of ex-Captain Dreyfus by court-martial, certain papers have continued to implicate foreign embassies in Paris, we are authorized, in order to prevent public opinion from going astray, to call to mind the note concerning this matter issued on November 30th, 1894: Certain newspapers having insisted in various articles on the subject of military espionage in implicating foreign embassies and legations, we are authorized to state that the allegations are devoid of all foundation.

Schwartzkoppen Is Unhappy and Confused
"I can only imagine. . . ."

Condensed from Die Grosse Politik, *vol. 13, pp. 290–291. Translated by the editor.*

Still in Paris as Military Attaché, Lieutenant-Colonel von Schwartzkoppen was much distressed when he read a *L'Éclair* article of September 14, 1896. He promptly sent to Berlin the following report. He professed to be perplexed by the "mysterious" affair. Obviously, he had no intention of clarifying the matter with an official statement of his own.

No. 3589

REPORT OF THE MILITARY ATTACHÉ IN PARIS—
LIEUTENANT-COLONEL VON SCHWARTZKOPPEN

Copy

No. 15   *Paris, September 20, 1896*

The article in *L'Éclair* on the 14th of this month in which its readers are given the supposedly true facts in the Dreyfus case bears the stamp of untruth. Nevertheless, there are supposed to be several new communications indicating guilt of the German Embassy and the German Military Attaché, with whom Dreyfus was said to have been in touch. Several serious newspapers, including *Le Temps,* have spread this news.

By and large it might be profitable for us to speak officially again about the Dreyfus matter, provided, of course, that a truthful clarification of this mysterious affair can be made. As long as the French press continues to make these lying reports accusing the German Embassy and the German Military Attaché, and affecting both the French and German publics, and as long as the French Government does not take any steps to deny such accusations, we should energetically defend ourselves against such articles.

I believe furthermore in this connection that an authoritative, binding declaration by the Embassy here and demand for an official denial make the only hope for counteracting the further publication of absolutely false reports. Apparently, official declarations, such as have appeared in the *Kölnische Zeitung,* are not reprinted in the press here. I regard it as completely false when the Parisian representative of the *Frankfurter Zeitung* [Dr. Goldman] believes he is doing us a service when he attacks on unfounded and insulting grounds the former War Minister, now Commanding General of the 3rd French Army Corps, General Mercier, and attributes to him conduct that is certain to injure the French people. We should be most careful not to make the same mistakes as the French press, which does not avoid charging certain persons with the lowest possible deeds without any substantiating evidence.

As for the Dreyfus case itself, it has not been possible for me, during the nearly two years that have elapsed since it began, to clear it up in my own mind. I can only imagine that either a forged document was introduced in evidence or that Dreyfus really sought to institute relations, and that such writing was discovered before it reached its destination. However that might be, the affair is very mysterious, and doubts on the guilt of the deported prisoner are ever arising. Although the noteworthy news in *L'Éclair* appeared while I was attending the French maneuvers, I did not see any changed attitude toward me on the part of the French officers or of the public.

The Minister of War, in fact, was strikingly amiable. Undoubtedly, he knows from the records of the case that I was in no way a participant in the entire affair, and the other officers undoubtedly will say to themselves that if there is the slightest suspicion against me on the part of the French Government, my continuance at this post would have been impossible.

My Italian colleague assures me repeatedly that Italy stands aloof completely from the Dreyfus affair.

(Signed) VON SCHWARTZKOPPEN

L'Intransigeant Accuses Dreyfus of Writing to the German Emperor

". . . he wrote directly to the German Emperor. . . ."

L'Intransigeant, *December 12, 1897. Translated by the editor.*

On December 12, 1897, *L'Intransigeant* (and *La Libre Parole*) published a sensational article saying that there was a secret document proving that Dreyfus had had direct contact with the German Emperor. This was, said the newspaper, the secret piece on which Dreyfus had been condemned. The *L'Intransigeant* article was written by Count Henri-Victor de Rochefort, chauvinist and anti-Semite.

THE SECRET DOCUMENT: THE TRUTH ABOUT THE TRAITOR

Dreyfus has been exasperated for some time by the anti-Semitic campaign pursued by several journals.

Very ambitious, he believed that he, as a Jew, could never attain the high position he wanted in the Army hierarchy.

And he thought that, under the circumstances, it would be preferable for him to recognize as definitive the results of the War of 1870, and he would return to live in Alsace, where he had interests, and where he would eventually adopt German citizenship.

That is the real reason why he decided to present his resignation and leave the Army.

But previously, *he wrote directly to the German Emperor* to present his sympathy for the person of the Emperor and for the nation of which he was the chief, and to ask his permission to enter the German Army in his current military grade.

William II made known to Captain Dreyfus through the mediation of the German Ambassador in Paris that it was preferable that he serve Germany, his true country, in the post that circumstances had designated for him, *and that he would be considered by the German General Staff to be an officer on mission to France.*

The promise was made to him, among others, that in the event of war he would immediately take rank in the German Army.

Dreyfus accepted those conditions.

And the treason commenced.

This preamble is necessary to know what followed.

One of the famous secret pieces is a letter from the German Emperor himself.

It was stolen, photographed, and replaced where it had been taken.

In that letter, addressed to M. de Münster, William II identified Captain Dreyfus by name as the purveyor of certain information, and he charged the agent of the Ambassador to communicate with Dreyfus to obtain certain information considered valuable by the German General Staff.

Such is the origin of the principal "secret document."

We have long since possessed a version which was furnished to us by a highly placed military personage.

We have been most careful to take every possible care in making public these important revelations, and we repeat that they emanate from authoritative sources.

A foreign Military Attaché has declared to us:

"I ignore the extremely curious details which you apparently possess on the relations of Dreyfus with the German General Staff, but I know that what I say corresponds admirably with your information.

"I, as well as most of my colleagues attached to military staffs of foreign powers here, have had friendly and even intimate relations with Colonel von Schwartzkoppen, and I myself have had numerous conversations with him on the Dreyfus affair."

He resumed: "Several days before the arrest of Dreyfus, Count von Münster, German Ambassador, had a talk with M. Charles Dupuy, President of the Council of Ministers, to the following effect: "A bundle of documents, including eight letters addressed to me, was stolen from the Embassy. This is a violation of our territory in time of peace. I regret to inform you that if these letters are not restored to me immediately, I shall leave Paris within twenty-four hours."

The documents were forthwith returned to Count Münster.

Only, they were photographed.

And those are the photographs which have been placed before the eyes of the Council of War.

That same day, December 12, 1897, *L'Agence Havas* issued this denial:

> The journal *L'Intransigeant* this morning published an article on the Dreyfus case titled: "The Secret Document: The Truth About the Traitor," which was inexact on several points.
>
> We are authorized to state that the Government issues a most formal denial and affirms that the documents described in that article do not exist and never have existed.

Ambassador Münster Reports Sensational Revelations

"The Parisian is completely irresponsible when it comes to politics, especially by anything concerning Germany."

Die Grosse Politik, *vol. 13, pp. 298–299. Translated by the editor.*

When Count de Rochefort, probably informed by the head of the General Staff, announced in *L'Intransigeant* the existence of the letter from William II to Ambassador Münster about Dreyfus, he was seeking to ease the discharge of Esterhazy. The document (forged, like many others in the Dreyfus *dossier*), caused a tremendous sensation. Münster immediately reported the incident to Reichs Chancellor Hohenlohe in the following dispatch.

No. 3597

THE AMBASSADOR IN PARIS COUNT MÜNSTER TO THE REICHS CHANCELLOR PRINCE VON HOHENLOHE

No. 286   *Paris, December 16, 1897*

The lies of Rochefort would have been recognized immediately as lies and disregarded in every other reasonable country and in every other capital.

The Parisian is completely irresponsible when it comes to politics, especially by anything concerning Germany. The superficiality and the passion of the Parisian leave him little time for reflection, and for that reason the yellow press here has a most dangerous influence.

As unbelievable as it might seem, reasonable Frenchmen, that is, those who must be regarded as reasonable, really believe Rochefort's revelations, and I have repeatedly been able to substantiate that they do believe them.

Chauvinism, anti-Semitism, compassion for a possibly innocent condemned man have made the Dreyfus Affair a political happening.

M. Méline [1] and his cabinet recognize that during this period of general excitement it cannot be tolerated that our Most Gracious Majesty and his representatives should be drawn into this quarrel, and that steps must be taken to oppose this misuse of the press. Unfortunately, the Government does not possess the means to oppose such misusage effectively, even though it is not deficient in good will.

Above all, a press law is necessary.

M. Méline told me that he has decided firmly [2] to lay such a law before the Chamber of Deputies. Whether or not that will take place before the elections seems very doubtful to me, although M. Méline and M. Hanotaux [3] say that at this moment the mood seems quite favorable.

I took the opportunity to remark about the respect that the French have for the energy of His Most Gracious Majesty, and how they fundamentally fear to begin a false struggle with us.

When I saw the *L'Intransigeant* article on Sunday morning, I wrote immediately to M. Hanotaux and asked him to see me. He suggested that I come at three o'clock.

When I came to him at three o'clock, he already had the printed denial of the *Agence Havas* in his hand and said that M. Méline had called him

---

[1] Jules Méline, Premier of France.
[2] Marginal notation by William II: "Right word?"
[3] The French Minister for Foreign Affairs.

and former Minister President Dupuy to come to him and advise him, which took place.

He regrets exceedingly this misuse of the press; the Minister-President is angered by it, and wants to express to me his regrets.

M. Méline, whom I then visited, said that he regards the matter as seriously as I do, regrets the incident, and has decided to put a stop to such misusages.[4]

That he is serious is shown by the enclosed lead article from *La République Française*.[5]

Rochefort seems to feel that the Government has serious intentions, and he has withdrawn now a little.

In these days we shall be able to see how the inquiry concerning Esterhazy proceeds, and whether a revision of the Dreyfus trial will be possible.

Excitement, especially among the students, is so great that the police have had to take special police measures on the Left Bank, and protection by strong contingents of police personnel have been given to the embassies as well as the house in which Scheurer-Kestner [6] lives.

I have been acting as if Dreyfus is no concern of mine at all. But when our Most Gracious Majesty is drawn into the quarrel, then I shall show with all my energy that I just will not tolerate it.

I am doing this on my own responsibility because I believe it to be proper and effective behavior under the circumstances, rather than await special instructions.[7]

I will not be put off by the assertion that such hostile accusations should be ignored because no one believes them.

MÜNSTER

German Secretary of State von Bülow Makes a Public Declaration
". . . between Captain Dreyfus and any species of German agency, no relations of any kind have ever existed."

Max J. Kohler, Some New Light on the Dreyfus Case, *reprinted from Freidus Memorial Volume (Vienna, 1929), p. 7.*

The *L'Intransigeant* article infuriated Ambassador Münster so much that he threatened a libel suit against the newspaper. A fresh

---

[4] Marginal notation by William II: "But he has not done it—"

[5] "The Press Law," in *La République Française*, September 16, 1897.

[6] Auguste Scheurer-Kestner, Vice-President of the Senate, who in the previous July was the first public official to take up the cause of revision.

[7] Marginal notation by William II: "Good."

debate in the French Chamber of Deputies, Esterhazy's acquittal, and Zola's *J'Accuse* letter brought new sensations in the press. On January 24, 1898, Secretary of State Bernard von Bülow, made a public declaration on the subject to the Budget Commission of the German *Reichstag* after an interpellation by Delegate Richter.

It was an evasive statement, with no word about Esterhazy's contacts with German organs and childishly denying the existence of the *bordereau*. The declaration indicated that everything on the case was meaningless or fabricated (though von Bülow knew better). This weak explanation was regarded by the German Government as its official attitude toward the case.

You will understand me, if I go into the subject only with much caution. A different course would be regarded as mixing ourselves up in the internal affairs of France. I confine myself therefore to saying most positively that between Captain Dreyfus and any species of German agency, no relations or connections of any kind have ever existed. The names Esterhazy and Picquart I heard three weeks ago for the first time in my life. The story of an alleged paper, found ostensibly in a paper basket from a mysterious agent, existed naturally only in fantasy, and in fact the incident never took place. I wish finally to declare with satisfaction that the so-called Dreyfus affair stirred up much dust, but has not been able to disturb the peaceful relations between Germany and France.

The German Ambassador Is Embarrassed

*"I do not know of this connection, and Colonel
von Schwartzkoppen kept it a secret from me."*

Die Grosse Politik, *vol. 13, pp. 301–302. Translated by the editor.*

Two months after Secretary of State von Bülow's "official" declaration on the Dreyfus case before the Budget Commission of the *Reichstag,* Count Münster, the German Ambassador, in great excitement telegraphed to the Foreign Office in Berlin that the *Siècle* in Paris had published a letter from a diplomat in Berne under the title "The Truth About Esterhazy." This letter revealed in detail the connections between Schwartzkoppen and Esterhazy, that the German Military Attaché had employed Esterhazy for some time without the knowledge of the Ambassador, and that Schwartzkoppen had received 162 documents from him. With indignation the Ambassador, obviously deceived by Schwartzkoppen on orders of the General Staff, complained that he had never known of the connection.

No. 3600

THE AMBASSADOR IN PARIS COUNT VON MÜNSTER TO THE FOREIGN OFFICE

TELEGRAM. DECIPHERED.

No. 54   *Paris, April 4, 1898*

Le Siècle today published an article from Berne concerning the relations between Major Esterhazy and Colonel Schwartzkoppen.

I did not know of this connection, and Colonel von Schwartzkoppen kept it a secret from me.

This publication promoted by the Dreyfus Syndicate is supposed to be followed by a similar article in English newspapers. But thus far it has not found any. A court-martial is supposed to meet today to consider a new accusation against Zola. That is apparently the reason for the publication of the *Siècle* article.

MÜNSTER

Von Bülow replied to the embarrassed Ambassador that nothing could be done about the matter "even if these connections did *not* exist and thus their refutation made easy." He said that it was, therefore, without any purpose for him (von Bülow) to approach the subtle question as to whether or not such connections "existed." Because Panizzardi, the Italian Military Attaché, was designated by the French press as originator of the disclosures on Esterhazy-Schwartzkoppen, von Bülow sent a telegram to the German Ambassador in Rome asking him to pass on to the Italian Government the word that Berlin expected the Italian king to undertake all necessary measures to prevent definitely similar acts in the future by persons who, at the time, were only doing their official duty.

This diplomatic exchange at the time when the Zola matter was being revived indicated the ambivalent attitude of the German Government in an embarrassing situation. Even more, the fact that the German Ambassador, Count von Münster, was bitterly complaining to the highest official in the Reich, indicated how the military had encroached upon the province of the diplomatic corps.

Chancellor Hohenlohe Reports on the Mood in Paris

". . . there would have been a revolution in Paris
should Zola have been acquitted."

William Herzog, From Dreyfus to Petain, *trans. Walter Sorell (New York: Creative Age Press, 1947), p. 234.*

In early June 1898, shortly before the second Zola trial, the German Chancellor, the 88-year-old Prince von Hohenlohe, was in Paris on his vacation. In contrast to Bülow, to Holstein the "grey eminence" of the Foreign Office, and to the German generals, the elderly Chancellor did not derive any satisfaction from the atmosphere in Paris. On June 11, 1898, he made the following entry in his diary.

Anti-Semitic mood. A. Meyer [the Jewish manager of the nationalistic and monarchistic paper *Le Gaulois*], whom I met in a salon, told interesting things about the Dreyfus Affair and maintained that there would have been a revolution in Paris should Zola have been acquitted. Münster did not believe it, but others said Zola was thrown into the Seine and the troops had not protected him. Now the general mood is calmer again. A. Meyer is enthusiastic about the monarchy and asserted that with it France would be quiet again. He spoke for Franco-German alliance. The Alsatian question had to be put aside and they had to fight together against one enemy, England. The hatred against England is greater than that against Germany. Déroulède, his friend, does not want any war of *revanche*.

Von Bülow Is Delighted by the Agony of France

"It would be best if the Affair would continue to fester. . . ."

Die Grosse Politik, *vol. 13, pp. 307–308. Translated by the editor.*

Although there was a widespread belief in France that Emperor William II was the villain on the German side in the Dreyfus Affair, actually the policy from Berlin was directed by Bernhard von Bülow, the responsible head of German foreign policy. On September 29, 1898, he sent by telegraph from the Semmering, the Alpine pass where he was taking his fall vacation, a document which could scarcely be surpassed for sheer undiplomatic depravity. Unaware that his telegram would eventually be made public, Bülow revealed his sense of joy in the maelstrom of troubles in which France found herself.

THE STATE SECRETARY OF THE FOREIGN OFFICE
BERNHARD VON BÜLOW, TEMPORARILY IN SEMMERING,
TO THE FOREIGN OFFICE

TELEGRAM. DECIPHERED.

No. 82   *Semmering, September 29, 1898*

Our chief interest in the Dreyfus Affair must be in keeping out of it as much as we can. A victory of the anti-revisionists is not to be wished for, because it might possibly lead to dictatorship and then to war with us. It should not sadden us that the French generals and the General Staff have been discredited—and especially the chauvinistic and the clerical officers who are militarily the most efficient ones among them. The story about the embezzlement of a million francs by the French General Staff, which was concocted by Bleibtreu and used with good effect yesterday by the *Neues Wiener Tageblatt* in its editorial, should continue to be spread. On the other hand, it is not to be desired that France should immediately win Liberal and Jewish sympathies by a quick and scintillating reparation of the Dreyfus Affair. It would be best if the Affair would continue to fester, to upset the Army, and scandalize all Europe. We must not admit Herr von Schwartzkoppen's alleged relations with Esterhazy, even if they did exist, because such an indiscretion would make it quite difficult in the future to maintain such information and agents.

BÜLOW

Mathieu Dreyfus Begs Schwartzkoppen to Break His Long Silence
"It is a moral obligation. . . ."

Kayser, The Dreyfus Affair, *p. 267.*

During the late summer and early autumn of 1898, Mathieu Dreyfus attempted to reach the ear of Schwartzkoppen and persuade him to end his silence and tell the truth. On several occasions he wrote to an intermediary, a M. Albert Sandoz of Mulhouse, who had agreed to contact Schwartzkoppen. It was all in vain. Schwartzkoppen refused to talk.

In a few days' time Picquart will be regarded by us and by our friends as a victim; to the majority of Frenchmen, however, he will have been branded, disgraced, covered with shame and mud.

Will Colonel Schwartzkoppen allow this fresh crime to be committed, when he could intervene by declaring openly, like a true soldier, that the famous *petit bleu* did indeed emanate from him and that Esterhazy was his agent?

If he does this, and he could do it in a variety of ways, either by writing direct to the French Government or by making a statement to the French Ambassador in Berlin, he will merely be doing his duty as a man of honor.

The whole of civilized Europe will be grateful to him for having borne witness in this poignant drama in which the part he has played has been an important, but, up to the present, a silent one.

It is a moral obligation, a duty he owes to his conscience, which he must fulfil; if he does not do so it may be said that his responsibility for the crimes now being committed is even greater than that of the Government of France.

Prince Alexander von Hohenlohe Attempts to Move Schwartzkoppen

". . . Yes, in my view you would be the most popular man and the German Government the most popular government in France."

The Truth About Dreyfus, *from* The Schwartzkoppen Papers, *edited by Bernard Schwertfeger (London and New York: Putnam, 1931), pp. 205–209. Originally published in Germany under the title:* Die Wahrheit über Dreyfus *(Berlin: Verlag für Kulturpolitik, 1930). By permission of G. P. Putnam Sons.*

Mathieu Dreyfus was not the only one seeking to convince Schwartzkoppen that a few words from him would bring about the collapse of the edifice of lies. Prince Alexander von Hohenlohe, son of the German Chancellor, Chlodwig Karl Victor Prince von Hohenlohe-Schillingsfürst, wrote to Schwartzkoppen on September 19, 1898, concerning a visit made to him by M. Albert Sandoz of Mulhouse on Dreyfus's behalf. The latter asked for information on several points which only Schwartzkoppen could answer. "Herr Sandoz was not only well recommended to me but made personally the impression of a most honorable man and one worthy of the highest regard."

Prince Hohenlohe wrote to Schwartzkoppen again on November 21, 1898, in the letter reprinted below. But no argument was enough to convince Schwartzkoppen to break the silence which he felt was imposed on him by his superiors.

PRINCE A. VON HOHENLOHE TO COLONEL VON SCHWARTZKOPPEN

(SECRET AND CONFIDENTIAL)

Colmar (Alsace), 21.xi.98

DEAR COLONEL,

May I trespass once more on your time in regard to the Dreyfus matter already mentioned? I am not coming this time to transmit to you a request or an application for an audience from some friend of Dreyfus, but to mention to you some ideas which have occurred to me in the course of attentive observation of the developments in this case.

According to all the newspapers there seems no doubt that Picquart is to be court-martialled on the charge of having falsified the address of the *petit bleu*. In view of the quality of the judges who are certain to be carefully picked for this purpose, and in view of their prejudice against the defendant, he will undoubtedly be convicted.

I am asking myself whether there is nothing that could be done to prevent this.

In all the past phases of the Dreyfus Affair it is clear that for many and various reasons there has been no possibility of any intervention from the German side, and particularly none of any deposition, or anything of that sort, from you. The state of public feeling in France was such that intervention would have been not only useless but absolutely dangerous. Since then there has been a considerable revulsion of feeling, and I think it can definitely be said that today the great majority of Frenchmen desire a thorough and impartial investigation of the whole of this dark affair; in a word, that those are now in the great majority who are demanding light and the truth in this case, and that the shouters like Rochefort, Drumont and their gang have lost ground considerably.

On the other hand, there is no doubt that the smack that France has just had from England in the Fashoda affair has done a good deal to lessen the tension with Germany and has even aroused among a section of the population a desire for a rapprochement with Germany; this is evident from the way some of the Chauvinist organs, such as the *Patrie,* are writing.

Bearing all this in mind, one involuntarily asks oneself, has not the moment perhaps come to strike a blow for us, i.e. for Germany?

In the present phase of the Dreyfus Affair the question at issue is no longer whether Dreyfus was employed in the service of Germany or

anything of that sort, on which it was impossible for us to say anything—
the reply was always easy: "Quite so, you have had nothing to do with
Dreyfus; but how do you propose to demonstrate to us that Dreyfus had
nothing to do with *you*, without your knowledge, through go-betweens,
without your having any notion that he was behind them?" It is no
longer a question of that, but the simple question: Did Picquart falsify
the address of the *petit bleu* or not? Did you write the address or did
someone else? The matter turns entirely on these simple questions.

Now, I am saying to myself: if in this situation, at this moment, amid
a complete *volte-face* of opinion, there is anything that we could do to
bring the truth to light, would not that have a good effect, would not
the great majority of the public in France recognize the honorable nature
of our action? I put the question, without answering it. For my part I
should be glad to answer it with a decided affirmative.

Suppose, for instance—I am only putting forward the hypothesis—you
were to write to the president of the court-martial a letter in some such
sense as this: "You are a soldier like myself; you will understand, therefore, why I feel bound to declare to you hereby on my honor that the
address to Esterhazy on the *petit bleu* has not been falsified but was
written by myself—Schwartzkoppen."

What would be the impression of such a letter or of a letter written
in that sense? In my view (though it carries no authority), the impression
would be an excellent one. Yes, in my view you would be the most
popular man and the German Government the most popular government
in France. For how long is another question; for nothing is stable in
France; but for twenty-four hours, and, indeed, for some days for certain.
That would make an end of the Picquart affair for good and all, and
Picquart would be acquitted amid acclamations.

In the other event, if Picquart is condemned, his conviction will be
the beginning of another Dreyfus case, this time called the Picquart case,
with, perhaps, a still more violent campaign for revision. The anarchy
in France, the strife and schism will assume yet greater dimensions; the
Army will be, perhaps, even more deeply discredited, and what the end
will be no one can foretell. We may then look on passively as unconcerned
spectators, do nothing whatever, and wait to see what will be the upshot
of the tragedy; that would be the other alternative.

Whether the latter course, considering it from a purely political
standpoint, would be of greater advantage for Germany, I do not venture
to decide.

Forgive me for taking up your valuable time with these lengthy
discussions. Do not resent my putting them forward. I felt that in view
of our old friendship I might venture quite unofficially to submit these

considerations to you. I have spoken to no one about them, nor have I seen M. Sandoz since he went to see you with my letter of introduction; nor have I heard from him save for a short letter of thanks. But I have followed the Affair attentively in the papers and have a keen interest in it, from a purely human standpoint. So it is that these ideas have occurred to me.

I should be grateful to you for a short acknowledgement of this letter.

Always yours sincerely,
A. HOHENLOHE

I will add that I am under no illusions as to the reception of my ideas. I know well that in this matter your hands are tied, and that you can do nothing without instructions. I only wanted to express my ideas to you as I have no one here to whom I can do it. So, no harm meant.

VI

Intermezzo: Picquart Versus Esterhazy

Until he became embroiled in the Dreyfus case, Georges Picquart was widely regarded as one of France's most promising young officers. An Alsatian from Strasbourg, he had served abroad in Tunis and had been promoted to the rank of major at 32. It was in all probability that due in part to the fact that he knew German, English, Italian, and Spanish, a rare accomplishment for a French officer, he was appointed in late 1895 as Chief of the Intelligence Department of the General Staff.

In this capacity Picquart was destined to be involved in a continuing confrontation with Esterhazy, the villain of the drama. It was not long before he became convinced of Esterhazy's guilt.

In December 1897, supported by his contacts on the General Staff, Esterhazy demanded an investigation to prove the "falsity" of the charges against him. The inquiry was entrusted to General Gabriel de Pellieux, who was convinced that Esterhazy was the victim of an abominable plot and that Picquart was an unwitting accomplice of the conspirators. De Pellieux had his mind made up even before he began his inquiry.

Esterhazy decided to bluff his way through. He sent a threatening and cynical letter to the President of the Republic. When he was denounced by Mathieu Dreyfus as the real author of the *bordereau,* Esterhazy brazenly requested a court-martial to meet "this shameful accusation." The Military Governor acceded to the request and gave orders for a court-martial.

The hearing was a farce, as judges, prosecution, and accused formed a united front. Most of the court's time in the two-day trial was spent examining depositions against Picquart. The judges retired, and before lawyers could rearrange their papers, the judges

117

returned and announced that Esterhazy was acquitted by unanimous vote.

Esterhazy emerged from the courtroom a free man as the crowds shouted: "Long live France!" "Down with the Jews!"

Picquart Seeks Action in the General Staff

"We must be careful especially to beware of first impressions."

William Herzog, Der Kampf Einer Republik: Die Affäre Dreyfus (*Zürich: Büchergilde Gutenberg, 1933), p. 416. Translated by the editor.*

As soon as he was certain that the *bordereau* was written not by Dreyfus but by Esterhazy, Picquart reported his discovery to General Raoul-François-Charles Le Mouton de Boisdeffre, Chief of the General Staff, and outlined his reasons. Boisdeffre listened, said nothing, and then referred Picquart to General Charles-Arthur Gonse, Deputy Chief of the General Staff. Because Gonse was on holiday, Picquart wrote to him on September 5, 1896, requesting authority to consult a legal expert.

Two days later, on September 7, 1896, General Gonse replied to Picquart and urged him to proceed with extreme caution. He told Picquart to give up the idea of submitting Esterhazy's handwriting to an expert and to await his own coming return to Paris.

September 7, 1896

MY DEAR PICQUART,

I have received your letter of the 5th, and I am hastening, after considering carefully what you have told me, to inform you that it seems to me that we must use extreme caution in this matter. We must be careful especially to beware of first impressions. . . .

I am returning on September 15. It would be much better if we discuss this matter orally. In short, it seems to me that we must proceed with extreme caution in this matter.

I heartily shake your hand, my dear Picquart.

Very truly yours,
A. GONSE

Picquart Repeats His Warning to General Gonse
"We can avoid all this. . . ."

Thalheimer, Macht und Gerechtigkeit, *p. 150. Translated by the editor.*

On September 8, 1896, Picquart wrote once more to Gonse, reminding him of his previous warning and repeating it in most urgent form.

September 8, 1896

MY DEAR GENERAL,

[I have read your letter carefully and I shall follow your instructions exactly. However], I believe it is my duty to tell you the following: A number of indications and a recent serious matter [1] concerning which I shall speak with you later, make it clear to me that the moment is near when people,[2] who are convinced that a serious error has been made, will make a great scandal. I believe I have done that which is necessary to see that the initiative comes from our side. If we lose too much time then the initiative will come from the other side, which could put us in a bad position. I should add that those people do not seem to me to be as well-informed as we are, and that their attempt at an embarrassing scandal will lead to a tremendous uproar, which, however, will shed no light on the case. It would be a deplorable crisis without any real value. We can avoid all this if we at the right time open the way to an act of reparation.

G. PICQUART

Gonse Recommends Prudence
"Prudence! Prudence! That is the word you must always keep before you."

Herzog, Der Kampf Einer Republik: Die Affäre Dreyfus, *p. 417. Translated by the editor.*

On September 10, 1896, General Gonse replied to Picquart's second letter and once again advised him to be most cautious. It was obvious that Gonse wanted Picquart to hush up the entire matter.

---

[1] At this point Picquart referred to the Weyler forgery. See page 90.
[2] The Dreyfus family.

September 10, 1896

MY DEAR PICQUART,

This will acknowledge receipt of your letter of the 8th. It is really not a matter of snuffing out the light, but one must act with the very greatest circumspection in order to reveal the truth.

Prudence! Prudence! That is the word you must always keep before you.

A. GONSE

When Gonse returned to Paris on September 15, 1896, Picquart called on him and repeated his recommendation for action. Gonse was not inclined to listen:

"Why do you concern yourself about getting this man off Devil's Island? The matter is finished and cannot be undone."

"But he is innocent" Picquart replied.

"If you say nothing, nobody will know."

Shocked, Picquart replied firmly: "General, what you tell me is abominable. I do not know what I shall do. But I won't carry this secret with me to the grave." *

L'Éclair Finds a "Traitor"

". . . that was the document in which Dreyfus was named."

L'Éclair, *September 14, 1896. Translated by the editor.*

On September 14, 1896, *L'Éclair* published a long, anonymous article obviously designed to put an end to doubts about the guilt of Dreyfus. Entitled "The Traitor," the article sought to demonstrate the fact of guilt by an analysis of Dreyfus's *dossier*. There were two letters, especially, said the article, which pointed to guilt. One was a decoded letter from Schwartzkoppen to Panizzardi, in which it was said: "That wretch Dreyfus is certainly becoming too exciting." The second was a letter to the German Embassy, an *"anonymous bordereau,"* which was supposed to show Dreyfus's handwriting. Both "documents" were later proven to be forgeries.

After implicating the German Embassy, the article then described the discovery of the *bordereau,* expert opinion on the handwriting in it, the dictation to Dreyfus, and the court-martial. It concluded as follows:

* See page 296 for Picquart's testimony on this incident before the court-martial at Rennes.

THE TRAITOR

It is true that Dreyfus did not know and perhaps still does not know today that the Minister of War has in his possession a photograph of a letter exchanged between the German and Italian Military Attachés, the only document in which Dreyfus's name appears. The letter, which he undoubtedly wrote but which he carefully avoided signing, can only be a moral element in the Affair. The experts Charavay and Bertillon said that it comes from Dreyfus, but the other three hesitated.

But a proof allows no hesitation: that was the document in which Dreyfus was named. It convinced the court and it weighed so heavily that the traitor can no longer speak against his condemnation. Because it was exceptionally confidential in nature, the Minister could not very well allow it to get out of his hands and be used at the court-martial.

There had to be an investigation in the Ministry itself. It took place. But in order to spare the Governmental representatives the corroboration of so many secret documents, it was set aside. The arrangement was made not to bring the document to the proceedings. Only the judges in the courtroom were able to see it.

This irrefutable proof led to a conclusive decision among the judges. When they were called upon for a verdict, and for the nature of the penalty, they were unanimous.

Bernard-Lazare's Pamphlet Opens the Offensive for Dreyfus

"I hope I have not spoken in vain."

Bernard-Lazare, Une erreur judiciaire, la vérité sur l'affaire Dreyfus (*Paris: Stock, 1897*), *p. xvi. Translated by the editor.*

Six weeks after the publication of the *L'Éclair* article on "The Traitor," there appeared a small, yellow brochure entitled: "A Judicial Error—The Truth About the Dreyfus Affair." Its author, Bernard-Lazare (pseudonym for Lazare Bernard), a talented Jewish journalist, who had become concerned about growing anti-Semitism, was convinced that the Jews were being attacked through Dreyfus. He got in touch with the Dreyfus family and soon became certain that a fearful judicial error had been committed. In sixty pages of penetrating, polemical prose, he published the text of the *bordereau*, discussed each document in detail, and analyzed the opinion of the experts. Three thousand copies of the pamphlet were printed and many were sent to other journalists as well as members of Parliament. From that moment on Bernard-Lazare became one of the central figures in the Affair. The final section of the Introduction follows.

The German Embassy never possessed that *bordereau* which is the subject of the accusation, and certainly not the documents mentioned in it. Never did the German Military Attaché in Paris write that letter to the German Military Attaché in Italy, * which is said to be the decisive indication of guilt. Captain Dreyfus is the victim of a terrible machination; he is innocent. I believe in his innocence with my deepest innermost soul, but I am only raising my voice because I am guided by my love for justice and my utter conviction. I hope I have not spoken in vain.

The Disgraced Picquart Draws Up a Codicil to His Will

"To my great stupefaction I found them identical."

Joseph Reinach, Histoire de l'affaire Dreyfus (*Paris: Librairie Charpentier et Farquelle, 1907*), vol. 2, pp. 701–704. Translated by the editor.

Major Henry, fearing Picquart above anyone else, managed to convince his superiors, Generals Gonse, Boisdeffre, and Billot, to get Picquart out of Paris. In November 1896 Picquart was ordered on a tour of inspection of the Eastern district and kept at a distance from Paris. In late December his mission was given a wider scope: he was ordered to organize the Intelligence Service in North Africa in the province of Constantine, in Algeria, and in Tunis. Picquart was well aware of what was going on, but as a disciplined soldier he obeyed without question. Returning from Tunis to Paris in the spring of 1897, he broke his left collarbone in a fall from his horse. He then drew up a codicil to his will and in an envelope gave an extract résumé of all his investigations. He left this material with his attorney to be brought to the attention of the President of the Republic in the event of his death.

In case of the death of the undersigned, forward this envelope to the President of the Republic, who alone should be made cognizant of its contents.

G. Picquart
Lieutenant-Colonel attached to the
4th Regiment of Tirailleurs.

---

* Obviously a misunderstanding or error on Bernard-Lazare's part: the real receiver of the message was supposed to be the Italian Military Attaché in Paris.

Sousse, April 2, 1897

I, the undersigned Marie-Georges Picquart, Lieutenant-Colonel of the *4th Tirailleurs,* formerly Chief of Intelligence in the War Ministry, certify on my honor the following facts which in the interest of truth and justice it is impossible to "smother," as has been attempted in the past.

In the month of May 1896 my attention was directed to Major Walsin-Esterhazy of the 74th Infantry Regiment because of a telegram-card which contained suspected information coming from someone in the German Embassy (probably from the German Military Attaché Colonel von Schwartzkoppen). A thorough investigation, which I undertook following a written order dated September 1, 1896, and given to me by General Gonse, revealed that Major Walsin-Esterhazy is an agent of Germany. The proof for that is abundant, and Esterhazy's desperate pecuniary situation, together with his complete lack of scruples in choosing the means for acquiring money that he needed, corroborate the material evidence already collected.

In the months of August and September Esterhazy got several Deputies to be active on his behalf and through his friend (perhaps his accomplice), Lucien Weil, he attempted to obtain through General Saussier [Governor of Paris] a place in the direction of the Infantry or in the Intelligence Department of the Ministry of War. The report which I made to the Minister on the subject of Esterhazy, made the latter goal impossible even though he made repeated efforts.

In my study of the Dreyfus Affair I was surprised by the following: that is, that certain deeds attributed to *Dreyfus* in fact coincide with deeds committed by Esterhazy.

Dreyfus was accused of writing a letter to the German Military Attaché in Paris. Out of curiosity I compared the handwriting of Esterhazy with that of this letter. To my great stupefaction I found them identical.

Three of five experts declared that the incriminating document bears the *modified and disguised* handwriting of Dreyfus. I, however, found that this was the *natural* handwriting of Esterhazy.

Because I did not wish to trust my eyes only, I showed one of the experts, M. Bertillon, a specimen of the handwriting of Esterhazy's without telling him the name. M. Bertillon declared immediately that the writing on that document was that of Dreyfus; he pressed me with questions seeking to find out where I had gotten this specimen of writing. Then he found, as he said, "that the disguised handwriting that Dreyfus has used is so well done that only an expert who has made special studies of the subject will not be fooled."

Now, all the specimens of Esterhazy's handwriting (and I have many of them from various times) are identical.

I reported these facts first to General Boisdeffre, then with his approval to General Gonse and finally to the War Minister General Billot. General Boisdeffre and General Gonse, who under the direction of General Mercier were the originators of the Dreyfus proceedings, were most embarrassed. The Minister admitted all my proofs, and told me that he would "put the hook" on Esterhazy [sic!]. For the time being I was to continue my investigations.

Meanwhile, the press campaign in favor of Dreyfus began, as well as the interpellation of Castelin. General Boisdeffre spoke with the Minister and the latter seemed very troubled after the conference. He told me bluntly (and I allowed myself to believe that this was not true) that he has received, from his special police, proof of Dreyfus's guilt, but he did not give it to me. General Gonse asked me with a certain anxiety if I believed what the Minister had told me.

As I always affirmed that I stuck to my guns on the material I had gathered, I was ordered one day (November 16) to go on a special mission to visit the 6th Corps; I was sent on this duty on the 7th, until the 14th, and then on the 15th. Finally I was detailed to the 4th *Tirailleurs,* all this without allowing me for an instant to draw my breath and in the evident intention to keep me as far as possible away from the Intelligence Service, which at that time had made a painful discovery.

All the proofs that I had in hand and which were taken from me several days before I began the aforementioned mission demonstrated in the most clear-cut fashion:

1. That Walsin-Esterhazy (and perhaps also his friend Weil) is an agent of Germany;

2. That the only palpable deeds that have been attributed to Dreyfus were performed by Esterhazy;

3. That the trial of Dreyfus was handled in an unbelievably frivolous manner and with the preconceived notion that Dreyfus was guilty, and with little attention to proper legal forms. The secret *dossier* communicated in the council room of the judges consisted of four documents, of which one pointed to Esterhazy, the second referred to the initial D, that could not possibly be Dreyfus, and the two others had no meaning whatever and were just nonsense. It concerns a *dossier* which was *not communicated* either to the accused nor to his lawyer and which led to the condemnation of Dreyfus. It had an effect on the indecisive judges who had no one to clarify it to them, and who were obliged to make a quick decision. It could not support a reasonable discussion and the defense had really completely refuted it.

I repeat: all these documents were taken from me one by one by General Gonse as soon as I discovered them. I even fear that the *dossier* brought to that courtroom has been destroyed.

G. PICQUART

Picquart Writes a Letter of Protest to Henry
"I have done nothing of which I am ashamed."

Herzog, Der Kampf Einer Republik, *p. 437.*

While in exile Picquart received many threatening letters, some of them coming from the Intelligence Department of the War Ministry. He was fairly certain that these were instigated by Major Henry, his former subordinate. Anxious to have his position defined, he wrote an official letter of protest to Henry.

May 18, 1897

Personal:

MAJOR HENRY:

Let anyone who asks after me be told once and for all time that I have been relieved of my duties, or that I no longer hold the appointment. I have done nothing of which I am ashamed. What I am ashamed of are the lies and mysteries with which my real position has been surrounded for the last six months.

G. PICQUART

Henry's Threatening Letter to Picquart
"As for the word 'lies,' . . . investigation has not yet determined where, how, and to whom this should be applied."

Quoted in Herzog, Der Kampf Einer Republik, *pp. 437–438.*

When he sent his brief note, Picquart had no idea that Henry was busily compiling a *dossier* against him. Henry now had to reply and he chose the course of insolence and threats. On May 31, 1897, he drew up a reply which he submitted to Generals Gonse and de Boisdeffre. His letter was sent out on June 3. In it he appropriated the word "mysteries" in Picquart's note and used it to apply to three different charges which were being made against Picquart in an "inquiry."

May 31, 1897

COLONEL

I take this opportunity to acquaint you with the following. After the receipt of your note of May 18 there was an investigation made here whether or not the term "mysteries" could be used to apply to several matters that have taken place in the year 1896 in the SS: [1]

1. The revealing of an outside correspondence, the purpose for which no one seems to understand.[2]

2. An attempt to suborn two members of the staff of the SS by inviting them to testify that "an official handwritten document was intercepted at a post office and that it came from a known person."

3. The revealing from motives foreign to the Department of secret documents showing indiscretions for unofficial purposes.

The material proofs of these facts are in existence here.

As for the word "lies," which was also used in the above-mentioned note of the 18th of May, investigation has not yet determined where, how, and to whom this term should be applied.

With highest esteem,

J. HENRY

General Gonse later stated before the Court of Cassation that, when Henry showed him the draft of this letter, he said: "I cannot allow you to send such a letter to a superior officer. Officially, I don't want to know anything about it." Henry always claimed that he had sent it with the full approval of Gonse.

Picquart Protests Again

". . . and against the tone used in it."

Quoted in Herzog, Der Kampf Einer Republik, *p. 439.*

As soon as he received Henry's insolent letter, Picquart answered him with the following protest.

Personal:

MAJOR HENRY:

Letter of May 31 received.

I protest in the most emphatic way possible against the representations included in it and against the tone used in it.

G. PICQUART

[1] Statistical Section.
[2] Henry refers here to Esterhazy's correspondence.

The *Espérance* Letter: Esterhazy Is Warned Anonymously
"Your name is going to be the object of a great scandal."

Quoted in Steevens, The Tragedy of Dreyfus, *p. 247.*

On October 18 (or 20), 1897, Esterhazy received an anonymous letter signed *"Espérance,"* which is quoted in full below. In the letter he was warned that he would soon be exposed and that the Dreyfus family was going to accuse him publicly of being the author of the *bordereau*. Curiously, the Dreyfus family at this time knew nothing about the name Esterhazy, although members were, indeed, searching for the writer of the *bordereau*. The anonymous letter tried to give the impression that Picquart had informed the Dreyfus family about Esterhazy.

Was this letter sent by the cabal against Dreyfus on the General Staff? Du Paty de Clam denied that he was the writer, yet later he testified that he had received orders from his chief to prepare two drafts of anonymous letters designed to warn Esterhazy. General Roget did not hesitate to say later that the anonymous communication was sent by du Paty de Clam.

Your name is going to be the object of a great scandal. The Dreyfus family are going to accuse you publicly of being the author of the writing which served as the cause of the trial of Dreyfus. This family has numerous models of your writing to use as points in the examination. A colonel who was at the Ministry last year, M. Piqart [*sic*] gave the papers to the Dreyfus family. This gentleman has now left for Tonkin, I believe. The Dreyfus family count on making you wild by publishing specimens of your handwriting in the journals, and making you flee to your relatives in Hungary. This will indicate that you are guilty; and then the revision of the trial will be asked for in order to have the innocence of Dreyfus proclaimed. It is M. Piqart who gave the information to the family. This M. Piqart brought your handwriting from sub-chiefs at Rouen last year. I hear all that from a sergeant of your regiment, to whom they gave money to have your handwriting. You are now well warned of what these scoundrels will do to ruin you. It is for you now to defend your name and honor of your children. Make haste, for the family are going to take steps to ruin you.

Your devoted friend,
Espérance

Do not show this letter to any one. It is for you alone, and to save you from the great dangers which threaten you.

Esterhazy Transmits a Letter to Minister of War Billot

"Although he [William II] is an enemy, he is a soldier."

Quoted in Herzog, Der Kampf Einer Republik, pp. 460–462.

In the General Staff there was intense worry that Esterhazy would not be able to withstand the blow when it came. He would have to be advised that his fate was very much linked up with the officers of the General Staff. It was decided that a member of the Ministry of War staff would send Esterhazy an anonymous summons for two days later at five o'clock in the afternoon in the neighborhood of the Parc Montsouris. Fearing a trap, Esterhazy called on Schwartz-koppen for help and demanded that the Military Attaché inform Mme. Dreyfus that her husband was a traitor and that any attempt to save him would be unsuccessful. Disgusted, Schwartzkoppen refused to comply, whereupon Esterhazy broke down, wept, and threatened to kill himself at the Embassy.

At the rendezvous Esterhazy met two men in disguise who told him that a Jewish conspiracy was working to ruin him. There were proofs of Dreyfus's guilt, and the General Staff was prepared to defend him. But first he must follow instructions of the General Staff. The next day du Paty de Clam advised him to request an audience of the Minister of War.

On October 25, 1897, Esterhazy was received in the War Ministry by General Millet, the officer in command of infantry. Esterhazy told of the anonymous letter stating that he would be the object of a slanderous denunciation. After listening to Esterhazy's account, Millet advised him to send a written report to the Minister of War.

That evening Esterhazy reported the result of his visit to du Paty de Clam. According to Esterhazy, du Paty then gave him the text of the letter to be forwarded to the Minister. With it was a written addendum by du Paty: "Copy your letter and learn it by heart. Keep the manuscript." Esterhazy later published a photograph of the original letter that du Paty gave to him.

October 25, 1897

Battalion Chief Esterhazy
to the Minister of War

DEAR MR. MINISTER:

I regret very much not being received by you today. In accordance with the instructions of the Director of Infantry I have the honor to report to you what I told those generals. I am moved by the thought not to justify myself against those disgusting intrigues but strictly to clarify the matter.

I was living quietly at my home in the country when fourteen days ago [1] I received the enclosed anonymous letter. My first reaction was to find Colonel Picquart, whose name I read for the first time, and when I found him to kill him. But he was not in Paris.

Thereupon, I examined all the documents published in the last year on the Dreyfus Affair, and I came to this conclusion based on the *bordereau* published in *Le Matin:* certain words are different from my handwriting, the whole handwriting differs from mine, but despite this, certain words were, indeed, of a striking similarity, and could only have been traced. In a published piece I read that the *bordereau* was, indeed, written on tracing paper.

I came naturally to the conclusion that someone was using my handwriting and Dreyfus himself was used to put the blame on me—in the event of discovery—for his dark correspondence.

I do not know Dreyfus. But for a long time specimens of my handwriting—unfortunately for me—lay in the files of bankers, moneylenders, jewelers, and other people, with whom Dreyfus could well have had close relations.

This explanation, however, does not quite satisfy me. At the time of the duel between Morès-Crémieux, Meyer, etc., I received many letters from Jewish officers, to whom I replied with a word of thanks. Maybe Dreyfus was among them, but I do not remember. All I can say is that he must have had many more specimens of my handwriting in order to write the words indicated in the *bordereau.*

Now I remember that I was asked by an officer of the Ministry at the beginning of 1894—I know the date exactly—because of something of an intimate nature that took place at the same time—to give a complete description concerning the role that the cavalry brigade led by my father during the Crimean campaign. This officer was working on a study of the operations at Eupatoria.

I drew up for him a very thoroughgoing report and sent it to him. Although at his wish I did not send it to the Ministry, it is very possible that he took it there with him, and that in this way it came under the eyes of Dreyfus or fell into his hands by the officer either lending him the report or in some other way. This officer can easily be found. It was Captain Bro. [2]

[1] This would be October 11, 1897, but in his testimony later Esterhazy gave the date as October 18 ("I was told to say it was the 20th").

[2] This memorandum existed only in Esterhazy's imagination. The officer declared that he had never received it—nor had seen it.

I have thought about this endlessly, and I can see no other source. Moreover, even the most simple examination of the documents mentioned in the *bordereau,* is enough to show that it was impossible for an infantry officer, especially one who is scarcely known in the military world, to obtain those documents or even to ask for the necessary secret information in order to identify them.

Only one was in my hands. However, I am just not certain whether it was a draft of a regulation for gunnery or the final version.

It was sent to me by a Jewish officer and at a time much later than the only maneuvers I was ordered to attend in 1894.

The only information that I could find there was concerned with documents for lectures that I was supposed to hold, and which I wanted to make as interesting as possible. As for the expedition to Madagascar, the conjecture is improbable that I could have been apprised about it at a time when it was not even decided upon. Finally, I must add how inadmissible it is to say that a man of my education and a man who knew his way around his milieu, would turn to a Military Attaché—as it is said that this document stems from the German Embassy—and address him as "My dear Sir" instead of using his rank and title.

If Dreyfus could have made use of my handwriting, then everything becomes clear. My difficult situation was known for some time in the Jewish world, my family relationships in the diplomatic world, my rare but wholly open relations with Colonel v. Schw . . . , who got to know my parents in Carlsbad,—all this helped make me the sacrifice of a hateful conspiracy. Indeed, I had so little to hide that I was in the German Embassy in broad daylight, and I have even been there many times in uniform in order to carry out orders of my Colonel. Is any such frivolous supposition permissible that I would be so stupid to write to him without disguising my handwriting?

I have said enough, Mr. Minister. To speak any longer about this matter will seem like a plea. That is the farthest thing from my mind. It only remains for me to ask you what I would have asked you had I had the honor to be received by you: whether you, in the event I am openly attacked, will help me protect my honor, or whether I must rely entirely upon myself.

My life means little to me. But I have a glorious heritage to defend. If necessary, I shall appeal to the German Emperor. Although he is an enemy, he is a soldier. He knows what the meaning of the name I carry represents, and I do not doubt that he will order his aide-de-camp to speak out against the infamy, whose sacrifice I am, and state on his honor that I never have had any relations with him—unworthy relations for him or for me.

ESTERHAZY

Du Paty de Clam and Henry were not altogether satisfied by the effect of this letter to the Minister of War. Henry soon informed Esterhazy: "Du Paty should have told you to send the letter to General B. immediately. He can do nothing without it. Hurry up! The matter is urgent. He is waiting for it."

Esterhazy's Testimony on His Relations with du Paty de Clam

"I am Colonel du Paty de Clam, of the staff of the Army. And you have only to do what I tell you."

Quoted in Steevens, The Tragedy of Dreyfus, *pp. 248–255.*

Esterhazy later gave his version of his mysterious relations with du Paty de Clam when he testified before the Criminal Chamber. When he was asked whether he knew who had written the text of his letter to the Minister of War, Esterhazy replied that he did not but that the addendum was certainly written by du Paty de Clam urging him to copy the letter, memorize it, and keep the manuscript. It is difficult to say, in view of Esterhazy's behavior throughout the case, whether or not all these assertions were exact. But they do shed some light on the relations between Esterhazy and the members of the General Staff who were worried about what he would do next.

In October, 1897, I was in the country, when I received on October 18th (I was told to say that it was the 20th) a letter; this letter was signed "Espérance."

On receipt of this letter, whose handwriting I did not know, I was very much surprised and started for Paris.

I went to the Rue de Douai. I would have it understood that, until then, I had concealed, in the strictest manner, my relations with Mme. Pays, and I thought that only a very few persons at the Ministry of War, and under conditions that I will explain later, could know of them.

I had telegraphed to Mme. Pays, who was in Normandy, to return.

The morning after my arrival I was very much occupied with this letter, and in the evening, on returning about the dinner hour, I learned from the concierge (animated at that time by different sentiments from those she has since manifested), that a gentleman had been to inquire for me. I was very much surprised; no one, in fact, knew of this address.

The concierge told me that she had declared to this gentleman that I was unknown; he replied that he knew perfectly well that I was in the house, that, furthermore, he had come in my interest, and that it was absolutely necessary for him to see me; he had told her that he would return in the evening.

I went to my home, 27, Rue de la Bienfaisance, where I could not get in, having left the keys in the country.

I asked the concierge if any one had been to inquire for me. I thought that any one who wanted to see me would first go to my only known residence.

The concierge said she had seen no one.

I returned then to the Rue de Douai, and waited all the evening.

No one came.

The next morning at an early hour (half-past seven) the concierge came up and told me that the gentleman who came the night before was waiting in the street, near the Square Vintimille.

I went down, and I found some one with blue spectacles, and whose whole bearing, in spite of his efforts, stamped him as a soldier.

This gentleman came to me and said:

"Commandant, I am charged with a very grave communication in your urgent interest."

The manner of this man, the certainty I had that no one outside of the Ministry could know that I might be at the Rue de Douai, caused me to at once suppose that I was in the presence of a messenger from the Ministry of War.

I replied to this man that I thought I knew the object of his visit, and that I had received in the country a letter containing a very singular announcement. This person then said:—

"Do not be uneasy, my Commandant; we know what there is in all that; you have defenders and protectors who are very powerful and *au courant* with everything. Will you come this evening to the rendezvous that I am going to indicate?"

I said to him: "Very willingly."

And he then showed me a piece of paper, indicating the angle of the Reservoir for the waters of the Vanne, opposite the Park of Montsouris.

The rendezvous was for five o'clock.

I went to the place at the time mentioned, and, at precisely five o'clock, I saw a carriage stop at a point about one hundred yards from where I was, in which there were three persons.

Two of these persons stepped out; the third remained in the carriage; the other two came to me. In one I recognized the man I had seen in the morning. The other had a false beard and spectacles. The latter person spoke to me quickly, saying:

"Commandant, you know what this means?"

And very rapidly, with great volubility, he related all that had been done against me since 1894 by Colonel Picquart, entering into numerous details on the maneuvers of many important persons—things which at that time were absolutely new to me.

This man also assured me, seeing the profound surprise that I manifested at all this news, that all these machinations were known, foreseen; repeated to me that I had the most powerful defenders, and that I must only obey strictly the instructions which would be given me, that my name would not even be mentioned.

I tried at various times to make him tell who he was, but without succeeding.

I saw, however, that he was an officer; I should have been glad to know who he was and from whom he came.

He told me at the end of half an hour's conversation, not to be disturbed; that I should be kept *au courant,* and that I should be every day in the waiting room of the Military Club at five o'clock, where the first man would come to find me if there was anything to tell me.

They left me, telling me to go away in a certain direction; they left from the side where the carriage was, so that I could not see the third person who had remained in the carriage.

The next morning, at the same hour as the day before, the concierge brought me a line in pencil saying:—

"In the cab, before a certain number, Rue Vintimille."

I went in all haste; I found the man with the false beard, who said to me: "Get in quickly," and told me to indicate a place where we could have a long talk without being disturbed.

I said to him: "I do not know any other place around here than the Cemetery of Montmartre, if you wish to go there."

We went there, and then this man said to me:—

"You must ask at once for an audience with the Minister of War, and we will state what you are to say to him" (because I had asked: "Demand an audience of the Minister, to tell him what? To show him this letter that I have received?") He then answered:

"No, we will arrange what you are to say to him."

I then said to him:

"But all this is very well, I see that you are an officer. I discern that you come from the Ministry, I should very much like to know who you are?"

The man replied:

"I am Colonel du Paty de Clam, of the staff of the Army. And you have only to do what I tell you."

I did not know Colonel du Paty de Clam.

I had met him once for an hour, sixteen or seventeen years before, at a meeting of two columns in Africa. In view of his grade and his capacity, I said to him:—

"This is sufficient, my Colonel; you can count on my absolute obedience."

Then Colonel du Paty de Clam dictated to me in the cemetery itself a request for an audience with the Minister, gave me to understand that he would have to make a report of what had passed, and gave me a rendezvous for the same evening.

He had said nothing about the rendezvous at the Military Club; I went there, however, and I found the first gentleman, who made me get into a carriage, and took me slowly as far as the Cirque d'Hiver.

He told me, with many details, all the machinations of which I knew nothing. He assured me that I was perfectly well known and laid great stress on the high protection of which he had spoken to me the day before.

I had addressed my letter to the Minister.

In the evening, I again saw at the meeting place indicated, Colonel du Paty de Clam, who made me write from his dictation, notes in regard to what I was to say to General Billot. The same evening I found Colonel Henry in a carriage before my door.

Colonel Henry was one of my comrades. I had been with him for more than twenty years in the Information Department, very soon after the organization of the department; I was there as lieutenant, and Henry also had the same grade and the same employment; I had seen him very frequently since.

I knew later that the third person who remained in the carriage at the park of Montsouris was Colonel Henry. Henry then very briefly told me not to be alarmed, that all that Colonel du Paty de Clam had told me was entirely correct, and that, in high authority, they well knew what was going on, and were determined to defend me by the most extreme measures against what he called "abominable manœuvers."

The next morning I was notified that I would be received the day after by General Millet, Director of Infantry, in the name of the Minister.

I saw Colonel du Paty, and I said to him:

"Why General Millet? The chief of a sub-direction has nothing to see in such a matter. If the Minister did not wish to receive me, he should have arranged for the Chief of his Cabinet to do so, or rather, the Chief of Staff of the Army."

In fact, the very wording of my request for an audience explained that it was on a matter important enough for the Chief of Staff.

The Colonel replied that it was not necessary to see General Boisdeffre, consequently, he must remain in reserve, thus indicating that General de Boisdeffre did not wish to take any active part.

I went to see General Millet; I presented the letter and I related to him what I had been instructed to say.

The General listened to me, and told me that he found it all very strange; that it was the first intimation he had of it; that he did not understand the story at all; that, in his opinion I attached a great deal of importance to an anonymous letter, and that he could only advise me to make a written statement of what I had just communicated to him, to enclose a copy of the anonymous letter that I had received, and to address the whole to the Minister.

The same evening I reported to Colonel du Paty de Clam the reply of General Millet, and he dictated to me the wording of a letter to address to the Minister; this letter, as well as all that I wrote in 1897, was given word for word as ordered.

This letter was dictated to me word for word. It contained a series of explanations agreed upon, and the wording was given me for approval, as is proved by the note from Colonel du Paty.

"Copy your letter and seal it well; keep the manuscript?"

At the same time Colonel du Paty said to me: "The Minister cannot do otherwise than tell General de Boisdeffre of the contents of this letter, and then we shall move."

The next morning at the post office in the Rue de Bac, opposite the Bon Marché, Colonel Henry informed me that General de Boisdeffre had not yet received from General Billot any communication from my letter.

I insist upon this fact because if Colonel Henry was aware that General de Boisdeffre had not been informed by the Minister of the letter that I had written to the latter, he could only have been notified of it by General de Boisdeffre, then awaiting the effect of my letter, and consequently knowing the sender.

Henry said to me:

"The Minister is going to keep that for five or six days before taking any decision, according to his custom. You will be told this evening what to do."

That evening I saw Colonel du Paty on the Esplanade of the Invalides, and he said to me:

"It is decided that you are to write to General de Boisdeffre directly; your letter will then permit General de Boisdeffre to intervene personally and to speak to the Minister of the letter that you have sent to the latter."

In other words, it would induce the transmittal of my letter to General de Boisdeffre, in order that this general officer could come upon the scene himself, thanks to the letter I had written him.

At this time, Colonel du Paty said to me one evening:

"The chiefs are trying to have with you a means of communication which will not be disclosed, because it is probable that you are watched. Having been informed of all that is preparing, it would be better to have, in case of necessity, an indirect transmission. General de Boisdeffre thought of the Marquis de Nettancourt, your brother-in-law."

I said: "No, my brother-in-law is in the country: I do not want to ask him to return for such a service."

Then he said: "We thought also of one of your comrades in the regiment"; and he asked me to mention one of them. I said:

"Really, one cannot ask a friend to run like that at all hours of the day or night."

And I thought, unfortunate inspiration it was, of my cousin Christian; but as he was at Bordeaux, and I could not make him come back, I said:

"I would propose to you some one devoted of whom I am sure, but I really do not dare to make the proposition." And I named Mme. Pays.

Colonel du Paty told me that he would report, and the next morning he told me that they would accept Mme. Pays as intermediary.

In the course of these interviews Colonel du Paty presented to me one evening a lady whom it is useless to name, and who also served as intermediary at various times.

At this moment I saw Colonel Henry, who said to me:

"All these people do not move. Méline [the Prime Minister] and Billot [the War Minister] and all the Government are taken up by the approaching elections and by the votes represented by Scheurer-Kestner, Reinach, etc., etc."

He was even very violent; I will not repeat the military terms in which he indulged. He ended by saying:

"If we do not put a bayonet in the back of all those people, they will sacrifice the whole French Army to their seat as Senator or Deputy!"

And, on leaving me, he said: "Saber in hand! We are going to charge!"

This occurred the day before my first letter to the President of the Republic, that is to say the 28th of October.

Colonel du Paty de Clam dictated the text of the letter to the President of the Republic.

I called his attention to the fact that the wording of this first letter was very extraordinary. (All the details of this letter were dictated to me word for word; this dictation took place on the Esplanade des Invalides, and I wrote with a pencil.)

M. du Paty replied:

"Everybody knows that you are queer. From you it will not appear extraordinary. It is in your style."

I remember very well that I said to him:

"Since it is like me, I don't care. . . . The moment that you command I obey."

Esterhazy's Three Letters to the President of the Republic
"An Esterhazy fears nothing and no one but God."

Rennes: Le procès Dreyfus, *vol. 2, pp. 150–152. Translated by the editor.*

During the summer of 1897 Auguste Scheurer-Kestner, Vice-President of the Senate, became convinced of the innocence of Dreyfus. By this time relations between the cabal on the General Staff and Esterhazy had become closer than ever. The conspirators informed Esterhazy that Scheurer-Kestner had requested an audience with M. Félix Faure, President of the Republic, in order to make him aware of discoveries made concerning certain falsifications in the Dreyfus *dossier*. Hoping to influence President Faure before Scheurer-Kestner could get to him, Esterhazy hastened to send him three letters. Alternately threatening and beseeching the President, Esterhazy gave the impression in these letters that he was on the verge of a nervous breakdown.

LETTER No. 1

Paris, October 29, 1897

TO THE PRESIDENT OF THE REPUBLIC—

I have the honor to send to you the text of an anonymous letter sent to me on October 20, 1897.

It is I who has been designated in that letter as the intended victim. I do not wish to wait until my name is brought to public attention to know what will be the attitude of my chiefs. I, therefore, addressed my chief and natural protector, the Minister of War, to learn if he would summon me the moment my name was pronounced.

The Minister did not reply. Now my house is sufficiently illustrious in the annals of history in France and in those of the great European courts, to make the Government of my country see to it that my name should not be dragged through the mud.

Therefore, I address myself to the Supreme Commander of the Army— to the President of the Republic. I urge him to stop the scandal, as it is right and duty to do.

I ask him for justice against the infamous instigator of this plot, who has given to the authors of this machination the secrets of his Department, and to attribute such evil deeds to me.

If I have to undergo the painful experience of not being listened to by the chief of my country, then I reserve the right to call upon the chief of my house, the suzerain of the family of Esterhazy, to the German Emperor. He himself is a soldier, and he will know how to place the honor of a soldier, even if he be an enemy, above mean and suspicious intrigues of politicians.

He will dare to speak loud and strong, to defend the honor of six generations of soldiers.

It is for you, Mr. President, to judge if you are to force me to carry the question on this ground. An Esterhazy fears nothing and no one but God. Nothing and no one will prevent my acting as I have indicated if I am sacrificed to I know not what political combinations.

(Signed) ESTERHAZY
Chief of Infantry Battalion

One might assume that President Faure would pay no attention to this threatening letter with its odor of blackmail. But du Paty de Clam and Henry, who undoubtedly encouraged Esterhazy to write it, were sound psychologists and knew exactly what would impress the President. When Scheurer-Kestner finally was received by the President, he was accorded an icy interview.

Two days after his first letter, Esterhazy, not having received a reply, decided to send a second letter this time to injure Picquart.

LETTER NO. 2

October 31, 1897

TO THE PRESIDENT OF THE REPUBLIC—

I regret to say that neither the Chief of Staff nor the Chief of the Army has given me a word of support, encouragement, or comfort in reply to a superior officer who places his threatened honor in their hands. I know that considerations of parliamentary politics prevent the Government from making a frank and clear declaration that would remove me at once and for all time from the quarrel and that would bring the defenders of Dreyfus to silence.

I do not desire that the services rendered to France during 160 years by five general officers whose name I bear, that the bloodshed, that the memory of these people of courage who were killed in the face of the enemy, the last just recently, that all these men should be repaid with infamy to serve such combinations and save a poor wretch. I am forced to use all means within my power.

A generous woman, who warned me of the horrible machinations woven against me by the friends of Dreyfus with the help of Colonel Picquart, has been able to obtain since then, among other documents, the photograph of a paper that she managed to get away from this officer. This document, stolen by Colonel Picquart from a foreign legation, is highly compromising for certain diplomatic personages. If I am to obtain neither support nor justice, and if my name is made public, this photograph, which is now in a safe place, will be published immediately.

Please forgive me, Mr. President, for having taken recourse to means so little in keeping with my character, but remember that I am defending something more precious than my life, more than my honor, the honor of a family without stain, and in this desperate struggle, in which all assistance has failed me, and which is driving me to insanity, I am obliged to make use of every possible weapon.

(Signed) ESTERHAZY
Chief of Infantry Battalion

President Faure apparently took this letter seriously. He ordered the Minister of War to telegraph to Picquart's chief that the latter "had allowed a woman to steal from him the photograph of a secret document of the highest importance compromising a foreign Military Attaché," and called for an interrogation of Picquart without delay.

By now Esterhazy had taken on the pose of a military hero, bearer of a document that could possibly plunge France into war if he were to publicize it. On November 5, 1897, he sent a third and final letter to the President.

LETTER NO. 3

Paris, November 5, 1897

TO THE PRESIDENT OF THE REPUBLIC—

Pardon me for writing to you a third time, but I fear that the Minister of War has not communicated to you my last letters, and I am most anxious that you should be familiar with the situation. Besides, it is the final time that I shall address myself to the public authorities.

The woman who informed me of the terrible plot against me has given me, among others, a document that is a protection for me. It proves the villainy of Dreyfus, and it poses a danger for my country, because if it were published with the facsimile of the writing it would force France to humiliate herself or to declare war.

You who stand high above party quarrels where my honor serves as ransom, do not leave me under the necessity of choosing between two alternatives equally horrible.

Force the Pontius Pilate of politics to make a clear and precise declaration instead of maneuvering to preserve the voices of the friends of Barabbas.

All the letters I have written will be placed in the hands of one of my relatives, who just this summer had the honor of being received by two emperors.

What will be thought throughout the world, when the cold and cowardly cruelty with which I have been left in my misery to defend myself, without support, without counsel, is known! My blood will fall on your heads. And when the letter about which the Government knows is published, and which is one of the proofs of Dreyfus's guilt, what will the whole world have to say to this miserable Parliamentary maneuver, which has prevented silence being imposed on the pack of hounds by some energetic words?

I utter the ancient French cry: *"Haro to me, my Prince! To my rescue!"* I address it to you, Mr. President, who, in addition to being Chief of State, are an honest man, and who ought to be moved profoundly by the cowardice you see before you.

Let them defend me, and I shall return the document to the Minister of War without anyone having laid eyes on it. But should they not defend me—for I can wait no longer—I shall stop at nothing to defend and avenge my honor which has been so shamefully sacrificed.

(Signed) ESTERHAZY
Chief of Infantry Battalion

Esterhazy Sends an Insolent Note to Picquart

"It is impossible that you can avoid an open and clear-cut declaration."

Quoted in Thalheimer, Macht und Gerechtigkeit, *pp. 250–251. Translated by the editor.*

Emboldened and assured of support by du Paty de Clam and Henry inside the offices of the General Staff, Esterhazy on November 7, 1897, sent an accusatory letter to Picquart in Algeria. Considering that he was certainly aware of his own guilt, Esterhazy deserved some kind of prize for this example of cool insolence.

COLONEL:

I have recently received a letter in which you were designated the author of an abominable plot to place me in Dreyfus's position. In this letter it was said among other statements that you corrupted certain officers of lower rank to obtain examples of my handwriting. That is a fact and I have checked on it.

It was also stated that you took from the War Ministry some documents that were entrusted to you in order to construct a secret file which you sent along to friends of the traitor. The existence of this file is revealed by the fact that today I possess one of the documents that comes from it. Because of the enormity of the accusation, I cannot believe—despite the proofs at hand—that a Staff officer of the French Army could have sold service secrets with the aim of putting a colleague in the place of a rascal, for whose crime he already had proof. It is impossible that you can avoid an open and clear-cut declaration.

ESTERHAZY

False Telegrams "*Speranza*" and "*Blanche*" Forwarded to Picquart ". . . all is discovered. . . ."

La revision du procès de Rennes, *vol. 1, p. 103.*

By now the forgery factory was working full blast. Three days after Esterhazy's letter to Picquart two telegrams, since called the "*Speranza*" and the "*Blanche,*" were sent to Picquart in Sousse, Tunis. As was intended, the telegrams were "intercepted" and placed in Picquart's *dossier.* They were forged after Henry had learned that the Countess Blanche de Comminges was one of Picquart's regular correspondents.

1

THE "SPERANZA" TELEGRAM—NOVEMBER 10, 1897

Colonel Picquart, Tunis

Stop the *demi-dieu;* all is discovered; very serious matter.

Speranza

2

THE "BLANCHE" TELEGRAM—NOVEMBER 10, 1897

Colonel Picquart, Sousse, Tunis

There is proof that the *petit bleu* was forged by Georges.

Blanche

Picquart, by now aware of what was going on, sent the Ministry of War a copy of Esterhazy's letter of November 7, and asked for an inquiry especially about an officer who claimed to be in possession of a secret document which he was not qualified to hold. At the same time he asked for an investigation of the "unknown parties" who had sent him the two false telegrams.

The Vice-President of the Senate Intercedes for Dreyfus
". . . I could never have lived in peace. . . ."

Le Temps, *November 14, 1897. Translated by the editor.*

In early November 1897 news vendors on the boulevards of Paris were selling leaflets reproducing the *bordereau* and letters from Dreyfus. It was clear from these facsimiles that there were differences between the two handwritings. By chance a banker, a M. Castro, who had bought one of the leaflets, noted a resemblance between the writing of the *bordereau* and that of one of his clients. Looking in his files, he was astounded to find that the writing of the *bordereau* was identical with that of a Major Walsin-Esterhazy.

Word soon flashed to Mathieu Dreyfus, who went straight to the home of Auguste Scheurer-Kestner, Vice-President of the Senate. The latter had arrived at the name of the traitor by other means but had been pledged to silence for a fortnight. Rushing to Scheurer-Kestner's home, Mathieu Dreyfus pushed a servant aside and cried in a broken voice: "Esterhazy!" "That is the man!" said Scheurer-Kestner.

Scheurer-Kestner now decided to break his silence. On November 14, 1897, he sent the following open letter to the *Temps*.

Never have I, either in thought or in word, doubted the loyalty or independence of those officers who sentenced Captain Dreyfus. However, new facts have been unearthed, which prove the innocence of the condemned man, and if, convinced as I am that a judicial error has been made, I had kept silent, I could never have lived in peace with the thought always present in my mind that the prisoner is paying for the crime of another man. . . .

On October 30, in a semi-official interview with the Minister of War, I showed, with the documents in my hands, that the document attributed to Captain Dreyfus was not written by him but by someone else. I urged him to make inquiries about the true culprit. However, the Minister, without requesting that I leave the documents with him, promised that an inquiry would be made which would refer only to events that took place after the sentence. I was careful to warn him about incriminating documents of more or less recent date, which might actually be the work of the real criminal or of persons interested in the misdirection of justice and of public opinion. On his part the Minister requested that I say nothing about our conversation for an interval of a fortnight, and said that he would advise me of the result of his investigation. I have waited vainly from that day on, and the fortnight requested is now over. That was the reason for what seemed to be the delay.

In addition, my request to see the documents proving the guilt of Captain Dreyfus was not honored. Nothing was given to me, nothing was shown to me, despite the fact that I stated voluntarily that, in the face of such proofs, I would be quick to make a public acknowledgement of my mistake. . . .

Hence, I repeat, without fear of being refuted, that a fortnight ago I gave to the Government documents showing that Captain Dreyfus is not the guilty man. If the Ministry of War would begin an organized inquiry and carry it through, it could prove without difficulty that another man is guilty.

Henry's "Dixi" Article in *La Libre Parole*

"Like a magician XY wanted to create a traitor in his place."

La Libre Parole, *November 15, 1897. Translated by the editor.*

The next day, November 15, 1897, Mathieu Dreyfus publicly named Esterhazy as "the traitor" who wrote the *bordereau*. By chance, on that same day, *La Libre Parole* published an article by Henry signed *Dixi*. The article was aimed at Picquart (indicated by the initials "XY") as an agent of the Dreyfus "Syndicate." The purpose obviously was to make it appear that Picquart was a paid agent of the defenders of Dreyfus and to bring upon him the hatred of the awakened and patriotic masses. The text repeated all the charges made against Picquart in Esterhazy's letter of November 7.

The "Dixi" article said that Dreyfus had kept in touch with his family and that he had given them the name of a man whose writing he had traced in the *bordereau*. The intended victim was "unmoved and without fear." Moreover, the Dreyfus *dossier* was "packed with evidence" which proved him to be the traitor.

. . . Like a magician XY wanted to create a traitor in his place. For this purpose he compiled an official *dossier* in which he included:

1. Examples of handwriting which he purchased from subordinates;
2. False documents, which apparently came from an embassy;
3. An incriminating document that his chosen sacrificial goat had written and sent to a diplomat. . . .

There are several other documents. Several of them incriminate Dreyfus. They then disappeared. Perhaps they will be found again.

Mathieu Dreyfus Publicly Accuses Esterhazy

". . . you will see to it that justice will be done without delay."

Le Figaro, *November 16, 1897. Translated by the editor.*

As soon as he was certain that the real traitor was Esterhazy, Mathieu Dreyfus addressed a letter to the Minister of War and sent a copy to *Le Figaro.* The letter appeared in that newspaper on November 16, 1897.

The only basis for the accusation directed in 1894 against my unfortunate brother is a letter-communication, without date, establishing that confidential military documents had been delivered to an agent of a foreign power.

I have the honor to make it known to you that the author of that paper is M. the Count Walsin-Esterhazy, Major of Infantry, currently since last spring on the inactive list because of a temporary infirmity.

The handwriting of Major Walsin-Esterhazy is *identical* with that of the document in question. It will be very easy for you, *Monsieur le Ministre,* to procure specimens of the handwriting of that officer. Moreover, I am ready to indicate to you where you can find his letters, of an incontestable authenticity and bearing a date before the arrest of my brother.

I cannot doubt, *Monsieur le Ministre,* that, having been informed of the perpetrator of the treasonable act for which my brother has been condemned, you will see to it that justice will be done without delay.

I beg to remain, sir

Your obedient servant
MATHIEU DREYFUS

With this letter naming the traitor, it seemed that the Affair was at an end. Surely the innocent officer would be brought home from Devil's Island promptly and justice meted out to the guilty Esterhazy.

But the Dreyfus case was by no means ended. It had only begun.

Esterhazy's "Uhlan Letter"

"I would not hurt a dog, but I would with pleasure have a hundred thousand Frenchmen put to death."

Le Figaro, *November 28, 1897. Translated by the editor.*

On November 28, 1897, *Le Figaro* published a sensational note by Esterhazy which soon became famous as the "Uhlan Letter." The French public was shocked to learn that the officer on the General Staff regarded by many as a patriotic hero had written to his mistress fifteen years earlier that he would gladly have witnessed a blood bath of Frenchmen. The letter was among many written by Esterhazy to his cousin and intimate friend, Mme. de Boulancy, who was one of his former mistresses. Esterhazy had borrowed 36,000 francs from the wealthy woman, after which the liaison broke up and the matter went to court. When Esterhazy was in the midst of his troubles, Mme. de Boulancy showed her friends some of his old letters. One of them, the "Uhlan Letter," quickly found its way to the press. On its publication Esterhazy lost confidence and decided to flee or commit suicide. Fellow officers urged him to wait before any such admission of guilt.

I am absolutely convinced that these people (the French) are not worth the cartridges necessary to kill them. My opinion is substantiated by those petty cowardices, worthy of drunken women, to which the men abandon themselves. There is only one human virtue which I value, and that is completely lacking in these people. If someone said to me today that I would be killed tomorrow as an Uhlan Captain while stabbing Frenchmen to death, I would be completely happy. I regret it from my whole heart not to be any longer in Ain-Draham, even though it is a terrible land, and that I must walk the soil of this damned France. I have made every effort to return to Algeria. . . .

You delude yourself entirely about my being and my character. The general impression is that I am worth much less than the least of your friends. But I am different from them. I am generally misunderstood. At the present moment I am exasperated, embittered, in a completely atrocious position. I am capable of doing great things if I had the chance but also of committing great crimes if they could avenge me.

I would not hurt a dog, but I would with pleasure have a hundred thousand Frenchmen put to death. Those cowardly, anonymous gossips, with their "They say's" go from one salon to another with their vile stories to which everyone listens. What miserable figures they would be under the red sun of battle in a Paris taken by assault, and abandoned to the pillaging of a hundred thousand drunken soldiers. That is an occasion about which I dream. Amen.

Judge Bertulus and Colonel Henry: "The Judas Kiss"

"Then he cried: 'Esterhazy is a bandit!'"

Rennes: Le procès Dreyfus, *vol. 1, pp. 340–368,* passim. *Translated by the editor.*

In the summer of 1898 M. Bertulus, a *juge d'instruction,* or magistrate, of the civil courts, was assigned to investigate all the criminal cases arising out of the Dreyfus case. For several months he conducted inquiries carefully and impartially, and came to the conclusion that Dreyfus and Picquart were innocent while Esterhazy was the guilty one. He was not able to make up his mind about Colonel Henry, who had been promoted and who had managed to get himself appointed by the Minister of War to assist the examining judge in reading the documents. Henry was very much worried about what a visit to Esterhazy's home might reveal.

In late July 1898, Henry came to the home of M. Bertulus for an interview. It was shortly before Henry was to commit suicide and the scene was a painful one. Bertulus later described it at the Court of Cassation and again at Rennes. The following testimony created a sensation in the audience.

Bertulus: I said to him: "After Esterhazy and du Paty de Clam there is yourself! You have had relations with Esterhazy! It would be quite possible to go so far as to maintain that the man who is keeping Esterhazy posted is none other than yourself!" Henry collapsed and burst into tears. He cried repeatedly: "Save us! Save us!" Suddenly, he raised himself, seized my head in his hands and kissed me directly on the mouth, while his tears ran over my face. I shoved him back and demanded that he sit down again. Then he cried: "Esterhazy is a bandit!"

And now I had him. It was my idea that now or never the question had to be put: "Is Esterhazy the author of the *bordereau?*" Henry did not say "yes" and he did not say "no." He never answered me on this point. He got up and said to me: "Don't press me any more! Please don't press me! Save the honor of the Army!"

When Bertulus again described this interview during his testimony on August 17, 1899, at the Rennes trial, the recital was naturally painful for Mme. Henry, the widow, who wept as he repeated the story. She ascended the platform and standing beside Bertulus said: "On the day my husband called on M. Bertulus, the colonel, in the course of a conversation that evening, told me that he had a friendly and charming reception. He described how the magistrate advanced to meet him and held out his arms. I said to my husband: 'Are you sure of this man? Are you sure he is sincere? I am very much afraid that his kiss was the kiss of a Judas.' I was not wrong: this man is, indeed, the Judas I had imagined."

There was much commotion in the court at this statement.

Bertulus said that he had no desire to reply to Mme. Henry. "She is only a woman."

"I am not only a woman," cried Mme. Henry furiously. "I speak in the name of my husband."

"How shall I reply to Madame?" asked Bertulus. "She is defending the name of a dead man and that of her child."

Bertulus then handed the court a letter which he had received the day before, warning him that it was the intention of Mme. Henry to create this scene by calling him a Judas. After gazing steadfastly at the magistrate, who was deeply moved, Mme. Henry descended the platform.

Confrontation Between du Paty de Clam and Esterhazy Before the Board of Inquiry, August, 1898

". . . Esterhazy was then in a rather queer mental condition."

Steevens, The Tragedy of Dreyfus, *pp. 260–262.*

On July 12, 1898, Esterhazy was arrested, and the next day Picquart, too, was placed in custody. Exhaustive inquiries were made in the weeks following. On August 24 Esterhazy appeared before a Board of Inquiry. On that day a confrontation took place between him and du Paty de Clam before the council presided over by General Florentin. The exchange revealed that du Paty de Clam had taken an undeniable part in the drawing up of the three letters which Esterhazy had sent to the President of the Republic.

The Witness (du Paty de Clam): Esterhazy wished to write to the Emperor of Germany; I told him that he had better write to the President of the Republic, who was the father of all the French people. This letter, I know it as I took a copy of it later at the Ministry of War. Esterhazy told me that it had been dictated to him.

Esterhazy: I want the Lieutenant-Colonel to tell who dictated it to me.

The Witness: Ah! I do not know! Would you say that it was I?

Esterhazy: Tell the truth.

The Witness: It was not I.

Esterhazy: Then, how did matters transpire?

The Witness: He wanted to look for foreign aid, from his relatives, and to ask the German Emperor through them if he had ever had relations with him, and to beg him to defend his honor as a member of an order of which this sovereign was grand master.

Esterhazy: That is it! I called upon the German Emperor as a vassal. Having decided to commit suicide, I wished first to call on all those who had any interest in defending an Esterhazy.

The Witness: Yes, it was then that I turned him away from this idea, and made him write to the President of the Republic.

The President: But these letters contained a sentiment of a threat?

The Witness: In my opinion, Esterhazy was then in a rather queer mental condition. I saw the letter at the Ministry, and told him that this letter, which he declared had been dictated to him, was crazy. Certainly it was not I who dictated it to him.

The President: But then who did dictate it to him? And furthermore, if it was dictated to him, what could have been his state of mind when drawing up this letter?

The Witness: It was not I. Esterhazy was admirably informed; but everything that he was told was of a nature to discourage him. They wished, he said, to ruin above all du Paty and General de Boisdeffre. As to making known to the Council if my relations with Esterhazy were ordered or were only a personal affair, I refuse to reply before Esterhazy.

The President: In any case, what did you do personally, and in what measure were you a party to the matter?

The Witness: As far as relates to the articles for the newspapers, he was assisted in his reply to the article "Vidi." I even corrected the reply.

The President: He did not act alone then, but with the help of officers in the active Army?

The Witness: Yes.

The President: We need to know in what measure he was guided, and therefore, responsible.

The Witness: Esterhazy never knew that he was defended by the General Staff, but only by individuals; I was one of those most interested in the manifestation of truth, and that is why I helped him. I did not see the letter to the President of the Republic until I saw it at the Ministry, after it had been received there.

The President: You approved of sending this letter?

The Witness: Yes; and I gave him the framework or substance. But, after having read the letter, I found fault with the composition.

Esterhazy: But, then, tell the truth! Say how these letters were dictated!

The Witness: I say that I do not know.

The President: Was it you who inspired what the threat contains?

The Witness: He spoke to me of writing it.

The President: You do not know who dictated it!

The Witness: No.

The President to Esterhazy: Where were they written?

Esterhazy: One back of the Caulaincourt bridge; another at the Invalides bridge; I do not know where the third was written. I wrote with a pencil at the dictation of some one; I recopied them quietly at home.

The President to Esterhazy: Do you know if du Paty knew this some one?

Esterhazy: Yes; the Colonel knew him.

The Witness: I knew him; I do not say that I did not; not being a sneak. Besides, I only knew from Esterhazy that they had been dictated to him.

Esterhazy: I beg the Colonel to say that he knew the author of the letter—that he knew him as well as I did; that it is absolutely exact that these letters were dictated by some one he knew, as well as the article "Dixi" (in the *Libre Parole*).

The President to the Witness: I ask you the question.

The Witness: I have said all that I had to say.

The President: Then, if you only knew it from Esterhazy, it is not your testimony. You only repeat the assertions of Esterhazy?

The Witness: It is impossible that the article "Dixi" should have been done by Esterhazy; therefore, it was given him.

The President: That is not testimony, but an opinion. We do not need it.

The Witness: I have nothing to say.

The President: To resume or sum up, you aided Commandant Esterhazy. Was it on your initiative?

The Witness: I do not wish to say before Esterhazy.

The President: Does Esterhazy lie in saying that the letter was dictated to him?

The Witness: He does not lie . . . or rather . . . I withdraw what I said.

Esterhazy: I assert that the article was brought to me all written, and that the letters were dictated to me.

The Witness: I am sure that he tells the truth as far as the article is concerned. As for the letters, I do not know. . . . I do not dare to confirm the statement of the Commandant Esterhazy. Was it on your initiative?

Letter from Picquart to the Minister of Justice, Keeper of the Seals

The General (Gonse): *"What business is it of yours if this Jew is on the Île du Diable? . . ."*

Steevens, The Tragedy of Dreyfus, *pp. 280–293.*

Certain that a tragic mistake had been made, Picquart with official approval wrote a narrative on September 14, 1898, of the circumstances which seemed to bring into question the stability of the verdict of 1894. His letter was addressed in confidence to the Minister of Justice. It was a masterful presentation of the facts to that date, written in clear-cut fashion from beginning to end.

Paris, September 14th, 1898

SIR,

I have the honor to indicate to you the reasons upon which I base my deep and firm conviction of the innocence of Dreyfus:

First, I give a summary of these reasons; I shall pass later to the detailed development of each of them in turn.

A. Dreyfus was arrested solely upon the suspicion of having written the *bordereau*. When the *bordereau* came into the hands of the bureau of information, it was supposed *a priori* and unjustly, that, in view of the documents enumerated therein, it could have been written only by an officer of the Ministry, preferably by an artillery officer, and the handwritings of the officers of the General Staff were compared with that of the *bordereau*.

After some hesitation, it was found that the writing of Dreyfus bore a likeness to that of the *bordereau*.

Dreyfus had never been suspected before; no previous supervision had admitted the suspicion of temptations, of questionable relations, of the need of funds; it had merely been remarked that he evinced a tendency to inquire indiscreetly into what was going on about him. But this tendency is not inexplicable in the case of an officer on probation who is attached to the General Staff of the Army for purposes of self-instruction, and who finds in his position a unique opportunity for familiarizing himself with our military organization.

The writing of the *bordereau* bears merely a resemblance to that of Dreyfus. On the other hand, it is identical with that of Esterhazy. The documents specified in the *bordereau* are, as a rule, of no small value.

Dreyfus, had he been inclined to treason, could have supplied himself much more. Moreover, the documents in question bear no relation to the particular ones which Dreyfus had in hand at the time the *bordereau* was written.

B. Admitting Dreyfus to be its author, certain phrases in the *bordereau* are inexplicable, for example, the following, "Provided you do not wish that I should have it copied *in extenso*." Dreyfus had no secretary at his disposition; Esterhazy, as Major, had one. Here is a point which can readily be understood, admitting the *bordereau* to be the work of Esterhazy.

II.—When Dreyfus was arrested, in an attempt to lend his *dossier* more weight, a secret *dossier* was made up, and this was communicated to the judges of the court-martial. Not one of these documents is applicable to Dreyfus.

III.—It has not been possible to arrive at the motives by which Dreyfus was actuated; he had never manifested unpatriotic feelings; he possessed a fortune, he had a home, he led a regular life.

IV.—Dreyfus has always protested his innocence, and moreover the alleged confession made by Captain Lebrun-Renault was nothing more than the result of an interested move on the part of his enemies.

V.—An attempt has been made to prove that Dreyfus was continually in a position to lay hands upon the documents mentioned in the *bordereau*. These documents were never thoroughly investigated when I was attached to the Ministry. They came altogether or nearly so, from du Paty de Clam, and were generally passed without any supervision. Moreover, they had no value.

VI.—The chiefs, Generals Billot, de Boisdeffre, and Gonse, have never raised an objection to any of the facts to which I drew their attention, with the exception of the false document brought to the Ministry of Colonies at the beginning of September, 1896, and the false document assigned to Henry which made its appearance at the end of October or the beginning of November of the same year.

VII.—Henry and du Paty de Clam have employed the most culpable measures to emphasize the guilt of Dreyfus and the innocence of Esterhazy.

I now take up in detail each of the paragraphs numbered above. . . .

[And Lieutenant-Colonel Picquart then proceeds to develop each of the paragraphs which we have just indicated. We are obliged to confine ourselves to the reading of the most interesting portions:] *

---

* These remarks were made by M. Alexis Ballot-Beaupré, who had been appointed President of the Civil Court in place of M. Jules Quesnay de Beaurepaire. Picquart's letter was part of a report made by M. Ballot-Beaupré.

When it became clear that there were no other charges against Dreyfus but that of the *bordereau,* documents which might be applicable to him were sought for among those of the service of information, and of these was formed a *dossier,* which I propose to consider in detail.

This *dossier,* which had been locked up in the file belonging to Henry toward the close of December, 1894, and which I received from the hands of Gribelin toward the close of December, 1896, was divided into two parts. The first, which had been communicated to the judges in the council chamber, was composed of four documents, accompanied by an explanatory commentary, made up, as Colonel Sandherr assured me, by du Paty de Clam. The second part of the *dossier* was of small value. It comprised seven or eight documents in all—to specify, several photographs, the secret documents, and several documents of no importance, having more or less reference to those of the first part.

I propose to take up in succession the documents of the first part, indicating so far as memory will admit, the terms of the commentary. For the rest, I maintain that my memory of these facts is very vivid, by reason of the profound impression made upon me by the sight of this *dossier.*

First document (torn in pieces, and when put together): a letter with a note written by a person whom we will designate by the initial "A," probably to his superiors. It was "A's" custom to sketch such plans, which he threw into the paper basket. This letter, written in a foreign language, was of the close of the year 1893 or 1894. I believe it authentic. It was worded, or approximately worded as follows:

"Doubts——what to do? Let him show his officer's certificate. What has he to fear? What can he supply? There is no interest in maintaining relations with an infantry officer."

The simple common sense shows that the author of this sketch had received propositions from an individual calling himself an officer; that he had some doubts as to the opportunity he was given of entering into relations with the latter, and that it concerned someone who was in the infantry.

The text, in a foreign language was faithfully translated in the commentary of du Paty de Clam, but he drew therefrom a most unexpected inference:

"A finds," says du Paty, "that there is no advantage in maintaining relations with infantry officers. He selects rather a Staff Officer, and takes one attached to the Ministry." This commentary enables one to note the treacherous spirit by which du Paty de Clam was actuated.

Second document: This was an authentic letter from (a person whom we designate by B) B to A, dating from the early part of 1894; it had been torn and then put together, and was worded approximately as fol-

lows: "I desire to have some information upon a question of recruiting."
This last reference [continues Lieutenant-Colonel Picquart] is to a
matter which was not absolutely confidential. "I shall ask Davignon"
[then sub-chief of the second division], "but he will tell me nothing.
Therefore ask your friend, Davignon must not know of it, because he
should not learn that we are working together."

That you may understand this matter, it should be said that the foreign
military attachés went about once a week to the second division, where,
at this time, they were informed very freely about everything which was
not confidential. The officers of the second division even complained of
working more for the foreign attachés than for the General Staff.

The commentator says: "At the time when B wrote to A, Dreyfus
was in the second division. Evidently it is he whom B designates as the
friend of A." This comment is absurd. In the first place nothing has ever
admitted the proof that A had relations with Dreyfus. Even if we admit
that the *bordereau* is the work of the latter, nothing in any event indicates that this friend was Dreyfus, nor who it was that furnished secret
documents to A. B dwells too lightly on that point, above all when he
says "Davignon must not know of it"—that is equivalent to saying that
the friend might be the chief of division, might be du Paty himself, who
had an understanding with A, might be the chief of the foreign section at
that particular time. All these officers were on excellent terms with A,
and would not have hesitated to give so futile a piece of information as
the one in question.

The third document was an authentic letter from B to A, dated 1894.
It had been torn and then put together. B said approximately: "I have
seen this blackguard D_____. He gave me for you some dozen plans."

The commentator says: "It was proved whether the plans were in
their place. They were. It was not proved whether the plans of the First
Division were also. It is allowable to believe that Dreyfus had taken
those of the First Division and had loaned them for the time being to B,
to be forwarded to A. As a matter of fact, Dreyfus was attached to the
First Division in 1893. He worked in the room where these plans were
kept, and since that time the combination of the locks had not been
changed."

This accusation is monstrous in the eyes of any one knowing the
routine of the offices of the General Staff. In the first place twelve plans
make up a considerable package, and in the vaults of the First Division
their disappearance must have been instantly noticed. How can we admit
that Dreyfus, who since a year was no longer attached to the First Division, could penetrate there and possess himself of such a package, an
act which was all the more dangerous in that the vault in question was

one of those often visited? How can we admit that, always unperceived, he could have carried off this package, when at the same time he had in his possession a quantity of other documents also of interest to A?

It may be remarked that nothing in the letter from B to A mentions the necessity of returning the documents, and that is why I am inclined to believe that they might have been taken from the Geographical Service, where it would have been possible to abstract them without too much difficulty. Whereas in the First Division, the thing is entirely impossible.

As regards the initial D, that suggests nothing. Foreign powers do not designate spies by the actual initial. I myself know a spy whose real name is C; he introduced himself to the foreigners under the name of L and by them he is called N. Finally the letter D could not be applied to a man having from the point of view of espionage, the importance of Dreyfus.

All the objections which I have enumerated, I made to my superiors, and Major Henry, and they were not able to deny their value. They accounted for much, I believe, in the origin of the false Henry document, where Dreyfus was named in full. I am not able to speak here except as my memory serves me, for there are some points which remain obscure. I earnestly urge that they be brought to my attention and that mention be made of the objections which may arise. I investigated all these documents thoroughly two years ago, with a complete understanding of the case, and I did not arrive at my absolute conviction of their inanity from the point of view of Dreyfus's guilt, until I had examined the question from all sides.

If one admits that these documents were able to decide the uncertain opinion of the judges of the court-martial of 1894, one must confess, that when the latter emerged from a debate of four days, which had greatly disturbed them, that they were searching for a clear and intelligible idea upon which to rely after the convinced discussions of the experts, and that they discovered this in the notes upon the *dossier,* whose origin was new, and in which they placed complete trust.

Then as they may not have been able to take account of the value of the documents which might be new for them, they accepted the explanations given them without suspecting the trap which their loyalty prevented them from perceiving. And further on, when at the end of August, 1896, the investigation upon Esterhazy and the secret *dossier* had convinced them of the innocence of Dreyfus, I made a report to General de Boisdeffre, who authorized me to explain these matters to Colonel X_____; he, however, told me to take into account a forged document of which I will speak later on, which had come in at the commencement of September 1896, to the Minister of Colonies. He asked me also to weigh the evidence of the forged Henry document, but he never brought forward any other objections. In fine, he was absolutely opposed to revision and to proceedings against Esterhazy, without being convinced of the absolute guilt of Dreyfus.

I said as much to General Billot, who for some time believed in the innocence of Dreyfus, and whose belief in his guilt was founded on the forged Henry document. He had always believed in the guilt of Esterhazy during the time that I was attached to the Ministry. So far as General Gonse, with whom I was able to speak freely, is concerned, I think I may enter upon some details. When, by order of General de Boisdeffre I went on September 3rd, 1896, to report to General Gonse the report of my inquiry on the subject of Esterhazy and Dreyfus, the General listened to my reasons and did not dispute them. He merely made a face and said to me, "Well then, we have been mistaken!" Then he instructed me not to concern myself with this matter. The letter of September, 1896, shows clearly that he brought forward no affirmation adverse to mine. At the time of his return to Paris on September 15th, he was still more explicit. I think I can repeat word for word the conversation I had with him on this subject, and which will never be effaced from my memory.

The General: What business is it of yours if this Jew is on the *Île du Diable?*

R: But if he is innocent?

G: How do you expect to go all over this trial again? It would be the most shocking story. General Mercier and General Saussier are both tangled up in it.

R: But, General, he is innocent, and that should be enough to revise the case. But, from another point of view, you know that his family are at work. They are searching everywhere for the true culprit, and if they find him, what will be our position?

G: If you say nothing, no one will ever know.

R: General, what you say is contemptible. I do not know what I shall do, but in any event I shall not allow this secret to be buried with me. And I left him instantly. From that moment I understood clearly the situation.

Once again General Gonse spoke to me of the guilt of Dreyfus apropos of the forged Henry document. Several days before General de Boisdeffre and General Gonse asked me if the Minister had made any special communication to me. Finally, one morning, the Minister told me he had a letter of B showing the guilt of Dreyfus. As I went out I met General Gonse, who said to me: "Well, are you convinced?" I replied: "Not at all," and I told him that it was a forged document, to which he replied: "When a Minister tells me something I always believe it."

In brief, my superiors never disputed openly the innocence of Dreyfus;

and they never brought forward but that one empty proof of his guilt—
the alleged avowals. For four months I was engaged upon an inquiry
upon Esterhazy without any incident arising to interfere with my investigation. But from the day when I reported to General de Boisdeffre
that Esterhazy was the author of the *bordereau,* there arose a series of
plots against Dreyfus and myself, of which I am the victim to this very
hour; and their principal authors, if not their actual instigators, I know,
can have been only du Paty de Clam and Henry—that is to say, the two
principal representatives for putting in motion the Dreyfus Affair. And
this, too, to my way of thinking, is one of the proofs of the emptiness of
the accusations against Dreyfus. If indeed, proofs of his guilt had been
available, it would not have been necessary to reinforce them by fraudulent means, nor to attack his defenders. Moreover, the maneuvers of
du Paty de Clam and Henry commenced from the very outset of the
Dreyfus Affair. We note that the first frauds were insignificant, but that
they grew little by little to end by arriving at actual forged documents.
The first maneuver was du Paty de Clam's interruption while Dreyfus
was writing. Du Paty de Clam felt it necessary that Dreyfus should seem
disturbed while he dictated the *bordereau* to him. As he was not disturbed du Paty de Clam addressed this question to him, "What is the
matter with you? You are trembling!" And this was intended to take
unawares the good faith of the two witnesses—Messieurs Cochefert and
Gribelin. Bad faith is here evident to any one who was accustomed to
matters of this kind. For any one who is posted on matters of espionage
the proof that the weakness of the *dossier* was well known, is that it is
much talked of, but not shown, and that General de Boisdeffre never
submitted to the Minister in 1898 the documents of which it was composed. Moreover, the General told me at that time, while the *dossier*
was still there, that no pains had been spared during the trial to influence the judges. Colonel Sandherr told him that he had said to one
of the judges: "I give you my guarantee that he is guilty." On the other
hand, Captain Gallet, one of the judges, was closely associated at this
time with Colonel Henry, who did not fail to post him on his understanding of the matter. That is how the thing happened. I was present
at all the Session, seated behind the judges. It was seen that the outlook
of the case was somewhat uncertain, and it was resolved to make a bold
stroke. Henry said to me: "As you are seated behind Gallet, tell him to
have me recalled to demand further information from me." As I refused to carry out this commission, Colonel Henry became angry, and
made the communication himself during adjournment of the trial. Captain Gallet brought up the question when the Session was resumed, and
Henry in making his deposition, said: "We had it from an honorable

person that an officer of the Second Division has betrayed information, and that officer is there," he added, pointing to Dreyfus. It was possible to surmise that the person in question had denounced Dreyfus, but that was not so. This person, a foreign spendthrift, to whom I had paid 1,200 francs for this service, had said to Henry that the foreign military attachés had friends in the Second Division from whom they got information, and this advice agrees entirely with the actual facts; for the foreign military attachés were received at the Second Military Division in the most friendly fashion, and there given all information which it was possible to accord to them.

But Dreyfus was attached to the Second Division simply as an officer of probation.

The alleged admission to Captain Lebrun-Renault make up in the same way a maneuver, the consequences of which have been recently felt. From the time of the deportation of Dreyfus to the *Île du Diable,* what it is proper to call "plots" increased. It was then that the forged Henry document was discovered at the Ministry of Colonies on the 25th of September, 1896. This forged document was a letter addressed to Dreyfus, which, as was the case with all the correspondence particularly personal, passed first through the hands of the Minister of Colonies, where it was examined. I myself saw it, the signature was that of one named Weyler. He told Dreyfus that his daughter was being married. This letter was written in strange characters resembling a drawing rather than writing and made to attract the eye. Although for more than a year I had read all the correspondence addressed to Dreyfus, I had never seen either this handwriting or this signature. But what was more serious, between the lines were written these words with sympathetic ink, sufficiently visible, however, for one to read them almost entirely: "We do not understand your communication, specify where are the vaults containing the—" This letter, which was a most rude forgery, was intended to start the idea of a counter plot launched by the friends of Dreyfus, with the intention of substituting a dummy. I gave it to M. Bertillon, who employed himself in having made by one of his employes an astonishingly accurate facsimile. As I looked at it against the light I noticed that the grain of the paper was identical with that of the original. M. Bertillon said to me with a smile—"We have thought of everything." The facsimile was sent to the *Île du Diable* in order to see what Dreyfus would do when he received it.

This forged document constitutes the serious fact of which I spoke to General Gonse in July, 1896.

Influenced by the chain of evidence, I thought for a moment that this document came really from the friends of Dreyfus, who, in order to

save him, had had recourse to the most clumsy means. However, upon
reflection, it did not take me long to become convinced of the character
of this document, and I believe that it was du Paty de Clam who was its
author, since it was to his interest at that moment to render my work
vain.

The idea of the dummy was one of those which du Paty de Clam mentioned most frequently. At any rate, at this time Henry was on leave
and could not intervene.

After this document, the false news reported in the press, particularly
the article in the *Éclair* of September 14th, which originated certainly
with du Paty de Clam, for in it are entire phrases which are word for
word similar to those which he uttered before me.

Finally the forged Henry document which is too well-known for me
to emphasize it further, not to mention the explanation recently given
by M. Bertulus, *Juge d'Instruction*.

What it is necessary to remember of all this is that the guilt of Dreyfus
was so uncertain that those in favor of his condemnation believed it
necessary to reinforce it by forged documents, or to attack by underhand
methods the methods of the prisoner.

In fine, Dreyfus was only arrested because it was unjustly believed
that the *bordereau* was the work of an officer of the General Staff. Once
arrested, nothing was found against him, but the accusation of the police
reports trumped up against him for the case, and which could not hold
water before the court-martial of 1894.

The reason for attributing the *bordereau* to Dreyfus was the similarity
of handwriting.

It has never been possible to discover the motive which would have
led him to commit such a crime resulting in inevitable conviction.

The Minister communicated to the judges in the Council Chamber
the secret *dossier* composed of documents inapplicable to Dreyfus, and
which could not be brought up against him unless one admitted the
commentaries which accompanied the *dossier,* they having been compiled by du Paty de Clam. The *dossier* was never submitted to the examination of the counsel for the defense. Dreyfus once convicted—attempts were made to elaborate this *dossier,* but so far without success.
In the autumn of 1896, when the inquiry upon Esterhazy destroyed the
grounds for attributing the *bordereau* to Dreyfus and broke down absolutely the accusation made against him, then it was that the start was
made with the system of the forged documents.

At the time when I left the Ministry, in 1896, there were no other
documents relating to Dreyfus besides those enumerated in the present
communication. I demand, that if other documents have come to light

since then, that I be placed in a position to report upon them. I demand also that all objections which may be applied to this Report shall be fully worked out, and that I be invited to furnish all such supplementary explanations as are necessary to bring the Dreyfus Affair into the full light of day.

In conclusion, Monsieur the Keeper of the Seals, allow me to express my gratitude. You have given me the opportunity of doing what I have wished to do for two years—to quieten my conscience by telling the entire truth to one who is the supreme arbiter of justice, and in consequence one of the guardians of this country's honor. I beg at the same time that you will accept the assurance of my deep respect.

(Signed) PICQUART

THE COMMUNICATION OF SECRET DOCUMENTS
TO THE COURT-MARTIAL OF 1894

(LETTER FROM LIEUTENANT-COLONEL PICQUART TO THE KEEPER OF THE SEALS, SEPTEMBER 15, 1898)

MONSIEUR THE KEEPER OF THE SEALS,

I have the honor to send you the supplementary information which you asked me to furnish on the subject of the communication of the secret documents to the Judges of the court-martial which condemned Dreyfus in 1894.

This communication was well known to all the officers intimately connected with the Dreyfus affair. I spoke of it at the time with General Mercier and General de Boisdeffre and du Paty de Clam. And later, when I assumed direction of the Service of Information, I spoke of it to General Gonse and Colonel Sandherr and Major Henry and to Gribelin, the Keeper of the Archives. Finally Vallecalle, the recorder of the first court-martial, spoke of it to me during the Dreyfus inquiry in these words:

"Was it not you who brought the secret *dossier* to Colonel Morel?"

"At the same time as I myself was not charged to make the delivery, I am unable to inform you except by hearsay and by what I have seen myself; albeit these details are true as a whole, they should nevertheless be checked."

"How was the delivery made?"

"Under sealed enclosure to the president of the court-martial, there was another enclosure containing—first, the four documents which I have specified in my *memoire;* second, the commentary written by du Paty de Clam on this matter. There is no doubt whatever about that."

When Colonel Sandherr spoke to me of this *dossier* in July, 1895, he said; "The small *dossier* which was delivered to the Judges of the court-martial is in the iron closet." When I asked Gribelin for it, I said to him: "Give me the *dossier* which was delivered to the Judges of the court-martial and which is in Major Henry's closet." He gave it to me immediately, and in a particular envelope the four documents and the Commentary. When I showed this *dossier* to General de Boisdeffre, he recognized it perfectly and asked why it had not been burned as before agreed. General Gonse also saw it in my possession, and we spoke of it as the *dossier* delivered to the judges in the council chamber.

2nd.—By whom was the delivery made? I am not entirely positive of the person who carried the *dossier* to the President of the court-martial. It might have been myself; it might have been du Paty de Clam. This uncertainty may seem curious, but is nevertheless natural. I had several deliveries to make at the time and I was not familiar with the exact appearance of the *dossier* in question.

3rd.—Where was the delivery made? At the court-martial at Paris, and it was opened in the council chamber. At what time? Assuredly after the close of the session. Because in reporting, the general impression of the deliberation to the Minister, I said to him that this impression was not unfavorable to the accused, but that at the time I was speaking the judges should be determined by the secret *dossier*. He did not contradict this reference, and moreover this secret *dossier* was always a clearly-understood thing at the Ministry. My declaration might be confirmed by Generals Mercier, de Boisdeffre and Gonse; Lieutenant-Colonel du Paty de Clam, Gribelin, the Keeper of the Archives and the recorder, Vallecalle.

Such, *Monsieur* the Keeper of the Seals, are the supplementary explanations which I had to offer you. I take the liberty of insisting in the same urgent manner that I should be allowed to furnish details which it is difficult to supply in writing.

VII

Enter Zola–The Conscience of France

He was a meek-looking, seemingly gentle little man, but behind the pince-nez glasses was a will of iron and a thunderous voice. Émile-Édouard-Charles-Antoine Zola was born in Paris in 1840, the son of an Italo-Greek engineer and a French mother. His father died when the boy was young and left him nothing but a lawsuit against the municipality of Aix. The lad went to Paris and Marseilles to complete his education, but he failed to get a degree. A period of terrible poverty ensued during which Zola merely existed in a Parisian attic. At the age of 22 he managed to get a position as a clerk in a publishing house at a miserable wage.

Later Zola became a journalist-critic and then turned to writing novels. From his pen there flowed a long series of naturalistic novels marked by scrupulous accuracy, psychological analysis, and powerful style. His work was attacked for "immorality and lack of taste," but there was no doubt about his reputation as one of the great novelists of France. Even more, he was a humanitarian and an honest man.

Zola was fascinated by the case that was convulsing French politics and social life. Convinced that Dreyfus was an innocent victim, he decided to do something about it.

Zola Addresses a Letter to the Youth of France

"Whither are you going, young men?"

Émile Zola, Four Letters to France, *trans. L. F. Austin (London and New York: The Bodley Head, 1898) pp. 1–11.*

On December 13, 1897, Zola published a letter directed to the youth of France. In it he expressed serious doubts about the guilt

161

of Dreyfus and he exhorted the youth of France to be concerned about the good name and future of their beloved country.

LETTER TO THE YOUTH OF FRANCE

Whither are you going, young men? And you, students, who parade the streets in bands, demonstrating in the name of your anger and your enthusiasm, feeling an imperious need to utter in public the cry of your outraged consciences—whither are you going?

Do you go to protest against some abuse of authority? Has some one offended the love of truth and equity which burns within you, ignorant as you are as yet of political truckling, of the basenesses of everyday life?

Do you go to redress some social wrong? Is it to throw the weight of your strenuous youth into the balance in which the lot of the fortunate and the disinherited of this earth are so unfairly weighed?

Do you go to insist upon tolerance, upon the independence of the human reason? Is it to cry down those narrow-minded sectaries who would like to lead your emancipated intellects back to ancient errors by proclaiming the bankruptcy of science?

Do you go to declaim beneath the windows of the shifty and the hypocritical your invincible faith in the future, in the coming century which you bring with you, and which should witness the realization of universal peace in the name of Justice and of Love?

"No, no! We go to hoot a man, an old man, who, after a long life of labor and loyalty, imagined that he might give his support with impunity to a generous cause, that he might seek to let light in upon the darkness, and to repair a judicial error for the honor of France."

Ah! when I, too, was young, I have seen the Latin Quarter thrilling with the lofty passions of youth, the love of liberty, the hatred of brute force, which crushes the spirit and constrains the soul. I have seen it under the Empire fulfilling its brave task of opposition, acting sometimes with injustice, but always through an excess of love for human freedom. In those days it hissed the favorite authors of the Tuileries, it shouted down those professors whose teachings appeared to it sinister, it rose against whosoever ranged himself on the side of darkness and of tyranny. There, in the Latin Quarter, burned the sacred fire of the beautiful folly of youth, when hope is a reality and tomorrow promises certain triumph of the perfect City.

And if we go further back in the history of the noble passions which have uplifted the youth of the Schools, we shall always find it filled with indignation against injustice, we shall always see it thrilling and rising in the defense of the humble, of the abandoned, and of the persecuted, against the mighty and the cruel. It demonstrated in favor of oppressed peoples, it stood for Poland and for Greece, it undertook the defense of all who suffered, of all who agonized beneath the brutality of a despot or of a mob. When one said that the Latin Quarter was on fire, you might be sure that some clear flame of youthful justice burned in the background, which, scorning caution, was impelled by its enthusiasm to labors of love. And what spontaneity there was then—an overflowing river pouring through the streets!

I know well that today, once more, the pretext is that the country is in danger, that France has been given away to the victorious enemy by a band of traitors. Only, I ask where shall we find a clear intuition of things, an instinctive perception of what is true, of what is just, if we do not find it in those fresh young souls now entering upon public life with honest and upright minds which nothing yet has come to sully? That politicians, perverted by years of intrigue, that journalists who have lost their mental balance through the perpetual chicaneries of their profession, are found to accept the most impudent lies and to shut their eyes to the most blinding light, can be explained, can be understood. But the youth of the country must be already badly gangrened if its natural candor and purity do not of a sudden pull themselves together in the midst of such untenable errors, and go straight for that which is self-evident, limpid, and full of the honest light of day!

The story is one of the simplest. An officer has been condemned, and no one impugns the good faith of his judges. They dealt with him according to their conscience, on what they considered to be certain proofs. Then one day it came about that first one man and then several men began to entertain doubts of these proofs, and ended by convincing themselves that one, the most important proof, the only one at least on which the judges had publicly relied, had been attributed falsely to the condemned man, and was most assuredly the work of another person. On expressing their conviction, this other person was denounced by the brother of the prisoner, who was thus doing his strict duty; and, in consequence, a new trial is held, which should it end in a verdict of guilty, must bring about the revision of the first trial. All this is perfectly clear, just, and reasonable, is it not? Where does one find in it a machination, a black plot to save a traitor? No one denies that there has been a traitor, all one asks is that it should be the guilty man and not the innocent one to expiate the crime. You will always have them, your traitors; the thing is to put your finger on the right ones.

A little common sense should be sufficient to do this. What is the motive actuating those who desire the revision of the Dreyfus case?

Put aside the imbecile anti-Semitism, with its ferocious monomania which sees a Jewish plot sustained by Jewish gold seeking to thrust a Christian in the place of the Jew into an infamous gaol. This will not hold water. The improbabilities, the impossibilities stumble over one another. There are certain consciences which all the gold in the world could never buy. We come perforce to the real motive, which is the natural, slow, and invincible expansion of every judicial error. There you have the whole story. A judicial error is a power which spreads, which conquers the conscience, which haunts it, which drives men to risk their fortune and their life, while they devote themselves more and more obstinately to the consummation of Justice. There is no other possible explanation of what is taking place amongst us today; the rest is nothing but the most abominable political and religious animosities, nothing but an over-flowing torrent of calumnies and abuse.

Yet what excuses shall avail our young men if they allow their ideas of Justice and of Humanity to be tarnished, were it only for an instant! When the French Chamber met on December 4th, it covered itself with shame by voting an order of the day "to brand with infamy the ring-leaders of the odious campaign which is troubling the public mind." For the benefit of those who, I hope, will read me in the future, I say boldly, that such a vote is unworthy of our generous country, and constitutes an ineffaceable stain. "The ringleaders" are those brave and conscientious men, who, certain that a judicial error had been committed, denounced it in order that reparation might be made in the patriotic conviction that a great nation, among which one innocent man agonized in torture, must be a doomed nation. "The odious campaign" is the voice of truth and justice on the lips of these same men; it is their pertinacity in wishing France to continue to be in the eyes of all who watch her, the humane France, the France who having accomplished freedom, will yet do justice. And as you see, the Chamber has fallen into crime, since it has corrupted the youth of the Schools, which deceived, led astray, let loose upon our streets demonstrates—a thing which has never been known before—against all that is noblest, all that is bravest, all that is most divine in the human soul!

After the meeting of the Senate on the 7th, the downfall of M. Scheurer-Kestner was talked of. Ah, yes, what a downfall must have taken place in his heart, in his soul! I can imagine his anguish, his torments, while he sees breaking up about him all that he has loved in our Republic, all that he has helped to conquer for her in the good fight of his whole life; first liberty, and then the manly virtues of loyalty, of frankness, and of civic courage. He is one of the last of his strong generation.

Under the Empire he knew what it was to belong to a nation submissive to the authority of one only, devouring itself in fever and impatience, and brutally gagged, while justice was denied it. He saw our defeats with bleeding heart; he knew their cause to be due to despotic blindness and imbecility. Later on, he was one of those who worked with the most ardor and wisdom to lift our country from its ruins and to restore her to her rank in Europe. He dates from the heroic times of our Republican France, and I picture him imagining that he had accomplished a good and durable work, in driving out despotism forever, and in achieving liberty, by which I mean that humane liberty which allows every man to follow the light of his own conscience amidst the tolerance of contrary opinions.

Yes, indeed! All has been conquered for us, and all is, once more, flung to the earth. Round about him, as well as within his own soul, he sees everything in ruins. To have fallen a prey to the necessity for truth is a crime. To have demanded justice is a crime. The most hideous despotism is back among us, again we are silenced with the most rigorous gag. It is not the heel of a Cæsar which crushes the public conscience, but it is a whole Chamber branding as infamous those who are fired with a passion for justice. We are forbidden to speak! Blows shut the lips of all who desire to defend the truth, the mob is stirred up that it may impose silence on individuals. Never before has so monstrous an oppression been thus organized and utilized against free discussion. And meanwhile a shameful terror reigns, the bravest turn cowards, and no one dares say what he thinks for fear of being denounced as a traitor and a bribe-taker. The few newspapers which at first stood out for justice are now crawling in the dust before their readers, people completely demoralized by all sorts of silly tales. And I believe that no nation has lived through a darker, a more turbid hour, or one more shattering for its reason and its dignity.

It is true, therefore, that the whole of the great and loyal past has crumbled away for M. Scheurer-Kestner. If he still believes in the goodness and equity of men, that is because he is of an incurable optimism. Daily, during the last three weeks he has been dragged through the mud for having sacrificed the honor and happiness of his old age in the desire for justice. There is no more grievous suffering for the honest man than to suffer martyrdom for his honesty. He sees his faith in tomorrow murdered, his hope poisoned, and, if he dies, he says, "All is over, nothing remains; all my good deeds vanish with me; virtue is but a word; the world is black and void!"

The better to give a slap in the face to patriotism, precisely this man is chosen, who is the last representative in our Assemblies of Alsace-

Lorraine! He, sold to the enemy, he, a traitor, he, insult the Army, when his very name should have sufficed to dispel the most somber suspicions! No doubt he was simple enough to think that the fact of his being an Alsatian, that his renown as an ardent patriot, were in themselves a guarantee for his good faith in the delicate rôle of justiciary, which he undertook. That he should have taken up this case at all was surely as much as to say that he considered its speedy settlement necessary for the honor of the Army and of the nation. Let it drag its weary course a few weeks longer, try to stifle the truth, refuse to do justice, and you will see whether you do not make us the laughingstock of all Europe, whether you do not degrade France to the last place among the nations!

But no! Pigheaded political and religious passions will listen to nothing, and the youth of our Schools gives the world the spectacle of its hooting M. Scheurer-Kestner, the traitor, the man who is sold to the enemy, who insults the Army and compromises the country!

I am, of course, aware that the handful of young men engaged in these demonstrations do not represent the whole of the youth of France; I am aware that a hundred turbulent voices in the street make more noise than ten thousand workers studiously shut up in their workrooms. But this noisy hundred is already a hundred too many, and that such a movement, no matter how restricted it may be, can take place today in the Latin Quarter, is a most distressing symptom.

Anti-Semitics among our young men! they do exist then, do they? This idiotic poison has really already overthrown their intellects and corrupted their souls? What a saddening, what a disquieting element for the twentieth century which is about to dawn. A hundred years after the Declaration of the Rights of Man, a hundred years after the supreme act of tolerance and emancipation, we go back to religious warfare, to the most odious and the most stupid of fanaticisms! One can understand this among a certain set who have a part to play, a pose to maintain, an ambition to satisfy. But to find it among the young who are born to aid the expansion of the rights and liberties with which we have dreamed that the coming century shall be splendid! Here are the laborers for whom we have waited, and behold, they proclaim themselves already as anti-Semites, that is to say, they inaugurate the century by a massacre of the Jews, merely because these are members of another race and another faith! A fine way, truly, to enter into the inheritance of the City of our dreams, the City of brotherly love and of equality! If, indeed, this were the real attitude of the young men, it would be enough to break one's heart, to make one renounce all hope, all human happiness.

Oh young men, young men! remember, I entreat, the great work which awaits you. You are the workmen of the future; it is you who will determine the character of the twentieth century; it is you who, we earnestly hope, will solve the problems of truth and equity that the dying century propounds. We, the old, the elder men, hand on to you the formidable results of our investigations, many contradictions, much perhaps which is obscure, but certainly the most strenuous effort which ever century made to reach the light, the most faithful and solidly based documents, and the very foundations of the vast edifice of Science, which you must continue to build up for your own honor and happiness. All we ask of you is to be more generous, more emancipated of mind than were we; to leave us behind in your love of a wholesome life, in your ardor for work, in the fecundity through which man and the earth will produce at length an overflowing harvest of joy beneath the glorious sunshine. And we should make way for you, fraternally, glad to go and take our rest after the day's toil in the sound sleep of death, if we knew that you would carry on our work and realize our dreams.

Oh young men, young men! Remember all your fathers suffered, the terrible battles which they fought and gained in order to win for you the freedom which you enjoy today. That you find yourselves independent, that you may come and go as you please, that you may say what you think in the press, is due to your fathers, who purchased liberty for you with their genius and with their blood. You have not been born beneath a tyranny; you do not know what it is to awake every morning with the heel of the master upon your neck; you have not fought to escape from the sword of the dictator, from the false scales of the unjust judge. Thank your fathers for this, and do not commit the crime of applauding lies, of joining the ranks of brute force, of fanatical intolerance, of ambitious greed. The dictatorship is at an end.

Young men, young men! side always with justice. Should the idea of justice grow dim within you, you expose yourselves to every peril. I am not speaking of legal justice, which is but the safeguard of social ties. Such justice, certainly, one must respect; but there is a higher justice than this, which accepts as fundamental principle the fallibility of all human judgment, and which admits the possible innocence of a condemned man without thereby in any way insulting the integrity of his judges. Have we not, then, here an enterprise which should uplift your burning love of righteousness? Who will get up and insist that justice be done if it is not you, who have no part in the conflict of personalities and interests, who are not yet engaged in or compromised by any crooked schemes, who dare to speak aloud in all sincerity and good faith?

Young men, young men! Be humane, be generous! Even if we are mistaken, stand by us when we say that an innocent man is enduring a most horrible penalty, of which it breaks our hearts to think. If you admit for one instant the possibility of a mistake, the tears rush to your eyes, and you feel yourself suffocating as you remember the enormity of his punishment. Let the convict-warders remain unmoved; but you, how can you so remain? You, who still can weep, who should be filled with pity for suffering of every kind. How is it that while one single martyr exists, no matter where, sinking beneath the burden of unmerited hate, the spirit of chivalry does not prompt you to espouse his cause and achieve his deliverance? Who, then, if it is not you, shall attempt the glorious deed, shall dare to fling himself into a dangerous and noble cause, and in the name of ideal justice, bid defiance to the mob? Ah! does it not cover you with shame that it is not you, but the old men, the men of a past generation, who, full of the enthusiasm which should be yours, are performing your work today?

Whither are you going, young men? And you, students, who parade the streets, flinging down, in the middle of our discords, the reckless courage and the high hopes of your twentieth year?

"We go to combat for Humanity, for Justice, and for Truth!"

ÉMILE ZOLA

Zola Speaks to the French Nation

"This is why, France, I entreat you, delay no longer but come back to your true self."

From Zola, Four Letters to France, pp. 12–24.

A week before sending his *J'Accuse* letter to the President of the Republic, Zola addressed the following "Letter to France" in a brochure. In emotional tones he beseeched his people to remain "the nation of honor, the nation of humanity, truth, and justice."

A LETTER TO FRANCE

During these terrible days of moral disturbance through which we are passing, at a moment when the public conscience appears to be obscured, it is to you, France, that I address myself, to the nation, to our native land!

Every morning when I read in the newspapers what you seem to think of this lamentable Dreyfus case, my stupor grows, my reason revolts more and more. What? It is you, France, who have come to this, that you forge for yourself convictions out of the most palpable lies, that you join hands with a horde of criminals against a few upright men, that you allow yourself to be driven mad by the imbecile pretext that your Army is insulted, and that there is a conspiracy to sell you to the enemy, when, on the contrary, the wisest and the most loyal of your sons desire to see you remain in the eyes of a watchful Europe, the nation of honor, the nation of humanity, truth, and justice.

And it is true that the great mass of the people has come to this, above all the poor and the humble; the inhabitants of the towns, nearly the whole of the provinces, and all the country folk; that great majority which accepts its opinions from the newspapers or the neighbors, and is equally incapable of getting at facts, or of reflecting thereupon. What then has happened, how is it that your people, France, with their good hearts and their common sense, have reached this ferocity of terror, this blackness of intolerance? They are told that there exists, undergoing the worst of tortures, a man, who perhaps is innocent; they are told that there are moral and material proofs which require a revision of his trial; and behold, your people refuse the light with violence, and shelter themselves behind fanatics and vagabonds, behind those to whose interest it is to leave the corpse in its grave; your people, who but a short while since, would have torn down the Bastille anew to set free a single prisoner!

What anguish and what desolation, France, in the souls of those who love you, and who long for your honor and your greatness! Brooding distressfully over the turbid and stormy sea of your people, I ask myself what are the causes of the tempest which threatens to carry away the better part of your glory? Nothing could be of a more deadly gravity; I see the most alarming symptoms. And I am going to speak out boldly, for the one passion of my life has been a love of truth, and I am here only carrying on my life's work.

Are you aware that the danger lies precisely in this somber obstinacy of public opinion? A hundred newspapers repeat daily that public opinion does not wish the innocence of Dreyfus, that his guilt is necessary to the safety of the country. And do you know to what point you yourself will be guilty, should those in authority take advantage of such a sophism to stifle the truth? It is France who will have desired it, it is you who will have insisted on the crime, and what a responsibility one day! Therefore, those of your sons who love and honor you, France, have but one pressing duty in this solemn hour; the duty of working

strongly upon public opinion, of enlightening it, of leading it back, of
saving it from the error into which blind passion flings it. And there is
no more necessary, no more holy task.

Ah yes! with all my strength I will speak to them, to the poor, to the
humble, to those who have been poisoned, and driven into delirium. I
will do nothing else but tell them where the real soul of the country
lies, where lie its indomitable energy and its certain triumph.

See how things now stand. A new step has been taken, and Commandant Esterhazy is summoned before a court-martial. As I have said
from the very first, the Truth must come out and nothing can prevent
it. Despite all ill will, every step taken will be mathematically a step
forward, when the right hour strikes. Truth possesses a power within
herself which overwhelms every obstacle. And should you stop her road,
should you succeed during a shorter or longer period in burying her
below the earth, this power augments, and becomes of an explosive force,
which, on the day that it breaks loose, will carry everything before it.
Try on this occasion to wall it up with lies, to keep it behind closed doors,
and you will see whether you do not prepare for the future the most
reverberating of disasters.

But, in proportion as truth advances, so do falsehoods accumulate, in
order to deny her progress. Nothing is more significant. When General
de Pellieux, commissioned to hold the preliminary inquiry, laid his
report on the table asserting the possible guilt of Commandant Esterhazy,
the reptile press pretended that because the latter chose so to have it,
General Saussier, undecided what to do, but convinced of Esterhazy's
innocence, agreed to submit the case to a court-martial, merely to please
him. Today the newspapers go one better, for they relate that three
experts having again declared the *bordereau* to be the undoubted work
of Dreyfus, Commandant Ravary in his judiciary information, saw himself face to face with the necessity of finding "no case"; if, therefore,
Commandant Esterhazy was going to appear before a court-martial, it
was because he had again forced the hand of General Saussier, and had
insisted on standing his trial all the same.

Is it not intensely funny, and perfectly idiotic? Behold the prisoner
managing the case and dictating the sentence! Behold this man, whose
innocence has been established after two investigations, and for whom,
nevertheless, the utmost trouble is taken to constitute a court, to no
other end than the production of a well-staged comedy, a sort of judicial
apotheosis! Justice becomes a mockery the moment you declare that an
acquittal is certain, for justice does not exist to try the innocent; and,
at the very least, the verdict must not be agreed on behind the scenes,

before the curtain goes up. Since Commandant Esterhazy is summoned before a court-martial, let us hope, for our national honor's sake, that the thing is serious, and not a mere parade got up for the amusement of noodles. My poor France! They must think you very foolish surely, when they tell you cock-and-bull stories, such as these?

Similarly, there are nothing but lies in the accounts published by the reptile press, and which should suffice to open your eyes. For my own part, I refuse, categorically, to believe in the three experts who failed to recognize, at the first glance, the absolute identity between the handwriting of Commandant Esterhazy and that of the *bordereau*. Stop the first little boy you meet in the street, bring him indoors, place the two documents before him, and he will tell you: "The same person wrote them both." There is no need of experts, be they ever so expert; there are certain words as like one another as two peas. And this is so true that Esterhazy himself, recognizing the terrifying resemblance, swore that many of his letters must have been traced with transfer paper; a whole laboriously complicated and puerile story, of which the press made copy for weeks on end. And now we are told that three experts have been found to declare that the *bordereau* is undoubtedly in the handwriting of Dreyfus. Ah, no! this is too much, such assurance excites suspicion, and at last, I hope, honest men will rise in their wrath.

There are certain newspapers which go so far as to say that the *bordereau* will be set aside, that there will be no question of it even before the court. Of what, then, will there be question? and why should the court sit at all? The *bordereau* is the nucleus of the case. If Dreyfus was condemned on the evidence of a document which was written by another, evidence which is sufficient to ensure his condemnation, the revision of his trial becomes an irresistible logical necessity, for there cannot be two criminals punished for the same crime. Maître Demange has repeated, categorically, that the *bordereau* was the only document shown to him, and Dreyfus was legally condemned on the *bordereau* alone. Even admitting that in defiance of all legality, other secret evidence exists, which I personally cannot believe, who will venture to refuse a new trial, from the moment it is proved that the *bordereau*, the only document which has been exhibited and avowed, is by the hand of another person? And this is why so many lies have been piled up round the *bordereau*, which constitutes, in a word, the whole case.

Here then, is the first point to note; public opinion is made up largely of these lies, of these far-fetched and stupid stories, which the press scatter broadcast every day. The hour of responsibility will come, when it will be necessary to settle up with this reptile press, that dishonors us in the eyes of the whole world. There are certain newspapers which thus fulfil their mission, for they have never carted anything but mud. But what a grief and what a surprise to find among them a paper like the *Echo de Paris,* a literary paper, so often in the vanguard of ideas, and which in the Dreyfus case is doing such dirty work! Its violent paragraphs, of a most scandalous unfairness, are not signed, but they are said to be inspired by the very persons who made the disastrous mistake of condemning Dreyfus. Is M. Valentin Simond aware that they are covering his paper with opprobrium? And there is another newspaper, the attitude of which should fill all honest men with disgust. I allude to the *Petit Journal.* That papers, which just manage to drag on their existence by the sale of a few thousand copies, should howl and lie in order to send up their circulation, can be understood; besides, the evil they do is a limited one. But that the *Petit Journal,* selling more than a million copies, addressing itself to the masses, and finding its way everywhere, should thus sow error and mislead opinion, this is of an exceptional gravity. When one has so many souls under one's care, when one is shepherd for a whole nation, one should be of a scrupulous intellectual honesty, under the penalty of falling into civic crime.

And here then, France, is what I find first of all in the madness which has seized you:—lies from the pressmen, and the reign of inept inventions, base insults and moral perversions, which they serve up to you every morning. How can you even wish for truth and justice, when they thus throw all your historic virtues, your clear intellect, your sound reason so completely out of gear?

But there are facts even graver than these, a whole consensus of symptoms, which turn the crisis that you now traverse into a terrifying object lesson for those who know how to observe and how to judge. The Dreyfus case is but one deplorable incident. The terrible thing is the way you conduct yourself in the matter. A man may seem in perfect health, when on a sudden little spots appear on his skin; death is in him. All the political, all the social poison which you have swallowed is beginning to show itself on your face.

Why did you permit the cry that your Army was insulted? Why did you end by shouting it yourself when on the contrary every ardent patriot only desired its dignity and its honor? Your Army—but, today, you yourself are the Army. The Army is not this chief, or that regiment, or the other gold-laced hierarchy, but it is every single one of your children who is ready to defend the territory of France. Examine your conscience. Was it in truth your Army which you wished to defend when none were attacking it? Was it not rather the sword that you felt the sudden need of extolling? For my part, I see in the noisy ovation accorded to the military leaders who were supposed to have been insulted, a revival—unconscious, no doubt—of Boulangerism still latent in your veins. At bottom, yours is not yet the real republican blood; the sight of a plumed helmet still makes your heart beat quicker, no king can come amongst us but you fall in love with him. Your Army—ah, yes indeed! It is not of your Army that you are thinking, but of the General who happens to have caught your fancy. And the Dreyfus case has nothing to do with this. While General Billot was getting the Chamber to applaud him, I saw the shadow of the sword drawn upon the wall. France, if you do not take care, you are walking straight to a dictatorship.

And do you know where else you walk, France? You go to the Church of Rome, you return to that past of intolerance and of theocracy against which the greatest of your children fought, and which they believed they had slain in sacrificing their genius and their blood. Today the tactics of the anti-Semites are very simple. Catholicism, seeking in vain to influence the people, founded workmen's clubs and multiplied pilgrimages; it failed to win them back or lead them again to the foot of the altar. The question seemed definitely settled, the churches remained empty, the people had lost their faith. And behold, circumstances have occurred which make it possible to inoculate them with an anti-Semitic fury, and having poisoned them with this virus of fanaticism, they are launched upon the streets to shout, "Down with the Jews! Death to the Jews!" It is true, the people are still unbelievers, but can we not see the beginning of belief in this return to the dark ages of intolerance, in this desire to see the Jews burned in our public squares? Here, at last, the poison is found, and when the people of France have been changed into fanatics and torturers, when their generosity and love of the rights of man conquered with so much difficulty, have been rooted up out of their hearts, then no doubt God will do the rest.

The clerical reaction has been audaciously denied. But one sees it on every side, it breaks out in politics, in art, in the press, in the street! Today it is the Jews who are persecuted; tomorrow it will be the turn of the Protestants, and already the campaign is begun. The Republic is invaded by reactionaries of every sort, who love her with a sudden and a terrible love, who wind their arms about her that they may strangle her. On every side one hears it said that the idea of freedom is bankrupt. And when the Dreyfus case began, this growing hatred found in it an extraordinary opportunity, and fanaticism began to flame up even among those least conscious of it. Can you not see that the reason for the fury of the attack on M. Scheurer-Kestner lies in the fact that he belongs to a generation which believed in freedom and insisted on having it? Today, men shrug their shoulders and sneer:—"Greybeards! Old fellows who are no longer the fashion." His ruin will consummate the ruin of the founders of the Republic, of those who are dead, and whom it is sought to bury in the mud. They struck down the sword, they left the Church, and that is why a great and honorable man like Scheurer-Kestner is treated today as if he were a blackguard. He must be drowned in shame that the Republic herself may be bespattered and swept away.

Then see, on the other hand, how the Dreyfus case exhibits in clearest daylight, the crooked chicanery of parliamentarism, a chicanery which soils and will extinguish it. The Dreyfus case comes up, unluckily for it, toward the end of one Parliament, when there are but three or four months in which to sophisticate the next one. The Ministry in office naturally wants to win the elections, and every deputy is equally anxious to be again returned. Sooner therefore than give up power, sooner than risk their chances at the polls, they are ready to go to any lengths. The shipwrecked man does not cling more tenaciously to the plank which shall save him. And this is the whole matter, everything is hereby explained; on the one hand, the extraordinary attitude of the Ministry in the Dreyfus case; its silence, its embarrassment; the evil action it commits in allowing the country to agonize beneath an imposture, when it is its paramount duty to make known the truth; on the other hand, the timorous disinterestedness of the deputies, who pretend to know nothing, whose one fear is to jeopardize their re-election by alienating the people, whom they believe to be anti-Semitic. You hear it constantly said, "Ah, once the elections are over you'll see if Government and Parliament don't settle the Dreyfus business in four-and-twenty hours!" And this is what the baseness of parliamentary chicanery can make of a great people!

France, it is then from this, too, that you fashion your opinions:— from the need of the sword, from the clerical reaction which is leading you centuries in arrear, and from the voracious ambition of those who govern you, who devour you, and who refuse to rise up from table!

I implore you, France, be once more great, come back to your true self.

Up to the present the only result of this anti-Semitism has been two sinister affairs; the Panama business and the Dreyfus case. Remember the accusations, the abominable scandals, the publication of falsified or stolen documents, by which the reptile press made of the Panama affair a hideous ulcer eating into and weakening the country for years together. It maddened public opinion. The entire nation, perverted, drunk with poison, seeing red, insisted on a reckoning, and shouted for the death of the whole Parliament because it was rotten. "Ah, if Arton could come back, if he could speak!" He has come back, he has spoken, and the lies of the reptile press have crumbled to such an extent, that public opinion, suddenly veering round, refused to suspect that a single person was guilty, and insisted on the acquittal of the lot. I certainly think that every conscience cannot have been altogether clean, since what happened then is what happens in every Parliament in the world, when gigantic undertakings deal with vast sums of money. But public opinion grew at length nauseated with such baseness. Too much mud had been thrown, too many denunciations had been made, and the imperious need was felt to bathe in pure air, and to believe in the innocence of everybody.

Well now, I prophesy that this is what will happen in the other social crime of anti-Semitism, the Dreyfus case. Once again the reptile press is oversaturating public opinion with lies and ignominies, and is too eager to proclaim that honest men are rascals, and that rascals are honest men. It floats too many idiotic stories which the very children end by disbelieving. It has been given the lie too often, it goes too directly against good sense and simple probity. And this is inevitable, that public opinion overgorged with filth, will end one of these fine mornings in a sudden revulsion of feeling; and with an outbreak of sovereign generosity, you will see it in the Dreyfus case as in the Panama business, leaning with all its weight to insist upon truth and justice. Thus shall anti-Semitism be judged by its works, by the two deadly occurrences through which the country has lost both dignity and wholesomeness.

This is why, France, I entreat you, delay no longer but come back to your true self. We cannot tell you what the truth really is; the courts alone know it, and we must suppose that they intend to make it public. It is for the judges alone to speak; it will only become our duty to do so, if they fail in giving us the entire truth. But do you not suspect that the truth is quite simple; a mistake at first, and then perversions to cover it? Facts speak so clearly, every phase of the inquiry has been a confession: Commandant Esterhazy inexplicably protected; Colonel Picquart treated as a criminal, and overwhelmed with insults; Cabinet Ministers playing upon words, official newspapers lying violently, the preliminary examination marching on tiptoe, with hopeless slowness. Does not this stink in your nostrils, does not this smell like a corpse? does it not seem as though, in reality, there were much to hide on the part of people, who thus openly allow themselves to be defended by all the rascality of Paris, while honest men, at the price of their own welfare, are asking for light?

Awake, France, remember your glory. How is it possible that your liberal-minded citizens, your emancipated people, do not perceive at this crisis into what mental aberration they are being flung? I cannot believe them to be accomplices, they are only dupes, because they do not realize all that there is in the background; on the one side the military dictatorship, on the other the clerical reaction. Is it your wish, France, to put in peril all that for which you have so dearly paid, religious tolerance, equal justice for all, and the fraternal solidarity of your citizens? That there should be doubts of the guilt of Dreyfus, and that you leave him nevertheless to his tortures, is sufficient to compromise your glorious conquests of right and liberty forever. What! shall there be but a handful of us to say these things, and will not all honest men rise to join us, all the emancipated minds, all the great hearts, who having founded the Republic, ought to tremble to see her in danger!

It is to such among your children, France, that I appeal. Let them gather together, let them write, let them speak. Let them work with us to enlighten public opinion, the poor, the humble, those whose minds have been poisoned and driven to delirium. The soul of our country, her energy, and her triumph are to be found only in justice and generosity.

My one fear is lest the affair should not be entirely cleared up, and at once. After proceedings held in secret, a verdict given behind closed doors cannot be the end. It is then only that the case begins, because not to speak out then would be to become an accomplice. What folly to imagine one can prevent the story from being written. It will be written, this story! And there is no responsibility, however small, which shall not be paid for.

And this will be for your final glory, France, because in my heart I have no fear. I know that, do what they will to injure your reason and your strength, you, nevertheless, are the future, and you will always have triumphant reawakenings to Justice and to Truth.

ÉMILE ZOLA

"J'Accuse . . . !"
"It is a crime to exploit patriotism for works of hatred. . . ."

L'Aurore, *January 13, 1898. Translated in* The Trial of Émile Zola *(New York: Benjamin R. Tucker, 1898), pp. 3–14.*

On January 13, 1898, Zola addressed a letter to the President of the Republic, in *L'Aurore,* a daily paper published in Paris under the editorship of Georges Clemenceau. The latter contributed the title. *"J'Accuse"* was a bitter denunciation of all those who had a hand in hounding Dreyfus. It quickly became one of the most sensational documents of the entire Affair. Zola's aim was to be prosecuted for libel and to stimulate a judicial inquiry into the whole unsavory business. He was to get his wish on both counts.

"I Accuse . . . !"

Letter to M. Félix Faure, President of the Republic

Monsieur le Président:

Will you permit me, in my gratitude for the kindly welcome that you once extended to me, to have a care for the glory that belongs to you, and to say to you that your star, so lucky hitherto, is threatened with the most shameful, the most ineffaceable, of stains?

You have emerged from base calumnies safe and sound; you have conquered hearts. You seem radiant in the apotheosis of that patriotic *fête* which the Russian alliance has been for France, and you are preparing to preside at the solemn triumph of our Universal Exposition, which will crown our great century of labor, truth, and liberty. But what a mud stain on your name—I was going to say on your reign—is this abominable Dreyfus affair! A council of war has just dared to acquit an Esterhazy in obedience to orders, a final blow at all truth, at all justice. And now it is done! France has this stain upon her cheek; it will be written in history that under your presidency it was possible for this social crime to be committed.

Since they have dared, I too will dare. I will tell the truth, for I have promised to tell it, if the courts, once regularly appealed to, did not bring it out fully and entirely. It is my duty to speak; I will not be an accomplice. My nights would be haunted by the specter of the innocent man who is atoning, in a far-away country, by the most frightful of tortures, for a crime that he did not commit.

And to you, *Monsieur le Président,* will I cry this truth, with all the force of an honest man's revolt. Because of your honor I am convinced that you are ignorant of it. And to whom then shall I denounce the malevolent gang of the really guilty, if not to you, the first magistrate of the country?

First, the truth as to the trial and conviction of Dreyfus.

A calamitous man has managed it all, has done it all—Colonel du Paty de Clam, then a simple major. He is the entire Dreyfus case; it will be fully known only when a sincere investigation shall have clearly established his acts and his responsibilities. He appears as the most heady, the most intricate, of minds, haunted with romantic intrigues, delighting in the methods of the newspaper novel, stolen papers, anonymous letters, meetings in deserted spots, mysterious women who peddle overwhelming proofs by night. It is he who conceived the idea of dictating the *bordereau* to Dreyfus; it is he who dreamed of studying it in a room completely lined with mirrors; it is he whom Major Forzinetti represents to us armed with a dark lantern, trying to gain access to the accused when asleep, in order to throw upon his face a sudden flood of light, and thus surprise a confession of his crime in the confusion of his awakening. And I have not to tell the whole; let them look, they will find. I declare simply that Major du Paty de Clam, entrusted as a judicial officer with the duty of preparing the Dreyfus case, is, in the order of dates and responsibilities, the first person guilty of the fearful judicial error that has been committed.

The *bordereau* already had been for some time in the hands of Colonel Sandherr, director of the bureau of information, who since then has died of general paralysis. "Flights" have taken place; papers have disappeared, as they continue to disappear even today; and the authorship of the *bordereau* was an object of inquiry, when little by little an *a priori* conclusion was arrived at that the author must be a staff officer and an officer of artillery,—clearly a double error, which shows how superficially this *bordereau* had been studied, for a systematic examination proves that it could have been written only by an officer of troops. So they searched their own house; they examined writings; it was a sort of family affair,—a traitor to be surprised in the war offices themselves, that he might be expelled therefrom. I need not again go over a story already known in part. It is sufficient to say that Major du Paty de Clam enters upon the scene as soon as the first breath of suspicion falls upon Dreyfus. Starting from that moment, it is he who invented Dreyfus; the case becomes his case; he undertakes to confound the traitor, and induce him to make a complete confession. There is also, to be sure, the minister of war, General Mercier, whose intelligence seems rather inferior; there is also the Chief of Staff, General de Boisdeffre, who seems to have yielded to his clerical passion, and the sub-Chief of Staff, General Gonse, whose conscience has succeeded in accommodating itself to many things. But at bottom there was at first only Major du Paty de Clam, who leads them all, who hypnotizes them,—for he concerns himself also with spiritualism, with occultism, holding converse with spirits. Incredible are the experiences to which he submitted the unfortunate Dreyfus, the traps into which he tried to lead him, the mad inquiries, the monstrous fancies, a complete and torturing madness.

Ah! this first affair is a nightmare to one who knows it in its real details. Major du Paty de Clam arrests Dreyfus, puts him in close confinement; he runs to Mme. Dreyfus, terrorizes her, tells her that, if she speaks, her husband is lost. Meantime the unfortunate was tearing his flesh, screaming his innocence. And thus the examination went on, as in a fifteenth-century chronicle, amid mystery, with a complication of savage expedients, all based on a single childish charge, this imbecile *bordereau,* which was not simply a vulgar treason, but also the most shameless of swindles, for the famous secrets delivered proved, almost all of them, valueless. If I insist, it is because here lies the egg from which later was to be hatched the real crime, the frightful denial of justice, of which France lies ill. I should like to show in detail how the judicial error was possible; how it was born of the machinations of Major du Paty de Clam; how General Mercier and Generals de Bois-deffre and Gonse were led into it, gradually assuming responsibility for this error, which afterward they believed it their duty to impose as sacred truth, truth beyond discussion. At the start there was, on their part, only carelessness and lack of understanding. At worst we see them yielding to the religious passions of their surroundings, and to the prejudices of the *esprit de corps*. They have suffered folly to do its work.

But here is Dreyfus before the council of war. The most absolute secrecy is demanded. Had a traitor opened the frontier to the enemy in order to lead the German emperor to Notre Dame, they would not have taken stricter measures of silence and mystery. The nation is awe-struck; there are whisperings of terrible doings, of those monstrous treasons that excite the indignation of History, and naturally the nation bows. There is no punishment severe enough; it will applaud even public degradation; it will wish the guilty man to remain upon his rock of infamy, eaten by remorse. Are they real then,—these unspeakable things, these dangerous things, capable of setting Europe aflame, which they have had to bury carefully behind closed doors? No, there was nothing behind them save the romantic and mad fancies of Major du Paty de Clam. All this was done only to conceal the most ridiculous of newspaper novels. And, to assure one's self of it, one need only study attentively the indictment read before the council of war.

Ah! the emptiness of this indictment! That a man could have been condemned on this document is a prodigy of iniquity. I defy honest people to read it without feeling their hearts leap with indignation and crying out their revolt at the thought of the unlimited atonement yonder, on Devil's Island. Dreyfus knows several languages—a crime; no compromising document was found on his premises—a crime; he sometimes visits the neighborhood of his birth—a crime; he is industrious, he is desirous of knowing everything—a crime; he does not get confused—a crime; he gets confused—a crime. And the simplicities of this document, the formal assertions in the void! We were told of fourteen counts, but we find, after all, only one,—that of the *bordereau*. And even as to this we learn that the experts were not in agreement; that one of them, M. Gobert, was hustled out in military fashion, because he permitted himself to arrive at another than the desired opinion. We were told also of twenty-three officers who came to overwhelm Dreyfus with their testimony. We are still in ignorance of their examination, but it is certain that all of them did not attack him, and it is to be remarked, furthermore, that all of them belonged to the war offices. It is a family trial; there they are all at home; and it must be remembered that the staff wanted the trial, sat in judgment at it, and has just passed judgment a second time.

So there remained only the *bordereau,* concerning which the experts were not in agreement. It is said that in the council chamber the judges naturally were going to acquit. And, after that, how easy to understand the desperate obstinacy with which, in order to justify the conviction, they affirm today the existence of a secret overwhelming document, a document that cannot be shown, that legitimates everything, before which we must bow, an invisible and unknowable god. I deny this document; I deny it with all my might. A ridiculous document, yes, perhaps a document concerning little women, in which there is mention of a certain D—— who becomes too exacting; some husband doubtless, who thinks that they pay him too low a price for his wife. But a document of interest to the national defense the production of which would lead to a declaration of war tomorrow! No, no; it is a lie; and a lie the more odious and cynical because they lie with impunity, in such a way that no one can convict them of it. They stir up France; they hide themselves behind her legitimate emotion; they close mouths by disturbing hearts, by perverting minds. I know no greater civic crime.

These, then, *Monsieur le Président,* are the facts which explain how it was possible to commit a judicial error; and the moral proofs, the position of Dreyfus as a man of wealth, the absence of motive, this continual cry of innocence, complete the demonstration that he is a victim of the extraordinary fancies of Major du Paty de Clam, of his clerical surroundings, of that hunting down of the "dirty Jews" which disgraces our epoch.

And we come to the Esterhazy case. Three years have passed; many consciences remain profoundly disturbed, are anxiously seeking, and finally become convinced of the innocence of Dreyfus.

I shall not give the history of M. Scheurer-Kestner's doubts, which later became convictions. But, while he was investigating for himself, serious things were happening to the staff. Colonel Sandherr was dead, and Lieutenant-Colonel Picquart had succeeded him as Chief of the Bureau of Information. And it is in this capacity that the latter, in the exercise of his functions, came one day into possession of a letter-telegram addressed to Major Esterhazy by an agent of a foreign power. His plain duty was to open an investigation. It is certain that he never acted except at the command of his superiors. So he submitted his suspicions to his hierarchical superiors, first to General Gonse, then to General de Boisdeffre, then to General Billot, who had succeeded General Mercier as Minister of War. The famous Picquart documents, of which we have heard so much, were never anything but the Billot documents,—I mean, the documents collected by a subordinate for his minister, the documents which must be still in existence in the war department. The inquiries lasted from May to September, 1896, and here it must be squarely affirmed that General Gonse was convinced of Esterhazy's guilt, and that General de Boisdeffre and General Billot had no doubt that the famous *bordereau* was in Esterhazy's handwriting. Lieutenant-Colonel Picquart's investigation had ended in the certain establishment of this fact. But the emotion thereat was great, for Esterhazy's conviction inevitably involved a revision of the Dreyfus trial; and this the staff was determined to avoid at any cost.

Then there must have been a psychological moment, full of anguish. Note that General Billot was in no way compromised; he came freshly to the matter; he could bring out the truth. He did not dare, in terror, undoubtedly, of public opinion, and certainly fearful also of betraying the entire staff, General de Boisdeffre, General Gonse, to say nothing of their subordinates. Then there was but a minute of struggle between his conscience and what he believed to be the military interest. When this minute had passed, it was already too late. He was involved himself; he was compromised. And since then his responsibility has only grown; he has taken upon his shoulders the crime of others, he is as guilty as the others, he is more guilty than they, for it was in his power to do justice, and he did nothing. Understand this; for a year General Billot, Generals de Boisdeffre and Gonse have known that Dreyfus is innocent, and they have kept this dreadful thing to themselves. And these people sleep, and they have wives and children whom they love!

Colonel Picquart had done his duty as an honest man. He insisted in the presence of his superiors, in the name of justice; he even begged of them; he told them how impolitic were their delays, in view of the terrible storm which was gathering, and which would surely burst as soon as the truth should be known. Later there was the language that M. Scheurer-Kestner held likewise to General Billot, adjuring him in the name of patriotism to take the matter in hand, and not to allow it to be aggravated till it should become a public disaster. No, the crime had been committed; now the staff could not confess it. And Lieutenant-Colonel Picquart was sent on a mission; he was farther and farther removed, even to Tunis, where one day they even wanted to honor his bravery by charging him with a mission which would surely have led to his massacre in the district where the Marquis de Morès met his death. He was not in disgrace; Gen. Gonse was in friendly correspondence with him; but there are secrets which it does one no good to find out.

At Paris the truth went on, irresistibly, and we know in what way the expected storm broke out. M. Mathieu Dreyfus denounced Major Esterhazy as the real author of the *bordereau,* at the moment when M. Scheurer-Kestner was about to lodge a demand for a revision of the trial with the keeper of the seals. And it is here that Major Esterhazy appears. The evidence shows that at first he was dazed, ready for suicide or flight. Then suddenly he determines to brazen it out; he astonishes Paris by the violence of his attitude. The fact was that aid had come to him; he had received an anonymous letter warning him of the intrigues of his enemies; a mysterious woman had even disturbed herself at night to hand to him a document stolen from the staff, which would save him. And I cannot help seeing here again the hand of Lieutenant-Colonel du Paty de Clam, recognizing the expedients of his fertile imagination. His work, the guilt of Dreyfus, was in danger, and he was determined to defend it. A revision of the trial,—why, that meant the downfall of the newspaper novel, so extravagant, so tragic, with its abominable *dénouement* on Devil's Island. That would never do. Thenceforth there was to be a duel between Lieutenant-Colonel Picquart and Lieutenant-Colonel du Paty de Clam, the one with face uncovered, the other masked. Presently we shall meet them both in the presence of civil justice. At bottom it is always the staff defending itself, unwilling to confess its crime, the abomination of which is growing from hour to hour.

It has been wonderingly asked who were the protectors of Major Esterhazy. First, in the shadow, Lieutenant-Colonel du Paty de Clam, who devised everything, managed everything; his hand betrays itself in the ridiculous methods. Then there is General de Boisdeffre, General Gonse, General Billot himself, who are obliged to acquit the major, since they cannot permit the innocence of Dreyfus to be recognized, for, if they should, the war offices would fall under the weight of public contempt. And the beautiful result of this prodigious situation is that the one honest man in the case, Lieutenant-Colonel Picquart, who alone has done his duty, is to be the victim, the man to be derided and punished. O justice, what frightful despair grips the heart! They go so far as to say that he is a forger; that he manufactured the telegram, to ruin Esterhazy. But, in heaven's name, why? For what purpose? Show a motive. Is he, too, paid by the Jews? The pretty part of the story is that he himself was an anti-Semite. Yes, we are witnesses of this infamous spectacle,—the proclamation of the innocence of men ruined with debts and crimes, while honor itself, a man of stainless life, is stricken down. When a society reaches that point, it is beginning to rot.

There you have, then, *Monsieur le Président,* the Esterhazy case,—a guilty man to be declared innocent. We can follow the beautiful business, hour by hour, for the last two months. I abridge, for this is but the *résumé* of a story whose burning pages will some day be written at length. So we have seen General de Pellieux, and then Major Ravary, carrying on a rascally investigation whence knaves come transfigured and honest people sullied. Then they convened the council of war.

How could it have been expected that a council of war would undo what a council of war had done?

I say nothing of the choice, always possible, of the judges. Is not the superior idea of discipline, which is in the very blood of these soldiers, enough to destroy their power to do justice? Who says discipline says obedience. When the Minister of War, the great chief, has publicly established, amid the applause of the nation's representatives, the absolute authority of the thing judged, do you expect a council of war formally to contradict him? Hierarchically that is impossible. General Billot conveyed a suggestion to the judges by his declaration, and they passed judgment as they must face the cannon's mouth, without reasoning. The preconceived opinion that they took with them to their bench is evidently this: "Dreyfus has been condemned for the crime of treason by a council of war; then he is guilty, and we, a council of war, cannot declare him innocent. Now, we know that to recognize Esterhazy's guilt would be to proclaim the innocence of Dreyfus." Nothing could turn them from that course of reasoning.

They have rendered an iniquitous verdict which will weigh forever upon our councils of war, which will henceforth tinge with suspicion all their decrees. The first council of war may have been lacking in comprehension; the second is necessarily criminal. Its excuse, I repeat, is that the supreme chief had spoken, declaring the thing judged unassailable, sacred and superior to men, so that inferiors could say naught to the contrary. They talk to us of the honor of the Army; they want us to love it, to respect it. Ah! certainly, yes, the Army which would rise at the first threat, which would defend French soil; that Army is the whole people, and we have for it nothing but tenderness and respect. But it is not a question of that Army, whose dignity is our special desire, in our need of justice. It is the sword that is in question; the master that they may give us tomorrow. And piously kiss the sword hilt, the god? No!

I have proved it, moreover; the Dreyfus case was the case of the war offices, a staff officer, accused by his staff comrades, convicted under the pressure of the Chiefs of Staff. Again I say, he cannot come back innocent,

unless all the staff is guilty. Consequently the war offices, by all imaginable means, by press campaigns, by communications, by influences, have
covered Esterhazy only to ruin Dreyfus a second time. Ah! with what a
sweep the Republican Government should clear away this band of Jesuits,
as General Billot himself calls them! Where is the truly strong and
wisely patriotic minister who will dare to reshape and renew all? How
many of the people I know are trembling with anguish in view of a possible war, knowing in what hands lies the national defense! And what a
nest of base intrigues, gossip, and dilapidation has this sacred asylum,
entrusted with the fate of the country, become! We are frightened by
the terrible light thrown upon it by the Dreyfus case, this human sacrifice of an unfortunate, of a "dirty Jew." Ah! what a mixture of madness
and folly, of crazy fancies, of low police practices, of inquisitorial and
tyrannical customs, the good pleasure of a few persons in gold lace, with
their boots on the neck of the nation, cramming back into its throat its
cry of truth and justice, under the lying and sacrilegious pretext of the
raison d'État!

And another of their crimes is that they have accepted the support
of the unclean press, have suffered themselves to be championed by all
the knavery of Paris, so that now we witness knavery's insolent triumph
in the downfall of right and of simple probity. It is a crime to have
accused of troubling France those who wish to see her generous, at the
head of the free and just nations, when they themselves are hatching the
impudent conspiracy to impose error, in the face of the entire world.
It is a crime to mislead opinion, to utilize for a task of death this
opinion that they have perverted to the point of delirium. It is a crime
to poison the minds of the little and the humble, to exasperate the passions of reaction and intolerance, while seeking shelter behind odious
anti-Semitism, of which the great liberal France of the rights of man
will die, if she is not cured. It is a crime to exploit patriotism for works
of hatred, and, finally, it is a crime to make the sword the modern god,
when all human science is at work on the coming temple of truth and
justice.

This truth, this justice, for which we have so ardently longed,—how
distressing it is to see them thus buffeted, more neglected and more obscured. I have a suspicion of the fall that must have occurred in the
soul of M. Scheurer-Kestner, and I really believe that he will finally feel
remorse that he did not act in a revolutionary fashion, on the day of
interpellation in the Senate, by thoroughly ventilating the whole matter,
to topple everything over. He has been the highly honest man, the man
of loyal life, and he thought that the truth was sufficient unto itself, especially when it should appear as dazzling as the open day. Of what use

to overturn everything, since soon the sun would shine? And it is for this confident serenity that he is now so cruelly punished. And the same is the case of Lieutenant-Colonel Picquart, who, moved by a feeling of lofty dignity, has been unwilling to publish General Gonse's letters. These scruples honor him the more because, while he remained respectful of discipline, his superiors heaped mud upon him, working up the case against him themselves, in the most unexpected and most outrageous fashion. Here are two victims, two worthy people, two simple hearts, who have trusted God, while the devil was at work. And in the case of Lieutenant-Colonel Picquart we have seen even this ignoble thing,—a French tribunal, after suffering the reporter in the case to arraign publicly a witness and accuse him of every crime, closing its doors as soon as this witness has been introduced to explain and defend himself. I say that is one crime more, and that this crime will awaken the universal conscience. Decidedly, military tribunals have a singular idea of justice.

Such, then, is the simple truth, *Monsieur le Président,* and it is frightful. It will remain a stain upon your presidency. I suspect that you are powerless in this matter,—that you are the prisoner of the constitution and of your environment. You have nonetheless a man's duty, upon which you will reflect, and which you will fulfill. Not indeed that I despair, the least in the world, of triumph. I repeat with more vehement certainty; truth is on the march, and nothing can stop it. Today sees the real beginning of the Affair, since not until today have the positions been clear: on one hand, the guilty, who do not want the light; on the other, the doers of justice, who will give their lives to get it. When truth is buried in the earth, it accumulates there, and assumes so mighty an explosive power that, on the day when it bursts forth, it hurls everything into the air. We shall see if they have not just made preparations for the most resounding of disasters, yet to come.

But this letter is long, *Monsieur le Président,* and it is time to finish.

I accuse Lieutenant-Colonel du Paty de Clam of having been the diabolical workman of judicial error,—unconsciously, I am willing to believe,—and of having then defended his calamitous work, for three years, by the most guilty machinations.

I accuse General Mercier of having made himself an accomplice, at least through weakness of mind, in one of the greatest iniquities of the century.

I accuse General Billot of having had in his hands certain proofs of the innocence of Dreyfus, and of having stifled them; of having rendered himself guilty of this crime of *lèse-humanité* and *lèse-justice* for a political purpose, and to save the compromised staff.

I accuse General de Boisdeffre and General Gonse of having made themselves accomplices in the same crime, one undoubtedly through clerical passion, the other perhaps through that *esprit de corps* which makes the war offices the Holy Ark, unassailable.

I accuse General de Pellieux and Major Ravary of having conducted a rascally inquiry,—I mean by that a monstrously partial inquiry, of which we have, in the report of the latter, an imperishable monument of naïve audacity.

I accuse the three experts in handwriting, Belhomme, Varinard, and Couard, of having made lying and fraudulent reports, unless a medical examination should declare them afflicted with diseases of the eye and of the mind.

I accuse the war offices of having carried on in the press, particularly in *L'Éclair* and in *L'Écho de Paris,* an abominable campaign, to mislead opinion and cover up their faults.

I accuse, finally, the first council of war of having violated the law by condemning an accused person on the strength of a secret document, and I accuse the second council of war of having covered this illegality, in obedience to orders, in committing in its turn the judicial crime of knowingly acquitting a guilty man.

In preferring these charges, I am not unaware that I lay myself liable under Articles 30 and 31 of the press law of July 29, 1881, which punishes defamation. And it is wilfully that I expose myself thereto.

As for the people whom I accuse, I do not know them, I have never seen them, I entertain against them no feeling of revenge or hatred. They are to me simple entities, spirits of social ill-doing. And the act that I perform here is nothing but a revolutionary measure to hasten the explosion of truth and justice.

I have but one passion, the passion for the light, in the name of humanity which has suffered so much, and which is entitled to happiness. My fiery protest is simply the cry of my soul. Let them dare, then, to bring me into the Assize Court, and let the investigation take place in the open day.

I await it.

Accept, *Monsieur le Président,* the assurance of my profound respect.

ÉMILE ZOLA

All Paris was shaken by this passionate indictment. Hundreds of news vendors distributed the paper, even in the more remote districts of Paris. Zola's story of the syndicate of traitors whose aim it was to ruin an innocent man created a sensation. "It was a breast bared," wrote one observer, "an indignant conscience calling other consciences to its aid." To Anatole France it was "a moment in the conscience of mankind." A revolutionary word was thrown into the midst of intrigue and lies and forgeries.

In his extraordinary letter, Zola had made it clear that he was wilfully exposing himself to a charge of defamation. He was quite right. Within five days that charge was made against him and Alexandre Perrenx, sub-editor of *L'Aurore*. They were summoned to appear before the Court of Assizes on February 7, 1898.

An Eyewitness at the Zola Trial

"The question will not be put!"

Maurice Paléologue, An Intimate Journal of the Dreyfus Case, *trans. Eric Mosbacher (New York: Criterion Books, 1957), pp. 130–140. Courtesy of Criterion Books.*

George Maurice Paléologue (1859–1944), expert in the Ministry of Foreign Affairs, was concerned with the Dreyfus case from its very beginnings. He was experienced as translator of various documents on the case. Later, representing the Foreign Office, he was to testify at the reading *in camera* at the Rennes court-martial, when he commented on some 400 documents by then assembled in the Dreyfus *dossier*. His secret diary on the Dreyfus case was published posthumously and translated into English in 1957.

Paléologue made several brief visits to the courtroom of the Zola trial. Entries in his diary reveal the highly charged emotional atmosphere in which the trial took place. Paléologue "re-worked" his diary in later life to improve its literary form; for this reason some historians are inclined to doubt its accuracy. Especially interesting is his account of the chief actors in the drama.

Monday, February 7, 1898

Today was the first day of the trial of Zola arising out of his letter to the President of the Republic entitled *"J'Accuse!"*

The president of the Assize Court is Delegorgue; the prosecution is in the hands of Van Cassel, the Advocate-General. Zola is defended by Maître Labori; and Maître Albert Clemenceau, the brother of the politician, is appearing for Perrenx, the manager of the *Aurore*.

The whole hearing was taken up with the usual formalities: selection of the jury by lot, calling of witnesses, reading of preliminary documents, etc.

A journalist who came from the Palais de Justice told me:

"You can imagine that the court was crammed, even to the window

sills. And what passion there was on people's faces! What looks of
hatred when certain eyes met! Outside, the *Libre Parole* gangs applauded the generals and hissed the Dreyfusards. If the police don't take
stricter measures tomorrow, there will be violence."

"Did you see Esterhazy?"

"Oh, yes, I saw him. . . . All eyes were fixed on him, but nobody
shook hands with him. The officers had actually been forbidden to talk
to him. He wandered alone between the groups, looking haggard and
ferocious. What a fine type of rogue!"

Tuesday, February 8, 1898

Second day of the Zola trial.

Casimir-Périer appeared and said: "I have come here only out of respect for the court. I cannot in fact take the oath to speak the whole
truth, for if I were asked about events that took place while I was President of the Republic, silence would be imposed on me by the Constitutional principle of non-responsibility."

During the evening Casimir-Périer telephoned me.

"I want to tell you that everything passed off very well," he said. "My
'Constitutional' excuse roused no protests. . . . On the way out the
Dreyfusards applauded me, which was probably an indirect way of demonstrating against my successor. . . . I've just been told that there have
been terrible brawls in the Rue de Harlay and the Place Dauphine.
When Yves Guyot, Reinach, and Zola left the Palais, they were set on
by a huge crowd yelling: 'Into the water with the traitors!' and 'Death
to Jews!' The Prefect of Police had to intervene in person to rescue
them."

Wednesday, February 16, 1898

The Zola trial has been going for nine days, but it is far from over.
I made three brief visits to the court in order to have at least a picture
of it in my mind.

As soon as the case opened, the court ruled the proceedings would be
restricted to consideration of the complaint by the Minister of War, that
is to say the alleged libel of the members of the court that tried Esterhazy.
The Advocate-General warned the accused and their counsel that "we
shall not under any pretext whatever permit a reopening of the question
of the verdict of 1894; the *res judicata* will be respected. If any attempt
is made insidiously to provoke a reopening of the case, the court will
not lend itself to it."

That is what has been done. Whenever the lawyers asked a leading
question, the president promptly stopped them in the driest tone with

the peremptory formula: "The question will not be put." I doubt
whether the annals of the Restoration or the Second Empire contain an
example of a political trial in which the Government's orders were more
rigorously carried out.

All the chief figures in the drama appeared on the scene:

Zola, nervous, sullen, sheepish, letting fall clumsy phrases such as:
"I don't know the law, and I don't want to know it" or, "I have gained
by my works more victories than the generals who insult me; I have
carried the French language to the ends of the earth!"

General Mercier, haughty, phlegmatic, severe, precise, superciliously
entrenched in awareness of his infallibility, hurling at the jury this terrible parting shot: "We have not the right to reopen the 1894 trial. But
if we had to return to it, and I were asked for my word as a soldier, I
should swear once more that Dreyfus was a traitor and was rightly and
legally convicted!"

Mathieu Dreyfus and his sister-in-law, *Mme. Lucie Dreyfus,* both very
dignified, inspiring everybody with compassion, or at any rate respect.

General de Boisdeffre, who in the public eye is the embodiment of
responsibility for the national defense and the secrets of the Russian alliance, very distinguished in manner, calm without stiffness, neatly evad-
ing all dangerous questions and concluding his testimony, like General
Mercier, with this solemn declaration: "In 1894 there was no doubt in
my mind about the guilt of Captain Dreyfus. Innumerable pieces of evidence that have since come to us have made my certainty unshakable."

Trarieux, the former Keeper of the Seals, a man of the greatest integrity, almost Jansenist in his austerity, a fervent advocate of reopening
the case, but too naïve in appearance, too emphatic, too verbose, expressing himself only in commonplaces, and thus losing all hold on his
hearers.

Colonel du Paty de Clam, pretentious, monocle in eye, well set-up,
abrupt in speech, and with mechanical gestures; a disturbing character,
with a morbid mentality, a shadowy and unhinged imagination, a strange
mixture of fanaticism, extravagance, and folly; it would not be surprising
to find him in "Tales of Hoffman."

General Gonse, a worthy man, a glutton for work, but weak, timorous,
and indecisive . . . and really too stupid.

Lieutenant-Colonel Henry, solid, sturdy, and thickset, with florid
cheeks and open features concealing plenty of cunning beneath his rude,
frank exterior.

Major Lauth, tall, slender, frigid, reticent, extremely intelligent, se-
cretive, the intimate collaborator, not to say the chief, of his chief, Henry.

Lieutenant-Colonel Picquart, tall and slim, with a rather stiff distinction, high forehead, eyes rather difficult to catch between his close eyebrows, expressing himself precisely, but obviously embarrassed in his behavior by the ferocious hatred of his comrades and perhaps even more by the delirious praise lavished on him by the fanatics of Dreyfusism, torn between the duties of professional discipline, on the one hand, and the risks of open rebellion, on the other, rather like a priest who, having gone astray in a theological controversy, felt hovering over his head the thunderbolts of anathema and excommunication.

General de Pellieux, superbly bold and plucky and a fine fencer, having not the slightest shadow of doubt about Dreyfus's guilt, and putting forth in the service of his belief the ardor, eloquence, and intrepidity of a believer testifying to his creed.

The archivist Gribelin, gentle, modest, self-effacing, and perfect servant, monastic in his docility, *perinde ac cadaver.* He could say a lot if he wanted to, for all the machinations of the intelligence department pass through his hands; it is he who registers documents, classifies them, keeps the files, makes payments, holds the keys of the ark and the tabernacle.

I nearly forgot the *handwriting experts,* absurd creatures incapable of agreeing on the most elementary deductions, flinging their extraordinary theories in one another's faces and running down and abusing one another like Molière's doctors. But one of them deserves special mention—Bertillon, who is a madman, a maniac, armed with the crafty, obstinate, and powerful dialectic that is the characteristic of interpretative psychosis.

As for the proceedings themselves, they are nothing but a long sequence of altercations and violent speeches, constantly interrupted by the automatic refrain of the president of the court: "The question will not be put!"

Thursday, February 17, 1898

According to police information which reached the War Ministry yesterday, the Assize Court jury, exhausted by the interminable arguments, in the course of which, moreover, they felt that the truth was eluding them, were inclining to acquit Zola.

General de Pellieux, who has definitely become the spokesman of the General Staff, accordingly felt that the hour had come to strike, and strike home.

On the pretext of desiring to supplement his previous evidence, he suddenly leaped toward the bar and declared in ringing tones:

"Dreyfus's crime is established by one piece of irrefutable evidence, which I have seen and held in my own hands. It is a letter addressed by a foreign military attaché to his colleague in another country. You will guess who it is of whom I speak. This is what the letter contains: 'I learn that there is to be an interpellation in the Chamber on the Dreyfus case. Never admit the dealings we have had with this Jew.' . . . I appeal to General de Boisdeffre to confirm what I have just said!"

This disclosure let loose such a violent tumult, such a din of applause, on the one hand, and anger, on the other, that the court adjourned until tomorrow to hear General de Boisdeffre.

Friday, February 18, 1898

At half-past two this afternoon, on the Quai d'Orsay on my way to the Ministry, I saw in front of me Lieutenant-Colonel Henry, walking in the direction of the Esplanade des Invalides. For a moment I was not sure that it was he, for he looked different from his usual self. He was walking slowly, hesitantly, and his back was bent.

I overtook him and tapped him on the shoulder. He turned abruptly. His face frightened me. He was hollow-cheeked and pale, and his eyes were drawn and feverish.

"What's the matter with you, my dear Colonel? Are you ill? You look bad!"

"Oh, I had an attack of my Tonkin fever again last night—a terrible attack. The result is that I can hardly stand up. But I had to go to the Assize Court, where General de Boisdeffre has just confirmed General de Pellieux's evidence. I left immediately afterward; I was feeling too ill to stay any longer. Now I'm going home to put myself to bed."

"Would you like me to walk a little way with you?"

"Certainly! But I shan't be able to tell you much. I'm feeling terrible, and my head is bursting."

Nevertheless it was he who started the conversation.

"What a day's hearing it was yesterday!" he said. "By . . . ! I haven't got over it yet!"

"You're referring to the Pellieux incident?"

"I certainly am! What Pellieux did was absurd! Documents as secret as that should not be disclosed in public."

"What? Do you mean to say General de Pellieux did not consult General Gonse or General de Boisdeffre before carrying out his *coup de théâtre?*"

"No! What happened was this. During an adjournment, General de Pellieux called Gribelin and said to him: 'You have a good memory, Gribelin? . . . Then repeat to me Panizzardi's letter to Schwartzkoppen —the letter that ends with the words: "Never admit that we have had dealings with this Jew."' Gribelin repeated the letter to him word for word, without suspecting the use the general was going to make of it.

Then the court resumed, and without consulting anybody, General de Pellieux asked permission to supplement his evidence. I was sitting next to General Gonse; we looked at each other in amazement. What on earth could Pellieux be going to say now? He advanced to the bar and repeated the letter, word for word. Gonse whispered into my ear: 'There! You heard that? What a fool!' As for myself, it took my breath away. . . . I'm sure it was that that gave me my attack of fever."

By this time we had passed the Boulevard de la Tour-Maubourg and were starting to walk down the Avenue de la Motte-Picquet. I said to Henry:

"You genuinely have no doubt about the authenticity of the Panizzardi letter?"

"None whatever."

"But you remember Tornielli's recent categorical and official statement that if Dreyfus is mentioned either by name or by any other description in a letter attributed to Panizzardi, that letter is bogus."

"But I've told you often enough that the authenticity of the document is demonstrated by a large number of similar documents!"

We had now reached the corner of the Avenue Duquesne, where Henry lives. There I left him to go to the Ministry.

Nisard, to whom I promptly reported this conversation, shut his eyes for a moment, as he does when he is concentrating his admirable intuitive faculties. Then, looking at me with that sharp look of his, he said:

"That document is bogus."

Clash Between Henry and Picquart

". . . Colonel Picquart is lying when he says that."

Le procès Zola devant la Cour d'Assises de la Seine et la Cour de Cassation (7–23 février et 31 mars, 2 avril 1890), 2 vols. (Paris: Siècle et Stock), entry dated February 12, 1898. Translated by the editor.

Picquart was the real prisoner in the dock at the Zola trial. He had aroused the contempt, anger, and fear of the General Staff, precisely because he would not do what he was supposed to do to protect the closed world of the Army. Henry was sent to the trial to question Picquart in a long cross-examination, during the course of which the latter had little trouble in gaining the advantage. Henry attempted to show that Picquart had been indiscreet in revealing "secrets of office" to the Dreyfusards. Angered by the course of the examination, Henry lost his temper. The following exchange took place during the session of February 12, 1898.

Henry: I say that my declaration is correct in every detail and I even say that Colonel Picquart is lying when he says that.

Picquart: (raising his arm and suddenly allowing it to fall) You do not have the right to say that!

The President: You are obviously not in agreement with one another.

Maître Clemenceau: Allow me, Mr. President, have I heard you correctly? You said: "Not in agreement!" Now this is the second time in this session that an offense has taken place. One witness is insulted by another, and the President has merely said: "The witnesses are not in agreement with one another."

The President: You can assume anything you wish.

Labori: Because Colonel Picquart after the attack to which he took exception heard only: "You are obviously not in agreement with one another," I demand that he be allowed to speak without interruption.

Picquart: I should like to make a statement to the jury concerning the meaning of all this. . . . Gentlemen of the jury, you have seen here how these people, Colonel Henry, Major Lauth, and the archivist Gribelin, have made shameful accusations against me. Yesterday you heard how Major Lauth without proof made the serious charge that I had "smuggled out" the *petit bleu*. Now, gentlemen of the jury, do you know why all this took place?

You will understand, when you come to know about it, how these people took part in the matter that is closely related to the Esterhazy affair. Perhaps it was with good intentions, as I am willing to grant, that Colonel Henry and the archivist Gribelin, supported by Colonel du Paty de Clam and guided by General Gonse, who had received from the deceased Colonel Sandherr a kind of testament, regarded it as their duty to defend this matter, which concerned the honor of the Intelligence Department against all attacks. Colonel Sandherr, already at the time of the matter, had been felled by a serious illness, from which he died. We are concerned here with the legacy of a critically sick man. The matter was handled by the Intelligence Department conscientiously because it believed itself to be in possession of the truth.

I had other ideas when I headed the Intelligence unit. Because I had doubts, I wanted to be absolutely clear in my mind, and I believed that there were better ways to defend a cause than by blind belief, which is often unfounded, in its truth.

Gentlemen of the jury, that is it, I don't know, a long time, several months, which is the cause of the insults which have been made on me by a press paid to spread libels and false accusations. . . . For months now I have been in a most unenviable position for an officer, for my honor has been besmirched without my having an opportunity to defend myself. Tomorrow, perhaps, I shall be thrown out of the Army, which I love and to which I have given 25 years of my life. That has not prevented me, after it became clear to me what my course of action must be, from finding the way to truth and justice. I have done this because I believed that in this way I was performing a great service for my country and for the Army. In this way I have come to the conclusion that as a decent human being I had to fulfill my duty. That is all I have to say.

On his honor as an officer, Picquart could not very well accept the designation of "liar" without seeking satisfaction. He had already refused to cross swords with Esterhazy; moreover, the Chief of Staff, fearing popular sentiment if Esterhazy were to be defeated, refused to sanction the encounter. But in the courtroom of the Zola trial Henry was able to win the undeserved honor of a duel with Picquart.

Summation by Georges Clemenceau

"Your verdict, gentlemen, will not decide our fates as much as your own."

Le procès Zola, *pp. 336–355.*

Actually, the trial was a judicial farce. The Government restricted its case to three passages in the *"J'Accuse"* letter, all relating to the court-martial. President Delegorgue, aware that both the Government and the General Staff wanted to shield certain key figures, suppressed any attempts of the defense to introduce new testimony. The presiding justice made legal history by his repeated remark in favor of the prosecution: "The question will not be put." In this atmosphere, covered with a smog of violence and hatred, Zola found his defense to be handicapped.

Georges Clemenceau, political radical and journalistic critic, had behind him a long, tempestuous career. A firebrand of mordant wit and unflagging energy, he had been the editor who published Zola's accusing letter. Originally, he had believed in Dreyfus's guilt, but by this time he was at the van of those defending the condemned officer. Following is Clemenceau's concluding speech to the jury at the end of the Zola trial.

Gentlemen of the jury, we are nearing the end of this exciting trial. After the magnificent summing up of the young orator, whom we all have applauded, I have no demonstration to add, and I should reproach myself for keeping you here longer, were it not absolutely necessary. M. Labori has told you the story of a great tragedy. Far away a man is in confinement who perhaps is the worst criminal conceivable, and who perhaps is a martyr, a victim of human fallibility. All the powers that are established to secure justice M. Labori has pictured to you in combination against justice. And he has appealed to you for the revision of a great trial. Yes, it is a great drama that has been developed in your presence. You, the judges, have seen the actors appear at this bar, and, after you shall have judged, you, in turn, will be judged by the public opinion of France. It was to obtain the verdict of that public opinion that M. Émile Zola voluntarily committed the act that brings him before you. After having reviewed with M. Zola all the phases of this drama, there remains still one thing to be done,—to try to free our minds from all impressions, and to inquire what we have thought and felt in order to determine our judgment.

To that end, gentlemen, would it not be well first to go back to the state of mind in which all Frenchmen, without exception, were when ex-Captain Dreyfus was convicted unanimously by a council of war. And, if you will permit me, I will begin my brief explanations by reading an article of mine with which I am confronted today, and which I wrote on the morrow of the conviction of Dreyfus. It seems to me that at that time all Frenchmen must have thought as I did, and, when I shall have shown that, I will inquire how a minority of Frenchmen have arrived at a different opinion. Here, gentlemen, is what I wrote on the day after the conviction of Dreyfus. The article is entitled "The Traitor."

Unanimously a council of war has declared Captain Alfred Dreyfus guilty of treason. The crime is so frightful that there has been an effort to entertain doubt to the very last moment. That a man brought up in the religion of the flag, a soldier honored with the protection of the secrets of the national defense, should betray,—frightful word,—should deliver to the foreigner all that can help him in his preparations for a new invasion,—that seemed impossible. How could a man be found to do such a thing? How can a human being so disgrace himself that he can expect only to be spat upon by those whom he has served? Such a man must have no relatives, no wife, no child, no love of anything, no tie of humanity, or even of animality,— for the animal in the herd instinctively defends his own. He must have been an unclean soul, an abject heart. Nobody wanted to believe it. Every chance for doubt was eagerly seized. Then they caviled; they calculated all the chances of error; they

constructed romances on the bits of information that reached
the public ear. They wanted complete light. They protested in
advance against closed doors.

In such trials, it must be admitted, publicity, with the comments that it involves, is liable to aggravate the evil that treason
does. The liberty to say everything, undeterred by any consideration of public order, may even be of advantage to the defence.

You see, gentlemen, that I then recognized that there are circumstances
when closed doors may be necessary. I have not changed my opinion. I
said that closed doors might even be favorable to the defense, for then
the defense would have the liberty to say everything; but on one condition,—that all the documents should be submitted to it. You know
that that condition was not fulfilled. I continue.

Consequently those who had most earnestly called for a public trial accepted without protest the statement of the president
of the council of war that there are interests higher than all
personal interests.

The trial lasted four days. The accused was defended by one
of the first lawyers at the Paris bar. By the unanimous decision
of his judges, Alfred Dreyfus has been sentenced to the maximum penalty. Such a decree is not rendered without a poignant
examination of conscience, and, if any doubt could have remained for the benefit of the accused, we should surely have
found a trace of it in the sentence. But the judge has said:
Death! But for Article 5 of the constitution of 1848, which abolished the death penalty for political offenses, Dreyfus would be
shot tomorrow.

Here a formidable question arises.

Can the crime of Dreyfus be likened to a political crime? I
answer boldly, No. Men entertaining different conceptions of
the interests of the common country may struggle with all their
might for a monarchy or for a republic, for despotism or for
liberty: they may struggle against each other; they may kill
each other; but they are not to be confounded with the public
enemy who betrays the very thing that each of them pretends to
defend. How is it that jurists have been able to establish an
identity between two acts which contradict each other? I do
not know, and I do not congratulate them on their discovery.

Undoubtedly I am as firmly opposed as ever to the death
penalty. But the public can never be made to understand why,

a few weeks ago, an unfortunate boy of twenty was shot for having thrown a button from his cloak at the head of the president of the council of war, whereas the traitor Dreyfus soon will start for *L'Île Nou,* where the garden of Candide awaits him. Yesterday, at Bordeaux, the soldier Brevert appeared before the council of war of la Gironde for having broken certain articles in the barracks. At the trial he threw his cap at the representative of the Government. Death. And for the man who helps the enemy to invade his country, who summons the Bavarians of Bazeilles to fresh massacres, who paves the way for incendiaries, and land stealers, and executioners of the country, a peaceful life given up to the joys of cocoanut-tree cultivation. There is nothing so revolting.

Truly, I wish that the death penalty might disappear from our codes. But who does not understand that the military code will of necessity be its last asylum? As long as armies shall exist, it probably will be difficult to govern them otherwise than by a law of violence. But, if, in the scale of punishments, the death penalty is the last degree, it seems to me that it must be reserved for the greatest crime, which, without any doubt, is treason. To kill a dazed unfortunate who insults his judges is madness when we allow a tranquil life to the traitor. Since unfortunately there are beings who are capable of treason, this crime must be made to appear in the eyes of all as the most execrable that can be committed. Unhappily, in our present state of mind, the sinister incident which has so deeply stirred opinion is for many but a pretext for declamation. It is so convenient to put the trumpet to the mouth and assume the attitudes of a disheveled patriot, while having treasures of indulgence for generals who indulge openly in anti-patriotic language. We were not capable of shooting Bazaine. A marshal of France who had the highest duties toward the Army of which he was the commander-in-chief pardoned the traitor, and relieved him of the penalty of degradation, after which they allowed him to escape. What excuse had he,—an army commander who had betrayed his army to the enemy? Strange patriotism that permitted this scandal. No less strange the tolerance that recently protected the abominable language used by another army commander in talking to two reporters.

Alfred Dreyfus is a traitor, and I offer no soldier the insult of putting him on a level with this wretch. But what weakness in regard to the high officer; and what severity toward a mere act of insolence before the council of war. Strike the traitor, but let the discipline be equal for all. To tolerate disorder in high places would end in the same result as treason. The privilege of some causes the revolt of others. That the Army may be united and strong, there must be one law for all. That was formerly one of the promises of the Republic. We await its realization.

Gentlemen, I told you just now that I believe that I then expressed the sentiments which animated all Frenchmen; and yet, when today they confront me with this article, I pretend that it contains my complete justification. What! We are to be suspected of desiring to outrage the Army, when, on the day when it declared its verdict, we showed confidence in its justice? Yes, a council of war unanimously decided that a man was guilty of treason. How could Frenchmen, on the day of the verdict, knowing nothing of the facts, doubt that the council had done its duty?

But, after the long, laborious, and luminous argument of M. Labori, have we not occasion to ask whether, since the day when I wrote this article, serious events have not occurred? These events M. Labori had put before you. He has discussed them, and it now seems to me impossible that your minds should not be flooded with a light almost complete. For, gentlemen, I confess that my ambition, since French opinion was unanimous on the day of the verdict, is that French opinion may be unanimous also in admitting that the most honest judges may have been mistaken, seeing that they are men.

Yes, gentlemen, many events have taken place since 1894. Did we then know the *bordereau?* Did we know the secret document of *L'Éclair?* Did I know of them when I wrote the article that I have just read? Did I know that a secret document had been communicated to the judges in the council chamber? I do not know, gentlemen, whether M. Labori has sufficiently insisted on this idea, but it is of a nature to so strike the opinion of all men, without exception, that I ask myself how we can help arriving at a unanimous opinion concerning it.

You are told that a document was communicated in the council chamber. Do you realize what that means? It means that we judge a man, condemn him, brand him, dishonor his name forever, that of his wife, that of his children, that of his father, the names of all whom he loves, on the strength of a document that has not been shown to him. Gentlemen, who among you would not revolt at the thought of being condemned under such conditions? Who among you would not cry out to us to ask justice, if, dragged before the courts of his country after a mere pretense at examination, after a purely formal trial, his honor and his life were to be passed upon by judges assembled in his absence to condemn him on the strength of a document with which he had not been made acquainted? Is there one of us that would willingly submit to such a verdict? If that is true, gentlemen, I say that it devolves upon all of us to see that such a trial should be reviewed. I do not care to consider at this moment whether or not there are any reasons for presuming innocence. I have listened to M. Labori's argument, and I do not conceal from you the fact that I am now inclined to think that there are strong reasons for believing Dreyfus innocent. I cannot affirm it absolutely; I have not the authority. And you, gentlemen, have not to pronounce upon the innocence of Dreyfus. All that you say is that there has been a verdict which was not rendered legally. In this case, in truth, form is of more importance than substance. When the right of a single individual is injured, the right of all is in peril,—the right of the nation itself. We love our country. That love no one monopolizes. But our country is not simply the territory on which we live. It is the home of right and justice, to which all men are attached, however different their opinions, be they friends or enemies. It is the common hearth of all, a guarantee of security, of equal justice for all. You cannot conceive of country without justice. The governors who represent it, the judges, the soldiers, however loyal they may be, are liable to err, and the whole question here is whether in this instance they have committed an error.

When I wrote the article which I have read to you, I knew nothing of the secret document first spoken of by *L'Éclair*. I was unacquainted with the *bordereau* reproduced by *Le Matin;* I had not heard the testimony of M. Salle, or its confirmation by M. Demange; I had been furnished no key to the reticence of General Mercier; I had not been informed of the prejudices of Colonel Sandherr against the Jews. [Murmurs of protest.] I am surprised to hear these protests. I have no desire to say anything that can wound anybody. A man came to this bar who, I regret to say, left the courtroom amid the silence of all. I wish that he had been hailed with our unanimous applause. I refer to M. Lalance, former protesting deputy in the *Reichstag,* who carried into the German assembly the protests of French patriotism. He came here to tell us that Colonel Sandherr, whom I never had the honor to know, and against whom I have absolutely nothing to say, had prejudices against the Jews,— prejudices which he shares with a very great number of very honest people. Therefore I have no intention of outraging Colonel Sandherr. I simply cite the testimony of a witness.

The Judge: M. Clemenceau, will you turn toward the jury?

M. Clemenceau: I beg you to excuse me, *Monsieur le Président;* I do so willingly. M. Lalance told us that in Alsace patriotic Jews voted for the protesting bishops, which honors them. He told us that at a military manifestation—at Bussang, I believe—a Jew wept, and that Colonel Sandherr, on his attention being called to it, remarked: "I distrust those tears." Now, it was Colonel Sandherr who prepared the Dreyfus trial.

I had no knowledge of the accusation against Major Esterhazy founded on this frightful similarity of handwriting; I had no knowledge of the indictment of Dreyfus; I did not know of the discovery by Colonel Picquart of a dispatch found in the basket where the *bordereau* was found, torn as the *bordereau* was torn, without a stamp as the *bordereau* was without a stamp, and which yet was deemed of no force against Major Esterhazy, while against Dreyfus so much was made of the *bordereau.* And yet, gentlemen, this dispatch contains the name of Major Esterhazy in full.

I had no knowledge of the first investigation made by General de Pellieux, which was concluded without any expert examination of handwritings, General de Pellieux alleging that M. Mathieu Dreyfus offered no proofs, although the only proof possible was to be looked for in the expert examination of handwritings. I had no knowledge of the examination conducted by Major Ravary. I did not know that Colonel Picquart had insisted in vain that an inquiry should be opened with a view to ascertaining who conveyed to *L'Éclair* the information concerning the secret document. I did not know that Colonel Picquart had asked an investigation concerning the "Speranza" and "Blanche" forgeries, and that this investigation was refused, so that he was finally obliged to carry the matter into the civil courts. I did not know, and I could not know, that the proceeding instigated against a man accused of treason by the chief of the bureau of information was going to be turned into a proceeding against this chief of the bureau of information. I could not foresee that a man of the importance of General de Pellieux would come to tell us that the closing of the doors was useless. I could not suppose that the archives of the Minister of War were so kept that the retention of a file of documents by M. Teyssonnières could pass unnoticed. I did not know that men would be struck on the threshold of this palace for shouting "Long live the Republic!" And there were many other things of which I was unaware. How could I have divined that a secret document, the document which they did not dare to show to M. Demange, the document that General Billot refused to show to his old friend, M. Scheurer-Kestner, could be stolen from the most secret drawer of the minister of war, and carried about Paris in the hands of a veiled lady, finally falling into the hands of a man suspected of treason? How could

I have believed that a man suspected of treason, or even any man whomsoever, you, or I, or anybody, could present himself with impunity at the war offices, in possession of a secret document of which the chief of the bureau of information was supposed to have sole care? And, finally, how could I believe, when they tell us that we insult the Army, that I should witness here the extension of a welcome to the only man who, beyond the possibility of dispute, has insulted France and the Army, Major Esterhazy? It matters little that he denies a letter whose authenticity will be proved later. I take those which he admits. They are sufficient, and they prove beyond a doubt that Major Esterhazy, who still wears the uniform—I know not why—is an abominable insulter of France and of the Army. I could not suspect that I should hear, as he left this courtroom, cries of "Long live Esterhazy!" and "Long live the Army!" Shall I offend honorable officers here present, if I say to them that it is high time to distinguish the Army from Major Esterhazy?

M. Labori just now shouted: "Long live the Army!" Why should we not shout: "Long live the Army!" when three-fourths of us here, lawyers or not, are soldiers. Yes, "Long live the Army!" but by what aberration of mind, when a man speaks of the French Army as Major Esterhazy has spoken of it, do the people dare to associate the two cries: "Long live Esterhazy!" and "Long live the Army!"

But, gentlemen, we have seen a still more unexpected spectacle. Two eminent commanders of the French Army, General de Pellieux and General de Boisdeffre, having come here, and, perhaps without fully realizing what it means, have used threatening language. The attorney general, in his summing up, recalling the fact that M. Zola had said that the council of war had condemned in obedience to orders, asked: "Where are the orders? Show us the orders." Well, I show them to you, Monsieur Attorney General. They have come to this bar in uniform, and have said: "I order you to convict M. Émile Zola." And I do not suppose that M. Émile Zola thought for a moment that some one appeared before the council of war and said to the judges: "I order you to condemn Dreyfus. I order you to acquit Esterhazy." There are different ways of saying a thing, and the state of mind of the speaker, and the state of mind of those to whom he speaks, create circumstances that must be taken into consideration. General de Pellieux, addressing the jurors directly, said to them; "Gentlemen, the crime—" he did not say the word, but that was certainly what he meant,—"the crime of M. Émile Zola consists in taking away from the soldiers their confidence in their commanders." Assuming an approaching war, he said to you: "Without this confidence we lead your children to butchery." What more direct threat could they have used? And the next day General de Boisdeffre stood at this bar, and told you that, if you ventured to acquit M. Émile Zola, he would not remain at the head of the staff. That manifestation was anti-military in the first degree, for you did not appoint General de Boisdeffre, and it is not for you to receive his resignation. General de Boisdeffre is a commander, but a subordinate commander. We know nothing of his military capacities; until we know more, we are bound to assume them to be good, and we have not to decide his fate. That is a matter between him and the minister of war, or parliament. Thus, to prove that no orders were given to the council of war, they have publicly dictated orders to this jury.

Well, since the first suspicions to which the publication of the *bordereau* gave rise, since the secret document spoken of by *L'Éclair*, since the indictments, and down to these last manifestations of the staff, have you not seen the light continually increasing regarding the Dreyfus case? For my part, as I told you, I at first thought Dreyfus guilty, *a priori*, without knowing anything about it; and I have nothing to eliminate from the expressions of my article. I even confess to you that I was much slower to harbor doubt than certain men who are not to be suspected of not loving the Army. Articles from the pen of M. Paul de Cassagnac, written in 1896, have been read to you, which more than hint that the verdict needs revision. M. de Cassagnac wrote several articles; I read them; they did not convince me; I remained silent; and not until the very late events, not until the day when I went to see M. Scheurer-Kestner, will you find a line from me in reference to the Dreyfus case.

I went to see M. Scheurer-Kestner under circumstances which I have publicly related. Although he is an old friend of mine, I was absolutely ignorant of the fact that he was taking an interest in the Dreyfus case. He had never said a word to me about it. When I learned through the newspapers that he was in possession of special information concerning it, and that he believed in the innocence of Dreyfus, I went to see him. He did not mention the name of Major Esterhazy; he showed me handwritings. I am not an expert, and these writings did not convince me at once. I said so the next day in my newspaper, and I continued to believe that Dreyfus was a traitor. I did more. I asked *L'Aurore* to insert extracts from articles that had appeared in *L'Intransigeant* containing arguments against Dreyfus. I said: "The truth must be known. Let us not hesitate to give the arguments for and against." You see, then, that I was slow in making up my mind. I should have only to show you the sequence of my articles to convince you that I long resisted the idea that Dreyfus could be innocent. But how was it possible to resist always, when the light was growing brighter every day, and when all the powers established for the doing of justice were combining to deny justice?

Gentlemen, I know that it has been said that this is a Jewish movement, and that many who do not say it think it. Well, what are the facts appearing from the testimony given at this bar as to the origin of the movement in favor of Dreyfus? I do not refer to his family, which believes in his innocence, and which naturally would move heaven and earth to prove it. But who were the first, outside of the Dreyfus family, to give body to this thought? Gentlemen, you know that it was in the Army that doubt was given birth. It was Colonel Picquart, whom I did not know until I saw him here, and who seems to me worthy of all respect, and for whom I am glad to testify my sincere affection,—it was Colonel Picquart who designated Major Esterhazy. It was Colonel Picquart who first conceived doubt.

M. Zola: And he is an anti-Semite.

M. Clemenceau: M. Zola tells me that he is an anti-Semite. I did not know it, and it does not matter. It was Colonel Picquart who submitted his doubts to his superior, General Gonse, and it is out of the scruples of those two men, expressed in the letters with which you are now familiar, that the whole matter which brings us here today has grown.

Now, gentlemen, what is the question before us? For my part, I consider it at once most simple and most complex. Most simple, for it is a question of legality, a question whether the law which is the guarantee of all of us, the law which protects us against the temptations of judges, the law which protects us against exterior passions, the law which safeguards all of us from the highest to the lowest,—it is a question whether the guarantees which this law furnishes have been observed in the case of Dreyfus. No, they have not. And that is all I want to know. I do not examine the presumptions of innocence, which are enormous, especially now that the present trial has shed full light upon them. I consider only the question of legality. And, the question being so simple, why has it aroused so many passions against it? It is because justice, while undoubtedly the most beautiful ideal to sing and to celebrate, is also the most difficult to realize.

The social organization is theoretically admirable. The people send to parliament men whose mission it is to represent their will. This will is formulated under the forms of law. The judges apply it, the police execute it. But it comes about that men invested with public power suffer themselves, because they are men, because they are weak, to be abused by the idea that they are more or less necessary men. Having some power, they want more. They confuse their own interests, individually and as a body, with the general interest, and, when it is pointed out to them that they have made an error, their first impulse is to resist *en masse*. Their entire profession is at stake.

May I be permitted this respectful criticism? They say to us: "You insult the Army." No, we do not insult the Army. The Army exists only through the law. We desire it to be great through the law, for we have duties toward it. But it has duties toward us, and there must be an understanding between military and civil society on the very ground of law and justice. Gentlemen, France for twenty-five years has been carrying on a double enterprise, which seems contradictory. We are a vanquished nation,—gloriously vanquished, it is true, but vanquished nonetheless,— and it has been our thought to re-establish the power of France. That is a matter of necessity. It must be, because there is no civil law, there is no means of doing right and justice, if we are not, in the first place, masters in our own house. And our second thought has been that of ridding ourselves of all personal despotisms, of every vestige of oligarchy, and founding in our own country a democracy of liberty and justice.

Then the question arose whether these two views are not contradictory. The principle of civil society is right, liberty, justice. The principle of military society is discipline, countersign, obedience. And, as each is led by the consciousness of the utility of his function to try to encroach upon his neighbor, military society, which has force at its disposal, tends to encroach on civil authority, and to look upon civil society sometimes from a somewhat lofty standpoint. It is a wrong. Soldiers have no *raison d'être* except as defenders of the principle which civil society represents. A reconciliation between these two institutions is necessary. The professional Army no longer exists. The universal Army, the Army of all, must be penetrated with the ideas of all, with the universal ideas of right, since it is made up of the universality of citizens. If, absorbed by the thought of defense, which is of the first legitimacy, civil society were to rush into military servitude, we should still have a soil to defend, it is true; but the moral country would be lost, because, abandoning the ideas of justice and liberty, we should have abandoned all that has been done hitherto in this world by the glory and renown of France. These two societies must come to an understanding. Military society must enjoy all its rights, in order to do all its duties. Civil society, conscious of its duties toward the country and the Army, must maintain its rights inflexibly, not only in the higher interest of the principle which it represents, but to insure a maximum of efficiency in the military institution. Yes, indeed, the Army must be strong, but, as the abnegation of some and the absolute command of others are destined to fuse in one immense effort of life and death for the defense of the territory, it is necessary that civil society, by the superiority of its principle, should preserve its full power of control.

Gentlemen, you belong to the Army. At what moment will the Army be most admirable? At the moment when, running to the frontier, it will have all our heart and all our hope. Suppose that a hundred thousand Frenchmen fall in the first battles. Ninety thousand of these will be men who today are not wearing the uniform, and only ten thousand of them will be men who call themselves soldiers. Will these men lie in two heaps? Will it be said that there is one honor belonging to the ten thousand military men, and another belonging to the ninety thousand civilians? No. There is but one honor for all, the honor that consists in the fulfillment of the supreme duty, total duty toward the country. Then let us not abuse a word which no longer has the significance that it had in the days of professional armies. The honor of the Army today is the honor of all. The Army has but one honor,—and it is potent for the national defense, that in peace it is always respectful of the law.

General de Pellieux asked us for confidence the other day. And, while he spoke, I reflected that, during the twenty-five years of the Empire, we had full confidence in the commanders of the Army. We never criticized them, we never controlled them. The men whom I saw start were full of confidence. You know to what disasters they ran. M. Zola has been reproached for having written *La Débâcle*. Alas! gentlemen,— and I say it very low,—if he wrote it, it was because before him there had been men of war to organize it and to bring it about. It is a return of that that is to be avoided, and patriotism does not consist in admiring, whether or no, everything that is done in the Army, but in submitting the Army to the discipline of the law. When General de Boisdeffre came to this bar, after General de Pellieux, to use toward this jury language that was threatening, he revealed to you what must have taken place before the council of war, and from what we have seen of the trial in the open day we may judge of the trial behind closed doors. The language of General Billot at the tribune was clear enough. It was the equivalent of an order; and did not Colonel Picquart say, to explain the insufficiency of the Ravary report: "General de Pellieux had concluded that there was no ground for a prosecution; Major Ravary could not do otherwise than come to the conclusion of his superior"? It is not necessary to conclude therefrom that the generals have wilfully failed in their duty. Nothing more than their own words is necessary to show us how, without intending it, without realizing it, they have stepped aside from the clear path of right and justice. General de Boisdeffre would have proved it superabundantly, if that had been necessary. He was asked for the proof, or, rather, he was not asked for it, for we were not allowed to ask it, but at the bottom of our hearts we wanted it revealed. If he had brought a decisive proof that would have compelled everybody to bow, for my part, I swear to you, I would have left this courtroom with a sense of relief. But what sort of proof did they bring us? A document later by two years than the Dreyfus verdict. What sort of justice is it, gentlemen, that discovers proofs of a just verdict two years after the verdict was rendered, and which produces, as convincing, documents that were never submitted to the accused? That is the philosophy of these closed doors. Behind them everything was known, even the secret documents, known to all except to him whom these documents were to condemn. They hide from us documents the revelation of which they say would be harmful to the national defense, and these documents, which they refuse to M. Scheurer-Kestner and to the chamber, traverse the highways in Major Esterhazy's pocket. M. Méline, to whom Jaurès said: "Yes or no, did you communicate secret documents?" replied to him: "We will answer you elsewhere." Elsewhere is here, and here they have not answered us, for I cannot consider as an answer the assertion that two years after the verdict they discovered a proof against the prisoner. M. Labori has told you that this document is a forgery. I tell you that, even if it is true, it is the first duty of all of us to see that this document is submitted to Dreyfus, whether he is a traitor or not,— to Dreyfus and to his lawyer; and, if you say that, because he is a Jew, he is not to be tried as others are tried, I tell you that the day will come when you will be similarly treated because you are a Protestant or a Freethinker. This is a denial of the French idea born of the Revolution, the idea of liberty for all, the idea of tolerance for all, the idea of equality of guarantees, equality of rights, equality of justice. If you once condemn a man without the forms of justice, some day the forms of justice will be abrogated by others to your harm. How justly the historians have cried out against the abominable law of the 22d of Prairial, made by Robespierre to rid himself of his enemies! All thinkers have handed over to the execration of mankind this abominable law that abolished the right of defense. It is odious, it is infamous; but at least it allowed the prisoner to know the charge against him. Why do you not do as much, you in times which are not of revolutionary violence, in peace, in tranquillity, when all the machinery of the public powers is operating freely? Yes, we condemn a man, a French officer, for he is a French officer, and not of the least distinguished, belonging to a family which has given proofs of patriotism. I do not know the Dreyfus family. I only reproduce the testimony of M. Lalance, which M. Labori has read to you.

Even if Dreyfus is a traitor, I do not see what interest we can have in refusing to honor people who are not responsible for the crime committed, and who have given manifest proofs of love for the French country. I cannot suffer the error of one to become a burden on all. If Dreyfus is guilty, let him be punished as severely as you will. You have my article, in which I say that I ask no pity for him. But, if he has broth-

ers, children, parents, who have behaved themselves as good Frenchmen, I hold it a point of honor to do them justice. It is the misfortune
of the times, in which all passions are furiously unchained, that we will
not listen to the voice of reason; that we insult each other, that we accuse each other. You have even seen here officers who are old comrades,
who tomorrow will vie with each other in deeds of valor and self-
sacrifice, if the country is threatened,—you have seen them accuse each
other, defy each other, and exchange retorts as if they were sword thrusts.
Tomorrow Colonel Picquart will cross swords with a companion in arms
whom at the bottom of his heart perhaps he loves. And we, who do not
wear the uniform, who are Frenchmen all the same, and who intend also
that France shall be effectively defended, what do we do? A few of us
assert that perhaps a judicial error has been committed. Then goes up
a great cry from the crowd: "Traitor! Scoundrel! Renegade! Agent of
the Jews!" And these are Frenchmen, gentlemen, who think to serve
France by pointing her out as a den of people who sell themselves; these
are Frenchmen, to whom it never occurs to suppose that their fellow
citizens are capable of French generosity. They hurl insults, they betray
hatred, and it is thus that they pretend to serve the country.

Gentlemen, if our enemies do not understand us, it is our duty to ourselves and to our country to understand them, in order that the prevailing
obscurity may be dissipated. For my part, I consider that the worst
treason, perhaps because it is the most common, is treason to the French
spirit, that spirit of tolerance and justice which has made us beloved by
the peoples of the earth. Even if France were to disappear tomorrow,
we should leave behind us one thing eternal, the sentiments of liberty
and human justice that France unchained upon the world in 1789. Gentlemen, when the hour of insults is past, when they have finished outraging
us, it will be necessary to reply. And then what will they offer us? The
thing judged. Gentlemen, look above your heads. See that Christ upon
the cross. There is the thing judged, and it has been put above the
judge's head that the sight of it may not disturb him. It ought to be
placed at the other end of the room, in order that, before rendering
his verdict, the judge might have before his eyes the greatest example
of a judicial error, held up for the shame of humanity. Oh! I am not one
of the worshippers of Christ, in the sense in which many among you
are, perhaps. But, after all, perhaps I love him more, and certainly I
respect him more than do many of those who preach massacre in the
name of the religion of love.

They also tell us of the honor of the Army. On that point I have
answered, but I wanted to cite to you, so odious are these words of
treason, and so revolting is it to me to see them flung so freely about,—

I wanted to cite to you the case of Marshal Bazaine. He was really a traitor, was he not? He betrayed French soldiers by hundreds of thousands, at the critical moment when it depended upon him to change the fortune of our arms and save his country. I wish to indulge in no declamation here, but I declare, and I defy any man to rise to contradict me, that Bazaine committed the greatest act of treason known to the world. Condemned to military degradation and to death, they spared him both. Tell me, do you think that the responsibility of commanders is greater than the responsibility of soldiers? Yes, undoubtedly. Well, if this responsibility is greater, why every day do they punish simple soldiers so pitilessly, and why do they pardon the traitor *par excellence,* the traitor who had no excuse, the traitor whose outstretched hand France awaited on the day of her supreme disaster. To what *régime* did they submit him? Let me read you a few words from a pamphlet by M. Marchi, keeper of the prison of the Sainte Marguerite Islands. Here are his instructions:

> You will treat the prisoner with the greatest regard: in short, at Sainte Marguerite one must be a man of the world, and not a jailer.

M. Marchi arrives at Sainte Marguerite. The temporary superintendent makes him familiar with the service, and informs him, among other things, that, supposing it to be his duty to watch the condemned man whenever he went to walk upon the terrace, Lieutenant-Colonel Valley went to Paris to protest against the conduct of the keeper, wherefore the keeper had been reprimanded. It would take too long to tell you of all the instructions. Suffice it is to know that cabinet ministers wrote to Bazaine, that they addressed him as *Monsieur* the Marshal, and that there was a question of pensioning him. Boats were allowed to come to the edge of the terrace, whence he conversed with visitors. On the eve of his escape he had obtained permission to go out with a guardian. Well, really, when I compare this tolerance, which is an outrage upon France and upon the Army, with the hatred unchained against the prisoner on Devil's Island; when I remember that an artillery officer named Triponé, who had not only delivered documents, but had delivered the Bourges detonator, of which we were the only possessors in Europe, by the complicity of the sub-officer Fessler, to the house of Armstrong, which then gave the benefit of it to Germany; when I see that Triponé was sentenced to five years in prison, and was pardoned after two years and a half, though his crime was certainly not less than that of Dreyfus,—I say that there is no equality of punishment between these Christians and this Jew.

Again, there is another fact. Adjutant Chatelain, who is now in New

Caledonia, perhaps is farming there and raising cattle; his crime, if I remember rightly, consisted in the sale of certain documents to Italy. He was not less guilty than Dreyfus. But what a difference in treatment! They talk of equality before the law. It is a phrase. We await the reality. They tell us that we have violated the law. I maintain, on the contrary, that we appear here in the interest of the law, and I say that we were unable to do otherwise. For the rectification of a judicial error application was made to the war department, to the executive power. You know how General Billot received the application; he refused to act. M. Trarieux applied to M. Méline; M. Scheurer-Kestner did the same thing; M. Méline would not even talk with them. In the Senate, discussion, leading to nothing. In the Chamber, discussion, leading to nothing. And similarly with the council of war, with the investigation by General de Pellieux, with the investigation by Major Ravary. Now, when all the powers that are the organs of the law fail in their legal duty, what was left for those who, like M. Zola, have undertaken the work of justice from which the powers of justice shrank? M. Zola's idea is an appeal to the people, an appeal to the people represented by twelve jurors whom he does not know, whose opinions none of us know, to pass upon his act, and say whether they will allow him to bring out the light. If he must be struck, he is very proud to be struck for this confession of justice and truth.

If the jury gives him its aid, the pacification of minds may be accomplished, and the agitation of this day finished by the legal reparation due to all who have been deprived of the guarantees of the law. Without truth, M. Zola can do nothing; he is powerless; he will be baffled on every hand. With a bit of the truth, M. Zola is invincible. It is for the jurors to answer to the appeal of truth.

I have said that the government is fallible. The jurors also have no higher light. They are men. They do their best. They have the advantage of being for a time unbiased by *esprit de corps,* and of being able thus, in perfect liberty of mind, to act in accordance with that need of superior justice which we all feel. We are before you, gentlemen. Shortly you will pass judgment. I hope that you may not be governed by the argument which now controls too many minds. How many Frenchmen there are who say: "Possibly Dreyfus was condemned illegally, but he was condemned justly, and that is sufficient; so let us say no more about it." Sophism of the *raison d'État,* which has done us so much harm,— which hampered the magnificent movement of the French Revolution by the guillotine and all sorts of violence. Ah! we have torn down the Bastille. Every 14th of July we dance to celebrate the abolition of the *raison d'État.* But a Bastille still remains within us, and, when we question ourselves, an illegality committed to the detriment of others seems to us acceptable, and we say, and we think, that this may be a little evil for a great good. Profound error. An illegality is a form of iniquity, since the law is guarantee of justice.

Gentlemen, all the generals together have no right to say that the illegality which comes from a certain form of justice, since it is a denial of it; all the magistrates together,—have no right to say that illegality can be justice, because the law is nothing but the guarantee of justice. To do justice outside of the law no one has either the right or the power. If you wish to render the supreme service to the country under the present circumstances, establish the supremacy of the law, the supremacy of justice. Cause to disappear from our souls that respect for the *raison d' État* so absurd in a democracy. With Louis XIV, with Napoleon, with men who hold a people in their hands and govern according to their good pleasure, the *raison d'État* is intelligible. In a democracy the *raison d'État* is only a contradiction, a vestige of the past. "France is a high moral person," said Gambetta. I do not deny it, monarchy or republic. But I say that the tradition of the *raison d'État* has had its day, and that the hour has come for us to attach ourselves to the modern idea of liberty and justice. After the original duty of defense of the soil, nothing can be more urgent than to establish among us a *régime* of liberty and justice, which shall be in accordance with the ambition of our fathers, an example to all civilized nations.

At the present hour, I admit, the problem presents itself to you in a bitter and sorrowful form. Oh! it is very sorrowful to sincere people to find themselves in hostility with brave soldiers who intended to do well, who wished to do well, and who, thinking to do well, have not done well. That happens to civilians not in uniform; that happens to civilians in uniform,—for soldiers are nothing else.

From this point of view you are at a turning point in our history, and you must submit military society to the control of the civil law, or abandon to it our most precious conquests. We have not to pass upon General de Boisdeffre or upon General de Pellieux. They will explain themselves to their superiors. It is not our affair. They have nothing to ask of us. But, however painful it may be to find ourselves for a day in conflict with them, take your course, since no danger can result, unless you yourselves abandon the cause of the law of justice which you represent. Thus you will render us the grand service, the inestimable service, of extinguishing at the beginning the religious war that threatens to dishonor this country. [Murmurs of protest.]

Since you protest, so much the better. I am willing to believe that it is your intention to renew the wars of religion; but, when I see in France, in our France of Algeria, a pillaging of warehouses; when I see it boasted in the newspapers that safes have been thrown into the sea, and that contracts have been torn up; when I see that Jews, while going to get bread for their families, have been massacred,—I have a right to say that religious warfare offered no other aspect in the Middle Ages; and I say that the jurors of today, in rendering a verdict in favor of liberty and justice for all, even for Jews, will signify their intention of putting an end to these excesses by saying to those who have committed these barbarities: "In the name of the French people, you shall go no farther."

Gentlemen, we are the law; we are toleration; we are the defenders of the Army, for we do not separate justice from patriotism, and the Army will not be strong, it will not be respected, unless it derives its power from respect for the law. I add that we are the defenders of the Army, when we ask you to drive Esterhazy from it. You have driven out Picquart, and kept Esterhazy. And, gentlemen of the jury, since there has been reference to your children, tell me who would like to belong to the same battalion that Esterhazy belongs to? Tell me if you will trust this officer to lead your children against the enemy? I need only ask the question. No one will dare reply.

Gentlemen, we have known terrible shocks in this century. We have experienced all glories and all disasters. We are now confronted with the unknown, between all fears and all hopes. Seize the occasion, as we have seized it, and determine your destinies. It is an august thing, this judgment of the people upon itself. It is a terrible thing also, this decision by the people of its future. Your verdict, gentlemen, will not decide our fates as much as your own. We appear before you. You appear before history.

After Clemenceau's final speech, prosecutor Attorney General Van Cassel replied bitingly: "For twelve days we have heard nothing here but insults to the Army, and now, for the last two days, in order that they might be tolerated here, they have done nothing but repeat that the staff is made up of brave generals." Defense counsel Labori, facing the audience, which was crying "Enough! Enough! Down with Labori!," made rejoinder. Turning to the jury, he concluded: "There are two ways of understanding right, gentlemen of the jury. The question before you is this: Is Zola guilty? Let these clamors dictate to you, gentlemen, the duty of firmness that is incumbent upon you. You are the sovereign arbiters. You are higher than the Army, higher than the judicial power. You are the justice of the people, which only the judgment of history will judge. If you have the courage, declare Zola guilty of having struggled against all hatreds in behalf of right, justice, and liberty."

The jury retired and returned within thirty-five minutes. The foreman arose and said: "On my honor and my conscience the declaration of the jury is: as concerns Perrenx, *yes,* by a majority vote. As concerns Zola, *yes,* by a majority vote."

Spectators began to cry: "Long live the Army! Long live France! Down with the insulters! To the door with the Jews! Death to Zola!" "These people are cannibals," said Zola.

Within a few minutes Perrenx was condemned to imprisonment for four months and the payment of a fine of 3,000 francs. Zola was sentenced to a maximum penalty of one year's imprisonment and a fine of 3,000 francs. His name was ordered struck off the rolls of the Legion of Honor.

After an appeal, a second trial was ordered for April 18 at Versailles. Before the trial could take place, Zola, following the advice of friends, left France and took refuge in London. During his absence all his property was confiscated. He returned to France on June 4, 1899.

How Rome Saw the Dreyfus Case

"There's no doubt about it. This time Judas is innocent!"

Paléologue, An Intimate Journal of the Dreyfus Case, *pp. 140–141. Courtesy of Criterion Books.*

Rome, like every other capital in the world, was stirred by reports from Paris. That the general impression was quite different from that of Vatican circles was noted in his diary by Maurice Paléologue, the French diplomat in the Ministry of Foreign Affairs.

FROM SATURDAY, MARCH 5 TO SUNDAY, MARCH 20, 1898.
TRIP TO ROME

The Italians are nearly as stirred by the Dreyfus case as are the French, but with the difference that here nobody believes Dreyfus to be guilty. People here do not understand how it is that it has not long since become obvious to the normally so quick and discriminating French mind that the 1894 verdict, the result of a genuine judicial error, was the result of a gigantic imposture. That is the impression I have gathered at the Duca di Sermoneta's, at the Contessa Pasolini's, at Signora Mazzoleni's, at the Contessa Bruschi's, at the Marchese Visconti-Venosta's, at the Duchessa Grazioli's, in fact everywhere; and that impression has been fully confirmed by Barrère, our Ambassador.

D'Annunzio himself, who hates the Jews, said to me during one of our walks on the Palatine:

"There's no doubt about it. This time Judas is innocent!"

In Vatican circles a different state of mind prevails. Here they avoid committing themselves on the crux of the matter, the question whether Dreyfus was legally and rightly convicted, but an insidious tenacity is shown in letting slip no opportunity of expressing pity for poor France, which is now discovering to its cost the ordeals and perils to which a nation exposes itself when it allows itself to be governed by Freemasons, atheists, and Jews!

Clemenceau and Drumont Meet in a Duel

"Six shots were exchanged, without result."

The New York Times, *February 27, 1898.*

Passion ran high during the Zola trial. Mobs gathered in the narrow streets around the Palais de Justice and there were fist fights and riots. The close of the trial brought no cessation. Incidents arising out of the case, accusations and libels, led to one challenge after another.

PARIS, Feb. 26. Ex-Deputy Georges Clemenceau and M. Drumont, editor of the *Libre Parole,* fought a duel this afternoon with pistols at Parc au Princes. Six shots were exchanged, without result. The dispute was brought about by an article on the Zola trial published in the *Libre Parole.*

Colonel Picquart Wins a Duel

The New York Times, *March 6, 1898.*

He Defeats Colonel Henry in an Encounter Resulting from the
Zola Trial in Paris
Wounds in Wrist and Arm
General Boisdeffre Waits at Colonel Henry's Residence for his Return
The Officers Fight at Close Quarters

PARIS, March 5. Colonel Picquart, who was disciplined for giving testimony favorable to the case of M. Zola at the recent trial of the author, fought a duel with swords today in the Riding School of the

Military School with Colonel Henry, who testified against M. Zola. The latter was wounded in wrist and arm. Colonel Henry succeeded Col. Picquart as Chief of the Secret Service at the War Office.

At the first encounter, Colonel Henry was slightly wounded on the forearm, and at the same moment his blade appeared to touch Colonel Picquart's neck. Senator Ranc, Col. Picquart's second, then intervened, but his principal was shown not to have been touched, and an encounter at close quarters followed. Colonel Henry was evidently wounded on the elbow, and the duel was brought to an end. After Colonel Henry's wound had been dressed, he went home, where General Boisdeffre was waiting for him. Officers acted as seconds for the two duellists and Colonel Henry's wound was dressed by a doctor.

VIII

The Tragic Fate of Colonel Henry

Perhaps the most tragic figure in the case, next to Dreyfus himself, was Hubert-Joseph Henry. Born in the small village of Pogny on the Marne canal, a few miles south of Châlons, Henry came of a farming family, and entered the Army in the ranks in 1865. In the 1870–71 war with Prussia, he was a sergeant-major and was taken prisoner twice, but escaped each time. His conduct under fire was so courageous that he was commissioned in the field. In 1876 he became aide-de-camp to General de Miribel. He took part as a Captain in the campaigns in Tunisia (1882) and Tonkin (1887). In 1891 he was promoted to Major and was assigned to the Intelligence Service of the Ministry of War.

A stout, bluff, hearty man with a booming voice, Henry never forgot his sense of subservience to the officer's caste. It was said that he possessed both the virtues and the defects of the peasant: on the one hand he was astute and courageous, on the other, he had simple cunning as well as shrewdness. Above all, he was anxious for promotion. Embroiled in the case from the very beginning, he was the first officer to see the incriminating *bordereau*. He collaborated with Bertillon and other "handwriting experts" to demonstrate that the original document was written by Dreyfus. He took it upon himself to inform the press about Dreyfus's arrest ("All Israel is in a state of agitation"). He testified at the first court-martial ("And there is the traitor!") and at the Zola trial ("We only did our duty as we understood it").

Worst of all, Henry took it upon himself to forge documents designed to implicate Dreyfus when proof was lacking. In some perverse way Henry was seeking to rescue his superior officers and "the honor of the Army" from what he believed to be unfair attacks by the Dreyfusards. Little by little Henry became enmeshed in coils of his own fabrication. Caught in a hopeless situation he finally committed suicide.

The Henry Forgery

"I did what I did for the good of the country."

On September 14, 1896, an article appeared in *L'Éclair* in which it was stated that a "decisive document" had emerged that proved the guilt of Dreyfus beyond a shadow of a doubt. By this time the cabal was seeking material to be added to the secret *dossier* to stifle any movement for revision and to assure the condemnation. At the end of August there appeared a letter ostensibly sent to Dreyfus on Devil's Island on which a message was added in invisible ink between the lines. Called the "Weyler forgery," the letter was so naïve that the censor of the Colonial Ministry rejected it immediately and it never reached the eyes of the General Staff.*

Perhaps Henry was encouraged by the words of General de Boisdeffre: "There is not much there." Included among his contributions was a document (October 31, 1896) which was supposed to constitute proof of Dreyfus's guilt. It was a forgery by Henry, reading: "I shall say that I never had any relations with that Jew. . . ." It was signed "Alexandrine," the code name used jointly by the Italian Military Attaché Panizzardi and by Schwartzkoppen. The name of Dreyfus was written out in full.

The letter was so clumsy that several officers of the General Staff, including du Paty de Clam, were suspicious of it from the very beginning. Esterhazy was delighted and hailed it as overwhelming proof of Dreyfus's guilt. His simple-minded supporter, General de Pellieux, also believed it to be genuine.

Henry's forged document had pieces joined together by gummed strips. It was made of two different pieces of paper: the cross lines in one were a bluish grey, in the other they were light mauve. Another paper (dated June 1894) in the file was used to establish the fact that the signature was that of Panizzardi. This document, too, was made up of different pieces: the bluish grey and the light mauve cross lines were both visible.

On July 7, 1898, M. Godefroy Cavaignac, Minister of War

* See page 90.

(October 1895—April 1896; June 1898—September 1898), a cousin of du Paty de Clam, presented the 1896 "document" to the Chamber of Deputies as "final" proof of Dreyfus's guilt. By a vote of 572 to 2 the Chamber ordered that Cavaignac's speech be posted in all the 36,000 communes of France. The public could now be assured that the "traitor" was in custody.

At this time Colonel Picquart sent a letter to the War Minister declaring that the document used against Dreyfus was a forgery. On August 30, 1898, to save face, Cavaignac ordered Henry, now Lieutenant-Colonel, to the war office for examination in the presence of Generals de Boisdeffre, Gonse, and Roget. The War Minister began his interrogatory by warning Henry that in the two documents concerned, one contained words belonging to the other, and reciprocally, that both must have been seriously altered. He advised Henry to tell the truth, and warned him that, because of the material character of the facts, the absence of explanation of them would be as grave in its consequences to him as an insufficient explanation.

1

HENRY'S FORGED LETTER

La revision du procès de Rennes, *vol. 1, p. 99. Translated by the editor.*

MY DEAR FRIEND:

I have read that a deputy is going to make an interpellation concerning Dreyfus. If I am asked in Rome for further explanations, I shall say that I never had relations with that Jew. That goes without saying! If anyone happens to ask you, say just that. Because it is necessary that no one should ever know what happened with him.

(Signed) ALEXANDRINE

2

MINISTER OF WAR CAVAIGNAC'S INTERROGATION OF HENRY

Translated in F. C. Conybeare, The Dreyfus Case *(London: George Allen, 1898), pp. 286–293.*

Cavaignac: When and how did you reconstitute the piece of June 1894? When and how that of 1896?

Henry: I received the first in June 1894. It was I that reconstituted it, as I did most of the pieces having the same origin, when they were written in French. I dated it to the time when I received it. As to the piece of

1896, I received it on the eve of Allhallows Day, and I reconstituted it myself. I put the date on it myself.

Cavaignac: Did you ever ungum and then put together again the piece of 1894?

Henry: No, never. Why should I have done so? It was a piece of no importance. It had been ranged with the *dossier* of 1894. I am quite sure I never ungummed it. What is more, I never ungum pieces.*

Cavaignac: Do you ever keep bits of paper without putting them together?

Henry: Sometimes, for a certain time—time enough to make out a little what the papers are. But I do not remember having kept bits of paper unarranged for more than eight or ten days.

Cavaignac: Did you have the piece of 1896 in your hands subsequently to your giving it to General Gonse?

Henry: No, I did not.

Cavaignac: How then do you explain the fact that the piece of 1894 has in it bits belonging to that of 1896 and *vice versa?*

Henry: I cannot explain it, and it seems impossible that it should be so. In fact, the 1896 piece never left the hands of General Gonse. As for the 1894 piece, which, as you know, is in the archives, I looked at it some days after I sent the other to General Gonse. At the moment they did not know where it was, and I was sent to look for it.

Cavaignac: Was the date which the piece bore written on it, or on the register of it?

Henry: There was no register of it, but a *dossier (i.e.* portfolio) in which bits of no importance were brought together.

Cavaignac: What you say is impossible. There is material proof that certain fragments have been interchanged. How do you explain that?

Henry: How? Why, if it is the case, I must myself have intercalated one in the other. For all that, I could not say that I fabricated a piece which I did not! I should have had to fabricate the envelope as well. How could that be?

Cavaignac: The fact of intercalation is certain.

Henry: I put together the papers in the state in which I received them.

Cavaignac: I may remind you that nothing is more serious for you than

---

* At this point Henry was apparently defending himself against any possible charge that he had ungummed the *petit bleu* in order to scratch out the address on it: "Commandant Esterhazy," etc. He had then re-written the same address over the erasure, and put it together again, in order to suggest that it had originally had another address, but that Picquart had obliterated it and written the address to Esterhazy, whom he wanted to implicate. This was the charge on which Picquart had been arrested in July 1898 and had been incarcerated in Cherche-Midi prison.

the absence of all explanation. Tell me what passed. What did you do?

Henry: What would you have me say?

Cavaignac: I want you to give me an explanation.

Henry: I cannot. . . .

Cavaignac: What did you do?

Henry: I did not fabricate the papers.

Cavaignac: Come, let us look. You put the fragments of one inside the other.

Henry (after a moment's hesitation): Well, yes, because the two fitted together perfectly. What led me to do it was this. I received the first piece in June 1894, and I reconstituted it then. When the piece of 1896 came, there were some words in it which I did not altogether understand. So I cut out some portions of the first piece to put them into the second.

Cavaignac: You forged the piece of 1896?

Henry: No, I did not.

Cavaignac: What did you do?

Henry: I added to the 1896 piece some words which were in the other. I arranged the phrases, *"Il faut pas qu'on sache jamais,"* but the leading phrase was left untouched, and the name of Dreyfus was in it all right.

Cavaignac: You are not telling me the truth.

Henry: I am. It was only the phrases at the end that I arranged.

Cavaignac: Was it not yourself that conceived the idea of arranging the phrases in such ways?

Henry: No one ever spoke to me about it. I did it to make the document more cogent.

Cavaignac: You are not telling me all. You forged the entire piece.

Henry: I forged nothing. Dreyfus's name was there all right in the piece of 1896. I could not take it out of the piece of 1894, since it was not there. I had not three pieces to work with—never more than the two. I swear that that is how it was all done.

Cavaignac: Your explanation is inconsistent with the facts themselves. Tell me all.

Henry: I have told you all. I only added this one phrase.

Cavaignac: Then this is your explanation: You forged the last phrase, *"Il faut pas qu'on sache jamais"*?

Henry: I cannot say that I made up the phrase. When I found the paper of 1896 I was very much stirred by it. There was on it, "I have seen that a deputy is going to interpellate about Dreyfus." Then, after a certain phrase I could not find the sequel. I then got out of the 1894 piece some words which completed the sense.

Cavaignac: It is not true; you forged the piece.

Henry: I swear I did not. I added the phrase, but I did not forge the piece.

Cavaignac: What you say is impossible; so own to the whole truth. . . . You made up the second piece, taking your idea of it from the first.

Henry: I swear I did not. The other pieces which we got at that time quite prove the authenticity of the next letter. "It is a bother that we have not had the end of the letter of ——" [here the name of a foreign officer].

I swear that the beginning of the letter in blue chalk is quite authentic.

Cavaignac: The beginning was invented as well. So tell the whole truth.

Henry: No, I only put in the last phrase: *"Il faut pas."* . . . I wrote it without tracing it.

Cavaignac: Come now, since the pieces speak for themselves, you had better confess. . . . What suggested it to you?

Henry: My chiefs were very anxious, and I wanted to reassure them and restore tranquillity in their minds. I said to myself: Let us add a phrase. Supposing we went to war, situated as we are now!

Cavaignac: That is the idea which led you to forge the letter?

Henry: I did not forge it. How could I have imitated a signature like that? It was the beginning of it which gave me the idea of adding the end.

Cavaignac: *"Il faut pas qu'on sache jamais personne.* Is that your language?

Henry: Yes, because I knew how he wrote.

Cavaignac: You did not date in 1894 the piece which bore that date?

Henry: Yes, I dated it in 1894. I do not think I dated it afterwards. I believed I had dated it in 1894, I think. I do not remember.

Cavaignac: You were alone in doing that?

Henry: Yes; Gribelin knew nothing about it.

Cavaignac: No one knew it, no one at all?

Henry: I did it in the interest of my country. I was wrong.

Cavaignac: Now, tell the truth, the whole truth. Tell me what passed.

Henry: I swear I had the beginning of it. I added the end to make it more cogent.

Cavaignac: Was the 1896 piece signed?

Henry: I do not think I made up the signature.

Cavaignac: And the envelopes?

Henry: I swear I did not make them up. How could I?

Cavaignac: It is very unlikely that you added only the phrase at the end.

Henry: I swear it. The beginning suggested it to me, and subsequently people were reassured.

There was here a pause, during which Henry retired. The Minister Cavaignac then recalled him, and continued his questions.

Cavaignac: Let us see. One of the pieces has crosslines of pale violet, the other of bluish grey, which shows that portions of it were regummed. But your explanation is impossible. The intercalations do not answer to what you say.

Henry: What portions do you say were intercalated?

Cavaignac: I do not wish you to ask me questions, but to answer mine. You forged the whole letter?

Henry: I swear I did not. I must have had the names which are in that of 1896 to do so. Why should I have taken a fragment of the 1894 piece to insert it in the other?

Cavaignac: You will not tell the truth?

Henry: I can tell you nothing else. I cannot say that I wrote the whole of it. As to the first letter, I found it; the second I intercalated, and only added the end.

Cavaignac: All you could have received was the heading and the signature.

Henry: I received the first part.

Cavaignac: You received nothing at all.

Henry: I had the first part, the heading and the signature.

Cavaignac: Impossible! You aggravate your situation by these concealments.

Henry: I did what I did for the good of the country.

Cavaignac: That is not what I asked. What you did was based on the documents themselves. Tell everything.

Henry: I cannot say I did what I did not. When I got the first part . . . .

Cavaignac: Impossible! I tell you it is written on the piece. You had better tell all.

Henry: Then you are convinced it is I.

Cavaignac: Say what is the case. . . . So then, this is what happened: You received in 1896 an envelope with a letter inside it, a letter of no importance. You suppressed the letter and forged another instead of it.

Henry: Yes.

It was a bombshell. After denying indignantly again and again that he was the author of the forged October 1896 letter, Henry broke down and gave the tremulous, scarcely audible response, "Yes," that he had suppressed the genuine letter and forged another.

Cavaignac immediately ordered Henry to be taken to the fortress of Mont Valérien under military arrest. General de Boisdeffre, who had been silent during the interrogation, at once offered his resignation: "I now know that my confidence in Colonel Henry was not justified. I have been misled." General de Pellieux, a member of the General Staff who had used the Henry forgery at the Zola trial as "absolute proof" of Dreyfus's guilt, also sent the following letter of resignation to Cavaignac:

> Having been the dupe of dishonorable people, I cannot hope to retain the confidence of my subordinates without which it is impossible to have authority; having, for my part, lost confidence in those of my superiors who have made me base my work upon forgeries. . . . I have the honor to request you to be so good as to arrange for me to retire on the grounds of seniority in service.

De Pellieux, at the request of General Zurlinden, who had intercepted his letter of resignation, consented to withdraw his application for retirement.

The Suicide of Henry

"*. . . this brave soldier, this heroic servant of the great interests of the State.*"

After breaking down in his interrogation by War Minister Cavaignac, Colonel Henry was escorted to a cell in Mont Valérien prison. On the way, as officially reported by the authorities, he gave way to hysteria:

> It is a shame! . . . What do they want of me then? . . . It is madness on their part. . . . My conscience reproaches me with nothing. . . . What I did I am ready to do again. . . . It was for the good of the country and of the Army. I have always done my duty. . . . In all my life I never met with such a pack of wretches. . . . They are to blame for my misfortune. . . .

Twenty-four hours later the Havas News Agency published a brief press report:

1
NEWS REPORT FROM HAVAS

Agence Havas, *August 31, 1898.*

It has just been stated that Lieutenant-Colonel Henry has committed suicide this evening at Mont Valérien [prison].

He has cut his throat with a razor which he had taken with him into his cell.

Henry left two notes: The first read:

> "I am like a crazy person. I have horrible pains in my head. I'm going to throw myself into the Seine."

The second, addressed to his wife:

> "I see now that everyone has deserted me except you. You know well in whose interests I worked. . . . I am completely innocent. They know it. And everyone will know it later. But at this time I cannot speak."

Henry had been found dead in his cell, his throat cut from right to left and from left to right, the razor beside him. Had he been his own executioner? Yes—was the decision of the police doctors. But skeptics suggested that when Henry threatened to name his accomplices, he signed his own death warrant and that the killing was arranged. Why had he been permitted to keep his own razor? Certainly no other prisoner had been allowed to retain a razor in his cell.

The anti-Dreyfusards went immediately into action. Colonel Henry, they said, was a "national hero," who should be praised for his "patriotic forgery" meant to save the Army. To them he was clearly a martyr for the cause of duty and patriotism. He was "a grand man of honor." His forgery was "a bank note with a credit value representing a bullion reserve of documents of *absolute authenticity*." Charles Maurras, fiery nationalist author, described Henry as sacrificing himself for France.

2
CHARLES MAURRAS IN THE "GAZETTE DE FRANCE," SEPTEMBER 6, 1898

We wait for justice to pay to Henry the public honors he deserves. Meanwhile the French have vowed a home worship (*culte domestique*) to this brave soldier, this heroic servant of the great interests of the State.

Henry divulged himself to none. . . . He readily consented to run the risk himself, but alone. In his self-imposed task of policing the relations of nations, *our energetic plebeian* could only have shocked the more delicate feelings of the high-bred *gentlemen* of the *état major* *
. . . . Henry sacrificed himself, with death before his eyes, to the task of deceiving for the public good the chiefs he loved, and whose complete confidence he enjoyed, M. de Boisdeffre, M. Gonse, perhaps others as well. . . . It would have been hard for him in such a matter to have pushed further his intellectual and moral scruples. . . .

They [the Dreyfusard journalists] are held back by the scruples of our mischievous half-Protestant education. . . .

During the month of September there was circulated in Paris and throughout the country an appeal for subscriptions for a "Henry Memorial." The solicitation was signed by M. Charles Leroux, 76 Rue Blanche, and was endorsed by M. Renaudin, Mayor of Pogny, where Henry was born.

3

APPEAL FOR A HENRY MEMORIAL

Conybeare, The Dreyfus Case, *pp. 297–298.*

Colonel Henry's Devotion to his Country

Public subscription for a monument to be raised to him.

When an officer is reduced to committing a pretended forgery in order to restore peace to his country and rid it of a traitor, that soldier is to be mourned.

If he pays for his attempt with his life, he is a martyr.

If he voluntarily takes his life,

HE IS A HERO

Within a month there were 15,000 subscribers to the Henry Memorial Fund, citizens who paid out 131,110 francs in the campaign to rehabilitate the "good name" of the forger. Among the contributors were Army officers (including General Mercier, 100 francs), four Senators, 53 Deputies, and literary figures, such as the nationalist Maurice Barrès and the poet Paul Valéry ("3 francs, not without reflection"). An officer sent 50 francs "awaiting the order to test the new guns and explosives on the 100,000 Jews who are poisoning the country."

---

* Maurras undoubtedly meant Major du Paty de Clam.

When Joseph Reinach, politician and publicist who headed the revisionist campaign for Dreyfus, accused Henry of having been Esterhazy's accomplice, Henry's widow, urged on by anti-Semitic editor Édouard Drumont, brought an action for libel against him. The hearing took place in the Court of Assizes in an atmosphere recalling that of the earlier Zola trial. The matter was finally dropped when on December 27, 1900, an Amnesty Law was promulgated stifling all the prosecutions arising out of the Dreyfus case.

Clerical Contributors to the Henry Memorial Fund
"The blood of Colonel Henry cries for vengeance."

Pierre Quillard, Le Monument Henry *(Paris: Stock, 1899), section marked "Clergy." Translated by the editor.*

Pierre Quillard compiled a simple list of subscribers to the Henry Memorial Fund. The names of the subscribers, their remarks, and the amount of their contributions were reproduced in separate categories in the columns of *La Libre Parole.* "There was," wrote Quillard, "an unparalleled outburst of ferocity, folly, and vile abuse." The following entries in the section marked "Clergy" were used by anticlericals to attack the Church and accuse it of playing an active role in the Dreyfus Affair.

	Francs	Centimes
—*Collot (L'Abbé)* Lorraine and prisoner of the Prussians who has confidence in the judgment of military justice and the five Ministers of War	5	
—*Cros (L'Abbé)* ex-lieutenant, for a bedside rug made of the skin of a Yid, to be trampled morning and evening	5	
—*Galey (L'Abbé H.)* for the defense of the eternal right against the bad acting of the Puritans and the knavery of the Jew-Huguenots	5	
—*Mancuert (L'Abbé) et M. Gely à Pessac (Gironde).* Two admirers of the beautiful campaign against the true enemies	1	20

—C. (*L'Abbé*). The blood of Colonel
Henry cries for vengeance   3

—*A parish priest of the country,* who
makes the most ardent vows for the
extermination of the two enemies
of France: the Jew and the Free-
mason   5

—*A parish priest of the diocese of
Bayeux.* Down with Republicans of
every kind: Yids, Huguenots, Free
Masons and all who have been
Judaized by them   1

The Man of Honor: Lieutenant-Colonel Georges Picquart (*Picture Post*, London, August 26, 1939)

The Guilty Officer: Major Ferdinand Walsin-Esterhazy (*Bibliothèque Nationale*)

THE "PETIT BLEU"
Reconstruction of the express post letter-card sent by Schwartzkoppen to Esterhazy through the Parisian system of pneumatic tubes. This message enabled Picquart to identify Esterhazy as the real traitor. (*Bibliothèque Nationale*)

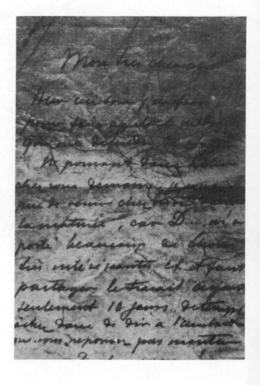

DOCUMENT NO. 371: FALSIFIED LETTER FROM PANIZZARDI TO SCHWARTZKOPPEN
So anxious was Major Henry to implicate Dreyfus that he manufactured evidence by adding forged documents to Dreyfus's *dossier*. In this document Henry erased the name "Dubois" and substituted the initial "D . . . " The letter was sent in September 1896, but Henry dated it "March 1894."

AUGUSTE SCHEURER-KESTNER (1833–1899), FIRST VICE-PRESIDENT OF THE SENATE IN 1896
Mathieu Dreyfus's greatest coup in the defense of his brother came when he was able to attract the interest of M. Auguste Scheurer-Kestner, Deputy to the National Assembly from Upper Alsace, Senator for life in 1875, and First Vice-President of the Senate in 1896. After a long and patient inquiry, Scheurer-Kestner became convinced of Dreyfus's innocence. From then until his death in 1899, he worked ceaselessly in behalf of Dreyfus. (*Illustrated London News*, September 30, 1899)

GEORGES CLEMENCEAU, DEFENDER OF DREYFUS
When Dreyfus was condemned, Georges Clemenceau was 53 years old. Behind him was a tempestuous career as political radical and journalistic-critic. At first he believed Dreyfus guilty, but he soon became aware that a gross miscarriage of justice had taken place. It was Clemenceau who gave the arresting title to Zola's "*J'Accuse.*" From the Zola trial on, Clemenceau became a most powerful voice in speaking for Dreyfus. (*Bibliothèque Nationale*)

MATHIEU DREYFUS, BROTHER OF ALFRED DREYFUS; HE WORKED INCESSANTLY TO VINDICATE HIS BROTHER

M. BERNARD-LAZARE (1866–1903), AUTHOR OF THE FIRST PRO-DREYFUS PAMPHLET, "A JUDICIAL ERROR" (*Illustrated London News*, September 30, 1899)

In this cartoon, Georges Clemenceau is shown receiving a bag of gold from a German officer standing before the "Espionage Bureau." Along with the gold is a set of "Instructions for the Dreyfus Syndicate." Clemenceau thanks his benefactor in German: *"Danke sehr, Herr Kamerad!"* and tells the officer to inform his chief that "I am going to send him my report." (*L'Antijuif*, September 15, 1898)

Eugène-Henri Brisson, Premier of France from June to October 1898, was won over as a Dreyfus adherent. The cartoon shows how Brisson was supposedly persuaded to the Dreyfus side. Rothschild and Reinach offer him dreams of a great future. A little band of *"Youpins"* ("Yids") dances around Brisson, tugging at his cloak. (*L'Antijuif*, September 22, 1898)

ÉMILE ZOLA

Prior to the Dreyfus case, Zola had studiously avoided public life, but he became convinced that Dreyfus was the innocent victim of a nefarious conspiracy; he decided to bring the truth into the open. In November and December of 1897, he published three articles in *Le Figaro*, followed by a number of pamphlets. Esterhazy's acquittal on January 11, 1898, spurred him to write his famous *"J'Accuse"* letter, published in *L'Aurore* on January 13, 1898, denouncing the conspirators by name and deliberately seeking prosecution for libel. Legal action followed promptly, and the fierce light of publicity was thrown on the case, which was exactly what Zola wanted.

ZOLA'S "J'ACCUSE" LETTER IN "L'AURORE," JANUARY 13, 1898

ANTI-DREYFUS CARTOON SHOWING "THE HOUSE OF ALFRED DREYFUS, JUDAS AND CO."
SELLING MILITARY SECRETS

DREYFUS DEPICTED AS "THE TRAITOR"

PICQUART SHOWN AS A CAMEL

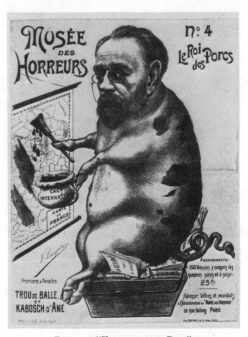

ZOLA AS "KING OF THE PIGS"

GENERAL DE PELLIEUX INTERROGATING ESTERHAZY (*Petit Journal*, December 19, 1897)

READING THE VERDICT AT THE TRIAL OF ESTERHAZY, JANUARY 11, 1898
The trial resulted in a prompt acquittal. Note that the spectators are cheering the verdict.
(*Petit Journal*, June 1898)

THE TRIAL OF ÉMILE ZOLA IN PARIS: SKETCHES MADE IN THE COURT-
ROOM

MAÎTRE DEMANGE, ZOLA'S COUNSEL
"Maître Salies has told me that an officer who was a member of the court-martial [of Dreyfus] said to him that a secret document was communicated to the court-martial."

MAÎTRE CHANTEREAU, ADVOCATE-GENERAL
"We have been present at fourteen sittings without a word having been said on the question we are here to decide: 'Has M. Zola been guilty of defaming the Army?'"

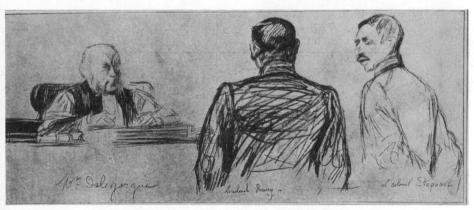

HENRY ACCUSES PICQUART AT THE ZOLA TRIAL
Left to right: M. Delegorgue, Presiding Judge, Henry, and Picquart. (*Illustrated London News*, September 30, 1899)

Anti-Zola Postcard Sold on the Streets of Paris
The workman's movable arm dunks Zola in the barrel (see illustration at right).

Anti-Zola Postcard Sold on the Streets of Paris
The workman's arm is movable (see illustration at left).

LA VÉRITÉ

Finira-t-on par la faire sortir?...

THE DREYFUSARDS STRIKE BACK IN CARTOONS

The goddess of truth, in the well, is being hauled out by the Dreyfusards (upper right), while the editors of the anti-Semitic journal, *La Libre Parole*, rush in from upper left with a huge candle snuffer. In the foreground, a French general peers through a telescope which is being covered by Bertillon, the handwriting "expert," dressed as a necromancer. Caption: "Will they ever get her out?" (*Le Grelot*, Paris)

PICQUART IN THE CHERCHE-MIDI PRISON
(*Graphic*, London, September 14, 1899)

COLONEL HENRY ON THE WITNESS STAND
Picquart stands to his right. (*Bibliothèque
Nationale*)

LIEUTENANT-COLONEL HENRY
Enmeshed in a web of forgeries and unable to extricate himself, the unhappy officer committed suicide on August 31, 1898. To the last, Henry insisted that he had worked in the interest of France, and that Dreyfus's guilt was necessary for the "honor" of the country. (*Bibliothèque Nationale*)

MME. HENRY
The devoted wife of Henry pathetically maintained a firm belief in her husband's innocence. Generals, politicians, clergy, and journalists honored the "patriotic forgeries" of her husband, and raised a considerable subscription fund for her use. (*Bibliothèque Nationale*)

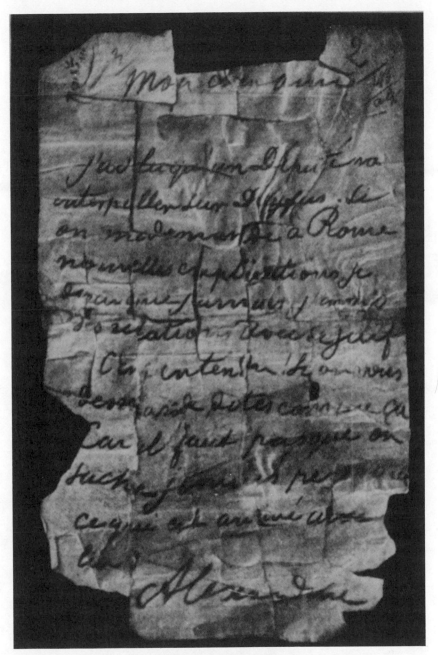

HENRY QUESTIONED BY MINISTER OF WAR CAVAIGNAC, AUGUST 31, 1898 (Fauret, Associated Press)

THE FUNERAL CORTÈGE OF COLONEL HENRY, SUICIDE (*Bibliothèque Nationale*)

IX

The Court of Cassation Orders
a New Trial

On September 3, 1898, following the suicide of Henry and the flight of Esterhazy from France, Mme. Dreyfus submitted a request for an appeal of her husband's case. Three weeks later the Cabinet decided to transmit the request to the Court of Cassation. This court was composed of three divisions, each with fifteen judges and a presiding judge. The Division of Requests and the Civil Division were concerned with appeals in civil suits, while the Criminal Division had jurisdiction over criminal appeals, including those coming from courts-martial.

The Criminal Division of the Court of Cassation decided that it would open an inquiry, which lasted from October 29, 1898, to June 3, 1899. Eventually it was decided that there was merit in the call for appeal and the case was remanded to a second court-martial.

The Times (London) Publishes Its Longest Letter-to-the-Editor, October 13, 1898

"I have thought it might be useful to readers of The Times . . ."

The Times (*London*), *October 13, 1898.*

Many an Englishman would rather see his own letter published in *The Times* than be the recipient of the Victoria Cross. It was considered a rare distinction to have one's letter appear in the great newspaper. Spellbound by the Dreyfus case, the English public sent hundreds of letters to *The Times,* which consistently regarded the conviction of Dreyfus as "not only an illegality, but an iniquity."

On October 13, 1898, while Dreyfus was still on Devil's Island, *The Times* published an extraordinary letter-to-the-editor. It was written by Sir Godfrey Lushington, then Permanent Undersecretary of State for Home Affairs, who believed, as did *The Times,* that all the facts known in the case should be presented to the public. The newspaper devoted a full page and a quarter of its large format to the letter, 10,000 words, in all probability the longest letter-to-the-editor ever published. It is presented here in full as an admirable summary of the case up to the second court-martial at Rennes.

THE DREYFUS CASE
AN EXAMINATION OF THE FACTS AND THE EVIDENCE
TO THE EDITOR OF "THE TIMES"

Sir,—I have thought it might be useful to the readers of *The Times* to have, in outline, a continuous narrative of the principal events of the Dreyfus case, and with this view I submit the following. It does not profess to be more than a compilation of what has already been given to the public, piecemeal, in the shape of news; for the most part it is presented without comment, and I have endeavoured to distinguish between established facts and what has been alleged with more or less probability.

The Charge Against Dreyfus

In October, 1894, Captain Alfred Dreyfus, an artillery officer on the staff, was arrested for treason. He belonged to a respected Jewish family in Alsace, his military character was unblemished, and he was in easy circumstances. At this time General Mercier and Minister of War General de Boisdeffre, Chief of the Staff (practically Commander-in-Chief of the French Army), General Gonse, Assistant Chief, Colonel Sandherr, well-known as an anti-Semite, was head of the Intelligence Department: under him were Commandants Picquart, Henry, and Lauth, also the archivist Gribelin. Commandant du Paty de Clam was an officer attached to the General Staff. Commandant Esterhazy was serving with his regiment. On October 15, on the order of the Minister of War, Captain Dreyfus was arrested by Commandant du Paty de Clam, and taken in the charge of Commandant Henry to the Cherche-Midi Prison, of which Commandant Forzinetti was governor. For a fortnight extraordinary precautions were taken to keep his arrest an absolute secret, from the public and even from his own family. His wife alone knew of it, but dared not speak, for Commandant du Paty de Clam is alleged to have forbidden her, with threats that her husband's life depended upon her silence. Even the prison officials, with the exception of the governor, were not to know who their prisoner was, or what he was charged with. The imprisonment was most rigorous. Captain Dreyfus was not allowed pen, ink, or paper, or to write to or receive a letter from anyone, even his wife or his lawyer; he was not so much as told what his offence was, beyond that it was treason in the betrayal of military secrets, and day after day he was subjected to long private interrogations by Commandant du Paty de Clam, who had been appointed, as officer of judiciary police, to make the preliminary inquiry into the case. So harsh was his treatment that Commandant Forzinetti felt it his duty to take the strong step of making a formal representation to the Minister of War and also to the Governor of Paris, at the same time declaring his own conviction that Captain Dreyfus was an innocent man. On October 31 Commandant du Paty de Clam made his report, which has not seen the light, and on November 3 Commandant d'Ormescheville was appointed *rapporteur* to conduct a further inquiry, and in due course to draw up a formal report, which practically constitutes the case for the prosecution. Not until then was Captain Dreyfus informed of the particulars and of the charges about to be laid against him. From this report of Commandant d'Ormescheville's we learn that the basis of the accusation against Captain Dreyfus was a document known by the name of the *bordereau*. Neither Commandant d'Ormescheville's report nor the *bordereau* has been officially published by the Government, but both ultimately found their way into the newspapers. The *bordereau* was a communication not itself addressed, nor signed. It began:

> *Sans nouvelles m'indiquant que vous désirez me voir, je vous adresse cependant, Monsieur, quelques renseignements intéressants:* *

Then followed the titles of the military documents, I, etc.

The report stated that the *bordereau* had fallen into the hands of the Minister of War, but how the Minister of War declined to say, beyond making a general statement that the circumstances showed that it had been sent to an agent of a foreign Power. It is now generally accepted that it had been brought to the War Office by a spy—an Alsatian porter who was in the service of Colonel von Schwartzkoppen, then the Military Attaché to the German Embassy in Paris. The report contained nothing

---

* The compositor of *The Times*, apparently faced with a quick deadline and not too familiar with the French language, made many errors in getting the letter ready for publication. The most glaring of these errors in French have been corrected. (*Editor's Note.*)

to show that Captain Dreyfus had been following treasonable practices to connect him in any manner with the *bordereau*. The sole question for the court-martial was whether the *bordereau* was in his handwriting. On this the experts were divided, three being of opinion that it was, two that it was not, in his handwriting.

The Trial and Sentence

The court-martial was duly held, and Captain Dreyfus had the aid of counsel, Maître Demange, but the first act of the court was, at the instance of the Government representative, to declare [secrecy] so that none but those concerned were present. After the evidence had been taken, the Court, according to custom, adjourned to consider their verdict in private. Ultimately, they found Captain Dreyfus guilty, and he was sentenced to be publicly expelled from the Army and imprisoned for life. Not till after his conviction was he allowed to communicate with his wife and family. The sentence has been carried out with the utmost rigour. Captain Dreyfus was transferred to *Île du Diable,* where he lives in solitary confinement. No one is allowed to communicate with him but his wife. Her letters, of course, pass through the hands of the Governor, who, it is reported, strikes out any reference they may contain to what is going on in France. For his services in the conduct of the prosecution Commandant du Paty de Clam was promoted to be Lieutenant-Colonel. The court-martial having been held within closed doors, the public at large knew nothing of Commandant d'Ormescheville's report or of the *bordereau*—nothing, it may be said, beyond the fact that Captain Dreyfus had been convicted of betraying military secrets to a foreign Power, and they had no suspicion that there had been any irregularities at the court-martial or that the verdict was a mistaken one. The Dreyfus family, no doubt, made representations, but for two years the Dreyfus question may be said to have slumbered.

Picquart and Esterhazy

In the course of time Colonel Sandherr, who died in January, 1897, had been compelled to retire for ill-health, and Commandant Picquart became head of the Intelligence Department. Commandant Picquart bore a distinguished record in the service and an excellent private reputation. He is a Catholic, and by birth an Alsatian. In May, 1896, there were brought to the Intelligence Department of the War Office some more sweepings from Colonel von Schwartzkoppen's wastepaper basket by the same Alsatian porter who had brought the *bordereau*. These were put by Commandant Henry into a packet, and given by him according to the usual custom to Commandant Picquart. Commandant Picquart swears that among these were about 60 small pieces of paper. These (also according to custom) he gave to Commandant Lauth to piece together. When pieced together they were found to constitute the document which is known by the name of *petit bleu,* a *carte télégramme* for transmission through the post office, but which had never been posted. It was addressed to Commandant Esterhazy, and ran as follows:

> *J'attends avant tout une explication plus détaillée que celle que vous m'avez donnée, l'autre jour, sur la question en suspens. En conséquence, je vous prie de me la donner par écrit, pour pouvoir juger si je peux continuer mes relations avec la maison R. ou non.*
>
> (Signed) C. t.
>
> *M. le Commandant Esterhazy,*
> *27, Rue de la Bienfaisance, Paris*

At this time Commandant Esterhazy was a stranger to Commandant Picquart, and the first step which Commandant Picquart took was to make inquiry as to who and what he was. His character proved most disreputable, and he was in money difficulties. The next was to obtain a specimen of the handwriting in order to compare it with other writings which had been brought by spies to the office and were kept there. In this way it came about that it was compared with the facsimile of the *bordereau,* when, lo and behold, the writings of the two appeared identical. It was Commandant Esterhazy, then, who had written the *bordereau,* and if Commandant Esterhazy, then not Captain Dreyfus. Commandant Picquart pushed on his inquiries and, among other things, had Commandant Esterhazy's letters intercepted in the post; but no further information seems to have been gained from this source. Commandant Picquart acquainted his chiefs of what had been done—namely, General de Boisdeffre in July, and his own immediate superior, General Gonse, in September, and about this time a correspondence on the subject took place between Commandant Picquart and General Gonse. The substance of it was that General Gonse was for continuing the inquiry, but for separating it from the Dreyfus case; he was against any writing being subjected to experts, and he enjoined on Commandant Picquart prudence, prudence. Commandant Picquart's reply of September 9 [the correct date is September 8, 1896] must be given in full:

> *Mon Général. J'ai lu attentivement votre lettre et je suivrai scrupuleusement vos instructions. Mais je crois devoir vous dire ceci: De nombreux indices et un fait grave dont je vous parletri*

*à votre retour me montrent que le moment est proche où des
gens qui ont la conviction qu'on s'est trompé à leur égard sont
tout tenter et falté un gros scandale.*

*Je crois avoir fait le necessaire pour que l'initiative vienne de
nous. Si l'on perd trop de temps, l'initiative viendra d'ailleurs,
ce qui, abstraction de considérations plus elévées pas le beau
rôle.*

*Je dois ajouter que ces gens-là ne me paraissent pas inform,—
comme nous le sommes et que leur tentative me parait devoir
aboutir à un gros gáchis, un scandale, un gros bruit qui n'ame-
nera pourtant pas la clarité. Ce sera une se facheuse, inutile
et qu'on pourrait éviter en faisant justice à temps.*

Veuiller, &c.

PICQUART

The Secret Documents

On September 15 of the same year, 1896, took place the first explosion.
This solely concerned the Dreyfus trial. On that day the *Éclair,* an anti-
Semitic newspaper, published an article titled *Le Traitre,* in which they
stated that at the court-martial the *pièce d'accusation* on which Captain
Dreyfus was tried was the *bordereau;* but that after the Court had retired to the "chamber of deliberation," there was communicated to them
from the War Office, in the absence of the prisoner and his counsel, a
document purporting to be addressed by the German military attaché
to his colleague at the Italian Embassy in Paris, and ending with a post-
script, *"Cet animal de Dreyfus devient trop exigeant";* further, that this
document was the only one in which appeared the name Dreyfus. This
at once had removed all doubts from the minds of the court-martial,
who thereupon had unanimously brought the prisoner in guilty; and the
Éclair called upon the Government to produce this document and thus
satisfy the public conscience.

This document has, for sufficient reasons hereinafter appearing, come
to be known as the *document libérateur,* and by this name we will distinguish it. As to the article in the *Éclair,* it must have proceeded from
a member of the court-martial or from some one in the War Office; but
whether its contents were true is a matter which to this day has not been
fully cleared up. This much, however, is known. We have the authority
of Maître Demange (Captain Dreyfus's advocate) that no such document
was brought before the court-martial during the proceedings at which
he was present. On the other hand, it has now been admitted that at the
date of Captain Dreyfus's trial there was, and that there had been for
some months previously, in the archives of the War Office a similar docu-

ment, not in the Dreyfus *dossier* proper, but in a secret *dossier*, only that the words therein are not *"Cet animal de Dreyfus,"* but *"Ce (sic) capitaine D———"* (initial only) *"devient trop exigeant."* And the explanation of this divergence which is suggested by the friends of Captain Dreyfus is that General Mercier, the Minister of War, did not lay the document itself before the court-martial but either read it or referred to its contents, in either case, however, expanding the letter D into Dreyfus, and that the informant of the *Éclair,* being able to speak only from memory, repeated the words as *"Cet animal de Dreyfus."* The Government have never yet either admitted or denied that General Mercier went down to the court-martial and made to them a secret communication. General Mercier himself at the Zola trial in 1898 held diverse language. First, he denied that he knew the document; when asked whether he had privately communicated a secret document to the Court, he refused to answer on the ground that it related to the *"affaire Dreyfus,"* to *"la chose jugée";* then he said that it was not true, and that Dreyfus was a traitor who had been *"justement et légalement condamné";* lastly, when called upon to speak precisely, and asked, *"M. le Général Mercier, dit-il qu'il n'est-pas vrai qu'une pièce secrète ait été communiquée? Ou M. le Général Mercier, dit-il qu'il ne la répété à qui que ce soit?"* His answer was—*"Je n'ai pas à repondre à la première question; mais en ce qui concerne la seconde, je dis que ce n'est pas exact."*

Publication of the *Bordereau*

As might be expected the article in the *Éclair* occasioned a considerable stir; both parties welcomed it, the one as showing Captain Dreyfus to have been really a traitor and therefore justly deserving his sentence; the other as a proof of whether guilty or not he had been condemned illegally on a document used behind his back. The public excitement was increased when on the 10th of November the *Matin*—a War Office journal—published what purported to be a facsimile of the *bordereau,* and a host of experts and others set to work to compare it with the accused's handwriting. The reproduction was no doubt made, not from the original *bordereau* which was in the sealed-up Dreyfus *dossier,* but from a photograph of it. And the photograph must have been obtained surreptitiously from some one in the War Office or from some one who had attended the secret court-martial. The correctness of the text has not been questioned, but there has been some controversy how far the form is sufficiently accurate for purposes of comparison, *i.e.,* to enable experts and others to judge whether the handwriting is identical or not with any other handwriting.

The natural sequel to these revelations was an interpellation in the

Chamber—the *interpellation Castelin* of November 18, 1896. On that day, M. Castelin, an anti-Semite deputy, by asking some question as to the safe custody of Dreyfus, gave the Government an opportunity. General Billot, then Minister of War, replied in general terms:—

> *1. Instruction de l'affaire, les débats, le jugement, ont eu lieu conformément aux régles de la procédure militaire. Le Conseil de Guerre regulierement composé, a regulierement déliberé, &c.*

The Parting of the Ways

There are now to be related a series of events which would be altogether mystifying to the reader unless he was acquainted beforehand with the two interpretations of them offered by the two opposite parties.

This view, as put forward by Maître Labori, M. Zola's counsel, who, in his defence of M. Zola was also defending Colonel Picquart, was this: —The *interpellation Castelin* was the parting of the ways. The Government by this time knew that General Mercier had interfered with the court-martial. They also knew, or had no doubt, that Commandant Esterhazy was the author of the *bordereau*. They should, therefore, after due further inquiry, have confessed—what was the fault of their predecessors—that the Dreyfus trial had been illegally conducted, and that an innocent man had been wrongly condemned. But they dared not do so. They therefore now resolved to uphold the Dreyfus verdict, to drop the case within the War Office against Commandant Esterhazy, and shield him if he were ever to be attacked from outside. To Commandant Esterhazy himself this, of course, was a matter of life and death, and in Colonel du Paty de Clam and others at the War Office he had powerful friends, who had command of the official documents, and who, from self-interest or fear, were ready to serve as tools in carrying out the War Office policy imposed by the chiefs of the Army,—viz., General Billot, the Minister of War, General de Boisdeffre and General Gonse, the chief and assistant chief of the Staff. The policy was one which, once adopted, had of necessity to be carried out through thick and thin to the bitter end. At present the world outside the War Office knew nothing of Commandant Esterhazy. But Commandant Picquart knew of him, was possessed of proofs of his guilt, and was incorruptible. Commandant Picquart, therefore, must be removed, discredited, silenced. The first step was to get him at once out of Paris, and this they did on the eve of the *interpellation Castelin;* the next to keep extending his mission, and, after an interval, to appoint him to a post of personal danger. The next was to compromise him by sending him anonymously, false telegrams and letters, which might be of use to support any charge that might afterwards be made that he was acting in conspiracy with a secret Drey-fusard syndicate. The next, to invent, as opportunity arose, false charges against him, as that he had intercepted Commandant Esterhazy's letters without authority; that he had disclosed or abstracted secret documents, and even that he had forged the *petit bleu* against Commandant Ester-hazy. Such charges would be heard before a secret military tribunal, and thus in some way or other they would get Commandant Picquart shut up in prison.

The opposite explanation which has always been put forward by the Government was, as might be expected, something like this: We were *bona fide* convinced that Captain Dreyfus was guilty and had been legally condemned; also that the suspicions of Commandant Picquart against Commandant Esterhazy were unfounded. The occurrence of the secret mission at the same time as the *interpellation Castelin* was a coincidence, and we chose Commandant Picquart for it simply because he was quali-fied to undertake it and, because we thought that to one who had Ester-hazy on the brain a change of scene and occupation would be salutary. At that time we gave credit to Commandant Picquart for being sincere, but on further inquiry we found that he was acting in league with the Dreyfusards, and that in order to save Captain Dreyfus he was bent on fastening the offence of treason falsely upon the innocent Commandant Esterhazy. We have made no false charge against Commandant Picquart; the charges have been true. If any false letters or telegrams have been sent to him, we have had nothing to do with that. We are honourable officers and throughout have acted as such; and the secrecy which we have been compelled to observe is in accordance with the French law, the rules of the service, and for the public good.

Picquart's Mission to Tunis

Let these theories be judged by the facts. On November 14, 1896, on the eve of the *interpellation Castelin,* Commandant Picquart was sent on a secret mission which has not been disclosed. He left his duties as head of the Intelligence Department nominally in the hands of General Gonse, his superior, but practically to be discharged by Commandant Henry, who was Commandant Picquart's subordinate. He requested his family to address their private letters for him to the War Office, whence they would be forwarded. His secret mission, or missions, took him first to Nancy, then to Besançon (permission being refused for him to return to Paris even for a night to renew his wardrobe), later on to Algeria and Tunisia, with instructions to proceed to the frontier. This is the account which Colonel Picquart gave on oath of a conversation he had with the General through whom were transmitted to him the instructions of the

War Office with regard to his frontier mission, and his account has not been contradicted:

> *Il me parla du prétexte pour lequel je devais aller sur la fron-*
> *tière, et me dit "Cela n'existe plus; cela vient d'être dementi.*
> *Tout cela ne tient pas debout, et je ne veux pas que vous alliez*
> *plus loin que Gabes."*

The frontier was not one of the easiest places in the world, and the General of the district would not allow him to go there, and accordingly telegraphed home for further instructions concerning him. In March, 1897, Commandant Picquart was appointed Lieutenant-Colonel of the 4th Tirailleurs, the appointment being represented to him as a favour. He was the youngest Colonel in the service. In his stead Commandant Henry became Chief of the Intelligence Department.

Mysterious Communications

Shortly after Commandant Picquart started from Paris a letter, dated November 20, 1896, had been forwarded to him from the War Office, having first been opened there. It was a genuine letter from the secretary to Mlle. Blanche de Comminges, a lady of rank and position, a friend of Colonel Picquart's. The letter, with much else of a commonplace character, contained the following passage:

> *Le demi-dieu demande tous les jours à Mlle. la Comtesse*
> *quand il pourra voir le bon-dieu.*

Words very enigmatical to strangers, and readily lending themselves to use by anyone who fancied or was trying to prove that the recipient was party to a secret conspiracy: but inside the circle of Mlle. Blanche de Comminges they were familiar enough. The lady has explained them on oath. *Demi-dieu* was the nickname of a Captain de Lallement, *bon-dieu* that of Colonel Picquart. Mlle. de Comminges was, of course, *Mlle. la Comtesse*. This, so far as appears, is not now questioned. From the first Colonel Picquart had, of course, felt some uneasiness at being sent on those missions away from his ordinary duties, and various little circumstances occurred to increase it, and in May, 1897, having occasion to write unofficially to Commandant Henry, now Chief of the Intelligence Department, he expressed himself strongly as to the mystery and falsities with which his departure had been surrounded; and he received a reply dated June 3, in which Commandant Henry said that the mystery he could well enough explain by what had come to his knowledge after some inquiry, and he alluded in general to three circumstances— (1) Opening letters in the post; (2) attempt to suborn two officers in the service to speak to a certain writing as being that of a certain person; and (3) the opening of a secret *dossier*. The first Colonel Picquart knew to refer to his having intercepted Commandant Esterhazy's; the other two allusions he did not at the time (June, 1897) fully understand; but the letter, couched in such terms and coming from one who had until lately been his subordinate, and now was the head of the Department, convinced him that he was the object of serious and secret machinations in the War Office. He immediately applied for leave and came to Paris. There he determined, with a view to his self-defence, to obtain legal advice from an advocate, M. Leblois; saw him, and showed him Colonel Henry's letters, and whilst abstaining (according to his own account and that of M. Leblois) from touching on the third matter, the secret *dossier*, spoke freely on the other two—on the *affaires* Dreyfus and Esterhazy generally; also in order to explain how far he had acted with the sanction or recognizance of his superiors, he placed in his hands the correspondence—not official but confidential—about Commandant Esterhazy which he had had with General Gonse in 1896. He left it to M. Leblois to take what course he might think, and returned to Sousse. In the course of the autumn he was summoned to Tunis and asked by the military authority there whether he had been robbed of a secret document by a woman. The question seemed a strange one and was answered by him with a simple negative. Later on he received at Sousse two telegrams from Paris, dated November 10. One:

> "*Arrêtez le demi-dieu; tout est découvert; affaire très grave.*
> *Speranza.*"

The other:

> "*On a preuve que le petit bleu a été fabriqué par Georges.*
> *Blanche.*"*

This was addressed to Sousse.

And two days after he received a letter, likewise of November 10,

---

* Either Sir Godfrey Lushington, writer of the letter, or *The Times* itself made many errors in giving the texts of both telegrams. In the *Speranza* telegram the word *Bondieu* is used instead of the correct *demi-dieu*, and the phrases are separated by periods instead of semicolons. In the *Blanche* telegram, "*est fabriqué*" is used instead of the correct "*a été fabriqué.*" Accurate rendition of such documents has long been a problem in quick journalistic reproduction. (*Editor's note.*)

from Esterhazy, an abusive one, charging him with conspiring against him, &c. He felt certain that the telegrams were sent in order to compromise him. His Christian name was Georges: Blanche that of Mlle. de Comminges. The second telegram certainly came from within the War Office, for it referred to the *petit bleu,* which no one outside the War Office knew anything about, M. Leblois excepted. Colonel Picquart suspected Commandant Esterhazy to be the author of the telegrams, the more so that in Commandant Esterhazy's letter and in one of the telegrams his own name Picquart was spelled without a *c.* He at once telegraphed to Tunis for leave to come and see the General there. He did see him and forwarded to the Minister of War the three documents with a covering letter in which he demanded an inquiry. He then obtained leave to go to Paris, but the condition was imposed on him that he should see no one before presenting himself to General de Pellieux. When he saw the General he learned for the first time and to his surprise that ever since he left Paris in November, 1896, his letters had been intercepted and examined at the War Office and he was called upon to explain various letters and documents. 1. The letter with reference to *demi-dieu* and *bon-dieu,* a copy of which had been retained at the War Office. 2. A bogus letter to him which had been detained at the War Office and never forwarded to him, dated December 15, 1896:—*"Depuis votre malencontreux départ, votre oeuvre est compromise; le demi-dieu attend des instructions pour agir."* 3 and 4. The two telegrams already described, received by him at Sousse.

M. Scheurer-Kestner's Intervention

Before June, 1897, Commandant Esterhazy's name had not been breathed to the public; it is now to come out, and from two independent sources.

Some little time after seeing Colonel Picquart, in June, 1897, M. Leblois had determined, in his interest, to consult M. Scheurer-Kestner, who was well-known to have taken an interest in the *affaire Dreyfus,* because of the suspicion that Captain Dreyfus had been condemned on a document which he had never seen and because of the discrepancies between Captain Dreyfus's handwriting and that of the *bordereau.* He was Vice-President of the Senate and a personal friend of General Billot, the Minister of War. M. Leblois communicated to him what he knew about Commandant Esterhazy and showed him General Gonse's letters to Colonel Picquart. In October M. Scheurer-Kestner communicated on the subject both with General Billot and with the President of the Council, M. Méline. He was now to learn the name of Commandant Esterhazy from another quarter. One afternoon in the end of October a

M. de Castro, a stockbroker, was seated in a *café* in Paris, and a boy from the street came up with copies of the facsimile of the *bordereau,* which had then been on sale for more than a year. M. de Castro bought a copy, and at once recognized, as he thought, the handwriting of the *bordereau* to be that of Commandant Esterhazy, who had been a client of his. He took the copy home, compared it with letters of Commandant Esterhazy, and all doubts vanished. His friends told M. Mathieu Dreyfus, who begged him to take the letters to M. Scheurer-Kestner, and he did so on November 12, 1897, and M. Scheurer-Kestner advised that M. Mathieu Dreyfus should go to General Billot and denounce Commandant Esterhazy as the author of the *bordereau.* And now to turn to Commandant Esterhazy. His own statement is this. In the month of October, 1897, when in the country, he received a letter from "Speranza" giving minute details of a plot against himself, the instigator of which was, Speranza said, a colonel named Piquart (without the *c*). He at once went to Paris, saw the Minister of War, and gave him Speranza's letter. Shortly afterwards he received a telegram asking him to be behind the palisades of the bridge Alexander III, at 11:30 P.M. He would there meet a person who would give him important information. He kept his appointment, met a veiled woman, who, first binding him over under oath to respect her incognito, gave him details of the plot of the "band" against himself. Afterwards he had three similar interviews, but not at the same place. At the second of these four interviews the unknown woman * gave him a letter saying:—

> "*Prenez la pièce contenu dans cette enveloppe, elle preuve votre innocence, et si le torchon brule, n'hésitez pas à vous en servir.*"

This document, henceforward called *le document libérateur,* was no other than the letter referred to in the *Éclair* (*ce canaille de D.*), which,

* On the authority of M. Leblois we have it that, in 1892, Mlle. Blanche de Comminges, who has already been mentioned, was pestered with offensive anonymous letters. Suspecting M. du Paty de Clam, she requested the intervention of a gentleman of her acquaintance. The general saw M. du Paty de Clam, and as a fact the anonymous letters thenceforth ceased. The lady was also desirous of recovering her correspondence from M. du Paty de Clam, and all the letters were restored except one, which he said had fallen into the hands of an unknown woman, who refused to give it up except on payment of 500 francs. Ultimately an appointment was made for a meeting at 10 P.M. on the banks of the Seine near the Jardin des Plantes. M. du Paty de Clam went to the spot with some friends, saw a lady, spoke apart for a moment with her, and came back, saying he had paid her 500 francs and she had given him the letter, which was then restored to Mlle. de Comminges. At the Zola trial M. du Paty de Clam refused to answer questions on this subject.

of course, ought to have been safe in the archives of the Intelligence Department. On November 14 Commandant Esterhazy returned this document to the Minister of War under a covering letter in which he called upon the chief to defend his honour thus menaced. The Minister of War sent Commandant Esterhazy a receipt. The next day the Minister received a letter from Mathieu Dreyfus denouncing Commandant Esterhazy as the author of the *bordereau*. The letter of Speranza to Commandant Esterhazy has not yet been divulged to the public; and the War Office, after diligent inquiries, have not been able to find the veiled woman. Very different was the interpretation put on this narrative by M. Trarieux, ex-Minister of Justice, and others interested in revision. Their suggestion was that Commandant Esterhazy was in the first instance apprised beforehand by his friends in the War Office of the coming danger and was for flying across the frontier, but that subsequently these same friends, finding that the chiefs of the Army were fearful of being compromised by his flight from justice and would make common cause with him, wished to recall him, and with this view took from the archives the *document libérateur,* and sent it to him as an assurance that he might safely return and stand his trial, and also with a view to his claiming the credit of having restored to the office a document which it is now intended to charge Colonel Picquart with abstracting.

More War Office Inquiries

On November 16, 1897, on a question being asked in the Chamber, General Billot, Minister of War, replied that he had made inquiries, and the result *"n'ébranlait nullement dans mon esprit l'autorité de la chose jugée,"* but that as a formal denunciation of an officer of the Army had been made by the *famille* Dreyfus, there would be a military investigation. A fortnight or so afterwards he repeated that the Government considered the *affaire Dreyfus comme régulièrement et justement jugée.* Here, as elsewhere, the reader will remember that the question at issue was who was the author of the *bordereau,* and that if Captain Dreyfus was, Commandant Esterhazy could not be. Consequently, a public declaration by the Minister of War that Captain Dreyfus had been justly condemned was as much as to say that Commandant Esterhazy must be acquitted. General de Pellieux, temporary Military Governor of Paris, was appointed to make the first preliminary inquiry into Commandant Esterhazy's case; and he, without stopping to have the writing of Commandant Esterhazy compared with that of the *bordereau,* made his report, which, though not published, was in favour of *non-lieu—* i.e., was to the effect that there was no ground for proceeding against Commandant Esterhazy, and that irregularities were proved against

Colonel Picquart. The next step was for a formal investigation and report; this task was assigned to Commandant Ravary. The report was afterwards read at the court-martial. But it is unnecessary to criticize it here beyond saying that it followed General de Pellieux in pronouncing in favour of *non-lieu* in the case of Commandant Esterhazy. It referred to the Dreyfus judgment as *"légalement et justement rendu"*; treated the story of the veiled woman as serious, and the origin of the *petit bleu* as suspicious; and threw out against Colonel Picquart a number of imputations which it suggested might properly form the subject of another investigation.

Notwithstanding these two reports, General Saussier determined that there should be a court-martial on Commandant Esterhazy. When the court met the Government representative prayed for the *huis clos,* but the court preferred a public hearing; ultimately a compromise was effected. Commandant Ravary's report (the case for the prosecution) was read, and two or three witnesses, including M. Mathieu Dreyfus and M. Scheurer-Kestner, were heard in public; then the doors were closed and Colonel Picquart, M. Leblois, the experts, and other witnesses gave their evidence in private; the three experts pronounced that the *bordereau* was not in Commandant Esterhazy's handwriting. Commandant Esterhazy was acquitted.

M. Zola's Letter

On the morrow of Commandant Esterhazy's acquittal, M. Zola launched his letter of January 13, 1898, which was addressed to the President of the Republic, and wound up with a series of formal accusations attributing the gravest iniquities to all concerned in either of the courts-martial, each officer in turn being pointedly mentioned by name. M. Zola's avowed object was to get himself prosecuted for defamation and to obtain an opportunity for bringing out *"la lumière"* on the whole situation. The Minister of War so far accepted the challenge as to institute a prosecution for the Assizes; but resolving to maintain the *chose jugée* as to the *affaire Dreyfus,* he carefully chose his own ground so as to avoid that subject, selecting from the whole letter only 15 lines as constituting the defamation. In particular as to one sentence, which ran:

> [*J'accuse le premier conseil de guerre d'avoir violé le droit en condamnant un accusé sur une pièce restée secrète, et*] *j'accuse le second conseil de guerre d'avoir couvert cette illégalité par ordre, en commettant à son tour le crime juridique d'acquitter sciemment un coupable:*

the prosecution omitted the first half of the sentence, the part within brackets. By French law it is for the defendants to justify the defamatory words assigned, and to prove their good faith. But this was a difficult task even for M. Labori, the counsel for M. Zola.

Difficulties of Procedure

There were several notable obstacles to be passed before light could reach the Court:

1. The *chose jugée* as applicable to the *affaire Dreyfus.* 2. The *huis clos;* the whole proceedings at the Dreyfus trial, and all the more important part of the proceedings at the Esterhazy trial, having been conducted within closed doors. 3. The *secret d'État* excluding all references to foreign Governments. 4. The *secret professionel,* pleaded not only by officers civil and military, but even by the experts employed by the Court for the identification of handwriting. 5. To these may be added the unwillingness of a witness for any reason whatever. Thus Colonel du Paty de Clam was allowed to refuse to answer questions as to his conduct in family affairs; and as for the Commandant Esterhazy, he turned his back on the defendants and and refused to answer any questions whatever suggested by them, although it was put to him by the mouth of the Judge. And, as M. Labori took no steps to enforce answers, it is presumed he had no power to compel an unwilling witness cited by himself. But, though the evidence was thus blocked at every turn, it should be mentioned that French law seems to place no restriction upon the pleading of counsel, and when M. Labori came to address the jury, he was allowed to place before them in full his own version of the whole case, except so far as related to the action of foreign countries or their representatives. Of the above-mentioned obligations to silence, three were such as it was within the competence of the Government to dispense from. No dispensation was given, and hence it was that the Minister of War even as prosecutor pressing his legal right to call upon the defendants, under pain of conviction, to prove the truth of the alleged libel, and at the same time, by the exercize or non-exercize of his official authority, preventing the witnesses for the defence from stating the facts that were within their knowledge and most material to the truth. But the *chose jugée* was a legal entity by which was meant not merely that the sentence could not be legally disputed, but that it was to be accepted as *la verité légale;* no word of evidence was to be admitted which in any way referred to any part of the proceedings—the whole affair was to be eliminated. The bar thus raised was very effectual in shutting out of Court larger classes of witnesses who would speak only of the *affaire Dreyfus,* but difficulty

arose in the case of other witnesses. It was not easy to show on what principle the *affaire Dreyfus* was a *chose jugée,* when the *affaire Esterhazy,* decided by an exactly similar Court, was not. The two cases could hardly be separated, for, if Captain Dreyfus was to be held the author of the *bordereau,* then Commandant Esterhazy could not be; and, lastly, the libellous words which the War Office through the law called upon the defendants to justify—

> *J'accuse le second conseil de guerre d'avoir couvert cette illégalité par ordre*

—involved one case just as much as the other. However, the Judge of Assizes was equal to the occasion. He ruled—

> *L'affaire Dreyfus, qui n'offre aucune connexité ni aucune indivisibilité avec les faits mentionnes dans la citation, etc.,*

and again:

> *Il n'est pas permis de prouver, soit directement, soit indirectement, soit par des voirs detournées, contre "la chose jugée," même pour établir des faits diffamatoires.*

The Military Witnesses

But of this there can be no doubt—whatever was the rule as to the *chose jugée,* it should have been enforced equally on both parties. This was not always the case. One single example of the contrary shall be given, which as will be shown hereafter, events have proved to be of the utmost significance. General de Pellieux had completed his long evidence, but having received from "a Juror" a private letter to the effect that the jury would not convict M. Zola unless they had some further proof of the guilt of Captain Dreyfus, on a subsequent day he asked leave to make a subsequent deposition. . . . And General de Pellieux called upon General de Boisdeffre and General Gonse to confirm what he said, and they did so. But when M. Labori asked to see the document and proposed to cross-examine the generals upon it, the Judge did not allow him: *"Nous n'avons pas à parler l'affaire Dreyfus."* It may be conceived what effect such a revelation, made by the chiefs of the French army in full uniform had upon the jury. They pronounced M. Zola guilty and found no extenuating circumstances; and he was sentenced by the Judge to the *maximum* penalty, viz., imprisonment for a year and a fine of 3,000 francs.

The Verdict against M. Zola Quashed

On April 2 the Zola case is brought up before the Court of Cassation and the Court quashes the verdict of the Assizes, on the technical ground that the prosecution had been instituted by the wrong person. The Minister of War was incompetent to prosecute: the only persons competent were those who could allege they had been defamed—in this instance the persons constituting the Esterhazy court-martial to whom M. Zola had imputed they had acquitted Commandant Esterhazy by order. Their rights, however, were not prejudiced by the mistaken protrusion of the Minister of War: they could still prosecute, if they thought fit. The officers who had sat at the Esterhazy court-martial were then called together again in order to decide whether M. Zola should be reprosecuted. To put a stop to any unwillingness on their part, M. Zola published in the *Siècle* April 17 a new declaration of Count Casella, which the Count said he would have deposed to on oath at the former trial if the Judge had allowed him to be a witness. This declaration gave a detailed history of various interviews in Paris with Count Panizzardi, the Military Attaché at the Italian Embassy, and at Berlin with Colonel von Schwartzkoppen, who had been the Military Attaché at the German Embassy. According to Count Casella, both these officers had declared positively to him that they had had nothing to do with Captain Dreyfus, but Colonel von Schwartzkoppen much with Commandant Esterhazy. It will be said that this declaration of Count Casella had not been sifted by cross-examination; but it is understood that at the end of 1896, immediately after the *Éclair* made the revelation of *document libérateur,* both the German and Italian Governments made a diplomatic representation to the French Government denying that they had had anything to do with Captain Dreyfus. At all events, in January, 1898, official denials had been publicly made by the German Minister of Foreign Affairs to the Budget Commission of the Reichstag and by the Italian Under-Secretary for Foreign Affairs to the Parliament at Rome.

Fresh Proceedings against M. Zola

The officers of the court-martial resolve to reprosecute, and the case is fixed for the May Assizes at Versailles. When the case comes on M. Zola demurs to its being tried outside Paris; the demurrer is overruled by the Court of Cassation, and ultimately, on July 18, the case comes on again at the Versailles Assizes. The charge, however, is now cut down from what it had been at the first trial in Paris. Of the whole letter of M. Zola now only three lines are selected as defamatory—viz:—

> *Un conseil de guerre vient par ordre, d'oser acquitter un*
> *Esterhazy, soufflet suprême à toute vérité, à toute justice.*

This selection was manifestly designed to shut out any possibility of reference to the *affaire Dreyfus,* and M. Labori, finding that any attempt to import it would be in vain, allowed the case to go by default, and M. Zola was condemned and, as before, sentenced to a year's imprisonment and a fine of 3,000 francs. He has appealed to the *Cour de Cassation,* and the appeal may be heard in the course of the autumn. To secure his own liberty in the meantime, M. Zola has avoided personal service of the order of the Assizes by removing beyond the frontier.

The *Petit Bleu*

We will now go back to Colonel Picquart. During the year 1897 he had become aware that in the Intelligence Department suspicions were expressed that the *petit bleu* was not a genuine document and insinuations made that Colonel Picquart had forged it. The reader will remember the letter of Colonel Henry of June 3, 1897, which was the first note of alarm to Colonel Picquart. The ground on which this imputation was rested came out clearly in the evidence which was given subsequently in the Zola trial, to which reference may now be made. The sweepings of Colonel von Schwartzkoppen's basket had been brought by a spy to the Intelligence Department, and were given first into the hands of Commandant Henry, who put them into a packet or *cornet* and passed them on to Colonel Picquart to examine. Colonel Picquart swore that on examination he had found among the papers a large number of documents, fifty or sixty. These he gave to Commandant Lauth to piece together and photograph. When pieced together they were found to constitute the *petit bleu* addressed to Commandant Esterhazy, who at that time was a perfect stranger to Colonel Picquart. At the Zola trial Colonel Henry had sworn that the pieces were not in the *cornet* when he gave it to Colonel Picquart, and the intimation was that Colonel Picquart has forged the document, torn it into pieces, and put the pieces into the *cornet.* Then it was pointed out that Colonel Picquart had not acquainted his superior immediately of his discovery. He had received the *cornet* in May: in July he informed General de Boisdeffre, and in September General Gonse. Then M. Gribelin, Archivist of the Intelligence Department, had sworn that Colonel Picquart had asked him whether it was possible to affix a postage stamp to the *petit bleu* to make it appear to have passed through the post (as though a written request for documents addressed by a foreign military attaché to a French officer by name would become more damaging evidence against him if it were proved to have been sent through the post office). Commandant Lauth had also sworn that Colonel Picquart had instructed him to arrange for the photograph not to show the marks of having been made up of little pieces, and had also asked him to swear (contrary to his opinion) that the *petit bleu* was in Colonel von Schwartzkoppen's handwriting. Such were the facts on which the imputation of forgery was made to rest, and they were stated or referred to by General de Pellieux and Commandant Ravary in their preliminary reports on Commandant Esterhazy's case.

Colonel Picquart Court-Martialed

Commandant Esterhazy was acquitted by the court-martial, and on the very next day Colonel Picquart was himself summoned to submit to a military inquiry. The court-martial sat with closed doors, so that neither the charges nor the proceedings would be known to the public, but the findings have found their way into the newspapers, and M. Demange, Colonel Picquart's counsel, certifies the report to be substantially correct. From these it may be inferred what were the charges brought before the Court. Among them forgery was not one. The court-martial first acquitted Colonel Picquart of impropriety in communicating to an *avocat* (M. Leblois) two *dossiers* which had nothing to do with Captain Dreyfus. There had been such a communication, but it had been made in conjunction with Colonel Henry, and was above-board, and not open to suspicion. 2. As to the question which, according to Commandant Lauth, Colonel Picquart had asked him respecting the *petit bleu*, the Court found that Colonel Picquart had given a satisfactory explanation. 3. As to the charge made by Colonel Henry and the Archivist, M. Gribelin, that in the autumn of 1896 they had separately seen M. Leblois closeted with Colonel Picquart and the secret *dossier* on the table before them (the *dossier* containing the *document*), the Court held that it fell to the ground, as M. Leblois was not in Paris at the time indicated. But (4) as to the charge (which had never been disputed) that in 1897 Colonel Picquart had communicated General Gonse's letters to M. Leblois, this the Court found to be proved; and for this military offence, Colonel Picquart was removed from the Army upon a pension of a little more than 2,000 francs, or 80 pounds per annum.

Other chastisements have followed which may be mentioned here. The Bar Council have suspended M. Leblois for six months for the use which he made of General Gonse's letters. The Council of the Legion of Honour provisionally suspended M. Zola in July—*i.e.*, while his appeal to the *Cour de Cassation* from his conviction at the Assizes is still pending. They have also appointed a commission to inquire into the conduct of M. de Pressonsé, whose criticisms of the Dreyfus case are alleged to be defamatory of officers. Commandant Forzinetti had been recalled for having declared at Rochefort the innocence of Captain Dreyfus. As to M. Grimaux, a veteran professor in the *École Poly-technique*, the Minister of War proposed to the Cabinet to remove him on the ground that he had signed a petition to the Chamber, but this the Cabinet refused to sanction, but M. Reinach, not in the regular Army, but in the reserve, had been brought before a military Court sitting with closed doors, and has been deprived of his rank for a breach of discipline consisting of his having published an article in the *Siècle* on the *affaire Dreyfus;* and M. Stapfer, Dean of the Bordeaux Faculty of Letters, has been suspended by the Minister of Education for a discourse on the same subject.

M. Cavaignac's Declaration

We now come to the famous declaration of July 7 (1898), made by M. Cavaignac, Minister of War. On the interpellation of M. Castelin, the Minister of War replied that hitherto the Government had respected the *chose jugée,* but now considerations superior to reasons of law made it necessary for them to bring before the Chamber and the country all the truth in their possession, the facts which had come to confirm the conviction of Captain Dreyfus. He made this declaration because of the absolute certainty he had of his guilt. He based his declaration first on documents in the Intelligence Department, and then on Captain Dreyfus's own confessions.

The latter will be dealt with first. The Minister relied on two witnesses. One was Captain d'Attel, who on the day of Captain Dreyfus's resigna-tion had told Captain Anthoine that Captain Dreyfus had just said in his presence, "As to what I handed over, it was nothing. If I had been let alone I should have had made an exchange." Captain Anthoine had, according to the Minister, immediately repeated these words to Major de Mitry. But Captain d'Attel is dead, and M. Cavaignac did not state to the Chamber at what date or on whose authority this informa-tion came to the War Office. The other witness was a Captain Lebrun-Renault, still alive, who had acted as captain of the escort on the day of degradation, January 5, 1895. This officer, according to M. Cavaignac, had on that day recorded a confession in his note-book; when he reported it to the War Office the Minister did not say, nor did he read to the Chamber, the terms of the note, but contented himself with saying that the substance of the confession appeared in a letter from General Gonse to General de Boisdeffre, and was that it was not original documents but copies that were handed over; and that if he (Captain Dreyfus) handed over documents, they were documents with no importance, and that he did so in order to obtain serious ones. Captain Lebrun-Renault had concluded by expressing his opinion that Captain Dreyfus made half-confessions mingled with reticences and lies. On this it is to be remarked that the Minister omits to specify the date at which Captain Lebrun-Renault first communicated to the War Office. It is believed to be in November, 1897, and against these allegations may act the testimony of Commandant Forzinetti, the governor of the prison in which Captain Dreyfus was confined, to the effect that there is no record of confession in the official report made at the time by Captain Lebrun-Renault, as captain of the escort, and that within the last year the captain had denied to him (Captain Forzinetti) that there had been any confession. Further, we know that throughout his imprisonment before trial, at the scene of the degradation, and in his letter written immediately afterwards to his wife, and to the Minister of War, Captain Dreyfus protested his innocence and that he had never committed even the slightest imprudence.

Then as to the documents confirmatory of the conviction of Captain Dreyfus, M. Cavaignac did not say whether by this term "guilt" he meant that Captain Dreyfus had been guilty of writing the *bordereau*, or had been guilty otherwise as a traitor. Indeed it has been remarked that he never as much as mentioned the *bordereau*. Was, then, the *bordereau* dropped, as a document no longer recognized to be in the handwriting of Captain Dreyfus? But he informed the Chamber that the Intelligence Department had during the last six years accumulated 1,000 documents and letters relating to espionage, the authorship of which there was no reasonable doubt. He would call the attention of the Chamber to only three, all of which, he said, had passed between the persons who had been mentioned (Colonel von Schwartzkoppen and M. Panizzardi). Here again it was noticed that the *"document libérateur (ce canaille de D.)"* was not mentioned. Had this, too, been dropped as no longer to be relied upon, because "D" did not mean Dreyfus, or was it now omitted because it had been produced at the court-martial by General Mercier and therefore could not be said to be confirmatory of his conviction? Of the three documents, which M. Cavaignac specified, the first, dated in March, 1894, made reference to a person indicated as "D"; the second, dated April 16, 1894, contained the expression *"cette canaille de D.,"* the same as that used in the *document libérateur*. The third was no other than *"la preuve absolue"* which General de Pellieux had imported into his evidence at the Zola trial as having been in the hands of the Government at the time of the Castelin interpellation in November, 1896. M. Cavaignac read out its contents, of which the following is an exact transcript:

J'ai lu qu'un deputé va interpeller sur Dreyfus. Si—je dirai que jamais j'avais des relations avec ce Juif. C'est entendu. Si on vous demande, dites comme ça, car il faut pas que on sache jamais personne ce qui est arrivé avec lui.

M. Cavaignac went on to say that the material authenticity of this document depended not merely on its origin, but also on its similarity with a document written in 1894 on the same paper and with the same blue pencil, and that its moral authenticity was established by its being a part of a correspondence exchanged between the same persons in 1896. "The first writes to the other, who replies in terms which left no obscurity on the cause of their common uneasiness." This Chamber was transported with the speech of the Minister of War, and, treating it as a *coup de grâce* to the *affaire Dreyfus* by a majority of 572 to two that a print of it should be placarded in the 36,000 communes of France.

Henry's Confession and Suicide

On the next day Colonel Picquart wrote a letter to the Minister of War undertaking to prove that the first two documents had nothing to do with Captain Dreyfus, and that the third, *la preuve absolue,* was a forgery. Within six weeks his words as to *la preuve absolue* came true. On August 31 the public are startled with the announcement that Colonel Henry has confessed to having forged it himself, and has committed suicide in the Fortress Mont Valérien, being found with his throat cut and a razor in his left hand. The discovery of the forgery was stated to have arisen from a clerk in the Intelligence Department having detected with the help of a specially strong lamp that the blue paper of *la preuve absolue* was not identical with the blue paper of a similar document of 1894 which M. Cavaignac had relied upon as a proof of its material authenticity. Nothing more is yet known, even now. But various questions have been asked. What was it that led M. Cavaignac to resume inquiry after the *affaire Dreyfus* had been supposed to have been extinguished by his speech? Was it, as given out, conscientious zeal to restudy the *dossier,* or was it that the German and Italian Governments had protested against their repeated repudiations of connection with Captain Dreyfus being treated as false? Again, how did the revelation from the strong lamp point to Colonel Henry as the forger? And what was the exact scope of his confession? Was it confined to *"la preuve absolue,"* or did it extend to the correspondence of which that document was said to have formed a part, or to any of the 1,000 espionage letters accumulated in the War Office? Again, as to Colonel Henry's death—a death so opportune if there were any more forgeries behind or if any other persons were implicated in the forgery found out—what were the exact circumstances concerning it and attesting the same to be a suicide? How was it that a prisoner in a military fortress was allowed to be in possession of a razor? Such questions were asked and have not been answered.

Anyhow, the fact remains that Colonel Henry, the Chief of the Intelligence Department, who had been one of the chief witnesses against Captain Dreyfus, the accuser of Colonel Picquart, and the upholder of Commandant Esterhazy, has confessed to having forged a document in order to prove treason against Captain Dreyfus, a helpless prisoner shut up in the *Île du Diable*. As a sequel to this confession, General de Bois-deffre, Chief of the Staff, has resigned, feeling he could not remain after having placed before the Minister of War as genuine a document proved to be a forgery. Commandant Esterhazy has been removed from the active list of the Army, having been brought by M. Cavaignac before a court-martial sitting with closed doors—his offence not disclosed, but conceived to be his anti-patriotic correspondence with a Mme. de Boulancy. A like fate has befallen Colonel du Paty de Clam from a similar court-martial instituted by M. Cavaignac's successor, his offence likewise not disclosed, but presumed to be improper communication of official secrets to Commandant Esterhazy. Commandant Esterhazy and Colonel du Paty de Clam have been also in trouble in the ordinary Criminal Courts. Commandant Esterhazy stands charged by his cousin with embezzlement of private moneys, and a prosecution was instituted against him, Mme. Pays, his mistress, and Colonel du Paty de Clam for having forged the *Speranza* telegrams and letters; but this has not been proceeded with on account of technical difficulties.

The First Step Towards Revision

However, notwithstanding the confession of Colonel Henry, M. Cavaignac insisted that Captain Dreyfus was guilty, and refused consent to revision. The Cabinet, not acceding to this view, M. Cavaignac resigned the Ministry of War, and is succeeded by General Zurlinden, then military Governor of Paris. General Zurlinden asks first to be allowed to study the *dossier,* and after a week's study and communication with the War Office staff he then declares his opposition to revision, retires from the Ministry of War, and resumes his post of Governor of Paris. With him also retires one other member of the Cabinet. Then the Minister of Justice takes the first formal step in referring the matter to a legal Commission, the technical question at issue appearing to be whether the confession by Colonel Henry—a witness in the case—of a forgery committed by him subsequently to the conviction with a view to its confirmation might be considered either as a new fact in the case or as equivalent to a conviction for forgery, so as to justify an application to the *Cour de Cassation* for revision. The Commission were divided in opinion, and the matter would have fallen to the ground if the Cabinet had not decided to take the matter into their own hands and apply to the Court direct. This has been done; the Court is making preliminary inquiries, and will then decide whether revision in some form may be allowed or a new trial ordered.

Colonel Picquart's Last Protest

With regard to Colonel Picquart, his public challenge of the documents put forward in the speech of the Minister of War was followed three days afterwards by an order of his Cabinet directing the Minister of War to set the Minister of Justice in motion, with a view that he should be criminally prosecuted in a non-military Court for communication of secret documents—the same offence as that for which he had been punished by the court-martial early in the year by removal from the active list of the Army—and M. Leblois was to be prosecuted with him as an accomplice. On the 13th of July Colonel Picquart is put into prison to await his trial, M. Leblois being left at large. The prison was a civil prison, where he was allowed to communicate with his legal adviser. About the 14th of September (Colonel Henry having in the meantime confessed and committed suicide) Colonel Picquart, whilst still in prison, applied to the premier, M. Brisson, to grant him an interview, and in reply was asked by the Minister of Justice to send him a written statement of all that he knew of the Dreyfus case, and Colonel Picquart complied with this request. On September 21 Colonel Picquart is taken from the prison to the Court for his trial. The Government Prosecutor rises and asks for an indefinite postponement on the ground that the military authorities are about to bring him before a military Court for forgery. This was the fact, and the explanation that has been given is this, that General Zurlinden when Minister of War had prepared a *dossier* for the arrest of Colonel Picquart, but had not sent it for execution to the Governor of Paris; that when he apprised the Cabinet of his intention, the Cabinet had refused their sanction; that almost immediately afterwards General Zurlinden had resigned the Ministry of War and returned to be Governor of Paris, leaving the *dossier* behind him, and that by some misunderstanding his successor at the War Office, General Chanoine, had sent on the *dossier* to the Governor of Paris, and it was then too late for the step to be recalled. Be this how it may, the military prosecution for forgery was ordered, and on the strength of it the Correctional Court acceded to the application for indefinite postponement of the other case of which it was seized; the military authorities claimed to take the prisoner out of the hands of the Civil authorities, and the Correctional Court acquiesced. Then it was that Colonel Picquart broke out:—

This perhaps is the last time my voice will be heard in public. It will be easy for me to justify myself as to the *petit bleu*. I shall perhaps spend tonight in the Cherche-Midi (military) Prison, but I am anxious to say if I find in my cell the noose of Lemercier-Picard, or the razor of Henry, it will be an assassination. I have no intention of committing suicide.

The same or the next day Colonel Picquart was removed to the Cherche-Midi Prison, there to await his court-martial, which is not expected yet for some weeks. He is not permitted to communicate with his legal adviser or anyone else. The charge of forgery relates, it is presumed, to the *petit bleu*. If so, we know the grounds on which up to February of the present year that charge was made to rest—chiefly the oath of Colonel Henry. We know, too, that at the previous court-martial of Colonel Picquart the War Office (General Billot, General de Boisdeffre, and others), having the facts before them, did not prefer a charge of forgery. It must also be mentioned that it is confidently asserted, whether with truth or not, that Colonel von Schwartzkoppen is ready to admit that it was he (Colonel von Schwartzkoppen) who wrote the *petit bleu*. What is now apprehended by Colonel Picquart's friends is that Colonel Henry may have suppressed the original *petit bleu* and substituted for it a forged *petit bleu* in the same words, but in a handwriting an imitation of Colonel Picquart's. In any case Colonel Picquart may, like Captain Dreyfus, be tried by court-martial with closed doors, and may, like Captain Dreyfus, be sentenced to be immured without permission to communicate with his friends. Such a court-martial would be subject to no review, as the proceedings would be unknown; and the fate of Colonel Picquart would probably determine the fate of Captain Dreyfus also, even if the Court of Cassation should order a new trial of Captain Dreyfus. For then his chief witness, Colonel Picquart, would appear before the Court as a convicted forger.

I am, Sir, your obedient Servant,

GODFREY LUSHINGTON

The Decision to Open an Inquiry

". . . there is ground for making a supplementary inquiry."

Text by The Associated Press, *in Harding,* Dreyfus: The Prisoner of Devil's Island, *p. 93.*

The Criminal Division of the Court of Cassation assembled on October 27. Two days later it declared that the request for revision was admissible and decided to open an inquiry. The text of the judgment follows.

In view of the letter of the Minister of Justice of September 20, 1898;

In view of the arguments submitted by the Public Prosecutor attached to the Court of Cassation, denouncing to the Court the condemnation pronounced by the first court-martial of the Military Court of Paris, on December 22, 1894, on Alfred Dreyfus, then captain of artillery, attached to the General Staff of the Army;

In view of all the documents of the case, and also of Article 443 to 446 of the Code of Criminal Procedure, amended by the law of June 10, 1895, on the admissibility, in proper form, of an application for revision—

Whereas, the court has had the matter brought before it by its Public Prosecutor, in virtue of an express order of the Minister of Justice, acting after having taken the opinion of the Commission established by Article 444 of the Code of Criminal Procedure;

Whereas, the application comes within the category of cases provided for by the last paragraph of Article 443, and has been introduced within the period fixed by Article 444;

Whereas, finally, the judgment, the revision of which is asked for, has the force of a *chose jugée*.

As regards the state of the case:

Whereas, the documents produced do not place the Court in a position to decide on all the merits of the case, and there is ground for making a supplementary inquiry;

For these reasons, the Court declares the application in proper form and legally admissible; states that it will institute a supplementary inquiry; and declares that there is no ground for deciding at the present moment on the Public Prosecutor's application for the suspension of the penalty.

The Court Decides on Annulment with Retrial

"*. . . the most grave presumptions about the suspicious conduct of Henry and Esterhazy.*"

France: Cour de Cassation débats, L'affaire Dreyfus, La revision du procès Dreyfus (*Paris: P. V. Stock, 1899*), *pp. 705–708. Translated by the editor.*

On October 29, 1898, the Court of Cassation began taking testimony on the revision proceedings. M. Quesnay de Beaurepaire,

President of the Civil Division of the Court, joined in the attacks made upon his colleagues. Matters became so complicated that de Beaurepaire resigned his position in order to have a free hand in carrying on his campaign against Dreyfus. Adjudication was transferred to the United Chambers of the Court of Cassation, in effect declaring that the highest criminal court in the country was incapable of dealing with the case.

On June 3, 1899, the judges of the United Chambers finally decided that the decision of 1894 condemning Dreyfus was to be set aside and the case remanded to a second court-martial for trial. The innocence of Dreyfus was demonstrated during the course of the investigation. The Court might have set aside the judgment of 1894 altogether, but Mme. Dreyfus, representing her husband, insisted that the case be re-tried by court-martial. The request was granted. It seemed that acquittal was near for Dreyfus.

Following is the text of the decision.

DECISION
RENDERED IN SOLEMN CONCLAVE
JUNE 3, 1899

In the Name of the People of France,

The Court of Cassation has rendered a decision on the requisition of the *Procureur-Général* to the following effect:

The *Procureur-Général* of the Court of Cassation states that the documents in the *bordereau* and notably the inquiries of the Criminal Division and the United Divisions result in the following facts which summarize the principal elements calling for a revision of the court-martial of December 22, 1894, condemning Dreyfus to deportation and degradation for the crime of treason.

These facts are as follows:

1. The Henry forgery renders suspect the sensational testimony made by Henry before the court-martial;

2. The date of the month of April assigned to the *bordereau* and the packet of documents, used in both the trial of Dreyfus and that of Esterhazy, was ground for the condemnation of the one and acquittal for the other, while today that date is reported to be the month of August—that removes every legal base from the judgment of 1894;

3. The manifest contradiction existing between the expert assessment of 1894 in the trial of Dreyfus and that of 1897 in the trial of Esterhazy, as well as the new opinion of one of the experts of 1894, having for a result the displacing of the majority of assessments of 1894;

4. The absolute identity of the type of paper on which the *bordereau* was written with the paper used by Esterhazy in writing his letters of 1892 and 1894 admitted by him;

5. The absolute proof resulting from several letters by Esterhazy about the fact that he was present at the August maneuvers at Châlons in 1894, and other documents proving that he alone could have written that phrase in the *bordereau:* "I am just about to leave for maneuvers," in addition to an official circular of May 17, 1894, not produced at the 1894 court-martial, indicating that Dreyfus not only did not go to the maneuvers or subsequent ones, that, therefore, he could not possibly have written that phrase;

6. The official report of Police Headquarters not produced in the proceedings of 1894 establishing that, contrary to the information furnished by Guénée * and held by the accusation as moral arguments, it was not Dreyfus who frequented gambling clubs but that he must have been confused with another man of the same name;

7. The dramatic scene produced in the inquiry by M. Bertulus justifying the most grave presumptions about the suspicious conduct of Henry and Esterhazy;

8. The dispatch of November 2, 1894, on the meaning of which everyone is in accord today, not being produced in the trial; it runs counter to another dispatch that was invoked against Dreyfus and it indicates that Dreyfus could have had no relations with the foreign power revealed in that dispatch;

9. The official documents establishing that Dreyfus could not have had any direct or indirect relations with any foreign power;

10. Finally, the protestations and grave presumptions of innocence resulting from the documents in the *dossier* and the correspondence of Dreyfus demonstrating that Dreyfus never admitted his guilt;

According to the terms of Article 443 of the Code of Criminal Instructions, No. 4, revision ought to be demanded:

"When, after a condemnation, new facts have been produced or revealed, or when previously unknown documents of a nature to establish the innocence of the condemned person are forthcoming."

Because all the facts cited here constitute precisely new facts or new documents in the sense of the law, the judgment of December 22, 1894, is hereby dissolved:

On these grounds,

The *Procureur-Général,*

---

* Guénée, a character of ill-repute, had been employed by the police to report on Dreyfus's passion for gambling. He produced no proofs, but only assertions which the Chief Commissioner of Police found to be groundless.

According to the documents of the *dossier* and the inquiry,

According to Articles 443, No. 4, 444, 445 of the Code of Criminal Instructions;

May it please the Court, the Court

Admits the new facts and new documents, etc., of a nature to establish the innocence of Dreyfus,

Declares as admittable and legally justifiable the demand for a revision of the judgment of the court-martial of December 22, 1894;

SETS ASIDE and ANNULS the said judgment and dismisses the case and orders that Dreyfus remain as the accused before another court-martial that it will be pleased to designate.

Done at Parquet, the 27th of May, 1899

Le Procureur-Général
(Signed) K. J. MANAU

After annulling the decision, the Court summoned the accused before another court-martial, especially appointed to sit in council for this purpose. Dreyfus was to be tried on the following question: "Is Dreyfus guilty of having, in the year 1894, entered into intrigues or maintained communications with a foreign power or one of its agents to induce it to commit hostile acts or enter into war with France, or to supply it with the means of doing so by handing over the notes and documents mentioned in the *bordereau?*"

In London Esterhazy Confesses that He Wrote the *Bordereau* "To Catch Dreyfus"

"That officer was named Dreyfus. He had to be caught."

Le Matin, *June 3, 1899. Translated by the editor.*

Shortly after the suicide of Henry on August 31, 1898, Esterhazy, fearing that all was lost, and without informing his accomplices on the General Staff, fled first to Belgium and then to England. There he assumed the name of Count Jean de Voilement and lived in a slum quarter in a room in a poor boardinghouse. He slept throughout the day and would walk the streets only at night. Once each month he would call at the post office to pick up a registered letter containing money: no one ever knew who sent it to him.

At the end of May 1899 a Parisian newspaperman named Serge Basset obtained an interview with Esterhazy in which the cashiered officer admitted that he had written the *bordereau* at the behest of his superior officer, Colonel Sandherr. Included with his confession was this statement: "There was on the General Staff an officer who committed treason. That officer was named Dreyfus. He had to be caught. And that is why I wrote the *bordereau*."

The interview appeared in *Le Matin* on June 3, 1899, the same day the Court of Cassation made its decision in favor of revision of the case.

[At the Rennes court-martial] I did not believe that Esterhazy was the author of the *bordereau*. I remember that, some time before I took the statement from Esterhazy, my colleague Philippe Dubois of *L'Aurore* attempted to convince me in every possible way that Esterhazy had written the *bordereau*. I gave him this reply: "I just cannot believe it. Please leave me alone."

On May 23 I went to London. It so happened that I had some very unpleasant news for Esterhazy. M. Ballot-Beaupré had just declared in his report before the whole Court of Cassation that to his best knowledge he held Esterhazy to be the author of the *bordereau,* and it seemed that the court also had come to this conclusion. In addition to this, the Countess Esterhazy, perhaps encouraged by her family, and as I had expected, had begun proceedings for a divorce. Major Esterhazy was shattered by this news and began to complain about the fate of his children.

"I am lost," he said. "I am at the end. My wife is going to divorce me and my children have been raised in an atmosphere of hatred and loathing for their father. And this last blow I owe to those generals for whom I did everything and sacrificed myself and who left me in the lurch. That is enough to make an end to it and to put a bullet into my head."

I assured him that I was deeply impressed as I heard him talk, no matter what anyone might say about him. And unintentionally, without being influenced by my professional interests, I said to him: "If these generals, who counted on your loyalty and who gave you the most difficult and dangerous of tasks to perform, left you in the lurch, as you say, then they are the greatest of evildoers, and they have the duty to take care of your children. They must tell the whole truth. Otherwise they will never have any peace and they will not be able to defend themselves against the accusation that they have thrown a shadow over the lives of your children."

I had spoken in all sincerity and the Major understood me. He thought for several moments and then suddenly (I remember the place—in the French quarter near Piccadilly, in front of the Criterion):

"Listen, Ribon [Basset's pen name], I believe that you are right. I shall tell the truth. I shall reveal something to you that few people have known until now. I prepared the *bordereau*." ["*C'est moi qui fait le bordereau*."]

This unexpected declaration surprised me very much. I cried out: "What, it was you!" He said: "Yes, I wrote the *bordereau* in the year 1894 at the order of Colonel Sandherr, my immediate superior officer. There was on the General Staff an officer who committed treason. That officer was named Dreyfus. He had to be caught. And that is why I wrote the *bordereau*. As for the real reasons, I shall reveal them later."

And he really gave them later. I told him that I was just dumbfounded. I trembled and had to gain control of myself again before I asked him: "How could you possibly carry the burden of such a secret for four years?" He replied: "If you understood all the demands that were placed on me, the pressure from the Dreyfusards, my relatives, my friends, my intimates, the generals, the General Staff. . . . A half year ago I wanted to speak out, but the General Staff ordered me in the strongest possible terms to remain silent. At that time there must have been a hundred people who riveted themselves to me and beseeched me not to talk, and to remain the devoted soldier that I have always been. . . ."

In the greatest excitement and utterly shattered I went to my hotel and the next day, after several hours of rest, I wrote down the interview and brought the text to Major Esterhazy. I asked him: "Will you give me permission to send this to my newspaper?" He read the manuscript and said to me: "Give me a little time to think about it. You will understand that such matters cannot be cleared up in one day."

Naturally, it is for us journalists a matter of conscience not to quote people against their will. So I took the manuscript back and did not speak of it any more.

On the following morning he came to my hotel to tell me: "I have come to a decision. I give you permission to publish my statement. I swear to you that I am not a traitor, and that I wrote the *bordereau* at the order of Colonel Sandherr, and that I am a sacrifice to passive obedience. I am hoping that after this declaration I shall be left in peace. Sit down at this table and we shall write the declaration once again, so that you will know the truth."

We, therefore, sat down together, and, with pen in hand, we worked out the details of the statement. Very quickly Major Esterhazy signed my manuscript in order to give it validity, and several days later he gave me a new assurance, dated and signed, in which he attested to the exact rendering of the remarks that he had made orally. . . .

X

The Second Court-Martial at Rennes

Brought back from Devil's Island in June 1899, Dreyfus was placed on trial at Rennes before a court-martial of seven officers. This time the proceedings were public. From August 7 to September 9 the attention of the entire world turned to the courtroom in the French city.

In conformance with the French code of laws, the witnesses were allowed to tell what they knew in their own way. They could voice their opinions, beliefs, prejudices, dislikes, all as if they were giving "evidence." Foreigners, especially those accustomed to Anglo-Saxon procedures, were puzzled.

After the reading of the Act of Accusation, Dreyfus testified in his own defense. The prisoner, who was fluent in German, assisted the judges in translating certain documents. Several former Ministers of War, supported by the foremost generals of France, took the stand to declare their unshaken belief that Dreyfus was guilty. General Mercier triumphantly produced a dispatch allegedly written by Colonel Schneider, the Austrian Military Attaché, confirming the guilt of Dreyfus, but the document was quickly proved to be a forgery. There was a confrontation between Mercier and Dreyfus, when the prisoner reminded the general of his duty as a gentleman and officer.

On August 14 an attempt was made on the life of Maître Labori, Dreyfus's counsel. That same day there was a clash in court between former President Casimir-Périer and General Mercier. The session of August 15 was devoted to an account of the prisoner's sufferings on Devil's Island. In the succeeding sessions the generals who opposed Dreyfus and such "experts" as M. Bertillon went down under counsels' fire. The witnesses for Dreyfus, skillfully led by Maîtres Labori and Demange, proved that Esterhazy had written the *bordereau,* that he had confessed, that he was at the maneuvers mentioned in the *bordereau,* and that many of the documents incriminating Dreyfus were actually forgeries.

All to no avail. The verdict was "guilty, with extenuating circumstances."

Order to Return Dreyfus to France

"In virtue of this decision, Captain Dreyfus ceases to be subjected to the convict régime. . . ."

Quoted in Dreyfus, Five Years, *pp. 291–292.*

On the morning of June 5, 1899, half an hour after noon, a warder opened the door to Dreyfus's hut on Devil's Island and handed him this telegram.

Please let Captain Dreyfus know immediately of this order of the Supreme Court. The Court quashes and annuls the sentence pronounced on the 22nd of December, 1894, upon Alfred Dreyfus, by the first court-martial of the Military Government of Paris, and remands the accused party to a court-martial at Rennes, etc.

The present decision is to be printed and transcribed on the Book of Records of the first court-martial of the Military Government at Paris on the margin of the annulled sentence.

In virtue of this decision, Captain Dreyfus ceases to be subjected to the convict régime; he becomes a simple prisoner under arrest, and is restored to his rank and allowed to resume his uniform.

See to it that the prison authorities cancel the commitment and withdraw the prison guard from the *Île du Diable.* At the same time have the prisoner taken in charge by the commandant of the regular troops and replace the guards by a squad of gendarmes, who will mount guard on the *Île du Diable,* according to the regulations of military prisons.

The cruiser *Sfax* leaves Fort-de-France [Martinique] today with orders to take the prisoner from the island and bring him back to France.

Communicate to Captain Dreyfus the details of this decision and the departure of the *Sfax.*

The Prisoner Is Brought Back to His Homeland
"That very day I had my first disillusionment."

Quoted in Dreyfus, Five Years, pp. 292–306.

Dreyfus was overjoyed by the news. He left the dismal island four days later. Believing that his innocence had at long last been established, he was shocked by his reception aboard the French man-of war. Although the telegram had stated that he was no longer to be treated as a prisoner undergoing sentence, but as an accused waiting for trial, he was shattered to realize that his day of justice had not yet arrived. He had expected only legal formalities before his release.

My joy was boundless, unutterable. At last I was escaping from the cross to which I had been nailed for nearly five years, suffering as bitterly in the martyrdom of my dear ones as in my own. Happiness succeeded the horror of that inexpressible anguish. The day of justice was at last dawning for me. The Court's decision terminated everything, I thought, and I had not the slightest idea that there remained anything to do but go through some necessary legal formalities.

Of my own story I knew nothing. As I said, I was still back in 1894, with the *bordereau* as the only document in the case, with the sentence of the court-martial, with that appalling parade of degradation, with the cries of "Death to the traitor!" from a deluded people. I believed in the loyalty of General de Boisdeffre; I believed in the Chief Magistrate of the State, Félix Faure; I thought both eager for justice. Thereafter a veil had fallen before my eyes, growing more impenetrable every day. The few facts I had learned during the last month were enigmas to me. I had learned the name of Esterhazy, I had learned of the forgery of Henry, and of his suicide. I had had only official relations with the true-hearted Lieutenant-Colonel Picquart. The grand struggle undertaken by a few noble minds, inspired by the love of truth, was utterly unknown to me.

In the Court's decision I had read that my innocence was acknowledged, and that nothing more remained but for the court-martial before which I was to appear to make honorable reparation for a frightful judicial error.

On the same afternoon, of the 5th of June, I sent the following dispatch to my wife:—

"My heart and soul are with you, with my children, with my friends. I leave Friday. I wait with uncontrollable joy the moment of supreme happiness, when I shall hold you in my arms."

That evening the squad of gendarmes arrived from Cayenne. I saw my jailers depart. I seemed to walk in a dream, to be emerging from a long and frightful nightmare.

I waited with anxiety for the arrival of the *Sfax*. Thursday evening I saw, far away, the smoke on the horizon and soon recognized the warship. But it was too late for me to embark that night.

Thanks to the kindness of the Mayor of Cayenne, I was able to get a suit of clothes, a hat, a little linen; in a word, the bare necessities for the journey.

On Friday morning, the 9th of June, at seven o'clock, the prison boat came for me. At last I was to quit that cursed island. The *Sfax*, a deep-draught ship for that harbor, was anchored far away. The prison boat took me out to her, but I had to wait for two hours before they would receive me aboard. The sea was heavy; the boat, a mere cockleshell, danced dizzily on the big waves of the Atlantic; I was seasick, and so were all the others on board.

About ten o'clock the order came to go alongside. I went on board the *Sfax*, where I was received by the executive officer, who took me to the non-commissioned officers' cabin, which had been specially prepared for me. The window of the cabin had been grated. (I think it was this operation which occasioned my long wait in the boat.) The glass door was guarded by an armed sentinel. In the evening I knew from the movement of the ship that the *Sfax* had weighed anchor and was getting into motion.

My treatment on board the *Sfax* was that of an officer under arrest *de rigueur*. For one hour in the morning and one hour in the evening I was allowed to walk on deck; the rest of the time I was shut up in my cabin. During my stay on board, I preserved constantly the attitude which I had maintained from the beginning, from a feeling of personal dignity. Beyond the needs of service I spoke to no one.

On Sunday, the 18th of June, we reached the Cape Verde Islands, where the *Sfax* coaled; we left there Tuesday, the 20th. The ship was slow and made not more than eight or nine knots an hour.

On the 30th of June, we sighted the French coast. After nearly five years of martyrdom, I was coming back to obtain justice. The horrible struggle was almost ended. I believed that the people had acknowledged their error; I expected to find my dear ones waiting to receive me on landing, and to see with them my comrades awaiting me with open arms and tearful eyes.

That very day I had my first disillusionment.

On the morning of the 30th the *Sfax* stopped, and I was informed that a boat would come to take me ashore. Nobody would tell me where the landing was to take place. A boat appeared; it merely brought the order to keep maneuvering in the sea. My disembarkation was postponed. All these precautions, these mysterious goings and comings, made a singularly painful impression on me. I had a vague intuition of something sinister underlying them.

The *Sfax,* having moved slowly along the coast, stopped toward seven o'clock in the evening. It was dark; the weather was thick, and it was raining. I was notified that a steam launch would come for me a little later.

At nine o'clock the boat which was to take me to the steam launch was at the foot of the *Sfax's* companionway, the launch being unable to come near on account of the bad weather. The sea had become very rough, the wind blew a gale, the rain fell heavily. The boat, tossed by the waves, was dancing by the ladder. I jumped for it and struck upon the gunwale, bruising myself rather severely. The boat pulled away.

Affected quite as much by the manner of the transfer as by the cold and penetrating humidity, I was seized with a violent chill and my teeth began chattering.

Butting our way crazily through the tossing waves, we came up to the steam launch, whose ladder I could scarcely climb, crippled as I was from the injury to my legs received when I jumped into the boat. However, I boarded the launch in silence. It steamed ahead for a time, then stopped. I was in total ignorance as to where I was or whither I was going. Not a word had been spoken to me. After I had waited an hour or two, I was requested to step into the small boat again. The night was still black, the rain kept pouring down, but the sea was calmer. I understood that we must be in port. At a quarter after two in the morning we landed at a place which I afterward knew was Port-Houliguen.

There I got into a carriage, with a captain of *gendarmerie* and two gendarmes. Between two ranks of soldiers this carriage drove to a railway station. At the station, always with the same companions, and without a word having been addressed to me, we got into a train which, after two or three hours of travel, arrived at another station, where we got out.

There we found another carriage waiting, and were conveyed swiftly to a city and into a courtyard. I got out, and looking about me saw that I was in the military prison at Rennes. It was about six o'clock in the morning.

The succession of emotions to which I was a prey may be imagined,—

bewilderment, surprise, sadness, bitter pain, at that kind of a return to my country. Where I had expected to find men united in common love of truth and justice, desirous to make amends for a frightful judicial error, I found only anxious faces, petty precautions, a wild disembarkation on a stormy sea in the middle of the night, with physical sufferings added to the trouble of my mind. Happily, during the long, sad months of my captivity I had been able to steel my will and nerves and body to an infinite capacity for resistance.

It was now the 1st of July. At nine o'clock that morning, I was told that in a few minutes I should see my wife in the room next to the one I was occupying. This room, like my own, had a wooden grating which shut out the view of the courtyard below. It was furnished with a table and chairs. Here it was that afterward my interviews with my own people and my counsel took place. Strong as I was, violent trembling seized me, my tears flowed,—tears which I had not known for so long a time.

It is impossible for words to express in their intensity the emotions which my wife and I both felt at seeing each other again. Joy and grief were blended in our hearts. We sought to read in each other's faces the traces of our suffering, we wished to tell each other all that we felt in our souls, to reveal all the feelings suppressed and stifled during these long years; but the words died away on our lips. We had to content ourselves with trying to throw into our looks all the strength of our affection and of our endurance. The presence of a lieutenant of infantry, who was stationed there, prevented any intimate talk.

On the other hand, I knew nothing of the events which had taken place during the past five years, and had returned with confidence,—a confidence that had been much shaken by the varied events of the previous night. But I did not dare to question my dear wife for fear of exciting her grief, and she preferred leaving to my lawyers the task of informing me.

My wife was authorized to see me every day for an hour. I also saw in succession all the members of our family; and nothing can equal the joy we had in being able to embrace each other after such a separation.

On the 3d of July Maître Demange and Maître Labori came to see me. I threw myself into Maître Demange's arms and was afterward presented to Maître Labori. My confidence in Maître Demange and in his wonderful devotion, had remained unchanged. I felt at once the keenest sympathy with Maître Labori, who had been so eloquent and courageous an advocate of the truth. To him I expressed my deep gratitude. Then Maître Demange gave me chronologically the history of the "Affaire." I listened breathlessly while they strung together for me, link by link, that fateful chain of events. This first exposition was completed by

Maître Labori. I learned of the long series of misdeeds and disgraceful crimes constituting the indictment against my innocence. I was told of the heroism and the great efforts of noble men; the unflinching struggle undertaken by that handful of men of lofty character, opposing their own courage and honesty to the cabals of falsehood and iniquity. I had never doubted that justice would be done, therefore Maître Labori's account of these events was a great blow to me. My illusions with regard to some of my former chiefs were gradually dissipated, and my soul was filled with anguish. I was seized with an overpowering pity and sorrow for that Army of France which I loved.

In the afternoon I saw my dear brother Mathieu, who had been devoted to me from the very first day, and who had remained in the breach during these five years, with a courage and wisdom that had been the noblest example of brotherly devotion.

On the following day, the 4th of July, the lawyers handed me the report of the trials of 1898, the investigation of the Criminal Branch of the Supreme Court, and the final hearings before the United Chambers of the same court. I read the Zola trial during the night that followed, without being able to tear myself away from it. I saw how Zola had been condemned for having upheld the truth, I read of General de Boisdeffre's swearing to the authenticity of the letter forged by Henry. But as my sadness increased on reading of all these crimes and realizing how men are led astray by their passions, a deep feeling of gratitude and admiration arose in my heart for all the courageous men, learned or ignorant, great or humble, who had cast themselves valiantly into the struggle. And history will record that the honor of France was in this uprising of men of every degree, of scholars hitherto buried in the silent labor of study or laboratory, of workingmen engrossed in their hard daily toil, of public officials who set the higher interests of the nation above purely selfish motives, for the supremacy of justice, liberty, and truth.

Next I read the admirable report prepared for the Supreme Court by Maître Mornard; and the feeling of esteem with which that inspired me for this eminent lawyer was strengthened when I made his acquaintance and was able to appreciate the rare quality of his intelligence.

Rising early, between four and five o'clock, I worked all day long. I went through the documents greedily, passing from one surprise to another in that formidable mass of facts. I learned of the illegality of my trial in 1894, the secret communication to members of the first court-martial, ordered by General Mercier, of forged or irrelevant documents, and of the collusion to save the guilty man.

During this time I received thousands of letters from known and unknown friends, from all parts of France, of Europe, of the world; I have not been able to thank all these friends individually, but I wish to tell them here how my heart melted within me at these touching manifestations of sympathy. How much good they have done! What strength I have drawn from them!

I have always been sensitive to change of climate, and I was now constantly cold and obliged to cover myself warmly, although we were in the midst of summer. In the last days of the month of July I was taken with violent chills and fever, followed by congestion of the liver. I was compelled to take to bed, but, thanks to vigorous treatment, was soon on my feet again. I then began to confine myself to a diet of milk and eggs, which I continued as long as I remained at Rennes. During the trial, however, I added kola to it, so as to be able to withstand the strain and remain on my feet throughout the long and seemingly interminable sittings.

The opening of the trial was fixed for the 7th of August. I had to exercise great restraint, for I was anxious about my dear wife, who, I saw, was exhausted by the long-continued strain and impatient to see the end of this frightful situation. I was longing to see again my beloved children, who were still in ignorance of everything, and to be able to forget in a peaceful home life all the sorrows of the past, and to be born again to life.

Dreyfus Receives Expressions of Support
"Soon you will achieve complete justice!"

Alfred Dreyfus, Souvenirs et correspondance, *Appendix. Translated by the editor.*

The return of Dreyfus from Devil's Island was greeted with enormous publicity throughout the world. For a time he and Mme. Dreyfus received more than a thousand letters a day from many countries. Three communications most appreciated by Dreyfus and his family were from Anatole France, the novelist, Joseph Reinach, the publicist, and Auguste Scheurer-Kestner, former Vice-President of the Senate, all of whom were his early champions.

FROM ANATOLE FRANCE

Paris, July 4, 1899

Capitaine:
Although I do not happen to know you personally, please allow me to send to you my respectful greetings upon your return to France.

Aware of the terrible wrong of which you have been the victim, I feel that I am merely doing my duty as a man and a Frenchman when I express to you my deepest sympathy for the frightful sufferings you have undergone, and my profound admiration for the unwavering constancy with which you have endured these adversities. I know that you have been sustained by the feeling that you are innocent, and by the hope that one day that innocence will be recognized. Be assured that that hope will not be disappointed.

Please accept, *Capitaine,* this expression of my greatest esteem and my profound sympathy.

ANATOLE FRANCE

FROM JOSEPH REINACH

Paris, July 5, 1899

Mon Capitaine:

I was just delighted by the news sent by your good brother to me this morning through my friend, Bernard-Lazare. This is the first letter you will receive from me telling you of my deep regard and my absolute confidence that justice will crown the triumph of truth. . . .

Since 1894 I have never doubted your innocence. . . . When I wrote you that first letter in September 1897, I had on two or three occasions seen Mme. Dreyfus, for whom I had the deepest and most devoted respect. Only later did I meet your brother Mathieu, that man of noble heart and with one of the finest minds of our time.

After the awful trials you have undergone with such courage, I do not believe it to be necessary to remind you: "Have confidence!" You are approaching the end, *Capitaine,* and your vindication will be a solace to you, not only in itself, but because it will add to the glory of France, which is still the great land of justice, and of the Army, which will proudly make amends for the wrong done to one of her finest sons. For me it will have been the honor of my life to have contributed my own share to this patriotic work.

I express here, *Capitaine,* my sincere and profound affection.

JOSEPH REINACH

FROM AUGUSTE SCHEURER-KESTNER

Biarritz, July 9, 1899

Mon Capitaine:

While you are receiving many tokens of sympathy, I do not want my own to be absent.

I send you these with a full heart, as I include myself among those who rejoice most deeply that the hour of justice has finally come for you.

I have long been convinced of your innocence, and I have followed with deep anxiety the events that have finally brought the truth to light.

The terrible martyrdom to which you have been subjected you have endured with a courage that could have been given only by a clean conscience. Fortunately you have had to support yourself, to uphold your honor and the honor of your children's name, a brother, and a most admirable wife, all of whom are worthy of you. I have been able to appreciate the courage they have shown in the hour of your great misfortune.

It is to be hoped that this sweet solace will be for you the beginning of justice.

Soon you will achieve complete justice!

I express, *mon Capitaine,* my deepest sympathy.

A. Scheurer-Kestner

The Court-Martial of Rennes Begins

"There came in a little old man—an old, old man of thirty-nine."

Steevens, The Tragedy of Dreyfus, *pp. 41–43.*

The second court-martial of Dreyfus at Rennes opened on August 7, 1899. A capable reporter, G. W. Steevens, who was present, described the courtroom and the opening scene.

The trial was to begin at half-past six. It wanted a quarter of an hour of the time when a line of mounted gendarmes, pushing the crowd out of the neighboring streets, proclaimed that they were taking Dreyfus across the road from the military prison to the High School, in whose lecture hall he was to be arraigned.

A moment later the line opened, and the crowd of journalists, waving their passes, pushed through. They jammed in at a narrow door, up stone steps, through another doorway, round a corner, inside a cordon of infantry, and they were in the court. It was a lofty, oblong, buff-plastered hall larger than the Prince's Restaurant, smaller than St. James's Hall. With large windows on each side—square in the lower tier, circular in the upper—it was almost as light as the day outside; round the cornice were emblazoned the names of Chateaubriand, Lamennais, Renan, and the intellectuals of Brittany. At the top was a stage, its front filled with a long table, behind this seven crimson-covered seats for the judges.

A white Christ on a black cross, hanging on the back wall above the President's chair, proclaimed the place a Court of Justice. On the right, as you faced the stage, were a small raised table and seats for the counsel of the accused; on the left a similar erection for the prosecuting Commissary of the Government and his assistants. Down each side of the body of the hall was a strip of extemporized matchboard bench and desk for the Press. In the broader center were seats for the witnesses, then, behind a bar, for the favored public. Behind all this ran another bar lined by a guard of the 41st Infantry. Behind their homely peasant faces and between their fixed bayonets peered the general public, five deep, in the shallowest of strips at the very back of the hall.

The Press stampeded and trampled over the matchboard, and in the fulness of time sorted itself into its appointed places. The general public shifted and scrunched behind the barrier. The center of the hall began to fill up with witnesses, with officers of infantry in red pantaloons and gunners in black. Behind the daïs appeared a sprinkling of selected spectators. Then, on the waxing bustle of the hall, came in men in black gowns with little white-edged tippets and white bands, with queer high black caps like birettas. Now we should see. And next moment—it was already past seven—there was a hoarse cry from behind—present arms!—rattle—and there filed in the seven officers in whose hands rests the conscience of France. The President—a small but soldierly man in eyeglasses, with black hair and a small face, a huge white moustache and imperial—saluted and sat down. Bring in the accused.

Instantly the black, rippling hall is still as marble, silent as the grave. A sergeant usher went to a door—the tramp of his feet was almost startling—on the right hand of the top of the hall. It opened and two officers stepped out. One of them was the greatest villain or the greatest victim in France—and for the moment men wondered which was he. It seemed almost improper that the most famous man in the world was walking in just as you or I might.

Then all saw him, and the whole hall broke into a gasp. There came in a little old man—an old, old man of thirty-nine. A middle-statured, thick-set old man in the black uniform of the artillery; over the red collar his hair was gone white as silver, and on the temples and at the back of the crown he was bald. As he turned to face the judges there was a glimpse of a face both burned and pale—a rather broad, large featured face with a thrusting jaw and chin. It was not Jewish in expression until you saw it in profile. The eyes under the glasses were set a trifle close together, and not wholly sympathetic either; you might guess him hard, stubborn, cunning. But this is only guessing: what we did see in the face was suffering and effort—a misery hardly to be borne, and a tense, agonized striving to bear and to hide it. Here is a man, you would say, who has endured things unendurable, and just lives through—maybe to endure more.

He walked up two steps to his seat with a gait full of resolve yet heavy, constrained, mechanical—such a gait as an Egyptian mummy might walk with if it came to life in its swathing grave-clothes. He saluted the President with a white-gloved hand, took off his *képi,* sat down. An officer of gendarmes followed and sat down behind him. The recorder, rising from beside the prosecuting officer, read out the general order constituting the court; then the white moustache and imperial twitched as the President, in a small voice, put a question to the prisoner. Another sudden stillness; then came the voice of Dreyfus. No one heard what he said—thin, sapless, split, it was such as might rustle from the lips of a corpse.

What he had said was, "Alfred Dreyfus; Captain of Artillery; thirty-nine years." With these three common phrases he broke the silence of four and a half years.

Dreyfus Testifies on the Opening Day

"It is iniquitous to condemn an innocent man. I never confessed anything! Never!"

Conseil de guerre de Rennes, Le procès Dreyfus, August 7–September 9, 1899 *(Paris: P. V. Stock, 1900), vol. 2, pp. 21–45. From the complete stenographic report. Translated by the editor.*

After answering the formal questions concerning his name, age, and other matters, Dreyfus listened as the clerk of the court read M. d'Ormescheville's bill of particulars of 1894 (the Act of Accusation), which accused Dreyfus of writing the *bordereau,* charged him with transmitting it with the concerned documents to an agent of a foreign power, and made serious accusations about his personal character.

The entire first day was devoted to questioning by Colonel Jouaust, who treated Dreyfus brusquely, almost brutally. Most of the time Dreyfus sat with his legs stretched out, his spurs resting on the ground, his hands clasped together and resting on his lap. When he uttered the words: "I never confessed anything! Never!" he raised his right, white-gloved hand and held it aloft as if appealing to Heaven to vindicate him.

Dreyfus's testimony concerning the *bordereau* is reproduced in full here. The rest of the day's testimony is condensed.

The President: The accused, stand up!

You are accused of the crime of high treason, of having given to an agent of a foreign power the documents enumerated in the *bordereau*. I hereby inform you that the law gives you the right to say during these proceedings anything that appears to be useful for your defense. I caution your defenders that they must express themselves with decency and moderation.

As I have just said, you are accused of having given to the agent of a foreign power the documents enumerated in the *bordereau* which is here:

[*The original of the* bordereau *was then presented to Captain Dreyfus.*]

The President: That document that has just been given to you—do you recognize it?

Captain Dreyfus: It was shown to me in 1894. As for recognizing it, I affirm that I do not. I say again that I am innocent, as I have always said it, as I cried out in 1894. For five years I have said that, Colonel, now I say it again for the honor of my name and that of my children. I am innocent, Colonel!

The President: Then you deny it.

Captain Dreyfus: Yes, Colonel.

The President: We are going to examine successively the different documents enumerated. First that piece is in a handwriting that resembles yours. The first persons who saw it were struck by the resemblance. It is that same resemblance which at the Ministry led to your designation as the author of the piece in question.

First is the note on the hydraulic brake of the 120-gun and the way in which this gun behaves.

The question of the hydraulic brake of the 120-gun is evidently of interest to an artillery officer.

You are such an officer, a graduate of the Military School, and it is not at all impossible that you are well acquainted with that subject.

In 1890 you were at Bourges.

Captain Dreyfus: Yes, Colonel.

The President: At the Pyrotechnical School?

Captain Dreyfus: Yes, at the Pyrotechnical School.

The President: You were in frequent contact with officers of the garrison?

Captain Dreyfus: Yes, Colonel.

The President: And consequently with the officers of the foundry at Bourges.

Well now, it was in 1890 that the first specimens of the hydro-pneumatic brake of the 120 were constructed; it is not at all impossible that this subject came up in your conversations with the officers of the garrison.

Captain Dreyfus: I knew the principle of the hydro-pneumatic brake as early as 1889. But I did not know at all anything about its real structure.

The President: But in your conversations did you not have information on the subject of the brake?

Captain Dreyfus: No, Colonel. Not any information on the details.

The President: But you had certain ideas about the subject?

Captain Dreyfus: Yes, I knew the principle of the brake of the 120, but I have never seen the piece, nor fired it, nor worked it.

The President: At the Military School, did you not speak about the 120-gun?

Captain Dreyfus: I do not remember. But on one occasion at the Military School we saw the artillery at Calais on a trip which the officers took to Calais.

The President: It was in the spring of 1894 that the 120 was first the object of extensive testing in the batteries. Now, the reports were addressed to the Ministry. At that moment were you at the Ministry?

Captain Dreyfus: Yes, Colonel, on the General Staff.

The President: At the beginning of 1894 you were in the First Bureau?

Captain Dreyfus: No, Colonel, in the Second Bureau.

The President: All right, the Second Bureau. It is then not impossible that you would have known about the way in which the 120-gun operated.

In that case it was a matter about which one spoke at the Ministry, and that you might well have known of such technical matters because of your relations with officers of the Third Bureau.

Captain Dreyfus: I have never had any conversations either with artillery officers or with officers of the technical section; consequently, I could never have repeated it to an officer. Since my stay at the First Bureau in 1893, I have absolutely never been occupied with technical questions.

The President: Come now, is it not at all impossible that you could have had some knowledge of that gun in your conversations in the passageways of the Bureau?

Captain Dreyfus: But, in the First Bureau one never was concerned with technical questions. It is, of course, not impossible that an officer in the Ministry might have heard someone speak of such things.

The President: "Some modifications will be made under the new plan." Again that is a matter which comes under the competence of the Ministry, in the bureau in which you worked, that is to say, in the Fourth Bureau.

Captain Dreyfus: That was not in 1894, it was during the first semester of 1893.

The President: You were then in the Fourth Bureau, concerned with transportation lines to the East. You were well-informed there. Commandant Bertin was struck by the special interest you took in those questions. You were absolutely well-informed about the transport situation.

Well now, when the organization of covering troops was modified in 1894, the main difficulty was to assure their transport without upsetting the manner of transport of the others. For that reason it was necessary to make provisional dispositions which could be changed in favor of more definite dispositions. You could well have known the plan for transport, about its difficulties, about what it was necessary to do in changing from the old dispositions to the new.

Captain Dreyfus: Pardon, but in 1893 there weren't any new plans.

The President: I am speaking of 1894.

Captain Dreyfus: It was in 1894 that the new plan was agreed upon.

The President: Do not confuse the questions. Your knowledge acquired in 1893 in the Fourth Bureau permitted you to understand these questions well.

Captain Dreyfus: But I was not responsible for it; it was only in September 1894 that I was charged with inspecting the printing of the documents, concurrently with the other ministries.

The President: What were those documents?

Captain Dreyfus: The Tables for Supplies.

The President: You had them in your possession for a certain time?

Captain Dreyfus: Yes, but I did not hold on to them. I returned the documents immediately to the Chief of the Bureau.

The President: But, during the preceding year, you were charged with printing the documents?

Captain Dreyfus: Yes, during the preceding year I had charge of inspecting the printing.

The President: You had them in your hands. It was necessary to bring them to the geographical printing service. You had them two times in your hands.

Captain Dreyfus: I returned them the same evening. We could handle only one table at each meeting. The service table for provisioning the covering troops was composed of a certain number of tables; at each meeting we could handle only one table and a certain number of examples.

The President: Not only could you have had very precise information concerning the effective forces, but the work of the covering troops was prepared, at least in part, in the Third Bureau, where you were stationed on July 1, 1894. Consequently, you would have had to have knowledge of that part of the work charged to the Third Bureau.

Captain Dreyfus: I was in the Third Bureau to the end of 1894. I had asked my Bureau chief to be charged with confidential work in May 1894; he replied: no.

The President: In that case you would have had information on the covering troops.

Captain Dreyfus: It is certain if I had asked it I would have had, but I never asked it.

The President: You have been charged with looking for information; it is probable that you knew what concerned the covering troops.

Captain Dreyfus: I have never asked anyone about it.

The President: The third document is a note on modifications of artillery formations. After the suppression of the service of pontoon-soldiers, there were available two regiments of artillery. Consequently, it was necessary to distribute these batteries throughout the Army corps. Officers of the General Staff were the only ones who knew about questions of general mobilization. You were perfectly placed in order to have information about that. Did you know anything about that?

Captain Dreyfus: At the beginning of 1894 I was in the Second Bureau. All I knew about that situation was the suppression of the two regiments of pontoon-soldiers and the creation of new batteries. The discussion was open for the suppression of the pontoon-soldiers; that is all that I knew about it.

The President: You did not know the given destination for those new batteries?

Captain Dreyfus: I was in the Second Bureau at the beginning of 1894, in the first semester.

The President: Yes, but in the second? . . . The *bordereau* was sent at the end of August!

At that moment, Commandant Mercier-Milon of the Second Bureau communicated that information to the personnel.

Captain Dreyfus: At the beginning of 1894, in the month of June.

The President: The communications were made from the 15th to the 20th of July, a month before the *bordereau* was set up.

Captain Dreyfus: The suppression of the pontoon-soldiers was during the month of March.

The President: It is possible, but the distribution of the batteries took place in June. It was at that time that Commandant Mercier-Milon conveyed his note to the officers.

Captain Dreyfus: The note was not distributed to the probationers.

The President: When something was communicated to the officers, the probationers could well have known of it.

At the end of 1893 did you have any knowledge sent by the Third Bureau to the Fourth on the subject of the effectiveness of the 120-batteries?

Captain Dreyfus: No, Colonel.

The President: Yet, it was the Third Bureau which sent along the information to the Fourth; consequently, you could have known about it.

Captain Dreyfus: I was in the section on maneuvers.

The President: It is possible that under the circumstances one Bureau could know what went on in another.

Captain Dreyfus: One never knew what went on in another section, except when one asked for information.

The President: In the First Bureau you were under Commandant Besse?

Captain Dreyfus: I was under his orders for three semesters.

The President: At the time he was studying the distribution of the 120-batteries between the different corps of the Army, and he sent out a note of which you should have known.

Captain Dreyfus: I did not know about it.

The President: You worked with him; that note has disappeared, and it cannot be found in the archives of the Ministry. You never knew about it?

Captain Dreyfus: One never spoke of it in 1894.

The President: The fourth document is a "note on Madagascar."

When you were at the Ministry in 1894, two studies were made on Madagascar; the first one, which had purely a geographical character, was made in the Bureau; it was copied by a corporal who worked in the anteroom of Colonel de Sancy. You were seen passing there several times while going to see the colonel.

Captain Dreyfus: I would comment that the antechamber is in front of the colonel's office and, therefore, everyone was obliged to pass it.

The President: Because it was the corporal who copied the note, it stands to reason that anyone going in or out of the office could have known of it. That is not an impossibility.

In any case, that note was of little importance; it was a simple geographical study. But in the month of July 1894 a more serious study was made, a study of the expedition itself. The study concerned the route to follow, the means to be employed, the material to be used; it was, in sum, a study for an expedition. It was made by different bureaus, but in particular by the Third Bureau, to which you were attached. Did you know about it?

Captain Dreyfus: Not at all.

The President: If the matter passed through your bureau, you would have known of it.

Captain Dreyfus: I was in the section on maneuvers.

The President: And you did not know anything about what went on in other bureaus.

Captain Dreyfus: Absolutely not. No officer communicated anything about it to me.

The President: The work was ended on August 20. The definite revisions were made on August 29, at the moment when the *bordereau* was being sent by its author. There is, therefore, a complete coincidence between that information and the work on Madagascar. As you were then in the Third Bureau, it was not impossible that you knew of it.

Captain Dreyfus: Nothing is impossible under such conditions, Colonel.

The President: No, but together these things lead at least to an assumption.

We pass now to the fifth document. It concerns "a Field Artillery Manual." Do you know anything about that manual?

Captain Dreyfus: No, Colonel.

The President: You have never known anything about it?

Captain Dreyfus: Never.

The President: There is a witness who claims that he had possession of the manual for forty-eight hours and that you had lent it to him.

Captain Dreyfus: I am convinced that that is an error. At the court-martial of 1894 I demanded that the witness be summoned but he never was.

The President: He is going to be summoned in the course of the trial.

Captain Dreyfus: I shall say it again: it is in the report of Commandant d'Ormescheville, as you have heard, where it is said that I had conversations with that officer during the month of February or March. Well, I have seen in the deposition of the Court of Cassation that the project of the manual is dated March 14 and that it was not submitted to the General Staff until the month of May. Therefore, I could not have had a conversation on that subject during the month of March.

The President: It was in the month of July 1894 that Commandant Jeannel sent you a copy of that manual?

Captain Dreyfus: But the reference was to the conversations I have had with him.

The President: No matter: what I ask of you is not what M. d'Ormescheville says. These are your replies: let me interrogate you, and do not pose any questions.

It was you yourself who complained to the Commandant Jeannel that the probationers of the General Staff did not know about the Firing Manual which was in the hands of all the officers of the regiment. Well! Ten copies were delivered, two of them to the Bureau to which you belonged. Do you grant that, as it was necessary to share the manual among the different officers, the Commandant gave you a copy?

Captain Dreyfus: No, Colonel.

The President: You deny it?

Captain Dreyfus: Yes, Colonel. Will you allow me an observation?

The President: Yes.

Captain Dreyfus: I should remind you that in July 1894 I did not belong any more to the Second Bureau of the General Staff nor did Commandant Jeannel, but to the Third Department. Well, after the depositions of the Court of Cassation, the Firing Manuals were given to all the bureaus. I just do not understand. . . .

The President: You can discuss the contradictory question with the witness.

Captain Dreyfus: Yes, but it was just an observation I wished to make.

The President: In the *bordereau* the author says that it is extremely difficult to obtain the manual. That was not the case for officers of the artillery corps whereas the officers of the Ministry really were not able to get the manual easily. There is again a coincidence with your personal situation.

Captain Dreyfus: Colonel, as I told the court-martial in 1894, it was easy to obtain the Firing Manual. It is certain that any officer might have asked for it and it would have been given to him.

I did not have it and I did not ask for it. I was not going to the Firing School and besides I was doing different work. Therefore, if I did not ask for the Firing Manual, it was because I had no need for it; it was quite easy for an artillery officer to get it. Consequently, that could not apply to an officer. . . .

The President: That is the core of the matter. The *bordereau* ended with the words: "I am just about to leave for maneuvers."

Well, have you ever been on maneuvers?

Captain Dreyfus: No, Colonel.

The President: It was the custom for only probationers to go. But at the date of the *bordereau* you did not know that you would not go?

Captain Dreyfus: There were no fresh orders. . . .

The President: At the Military School you were reproached for saying that the Alsatians were happier as Germans than as Frenchmen?

Captain Dreyfus: No, I never said any such thing.

The President: How do you explain the poor military performance report written about you by a certain general?

Captain Dreyfus: He said that he wanted no Jews on the General Staff.

The President: In 1892 you went to Mulhouse, Alsace. What did you do there?

Captain Dreyfus: I went there three times, via Basle, without a passport. Once I arrived at my home, I never went out of it.

The President: You went there in 1886?

Captain Dreyfus: Yes, possibly.

The President: Did you follow the German maneuvers?

Captain Dreyfus: No.

The President: Did you talk with German officers?

Captain Dreyfus: I deny it absolutely.

The President: What was your object in going to Alsace?

Captain Dreyfus: For instruction.

The President: You wrote certain information concerning the manufacture of the Robin shell. You said that this information was requested by a professor of the Military School. That was false. I am told that you asked officers indiscreet questions.

Captain Dreyfus: It is not true.

The President: Did you have any relations with a lady living in the Rue Bizet?

Captain Dreyfus: I had no intimate relations with her.

The President: I do not mean from a moral point of view, but in a military sense. This woman was suspected of being a foreign agent. Why did you visit her?

Captain Dreyfus: I only learned that at my court-martial in 1894. Major Gendrion introduced me to her. Because Gendrion belonged to the Inquiry Bureau he should have known if she was a suspected person.

The President: Passing through the Champs Elysées in 1891, you said: "Here lives a certain lady. Suppose we call on her. I have lost heavy amounts of money at her house."

Captain Dreyfus: It is false! I have never gambled. Never! Never!

The President: Did you know Colonel du Paty de Clam?

Captain Dreyfus: No.

The President: Did you know Lieutenant-Colonel Henry?

Captain Dreyfus: No.

The President: You have no animosity against them?

Captain Dreyfus: No.

The President: And Colonel Picquart?

Captain Dreyfus: I do not know him.

The President: And Lieutenant-Colonel Esterhazy?

Captain Dreyfus: I do not know him.

The President: Colonel du Paty de Clam said that your handwriting at his dictation was less firm when he examined you on the day of your arrest.

Captain Dreyfus: My handwriting has not changed much.

[*On being given a copy of his handwriting written on the day of his arrest, Dreyfus, tremendously excited, swayed to and fro for a moment, and then cried out in a piercing voice.*]

Captain Dreyfus: It is iniquitous to condemn an innocent man. I never confessed anything! Never!

The President: Did you say: "If I handed over documents it was to have more important ones in return?"

Captain Dreyfus: No.

The President: Did you say: "In three years they will recognize my innocence?" Why did you say "three years"?

Captain Dreyfus: I asked for all means of investigation. They were refused me. I was justified in hoping that at the end of two or three years my innocence would come to light.

The President: Why three years?

Captain Dreyfus: Because a certain amount of time is necessary to obtain light.

The President: Coming to the day of your degradation, what passed between you and Captain Lebrun-Renault? What did you tell him?

Captain Dreyfus: Nothing. It was really a kind of broken monologue on my part. I felt that everyone should know of the crime with which I was charged, and I wanted to say that I was not the guilty party. I wanted to make it clear that the criminal was not he whom they had before their eyes. I said: "Lebrun, I shall cry aloud my innocence in the face of the people."

The President: Did you not say: "The Minister knows I handed over documents"?

Captain Dreyfus: No. If I spoke of a minister who knew I was innocent, I referred to a conversation I previously had with du Paty de Clam.

The "Annotated *Bordereau*": The Mysterious, Non-Existent
"Key Document" of the Case

". . . this dog of a Dreyfus is shameless. . . ."

Rennes: Le procès Dreyfus, *vol. 1, pp. 76–77. Translated by the editor.*

On Saturday, August 12, 1899, General Mercier, the Minister of
War at the time of Dreyfus's first court-martial, and implacable in
his belief in Dreyfus's guilt, began his testimony as the third and
final witness of the second public session at Rennes. He wore on
his breast the decoration of a Grand Officer of the Legion of Honor.
As he sat down he placed on the witness rail his *képi* of brilliant
crimson and gold. He spoke almost inaudibly, in a weak, monotonous
tone. His deposition lasted from 8:10 A.M. until noon.

Mercier began by stating that in 1893 (he came into office
December 3, 1893), he was informed by Colonel Sandherr of the
conduct of foreign officers in France and of espionage operations
in various centers. He produced a note written in pencil and in
German by Colonel Schwartzkoppen on August 29 of that year
directing that 300 francs each should be given to 22 men if they
brought certain military information.

General Mercier: I am obliged to add, for this will have some
importance in the course of my deposition, that His Majesty, the German
Emperor personally busied himself with these espionage affairs and that
in certain exceptional cases the espionage chiefs in centers like Paris,
Brussels, and Strasbourg corresponded even directly and personally with
the Emperor. This is shown by certain documents of the secret *dossier,*
especially by a letter written by X., Colonel Sandherr's predecessor, to
the Emperor. This will enable you to appreciate the importance of
M. Mertian de Müller's statement as to seeing the fact of Dreyfus's arrest
pencilled on a newspaper on the Emperor's desk at Potsdam.

At this point General Mercier was setting the groundwork for the
existence of an "annotated *bordereau,*" a new document that was
supposed to prove Dreyfus's guilt beyond a shadow of a doubt. Before
testifying he let it be known in Army circles and in the press that
there was a crushing ultra-secret document in the *dossier* of Dreyfus.
He intimated that the *bordereau* used at the original court-martial
was only a tracing made by Esterhazy of the real *bordereau.* The
latter bore marginal "annotations" in the hand of the German

Emperor himself. If the document were to be made public, it would implicate many prominent Germans, including the daughter of the German Ambassador.

In his opening testimony, Mercier suggested that France and Germany were on the verge of war. This was heatedly denied by ex-President Casimir-Périer. Mercier also stated that the German Emperor William II was seriously implicated in espionage. He also repeated the canard that a certain M. Mertian de Müller had found in the study of William II a copy of the *Libre Parole* with a note in the margin by the Kaiser: *"Dreyfus ist gefangen."* ("Dreyfus is imprisoned.") Throughout the trial at Rennes the mysterious fable of the "annotated *bordereau*" existed only in the murky atmosphere: it was never produced. This supposed "document" did a great deal of harm to Dreyfus and undoubtedly influenced the judges.

Evidently, Mercier could not present the "annotated *bordereau*" at Rennes, but a clue to the mystery came the following Monday morning in an article in the newspaper *Le Gaulois* titled "An Open Letter to General Mercier." Apparently, it was a means of passing on to the judges at Rennes the entire story of the "annotated *bordereau*" which General Mercier felt he could not give in court. Following is the text of the article in *Le Gaulois*.

Le Gaulois, *August 14, 1899. Translated by the editor.*

GENERAL: In your intrepid, overpowering, and irresistible testimony you told a large part of the truth. But have you told the whole truth? I doubt it, and I tell you my reasons:

You declared that the German Emperor personally took part in espionage matters, and that on the matter of the *bordereau* he broke out into a rage reaching so intense a form that he brought us for a few hours to the very abyss of war.

But you did not clarify why the Kaiser was brought to a point where he could threaten us with war, and what definitely disturbed him.

Your silence on this point obscures your testimony and throws the entire matter into unfortunate darkness.

An especially trustworthy individual described to me the drama, of which you only revealed a small part:

The *bordereau* was written by Dreyfus on heavy paper and it was sent to the Kaiser, the chief of German espionage. On the column of the list, near each individual offer, was the demanded price. The Kaiser sent the *bordereau* together with a personal comment in German back to Paris, that "this dog of a Dreyfus is shameless" and that one should force him "as soon as possible to hand over the proffered documents." The *bordereau* with the remarks came into possession of Colonel Henry. One can imagine the excitement in the German Embassy when the loss of these documents was discovered. Herr von Münster hurried to the Élysée, fumed and threatened. He calmed down only when the *bordereau* was returned to him and when he was promised absolute silence about the incident.

But before the Minister of War showed the *bordereau* to his ministerial colleagues whom it concerned, he had a photograph made of it.

You possess a copy of this photograph and you have brought it with you to Rennes.

These facts clarify the puzzle of Esterhazy. In order to give some ground to the charges against Dreyfus, without implicating the German Kaiser, Esterhazy was ordered to photograph the *bordereau* on thin paper, without, however, including the remarks of the Kaiser.

In this way Esterhazy, without lying, could say that he was responsible for writing the *bordereau,* and you can quite rightly state that Dreyfus was the author of the *bordereau.*

If this believable explanation is correct, do not hesitate to confirm it. If there are errors in it, then you must correct them. If it be false, then it would be necessary to deny it. Whatever you do say, all decent and patriotic Frenchmen will take your own explanation as the conclusive truth.

Confrontation Between General Mercier and Captain Dreyfus

Captain Dreyfus: *"That is exactly what you ought to say!"*

Rennes: Le procès Dreyfus, *vol. 1, pp. 142–143. Translated by the editor.*

For nearly four hours General Mercier continued his testimony, most of which was intended to show the guilt of Dreyfus. At the end of his evidence, the former War Minister made a final personal assault on the accused. The tension building up in the courtroom finally exploded in a bitter confrontation between accuser and accused.

General Mercier: . . . In my estimation, the treason clearly results— first, from the contradictions and perpetual falsehoods of the accused; next, with moral certainty, from the technical examination of the *bordereau*. It results with material certainty from the cryptographic examination of the same *bordereau*. It results from the confessions.

Under these conditions, I am going to terminate my testimony which is already too long, and thank you for having permitted me to testify at length.

I should like to add one word. I have not reached my age [65] without having the sad experience of learning that all that is human is liable to error. If, moreover, I am weak-minded, as M. Zola has charged, I am at least an honest man and the son of an honest man. When, therefore, I saw the campaign for revision begin, I watched with poignant anxiety all the polemics, all the debates of that campaign. If the least doubt crossed my mind, Gentlemen, I would be the first to declare before you to Captain Dreyfus: "I have been honestly mistaken."

Captain Dreyfus: That is exactly what you ought to say!

General Mercier: I would come and say to Captain Dreyfus: "I have been honestly mistaken. I come with the same faith to admit it, and I shall do all in human power to repair it."

Captain Dreyfus: That is, indeed, your duty!

General Mercier: Well, not so. My conviction since 1894 has not undergone the slightest change. It is in fact deepened by intense study of the *dossier* and it has been strengthened also by the inanity of the means resorted to for the purpose of proving the innocence of the condemned man of 1894, in spite of the immensity of the accumulated efforts, and in spite of the millions senselessly expended.

The President: You have finished?

General Mercier: Yes.

The cold print of the stenographic record cannot possibly show the dramatic intensity of this moment. Eyewitnesses reported that throughout the morning Dreyfus had listened with sphinx-like silence. He looked at Mercier as a cat watching a mouse. The audience could scarcely suspect the volcano slumbering inside the accused officer. Occasionally, he moistened his lips with his tongue.

As Mercier began his final summation, Dreyfus's suppressed feeling of rage and anger won mastery over him. When the witness declared that he would be the first to admit that he was honestly mistaken, Dreyfus electrified the spectators by jumping to his feet, and his voice resounded throughout the courtroom like a trumpet note: "That is exactly what you ought to say!" It was almost like the cry of a wounded animal.

The audience, sensing the agony of the accused, broke into wild applause, only to be hushed by the ushers. As the session ended there was a demonstration in the courtroom. A part of the audience rose *en masse*, hissing and cursing the former Minister of War as he left the hall. Gendarmes immediately placed themselves between the General and the audience.

Outside, natives of Rennes who had always been anti-Dreyfus, and who had not heard General Mercier's lame performance, cheered him with shouts of *"Vive la République!"* and *"Vive la Justice!"*

An American Psychologist Reacts from Bad Nauheim

"Picquart is a real hero—a precious possession for any country."

Quoted in Nicholas Halasz, Captain Dreyfus: The Story of a Mass Hysteria *(New York: Simon and Schuster, 1955), pp. 229, 233. By permission of Simon and Schuster.*

The attention of people all over the world turned to the courtroom at Rennes. While taking the cure at Bad Nauheim, William James, American psychologist and philosopher, one of the founders of pragmatism, and brother of the novelist Henry James, sent these two letters in mid-August 1899 to friends in the United States.

WILLIAM JAMES TO MRS. E. P. GIBBINS FROM BAD NAUHEIM

The still blacker nightmare of a Dreyfus case hangs over us; and there is little time in the day save for reading *Le Figaro's* full reports of the trial. Like all French happenings, it is as if they were edited expressly for literary purposes. Every witness so-called has a power of statement equal to that of a first-class lawyer, and the various human types that succeed each other, exhibiting their several peculiarities in full blossom, make the thing like a novel. Esterhazy seems to me a fantastic scoundrel—knowing all the secrets, saying what he pleases, mystifying all Europe, leading the whole French Army (except apparently Picquart) by the nose, a regular Shakespearean type of villain, with an insane exuberance of rhetoric and fancy about his vanities and hatreds that literature has never yet equalled. It would seem incredible that the court-martial should condemn [Dreyfus]. Henry was evidently the spy, employed by Esterhazy, and afterwards du Paty helped their machinations in order to protect his own record at the original trial—at least this seems the plausible theory. The older generals seem merely to have been passive connivers, stupidly and obstinately holding to the original official mistake rather than surrender under fire. And such is the prestige of caste-opinion, such the solidarity of the professional spirit, that, incredible as it may seem, it is still quite probable that the officers will obey the lead of their superiors and condemn Dreyfus again. . . .

Picquart is a real hero—a precious possession for any country. He ought to be made Minister of War, though that would doubtless produce a revolution. I suppose Loubet will pardon Dreyfus immediately (if the court recommends it). Then Dreyfus, and perhaps Loubet, will be assassinated by some anti-Semite, and who knows what will follow?

WILLIAM JAMES TO MRS. R. MORSE FROM BAD NAUHEIM

Talk of corruption! We don't know what the word corruption means at home, with our improvised and shifting agencies of crude pecuniary bribery, compared with the solidly entrenched and permanently organized corruptive geniuses of monarchy, nobility, Church, Army, that penetrate the very bosom of the higher kind as well as the lower kind of people in all European states (except Switzerland) and sophisticate their motives away from the impulse to straightforward handling of any simple case. *Témoin* the Dreyfus case. But no matter! Of all the forms of mental crudity, that of growing earnest over international comparisons is probably the most childish. Every nation has its ideals which are a dead secret to other nations, and it has to develop in its own way, in touch with them. It can only be judged by itself. If each of us does as well as he can in his own sphere at home, he will do all he can do; that is why I hate to remain so long abroad. . . .

Attempt to Kill Maître Labori

(*From our Special Correspondent*)

The Times (*London*), *August 15, 1899.*

Rennes, August 14 (1899)

. . . Suddenly a hubbub at the entrance arrested our attention. We turned and saw the tall form of M. Taunay, of the judicial police, clambering upon a bench, and then instantly this announcement rang through the Court: "M. Labori is wounded." It was like a pistol shot in the Court itself. The faces of half the audience became white with consternation. Several persons rushed out, among them doctors who were present. . . .

What had happened was this. M. Labori, who had yesterday received two letters threatening to kill him, but who had paid little heed to them, as to the scores of others he had received during the last two years, left his house this morning at 6 o'clock alone, his wife, who attends all the sittings of the Court, intending to follow him in a few moments. On the way he fell in with Colonel Picquart and M. Gast, the colonel's cousin. The three had passed the bridge of La Barbetière and, leaving the low path, had arrived on the Quai Richemont near the bridge across the Vilaine, when a pistol shot was heard behind them, and M. Labori, uttering the familiar French ejaculation: *"Ooh, la, la!"* tottered and fell. He had received a bullet in the back.

The details which I am about to give I have from Colonel Picquart and M. Gast themselves. Their first thought was of their companion. A few moments were therefore lost in assisting M. Labori. Moreover, neither Colonel Picquart nor his friend was armed.

With a scrupulous correctness intelligible enough at a moment when the slightest violation of the law of the land may entail the most serious inconveniences, but with a loyalty which the present event had proved to be quixotic, and which they profoundly regret at this hour, they were without their revolvers, in spite of the threatening letters which the colonel has never ceased to receive for many months. Had they been armed they might easily have killed the assailant.

The would-be murderer, darting off at full speed, had, however, already put 100 yards between himself and his victim. Yet as soon as M. Labori had been laid out on the pavement both his companions started out in pursuit. There were workingmen, early risers, nearby who heard the shot and can help to identify him, but not one of them made the slightest effort to capture him. M. Gast is a solid, somewhat heavily built man, who soon found pursuit futile, and even Colonel Picquart, although he is more active, and although in M. Gast's words, he "ran like a deer," had to abandon the chase.

The assailant had dashed along the river, unarrested by the slightest obstacle, human or otherwise, until he met on the banks of the Vilaine a company of workingmen unloading a barge. Seeing the man running toward them, and hearing the cries of "Assassin!" which had followed him from afar, they sought to capture him. But aiming his revolver, he cried: *"Laissez-moi!* I have just killed Dreyfus." For the shame of France it was an "open sesame" and the man rushed on.

He gained the open fields, making in the direction of Châteauaugiron. The forests of Rennes lay there rich in lurking places, a far finer refuge for a hunted criminal than the clear spaces of the little wood where, in Zola's novel, *Paris,* the anarchist Salvat is surrounded and tricked by the police. The would-be assassin, who according to the impression of Colonel Picquart is not yet 30, is red-haired, and wore a short black coat and a sort of round white skullcap, capable, however, Colonel Picquart says, of being rolled down like a turban upon the brow and ears. He sped on into the country, finally followed by no one, left fairly to himself to choose his lair. For Colonel Picquart had given up the pursuit and returned to his friend.

He found M. Labori still lying on the pavement but his wife had arrived, and she was holding his head and shoulders on her knees, while with a little Japanese fan, hastily snatched up as she left the house, she fanned the handsome pallid face of her husband.

A half hour passed before a shutter was brought, and it was almost as long before a doctor arrived. Four soldiers had been ordered to the spot with the shutter to transfer M. Labori to his house. He had not lost consciousness, and he spoke to his wife of the trial, urging her immediately to inform the Court and have the proceedings interrupted. . . .

The wound was at first thought to be fatal. It was feared that the bullet had perforated a lung and in its passage perhaps affected the spinal cord. Later more accurate details were known. The bullet entered the back a little to the right of the backbone on a level with the fifth or sixth rib. The state of the wound for the moment prevents surgical search for the bullet. The doctors hope that it is lodged in the muscle of the back, but at the hour at which I write, late in the afternoon, the condition of the patient is very feverish, and the fact that he has not moved his leg since the morning makes the doctors fear that even if he recovers one side of his back may be paralyzed.

M. Labori, it should be remembered, has only just recovered from typhoid fever, during which he was for a time in a critical state. His ardent, nervous, high-pitched organism, wrought up as it is to a pitch of terrible tension by the anxieties over the work in the Dreyfus Affair, is in an extremely unsatisfactory condition for combating this fresh shock. . . .

10:40 P.M. The father and mother of M. Labori arrived tonight, thinking him dead. The patient has received M. Mathieu Dreyfus, but the decision as to the choice of a fresh lawyer, whether M. Clemenceau or M. Mornard, is deferred till tomorrow.

The following is the official bulletin published at 10 o'clock: "Condition unchanged. No fever; temperature 99.5. Situation, on the whole, favorable since the last bulletin."

Fortunately, X-rays taken the next day showed that the bullet had penetrated the skin and the subcutaneous tissues and had lodged in the dorsal muscles. *The Times* reported that while M. Labori was lying on the ground, he had his pockets picked and his papers stolen.

The news of the attempted assassination created a sensation. It was decided to continue the case after the President of the Court and even the generals had expressed their regret. The press war, too, went on: the Dreyfusards claimed that the culprit was a hired

assassin of the General Staff, while the anti-Dreyfusards planted the
rumor that Labori had arranged to be shot by a confederate in order
to arouse sympathy for his cause.

Labori was able to resume the defense after a week. He was
greeted with enthusiasm in the courtroom. "I am getting on well,
my friends, thank you, thank you!" He walked briskly, but held his
left arm close to his side, in order not to disturb the wound.

The Imperial Chancellery Refuses to Hand Over Documents of 1894

". . . the conclusion would be drawn that he was our spy."

Kölnische Zeitung, *August 16, 1899. Translated by the editor.*

On August 16, 1899, nine days after the opening of the Rennes
court-martial, the semi-official *Cologne Gazette* published a statement
which peremptorily rejected the possibility that the incriminating
documents handed over to the Germans in 1894 might be made
available to the court-martial. Obviously, the Imperial Chancellery
had no wish to expose itself to such documents being declared false.

If, subsequent to the statements made by the German Government
and the proceedings in the Court of Cassation, there is any person who
believes Dreyfus to be guilty, all that can be said is that he is obviously
either suffering from mental illness or deliberately wants to convict an
innocent man. One is helpless when confronted with such persons, and
nothing that the German Government could publish would make any
impression whatever on them. The documents supplied by us would be
declared false, and from the fact that Germany was trying to save
Dreyfus the conclusion would be drawn that he was our spy.

Piquart Recounts the Plots Against Dreyfus

"Beyond the bordereau *there was nothing against Dreyfus—
absolutely nothing."*

Harding, *Dreyfus, The Prisoner of Devil's Island, pp. 162–175. The stenographic report is in* Rennes: Le procès Dreyfus, *vol. 1, pp. 368–484.*

Colonel Picquart was called to the stand and testified on the afternoon of August 17, 1899, and five hours the next day. Giving his
testimony in a loud voice, he at first replied to the various attacks
made on him and then discussed in detail the documents in Drey-

fus's secret *dossier*. The following condensation was made by William Harding, cable editor of *The Associated Press*.

August 17, 1899

Colonel Picquart was then called to the witness stand. He protested most formally against all suspicion of having caused the disappearance of any document relating to Dreyfus. Documents, he added, had disappeared, but he was not connected with their disappearance. He also repelled with scorn the assertion that he had endeavored to put another officer in the place of the real author of the *bordereau*.

"It is true," the witness continued, "that the name of Captain Dorval being mentioned to me as a dangerous man, I had him watched; and do you know, gentlemen, by whom Dorval was denounced? By his own cousin," continued Picquart, "Major du Paty de Clam."

Colonel Picquart then next proceeded to reply to the various attacks made upon him. "These tactics," he said, "are evidently pursued with the object of lessening the value of my testimony."

The colonel next outlined his connection with Dreyfus at the Military College, and afterward at the Ministry of War, where, owing to the anti-Semite prejudices of the General Staff, he first appointed Dreyfus to a department where probationers had no direct cognizance of secret documents.

He then described the consternation in the War Office when the treason was discovered, and the relief experienced when it was thought the guilty person had been discovered. It was then the witness discovered the similarity between the handwriting of Dreyfus and that of the *bordereau*, and he had recourse to du Paty de Clam, "who was supposed to have geographical knowledge." [Laughter.]

Then the witness described what he characterized as the "irregular steps" taken by General Mercier to accomplish the arrest of Dreyfus.

Referring to the dictation test, the witness earnestly and emphatically affirmed that he saw no signs of perturbation in the handwriting of Dreyfus on that occasion, and, moreover, shortly afterward du Paty de Clam admitted he had not found a fresh charge against Dreyfus.

"Beyond the *bordereau*," added the witness, "there was nothing against Dreyfus—absolutely nothing."

The colonel next declared that in 1894 he did not know the contents of the secret *dossier*. But he believed, like all other officers, that it contained frightful proofs against the prisoner. But when he became acquainted with its contents he found that his earlier impressions were entirely wrong.

The witness also declared he was quite ignorant of the confessions Dreyfus is alleged to have made to Captain Lebrun-Renault.

Next the colonel examined the *bordereau* and declared Dreyfus could not have disclosed part of it.

Regarding the Madagascar note, the witness disputed its value, and said he did not believe it was a confidential note. He added that if Dreyfus, in his capacity of a probationer, had asked the witness for the note, he would have handed it to him immediately. Therefore, he [Picquart] was unable to understand the sentence in the *bordereau* reading: "This document was very difficult to obtain."

Colonel Picquart declared he had never seen Dreyfus copy the smallest document in the War Office. In the opinion of the witness the department where the *bordereau* was discovered ought to have been searched when the discovery was made. This, he explained, was the department in which du Paty de Clam worked, and that was the department which was working on the plan of the concentration of the troops and the Madagascar expedition. He added:

"It was in Major du Paty de Clam's department that the search should have been made, or rather in his private room, where he worked quite alone." [Sensation.]

Du Paty de Clam, continued the witness, had been guilty of grave impudence in having, contrary to the regulations, had confidential documents copied by simple secretaries, non-commissioned officers, and even private soldiers, whereas the custom was that such work was done solely by officers.

Later on the witness said he wondered if it was not to avoid the risk of punishment that du Paty de Clam advanced the date of the reception of the *bordereau* at the Intelligence Department, so as to make it prior to the date of his, du Paty de Clam's, arrival in the Third Department. [Sensation.]

August 18, 1899

Picquart then proceeded to discuss the secret *dossier* as being the mainspring of the condemnation of Dreyfus.

The colonel practically occupied the whole of the sitting with a masterful presentation of his side of the case. He spoke for five hours, and his voice at the end of that time began to show signs of fatigue.

His testimony was followed with the closest attention by the members of the court-martial and by the audience, and during the brief suspension of the court Generals Mercier, Roget, Billot, and de Boisdeffre, and other witnesses sauntered together up and down the courtyard of the Lycée or gathered in little groups, animatedly discussing Picquart's evidence, which, although it contained but few facts, was so cleverly placed before the tribunal and was spoken so effectively that it could not fail to repeat the impression he had made the day before.

Dreyfus naturally drank in all the witness's words, which came as a balm to the wounds inflicted upon him by Generals Mercier and Roget; and the prisoner frequently and closely scanned the faces of the judges, as though seeking to read their thoughts.

Before resuming his deposition, Colonel Picquart said:

"For the moment I shall confine myself to the following explanation: The Quenelli case occurred between May 30 and July 17, 1896, at which period, on account of a family bereavement, I was able to pay very little attention to my official duties. In my absence, Colonel Henry acted for me. Moreover, I devoted most of the month of July to a journey of the Headquarters' Staff, which also prevented me from attending to my ordinary duties. I was, therefore, able to give only very intermittent attention to the Quenelli case. Besides this, Quenelli was a returned convict, who had contravened a decree of expulsion and had been caught red-handed in another criminal act. He was, at first sight, a not particularly interesting personage.

"I protest absolutely against the allegation that I consented to the communication of secret documents to the members of the Dreyfus court-martial without the prisoner's knowledge. I never ordered such communication, and if it was done it was not with my cognizance. Having thus explained certain matters I will continue my deposition."

Then the colonel proceeded to discuss the phrase occurring in the *bordereau*, "I am going to the maneuvers." He said there was no question of probationers going to the maneuvers in September. This, he pointed out, would have curtailed their period of probation in an entirely unusual manner. It was for this reason that D'Ormescheville, who drew up the *acte d'accusation*, or indictment, against Dreyfus in 1894, changed the date of the *bordereau* from September to April. When, however, it was discovered that Dreyfus knew as early as March that he would not attend the maneuvers, the correct date was resumed. Later this was found untenable, and so, in their testimony before the Court of Cassation, Generals Mercier, Gonse, and de Boisdeffre reassumed the date of the *bordereau* to have been April.

After dealing with the testimony of the experts at the court-martial of 1894, Picquart proceeded to examine the secret *dossier,* a close analysis of which, he asserted, was particularly necessary, "owing to the weight the document had with the members of the court-martial in 1894."

"This *dossier,*" continued the witness, "may be divided into two parts.

The first contains three documents: One, a document known as the d'Avignon document, the terms of which are about as follows: 'Doubt; proof; service letters; situation dangerous for me with French officer; cannot personally conduct negotiations; no information from an officer of the line; important only as coming from the Ministry; already somewhere else.' "

This is a literal translation of a cipher dispatch in German, which was intercepted early in 1894. It was sent by Schwartzkoppen in reply to a message which had been intercepted December 29, 1893, and which contained the words: "The documents; no sign of the General Staff."

"Service letters" in the reply is translated from the German original "patent," *i.e.,* an officer's brevet. Both dispatches have been paraphrased by Picquart as follows: The documents received. There is no evidence that they come from the War Office."

To which the reply was: "You doubt? My proof is that my informant [Esterhazy] is an officer. I have seen his brevet. True, only a regimental officer; but I assure you he brings his information, every bit of it, from the Intelligence Bureau. I cannot communicate directly with Henry."

"Two, the document containing the words, '*Cette canaille de D——.*'

"Three, a document which is nothing but the report of a journey to Switzerland, and made in behalf of a foreign power.

"The second part of the *dossier,*" continued Picquart, "consisted partly of a supplementary review of the first. It contained the gist of seven or eight documents, one of which, '*Cette canaille de D——,*' will serve for the purposes of comparison. It also contained the correspondence of Attachés 'A' and 'B'." [These initials represent Colonel von Schwartzkoppen, formerly German Military Attaché, and Major Panizzardi, the former Military Attaché of Italy, at the French capital.]

The witness next explained why Major du Paty de Clam's translation of the d'Avignon document, which has been classed as idiotic, was open to doubt and why the document, if it had any meaning whatever, was as applicable to Esterhazy as to Dreyfus. Du Paty de Clam's translation or paraphrasing reads as follows:

"You say the documents do not bear the mark of the General Staff. There are doubts; proof is therefore necessary. I will ask for '*la lettre de service,*' but, as it is dangerous for me personally to conduct the negotiations, I will take an intermediary and tell the officer to bring me what he has. I must have absolute discretion, because the Intelligence Bureau is on the watch against us; there is no good of having relations with a regimental officer. Documents are only of importance when they come from the Ministry; this is why I continue my relations."

Regarding the correspondence of the Military Attaché, the witness demonstrated the insignificance of the information asked for.

Colonel Picquart then took up the *"Cette canaille de D——"* document. He called the attention of the court to the fact that it was addressed by Schwartzkoppen to Panizzardi, and not *vice versa,* as long believed.

After giving his reasons for believing Dreyfus was not the person referred to in that document, Picquart showed how du Paty de Clam endeavored to ascribe the authorship of the document to Panizzardi with the view of establishing a connection which in reality did not exist between the various documents in the indictment against Dreyfus.

The former Chief of the Intelligence Department concluded his examination of the first portion of the secret *dossier* by saying:

"May I be allowed to express deep regret at the absence of Major du Paty de Clam? It seems to me indispensable that this officer, who wrote the commentaries on the secret *dossier,* should be summoned to give evidence here. He would give us his reminiscences, and I would help him." [Laughter.] "But," added Picquart, "since I am dealing with this question of the commentaries of Major du Paty de Clam, permit me to point to you, gentlemen, that this document was not the property of any particular minister. It was classified as belonging to the Intelligence Department, and, as you see, it formed part of a well-defined *dossier*—a *dossier* which was shut up in one of the drawers of my desk and which was abstracted from it. This commentary, therefore, is upon a secret *dossier* document which was improperly removed from my department."

Continuing, the witness remarked: "Mention was made yesterday of the disappearance of documents. That is the case in point."

Turning to the second portion of the *dossier,* Picquart described a number of documents in it as forgeries, and said the police reports therein contained nothing serious against Dreyfus. He explained that they embodied the theme mostly utilized by police spies in order to dupe the Intelligence Department, and asserted that their information was mostly worthless or false, and prepared in order to make interesting reading.

"In the inquiry made by M. Quesnay de Beaurepaire" (former President of the Civil Section of the Court of Cassation), continued Picquart, "you have an excellent example of the sort of people who can present in the most specious guise what amounts absolutely to nothing. You cannot imagine, gentlemen, what people, in order to get money, if only a modest twenty-franc piece, have brought to the Intelligence Department in the shape of so-called 'information,' which examination has proved to be worthless."

Concluding his examination of the secret *dossier,* Colonel Picquart explained how he had acquired the conviction that the *bordereau* was written by Esterhazy, and how he ascertained that the anti-Dreyfus proofs were worthless. He began by detailing how he first learned of the existence of Esterhazy and his efforts to discover something about him. The witness earnestly asserted that the first occasion on which he saw Esterhazy's name was when he read the address of the *petit bleu.* He said he was not acquainted with Esterhazy, and never had Esterhazy watched. Previous to this the utmost efforts had been made to prove the contrary, and to show that Picquart knew Esterhazy before the discovery of the *petit bleu.*

What Picquart gathered about Esterhazy's character, he continued, created the worst impression upon him, but he learned nothing to connect Esterhazy with any act of espionage. Therefore he did not mention his suspicions. An agent, however, was ordered to watch Esterhazy, who had completely compromised himself through his relations with an English company, of which he had agreed to become a director.

"That could not be permitted in the case of a French officer," said Picquart. "Moreover, Esterhazy gambled, led a life of debauchery, and lived with Mme. Pays."

Turning to the leakage at Headquarters, the witness described the negotiations of Major Lauth with the spy Richard Cuers, at Basle, showing how the spy promised to inform him about the leakage, and how he, Picquart, was induced to allow Lieutenant-Colonel Henry to accompany Major Lauth to Basle.

Picquart also described the vague replies of Henry when questioned on the subject of Esterhazy before his departure, and the futility of the visit to Basle, because of Cuers's refusal, when he saw Henry, to impart the promised information. This incident caused the witness to wonder whether, instead of trying to make Cuers speak, Henry and Lauth had not done everything possible to impose silence upon him.

"I affirm," continued Picquart, "that General de Boisdeffre knew that this question was to remain a secret between us, and that I was not to mention it except to the Minister of War. I knew Esterhazy was anxious to enter the War Office, and I did not regard his desire favorably. I communicated my impressions to my chiefs, who approved all my steps, and the application of Esterhazy was rejected.

"His insistence, however, only increased my uneasiness regarding him, and I resolved to obtain a specimen of his handwriting. I was immediately struck with the similarity of his handwriting and that of the *borde-*

reau, and forthwith I had the letters of Esterhazy which were in my possession photographed, and showed the photographs to Major du Paty de Clam and M. Bertillon between August 25th and September 5th."

The colonel emphasized this point, because M. Bertillon affirmed that he saw the photographs in May, 1896, and made a note of them, whereas the letters were not written on that date. The conflicting testimony of Picquart and Bertillon on this point had been used to discredit the former's evidence.

Colonel Picquart also said du Paty de Clam, on seeing the writing, forthwith declared it was that of Mathieu Dreyfus, the brother of Captain Dreyfus.

The witness, continuing, said:

" 'You know,' du Paty de Clam maintained, 'that the *bordereau* is the joint work of Alfred and Mathieu Dreyfus.'

"M. Bertillon said: 'That is the writing of the *bordereau.*'

"M. Bertillon tried to discover where I had obtained the handwriting, but the only information I imparted was that it was current and recent handwriting.

"M. Bertillon then suggested that it was a tracing, and ended by saying that if it was current handwriting it could only have emanated from some one whom the Jews had been exercising for a year in imitating the writing of the *bordereau.*

"At M. Bertillon's request I left the photographs with him. When he returned them he said he adhered to his opinion and earnestly asked to see the original. When I saw beyond a doubt that the handwriting of the *bordereau* was Esterhazy's, and seeing that the documents mentioned therein might have been supplied by Esterhazy, that the words, 'I am going to the maneuvers' could perfectly well apply to Esterhazy, and that Esterhazy had secretaries at his disposal to copy a document so voluminous as the Firing Manual, I resolved to consult the secret *dossier* to see what part of the treachery might be ascribed to Dreyfus, and to assure myself whether the *dossier* contained anything implicating Esterhazy. I frankly admit I was stupefied on reading the secret *dossier.* I expected to find matters of gravity therein, and found, in short, nothing but a document which might apply just as much to Esterhazy as to Dreyfus, an unimportant document mentioning Davignon, and a document which it seemed absurd to apply to Dreyfus, namely, the '*Cette canaille de D——*' document.

"Lastly, I recognized a report appended in the handwriting of Guénnée, an agent, which appeared to be at least as worthless as the second document.

"It was then evening. I had stayed late at the office in order to examine the documents thoroughly. I thought it over during the night, and the next day I explained the whole situation to General de Boisdeffre. I took to his office the secret *dossier,* the facsimile of the *bordereau,* the *petit bleu,* and the principal papers connected with my investigation of Esterhazy.

"I wonder now if I had one or two interviews? But I still see General de Boisdeffre, as he examined the secret *dossier* with me, stop before he reached the end, and tell me to go into the country, give an account of the Affair to General Gonse, and ask his advice.

"When I informed General Gonse of all which had occurred, he remarked: 'So a mistake has been made?'

"After my interview with General Gonse I did not work any longer on my own initiative. I said nothing more until the return of General Gonse, September 15th. At this time Esterhazy was at the great maneuvers."

Next the witness dwelt on the rumors in September, 1896, of the project of replacing Dreyfus by a man-of-straw, and the discovery of the forged Weyler letter, supposed to be connected with the same project.

At about the same time the campaign for and against Dreyfus was started by the newspapers.

The witness then turned to the newspaper attacks on Dreyfus, saying that the information regarding the *bordereau* contained in them convinced him that they had been inspired by some one closely connected with the Dreyfus Affair. They could not, he added, be attributed to the Dreyfus family, while they contained expressions familiar to du Paty de Clam, whom it would be interesting to hear on the subject.

The witness next said he asked permission to inquire into the sources of the articles, but was forbidden to interfere in any way whatever.

Describing his interview with General Gonse, on September 15th, Picquart said:

"When I asked General Gonse for permission to continue the investigation, insisting on the danger of allowing the Dreyfus family to proceed with their investigation alone, the general replied that it was impossible, in his opinion and in the opinions of General de Boisdeffre and the Minister of War, to reopen the Affair. When I pressed the point, in order to make General Gonse understand that nothing could prevent its reopening if it could be believed Dreyfus was innocent, General Gonse replied:

" 'If you say nothing, nobody will know.'

" 'General,' I replied, firmly, 'what you tell me is abominable. I do not know what I shall do. But I won't carry this secret with me to the grave.'

"I at once left the room," added the witness. "That is what occurred.

I know my account is disputed, but I positively swear it," said Picquart, as he emphatically smote the bar in front of the witness box, and looked in the direction of the generals.

The colonel next described his intentions with regard to Esterhazy, which Generals Gonse and de Boisdeffre had forbidden him to carry out. He attached particular importance to this point, as it contained a clue to subsequent occurrences. Later, the witness said, that while du Paty de Clam evidently acted wrongly in disguising himself during the investigations with a false beard and blue spectacles, perhaps he was authorized to do so.

Colonel Picquart also showed how, through an article in the *Éclair* of September 14, 1896, he was satisfied Esterhazy had been warned of the suspicions against him.

In order to make the proofs complete, the witness continued his investigations with the utmost discretion. In his opinion, the only event of importance in the Dreyfus affair since the discovery of the *bordereau* was the Henry forgery, perpetrated on October 31st, 1896. He added that it must have been handed immediately to General Gonse.

Shortly before Henry perpetrated the forgery, the agent Guénée, Henry's right-hand man, prepared a report declaring that M. Castelin (Republican Revisionist, Deputy for Laon, division of Aisne) was about to play the hand of the Dreyfus family by unmasking, in the Chamber of Deputies, the prisoner's accomplices, thus having the Affair reopened.

Then, turning to the distant mission upon which he was dispatched, Picquart described the irritation he felt when he saw he was being removed because he was no longer wanted as head of the Intelligence Department. He explained that if this disgrace had been frankly avowed it would have been much less painful to him. The colonel also said that during his absence his correspondence was tampered with.

Dealing with his mission to Tunis, which Picquart said ought to have been entrusted to a commissary of police, the witness declared it was then that Henry, abandoning his underhand intrigues, began a campaign of open persecution. Henry wrote to the witness, accusing him of communicating information to the press, with disclosing the contents of secret documents, and with attempting to suborn officers in connection with the *petit bleu*.

It was then Picquart learned of the existence of the forged secret documents directed against himself, and foresaw his own ruin if the Dreyfus Affair was reopened; and, to safeguard himself, he entrusted to a lawyer friend, M. Leblois, a certain letter from General Gonse, at the same time acquainting the lawyer with what he knew of Esterhazy, and instructing the lawyer how he should intervene, "if the occasion demanded it." This lawyer communicated with M. Scheurer-Kestner, then one of the Vice-

Presidents of the Senate, and the representations of the latter to Premier Méline's Government followed.

When Picquart's furlough was due, General Leclerc, commanding in Tunis, was ordered to send Picquart to the frontier of Tripoli. Leclerc commented to the witness on the abnormal order, and Picquart confided to the general the probable reasons for it, and his belief in the innocence of Dreyfus. General Leclerc thereupon ordered Picquart not to go beyond Gabes.

Picquart created a sensation by incidentally remarking that the judges in 1894 were shamefully deceived in having the document containing the words, *"Cette canaille de D——"* communicated to them.

Witness then bitterly recited the details of the various machinations with the view of incriminating him, instigated by Henry, Esterhazy, and du Paty de Clam.

"I have almost finished my task," added Picquart, "but I ask permission to refer to the way the *bordereau* came to the War Office. I have doubts in regard to the person who brought the *bordereau*. Two quite different persons could certainly have delivered the *bordereau* in 1894. But, if an intelligent person had delivered it, he would certainly have insisted on the value of its contents."

In reply to questions of General Roget, Picquart admitted sending documents to Belfort for the use of the Quenelli case. "But," Picquart added, "they were handed to the Public Prosecutor."

General Roget's questions were evidently with the view of eliciting the confession from Colonel Picquart that, in the Quenelli case, he communicated to the judges documents unknown to the defense, as he now accuses the General Staff of doing in the Dreyfus case.

General Mercier promptly replaced General Roget.

"Picquart," Mercier said, "has stated that I ordered him to convey documents to Colonel Maurel-Pries. That is false. I never handed any packet to Colonel Picquart for Colonel Maurel-Pries. I never mentioned secret documents to him."

In reply Colonel Picquart said:

"I remember perfectly that General Mercier handed me a packet for Colonel Maurel-Pries."

General Mercier next denied Colonel Picquart's statement relative to the meeting with General Gonse during the afternoon of January 6, 1895, when the latter was greatly excited at the prospect of war.

Colonel Picquart replied that he adhered to everything he had said. General Gonse, the witness explained, was excited because he knew of the action of an ambassador toward M. Casimir-Périer, then President of the Republic.

General Mercier next referred to Picquart's statement that the d'Avignon document was communicated to the court-martial of 1894. He said:

"I deny it positively. The only documents communicated were the Panizzardi telegram, du Paty de Clam's commentary, the note of the Italian attaché in regard to French railroads, and the report of Guénée."

Picquart here pointed out that he had only expressed his belief on this subject.

Maître Demange's cross-examination compelled General Mercier somewhat reluctantly to enumerate the secret documents submitted to the first court-martial. Among them was the "*Cette canaille de D——*" letter.

When asked why the commentary of Guénée was not attached to the document, Mercier replied:

"It was supplied for my personal use."

"Then," said Maître Demange triumphantly, "you could not have meant Dreyfus, but did mean Dubois."

M. Demange asked General Mercier why it did not occur to him to append to the comments information of the existence of a man named Dubois, who was suspected of having communicated information to foreign powers.

General Mercier replied:

"Because we had discovered that he could not have been the author of the documents mentioned in the comments."

"Ah," said Maître Demange, "because you considered that Dubois could not be the author, after study of the *dossier,* of the divulgations, consequently you did not reveal the fact that there was a person called D—— who might be meant?"

General Mercier: "Quite so."

The court then adjourned.

The Extraordinary Testimony of Alphonse Bertillon

"Now and again M. Bertillon's voice rose in hateful shrieks."

The Times (*London*), *August 26 and 28, 1899. The stenographic report is in* Rennes: Le procès Dreyfus, *vol. 2, pp. 318–386.*

Alphonse Bertillon (1853–1914), anthropologist, had achieved fame by inventing a system of identification of criminals known as Bertillonage. Utilizing anthropometry or the measurement of certain parts of the human body, Bertillon found it possible to identify an individual for the rest of his life. The essential elements included: (1) length of head; (2) breadth of head; (3) length of middle finger;

(4) of left foot; and (5) of forearm to tip of the middle finger. The measurements had to be extremely accurate and were slow and expensive. The development of identification by fingerprints led to the replacement of Bertillon's system.

Bertillon also fancied himself to be a handwriting expert. At the beginning of the Dreyfus case in 1894, he was asked to report on the handwriting of the *bordereau*. Immediately after the arrest of Dreyfus, the accusers General Mercier, Major Henry, and Major du Paty de Clam called in M. Gobert, handwriting expert of the Bank of France, who reported at once that the *bordereau* "might have been written by a person other than the one under suspicion [Dreyfus]." Dissatisfied, the officers, seeking a more accommodating expert, turned to Bertillon, then Chief of the Judicial Identification Department of the Prefecture of Police, and a notorious anti-Semite. Bertillon studied photographic prints of the *bordereau* and submitted his conclusions: "Setting aside the hypothesis of the documents having been most carefully forged, it seems clear to us that the same person wrote all the documents received, including the incriminating document."

As the case gathered momentum, Bertillon evolved a theory that the dissimilarities between the *bordereau* and the handwriting of Dreyfus were only another means of deception employed by the traitor. He worked out "scientifically" the "indisputable proof of an absolute, complete, and unreserved conclusion." At the Zola trial, Bertillon attempted to justify his "infallible and transcendent method of graphology" to the accompaniment of laughter from the audience.

On August 25, 1899, Bertillon was called as the 61st witness before the court-martial. As Dreyfus gazed on in stupefaction, Bertillon went into a long-winded defense in incomprehensible and unintelligible terms of his "infallible system." There was consternation in the courtroom, and the majority of the public left. The following two reports from *The Times* (London) reveal the extraordinary nature of Bertillon's testimony.

The Dreyfus Trial

M. Bertillon's Evidence

(from our special correspondent)

Rennes, Aug. 25, [1899]

Kismet. It was preordained that we should behold in this great trial every form of human passion, all types of human nature. Today has been the day of M. Bertillon. A friend said to me as we left the hall:—"In the great *cause célèbre* of the 18th century, that of the Queen's diamond necklace, a charlatan played a leading rôle, and so, in the Dreyfus case, a century later, we are placed at the mercy of the fantastic mystifications of a disordered visionary's brain, for such Bertillon is, the Cagliostro of the 19th century. Such cases as his are well-known to our *savants,* and in the treatises of our specialists in insanity they bear a learned tag defining the nature of their aberration from the normal." My companion went on to discourse learnedly to me the properties of special nerve ganglia and of the mystery of the localization of the functions of the brain. It was a great surgeon who happens to be at Rennes who passed this verdict on M. Bertillon. I shall not undertake to report the details of his diagnosis. But I hasten to add that the analysis which he had been making in scientific language so precise and instructive was but the translation into the idiom of a specialist of an impression which had been universal. Yet it is upon this system of M. Bertillon, to some extent at any rate, that General Mercier has based his faith in the guilt of Dreyfus.

M. Bertillon would have been diverting if we could have listened to him without the recollection still fresh in our minds of the respect in which only yesterday Colonel Maurel, President of the court-martial of 1894, had spoken of this dangerous inventor of one of the most pretentious hobbies on which the human brain ever rode to intellectual perdition. But if Colonel Maurel had been hypnotized by this madness, why not the Judges of 1899? It is impossible to take M. Bertillon seriously. He is absolutely, even ridiculously, unintelligible. And yet the very fact that he is imposed upon us by the Court obliges us to settle back into an attitude of attention in order to try to master the intricacies of his system. The Judges and the counsel for the defense assumed an attitude of unimpeachable correctness, and did their best to understand. The public and the journalists, on the contrary, after an hour's heroic effort to comprehend how "the artificial construction of the keyword 'interest' as well as the intercalation in the blotting paper letter seized at Dreyfus's house constituted a fresh proof, and a quite special one, of guilt," gave up the task and repaired to the courtyard of the Lycée, there to exchange ideas on the possibilities of human credulity. What they did agree upon was that this "fresh proof" was indeed "a quite special one." Major Esterhazy, as General Gonse had declared so justly, was a "special defendant." M. Bertillon's discovery is so "special" that the "keyword" of it remains locked up in the dim interstices of his own brain.

When he appeared there was merriment in Court. A pale, strange figure, sinister to behold, he mounted to the bar and took his place there, where M. Gobert, expert of the Bank of France, had just affirmed his absolute certainty that Dreyfus did not write the *bordereau*. M. Labori immediately rose and asked Colonel Jouaust if he could not lend him a photograph of the *bordereau* to enable the counsel for the defense to follow M. Bertillon's demonstrations. The latter volunteered amiably to supply the want, but the store of provision of this sort was so abundant that I despair of conveying any complete sense of the astonishment which was to be ours without evoking the picture of the miracle of the loaves and fishes. M. Bertillon spoke but a word, and lo! we beheld traversing the Court a sergeant with three soldiers tottering under such a load of portfolios as only the archives of the great museums of engraving of the world could in ordinary circumstances furnish. This procession of soldiers staggering under voluminous *dossiers* was so funny a sight that even the President could not resist a smile. Laughter ran through the courtroom. Yet M. Bertillon himself remained preternaturally grave. He arranged his portfolios all about him; leaning them up against chairs, spreading them out on tables, displaying them with portentous solemnity before us like a professor. We all stared like children in presence of the mysteries of a magic lantern. It is a thousand pities that Colonel Jouaust had not taken the precaution to authorize the presence of a photographer to record kinematographically all these preliminaries of the show.

I have no intention of trying to guide the reader through the mysteries of this exhibition. I could not do so if I would. And yet I had taken the precaution to refer again before coming to the courtroom this morning to the stenographic report of M. Bertillon's evidence before the Court of Cassation, as well as the effort to popularize the system which is embodied in the pamphlet published under the auspices of the League of the *Patrie Française,* whose committee is mostly composed of men who protest that what is clear is not French. M. Bertillon's exposition went on with preternatural gravity for hours. The little messenger of the Court had not an instant to himself. He was running constantly about all over the platform, handing the diagrams and photographs and enlarged projections now to the counsel for the defense, now to the President, now to the Government commissary. At one moment a Judge would rise and, with a polite smile, offer a photograph to M. Demange; at another the entire bench of the defense was up and making for the Judges' table, where, gathered about the central figure of the colonel, the members of the Court were one and all bending over an invisible chart, while M. Bertillon traced with his finger about the cryptographic map the logical routes by which he sought to lead them all into the very heart of that famous fortress where, by similar processes in 1894, he succeeded in burying Dreyfus alive.

Dreyfus himself meanwhile sat an amazed spectator of these maneuvers. If he were the author of the *bordereau* what thoughts would have been his. As he is not, according to M. Ballot-Beaupré, what thoughts must he have cherished. After all, this was not an amusing spectacle; it was not even one which the most serene and philosophic of us could regard with detachment. It was simply abominable. It was monstrous. It was picturesque, if you will, to behold these groups of black-robed advocates and epauletted officers bending there shoulder to shoulder over these mysterious multiplications of the little scrap of tracing paper which Esterhazy wrote in 1894. But it was awful as well. And the heart of the tortured prisoner must have been breaking with a racking and almost despairing grief as he sat there so "out of it all," witnessing the black spider weaving out of his own entrails his relentless web. No man can bear this sort of thing forever.

Now and again M. Bertillon's voice rose in hateful shrieks. There were interludes when he clenched his fist and struck the bar, swearing that Dreyfus was the traitor. The voice rang out with passion and excitement. You beheld in him the man vain unto madness with confidence in his atrocious phantasies. He was at last taking his revenge for all the insults of those who had called him a fit subject for an asylum of the insane. His time had come to browbeat the *"malheureux,"* as M. Gobert called him, who in 1894 had exclaimed, as M. Bertillon had unfolded his enormities, *"Oh le misérable!"* I assure you, the ridiculous side of the scene was not the side which remained long in the light. We beheld rather the inquisitorial aspect of it all, and we asked ourselves how in the inscrutable mysteries of human fate certain men should be exposed to drink thus to the dregs the cup of human sorrow.

And as we reflected on these things our thoughts wandered back to the long hours when Dreyfus, through those lonely hot afternoons under the shadow of his hut on the Devil's Island, turned the pages of a book or read over again the letters from home and was seen to drop hot tears on the blurred characters. And then we completed the chain and we looked forward with dismay to the fast-approaching moment of the verdict, scarcely daring to contemplate this hour even from afar, so lowering it seemed to become when we had thought to find it clear-browed and serene with the smile of peace.

Bertillon gave his testimony in the manner of a schoolboy reciting his lessons. The audience, in the dark regarding the meaning of his technicalities, punctuated his queer expressions with peals of laughter. He testified that when he spoke of the fabrication of the *bordereau,* Dreyfus exclaimed: "Oh, the wretch! He saw me write then." "I did not hear the remark," said Bertillon, "but when it was repeated to me it was a revelation. For, if innocent, the word 'fabrication' would have delighted instead of frightened him." This was Bertillon's "expert testimony."

When the court resumed its sessions on August 26, 1899, Bertillon began by striking a dramatic pose and declaring in a declamatory tone: "I am convinced that the writer of the *bordereau* is the prisoner sitting there." Then came other experts who proceeded to tear down Bertillon's vague technicalities.

THE DREYFUS TRIAL

EVIDENCE OF EXPERTS

(FROM OUR SPECIAL CORRESPONDENT)

Rennes, Aug. 28, [1899]

Today we have witnessed the exposure of the incredible charlatanry of the unspeakable Bertillon. M. Paray-Javal laid this last hope of the old General Staff of 1894 prone, and M. Bernard, a mining engineer who left the Polytechnic School at the head of his "promotion," finished him. As he lay there he raised piteous glances to the Judges on the bench, the Judges who had done their best hitherto to humiliate Colonel Picquart. He raised his hand asking to be allowed to reply. Colonel Jouaust was evidently in a new and unfamiliar mood. "If it is to reply to the experts I cannot allow it," he said. The sorried group around General Roget could scarcely believe its ears. Colonel Jouaust preferred an excuse. "We have 13 or 14 experts to be heard, and we shall never have done." But where there is life there is hope. "It is on a personal matter," explained M. Bertillon, and without waiting for a reply he pulled himself together and came to the bar. But, seeing M. Bertillon making fresh preparations with his strange paraphernalia of charts and maps and projections, the President became stern, and ordered him back.

M. Paray-Javal had found the words which M. Bertillon had not known how to forgive—"The *amour-propre* of M. Bertillon is very intelligent." The distinction thus implied with such bitter irony between the mental and moral qualities of the head of the Paris Anthropometric Bureau had not been to his liking. But it was swift little sword thrusts such as these, greeted by the cruel laughter of the spectators, which, coming intermittently in the depositions of M. Paray-Javal and M. Bernard, had in finishing M. Bertillon awakened the sporting instincts of the Judges. Moreover, neither M. Paray-Javal nor M. Bernard was too long. Both were clear, full of good humor, and brief, and they accomplished their purpose without too constant demands on the Judges' time. They thrust no necromancers' charts under the Judges' eyes. They had not the air of jugglers. M. Bernard, too, was a Polytechnician like the Judges themselves, a man who spoke their language, and was in a way their comrade. He inspired confidence. When the experts had done it was really too much for M. Bertillon to ask Colonel Jouaust to allow him to be heard afresh. If he had not stirred we might have forgotten him. He would certainly have been spared this and similar paragraphs in the press of the world, and he might have been decently buried in oblivion.

This treatment which he had received from the Court has its importance. It seemed to us all characteristic, typical, indeed, as evidence of that startling change which had come over things since Saturday. Similar little signs of the change were scattered all along through the depositions of the experts who succeeded. The President stopped M. Teyssonnières when he rambled, and he listened with the deference which was due to the admirable evidence of M. Charavay, the palaeographer, when he admitted his blunder in 1894, and when, turning to him who he said had been the victim of his mistake, he added amid general emotion:—"I declare here on my soul and conscience that the *bordereau* must be attributed to Esterhazy." M. Pelletier followed, and he, at least, is an expert who has nothing on his conscience, for he saw the truth five years ago. Then came the grandiloquent Couard, whom, with his fellow experts of the Esterhazy trial, M. Zola described in an immortal paragraph, and who, amid many an explosive phrase which aroused the unsuppressed hilarity of the Court, exhibited an *amour-propre* more magnificent than that even of M. Bertillon in the words, "I would lay my head on the block rather than swear that the *bordereau* was written by Esterhazy." M. Couard, it should be remembered, has not examined the handwriting of Dreyfus; yet, like M. Varinard and M. Belhomme, he sticks to his guns. They, none of them, however, can be made to say that the *bordereau* is the work of Dreyfus, and they thus leave the ground clear for the production of the arguments of the experts of 1894, one of whom, as we have seen, has changed his mind, agreeing with two others that Dreyfus did not write the *bordereau*. Let no one so insult the Judges as to imagine that they are not as competent as any one else to draw the necessary conclusions. And let the partisans of Dreyfus thank the fates for M. Bertillon, whose presence has served to discredit the maneuvers or the stupidity of those who would ascribe this document to another than to the man who has over and over again accepted its paternity.

The experts had done an effective job in ridiculing Bertillon's evidence. M. Paray-Javal, the draughtsman, demonstrated with the aid of a blackboard the fallacy of Bertillon's calculations. M. Bernard, an inspector of mines who had taken high honors at the Polytechnic School, aroused laughter by showing a page borrowed from a report by Bertillon himself and confusing him with it. M. Charavay, archivist and expert in ancient manuscripts, concluded his testimony with these words: "It is a great relief to my conscience to be able to say, before you and before him who is the victim of my mistake, that the *bordereau* is not the work of Dreyfus, but of Esterhazy." M. Pelletier, another expert, summed up his testimony: "There remains nothing but to maintain in their entirety my conclusions to the effect that there is no likeness between the writing of the *bordereau* and that of the prisoner."

Testimony of the "Little White Mouse"

"It is high time to end it."

Rennes: Le procès Dreyfus, *vol. 2, pp. 555–563. Translated and condensed by the editor.*

He was called the "Little White Mouse" and he was reputed to speak at length without saying very much. Yet he had held high office in the Third French Republic—as former Minister of War, former Minister of Foreign Affairs, and former Premier. When he was called to the stand, M. de Freycinet at first refused to reply to the questions put to him. From then on he carefully picked his way through the maze of questions.

M. Demange: May I remind you that General Mercier had said that you told General Jamont that 35,000,000 francs had been raised abroad for the defense of Dreyfus.

M. de Freycinet: I felt deep anguish at the sight of the trouble into which my country was plunged. My whole desire was to see peace and calm restored.

In regard to the conversations you mentioned, General Jamont paid me a courtesy call when I left office at the beginning of May. I received many such visits. I do not exaggerate when I say I received a hundred such visits. I made no notes of the conversations taking place on such visits.

Regarding General Jamont, of course we talked about the case and the campaign of speeches and press reports which had been going on throughout the world during the previous two years. On the Dreyfus matter I was led to say that our agents abroad reported that efforts had been made by private individuals on behalf of this campaign. It was a very disinterested campaign in France, to be sure, even less so abroad.

I reported the estimates I heard had been made by people who said they were well acquainted with the matter of advertising in reference to the probable money value of the entire campaign throughout the world since its beginning.

That, Mr. President, is a résumé as complete and as faithful as my memory permits of my talk with General Jamont. What impressed me most was the identity of our anxiety in regard to the Army. We both expressed uneasiness for it must not be concealed that the current attacks have had a deep echo which might eventually endanger the cohesion of the Army.

You will admit, Gentlemen, that there is a higher discipline than even the Military Code. As I have said before in the Chamber, it is that more intensive discipline that comes from the confidence of the soldier in his commander. How is it possible for that confidence to be maintained if those commanders are depicted each day in the blackest colors? Was it not to be feared that at a given moment this confidence would disappear, and what would be the outcome if we at the same time were troubled by external problems? [Sensation in the audience.]

I urge my countrymen to take part in these attacks under the impulse of a generous emotion and with the object of serving a noble high-principled idea to consider the dangers into which they might involve the country. In the words that General Jamont used to me: "It is high time to end it."

Let us stop throwing at each other accusations which discredit us in the eyes of our rivals. Gentlemen, let us prepare—and I would hope that my feeble voice will be heard by all—let us prepare to accept your judgment with respect and silence. May the judgment of this French court, upon which the eyes of the whole world are turned, open up an era of reconciliation which is necessary. [Intense excitement.]

Gentlemen, pardon me for telling you all this. It comes from my heart, a heart which had no longer much to desire here below, except to live and see our country great and honored.

I have finished. I have given an exact account of the interview with the Commander-in-Chief of our armies in time of war. I have nothing to add.

M. Demange: Won't you repeat in court your statements made in the Chamber of Deputies about the small importance of the alleged treason?

M. de Freycinet: No. The Court could indicate the sense of my speech. In my opinion most of the leakages could have been only of minute importance, though the information relative to covering the troops might have been important. The publication of secrets relating to arms and explosives was also dangerous. But when I made my speech in the Chamber of Deputies I wished above all to avoid increasing public excitement.

M. Labori: Is M. de Freycinet aware of any fact that led him to believe foreign money has played a part in the revision of the trial of 1894?

M. de Freycinet: No, no, Mr. President.

M. Labori: What do you think of the accusation of certain sections of the press against Mm. Scheurer-Kestner, Trarieux, Brisson, and Ranc, and by another section against the Court of Cassation, tending to attribute the opinion on the revision expressed by those persons to the influence of corruption?

Colonel Jouaust: I refuse to allow the question.

M. Labori: At least I should be allowed to question M. de Freycinet about M. Scheurer-Kestner, the former Vice-President of the Senate, whose statements about the letters Colonel Picquart wrote to him from Tunis have been contradicted by Savignaud, Picquart's former orderly.

Colonel Jouaust: The good faith of M. Scheurer-Kestner is not under discussion. Apparently, M. Labori wants to introduce passion into these proceedings.

M. de Freycinet: I do not scruple to say that M. Scheurer-Kestner is my friend, and I have the highest opinion of his character.

M. Labori: Thank you for this frank statement.

[At the close of M. de Freycinet's testimony, Colonel Jouaust addressed Dreyfus:]

Colonel Jouaust: Do you have any observation to make?

Dreyfus: No, Colonel.

Berlin Again Refuses to Become Involved

"Germany has done her duty and even more than her duty."

Kölnische Zeitung, *August 29, 1899. Translated by the editor.*

Once again, on August 29, 1899, the Imperial Chancellery made it clear in the semi-official *Cologne Gazette* that it refused to give any light from Germany. Despite these notices from Berlin, appeals were to be made a few days later to Emperor William II and King Humbert to send the concerned Military Attachés to Paris.

Many efforts have been made to move the German Government and to persuade Colonel Schwartzkoppen to drop his reserve. When one observes what credit is given in France to the statements of Colonel Panizzardi, it must be concluded that Colonel Schwartzkoppen's testimony would not be able to convince people who simply do not want to be convinced. Germany has done her duty and even more than her duty. When the Chancellor speaks, as Count von Bülow has spoken, he speaks in the name of the Empire and the Emperor, and there can be no question but that he is telling the truth. If there are persons in France for whom all this amounts to nothing at all, it only dishonors their character and does not reveal their good sense. It is impossible that Germany support the solemn declarations she has already made with any written evidence or any more new testimony.

More Witnesses in Favor of Dreyfus

"You suppress all awkward questions."

Harding, Dreyfus, The Prisoner of Devil's Island, *pp. 252–269. The stenographic report is in* Rennes: Le procès Dreyfus, *vol. 3, pp. 113–309.*

On the two opening days of September 1899 there was a long series of witnesses in favor of Dreyfus. It was becoming more and more clear that a terrible injustice had been done, but apparently the officers sitting in judgment were more concerned about the prestige and "honor" of the Army than about the guilt or innocence of the prisoner.

September 1, 1899

Immediately after the opening of the session of the court-martial on September 1st, Colonel Jouaust aroused the interest of the audience by remarking:

"Maître Labori the other day asked that information be obtained regarding the character of a certain witness. I would not have acceded if the witness had not expressed a similar desire. Information which has now reached me will be read."

The clerk of the court accordingly read a report regarding M. Dubreuil, the Parisian friend of M. de Beaurepaire, who testified on August 23d that Dreyfus met a German attaché at the house of a mutual friend named Bodson, and whose cross-examination reflected severely on his reputation. The report was to the effect that M. Dubreuil never was a horse dealer, as claimed by M. Labori, and that the character of the witness was most respectable, he being held in general esteem.

This was a very satisfactory session for Dreyfus. The Beaurepaire witness, Germain, who was to prove that Dreyfus attended the Alsatian maneuvers, found his statements denied by a reputable witness, while Germain himself, it was proved, had undergone two convictions for swindling.

In his deposition Germain declared he saddled a horse for Dreyfus to follow the maneuvers, and he said that his employer, Kuhlman, accompanied Dreyfus riding, and adding that the major told the witness the name of his companion.

Colonel Jouaust questioned Dreyfus on this point, and in reply to the usual question Dreyfus admitted that about 1886 or 1887 he spent a furlough at Mulhouse adding:

"Every year, both while studying and attending the gunnery and artillery training schools, I passed one or two months at Mulhouse. But I can positively affirm that I never was present either in an official or semi-official capacity at the German maneuvers. I was never invited to attend the German maneuvers, and I never dined or lunched with any German officer. On each visit I called on the general commanding at Mulhouse with my regular passport, in accordance with my duty.

"I would like to point out, in regard to the maneuvering ground to which reference is made, that the Mulhouse ground is not ground over which maneuvers could be carried out. It is merely a small drill ground, nothing more than a clearing in the Hartz Forest on the road from Mulhouse to Basle. It is true that in the course of my excursions in 1886 I might have seen regiments drilling. But I emphatically declare that while out riding in 1886 or 1887 I never dined or lunched with German officers, was never even invited to do so by foreign officers, and never spoke to foreign officers."

Replying to Colonel Jouaust, Dreyfus said that while he was at Mulhouse he rode his brother's horse, and did not remember anything about the horse mentioned by Germain.

During the cross-examination M. Labori asked the groom, Germain, if he was acquainted with M. de Beaurepaire, and the witness replied that he was not acquainted with him, but he added that M. de Beaurepaire knew the facts to which he testified, through the witness's friends, and he also admitted having written to M. de Beaurepaire giving information which the latter had published in the *Écho de Paris*.

The next two witnesses, however, gave strong testimony in favor of Dreyfus, and sadly knocked Germain's testimony about.

Kuhlman, the livery stable keeper, who employed Germain at this time, in his testimony said that he never rode with Dreyfus as stated by Germain; that he never went to the maneuvers in company with Dreyfus, and absolutely denied all Germain's statements. Germain, the liveryman added, was in his employ, and possibly the groom accompanied Dreyfus. But the witness had no knowledge of it.

In conclusion, Kuhlman emphatically reiterated that he never rode with Dreyfus. He said he was well acquainted with the whole Dreyfus family.

Major d'Infreville testified that he had known Germain since 1894. He added that Germain informed him that Dreyfus attended the German maneuvers. Witness had never said that an officer Germain saw in the Bois de Boulogne was Dreyfus, for the simple reason that he did not know Dreyfus.

Germain, on being recalled, asserted that he certainly thought Major d'Infreville told him the officer referred to was Dreyfus.

The next witness, Captain Le Monnier of the Headquarters Staff, who was a probationer at the same time as Dreyfus, deposed that while they were at the School of War in 1894, Dreyfus, in the course of a conversation referring to the covering of troops in the Vosges region and the movements necessary for the invasion of Alsace, said that he was well acquainted with a certain position to which the Germans attached great importance as a means of checking a French advance. This position, witness continued, was westward of Mulhouse, and Dreyfus said he reached this opinion after following the German maneuvers on horseback.

The prisoner at this point quietly pointed out that the position mentioned by Captain Le Monnier was situated in an entirely different locality from where he, the prisoner, is supposed to have followed the maneuvers. Dreyfus added:

"Captain Le Monnier must have confused it with a position which I described from knowledge acquired when traversing the whole district on horseback while a youth."

The prisoner reiterated that he never attended the maneuvers in question.

The next witness, M. Villon, another of the friends of M. de Beaurepaire, declared that when in Berlin during the year 1894 he overheard a conversation of some German officers who were lunching in an adjoining room of a café in that city. One of the officers, the witness added, expressed indignation that a French officer was guilty of treason, and his companion replied:

"It is a good thing for us. You know we are getting the plans of mobilization from Dreyfus." [Murmurs of assent and dissent.]

At the request of M. Demange, M. Villon detailed the alleged conversation, and said he had not mentioned the conversation in 1894, because Dreyfus has been arrested, and, knowing him to be guilty, the witness foresaw he would be convicted.

The café, however, in which the above conversation is reported to have occurred has since disappeared, and, as there are no means of verifying Villon's testimony, it certainly should not have had much effect on the judges.

Two or three witnesses, in support of Dreyfus on artillery questions, were next heard, and special Commissary Fischer of the Eastern Military Railway System testified that he was charged to investigate the leakage of documents at the gunnery school at Bourges, and found nothing to incriminate Dreyfus.

Fischer asserted that he was not long in finding out that a former artilleryman named Thomas had communicated to a foreign power documents affecting the national defense. Thomas, he added, was sentenced to death for attempted murder in 1886, but the sentence was commuted to penal servitude for life. The witness went to Avignon and secured the convict's confession that he communicated sketches of "shell 80" of the horse artillery and of the "120 siege-gun," for which he had received one thousand francs.

Replying to Colonel Jouaust, the witness declared that, as Thomas was arrested in 1886, he could not have been a spy at a later date.

Fischer was followed by Lieutenant Bernheim, who testified that, while in garrison at Rouen, he furnished Esterhazy with information and documents regarding the artillery, in which Esterhazy was much interested. The witness was never able to recover the documents. He supposed at the time that Esterhazy was anxious to increase his military knowledge.

Replying to M. Demange, Lieutenant Bernheim said he had not testified at the Esterhazy trial, because his testimony was then considered to be of no great value.

Lieutenant Brugère, of the Artillery Reserve, the next witness called, said it was perfectly easy for any officer to inspect closely the "120-short" gun. Moreover, he added, detailed explanations and information regarding the brake were given to the officers present when the gun was fired. On two occasions, witness also said, when the gun was fired he noticed the presence of a group of non-artillery officers. Therefore, the lieutenant pointed out, it was plain that access to the gun was quite easy.

In May, 1894, Lieutenant Brugère continued, the new Firing Manual was distributed. A copy was given to each battery, and, as the captain's lectures were not fully understood, other copies of the Firing Manual were printed, and all officers and non-commissioned officers so desiring could obtain as many as they liked. In some regiments even the ordinary gunners secured copies, and among those favored regiments, Lieutenant Brugère pointed out, was the Sixth Artillery, stationed at Rennes. [Excitement.]

The witness said he gave his copy of the Firing Manual to an infantry officer on May 17, 1894. The *Société de Tir à Canon,* of Paris, also reprinted the manual and distributed it among its members.

Captain Le Rond here interposed, saying that no batteries of the "120-short" gun were at the Châlons camp in 1894, and Lieutenant Brugère retorted that he only referred to what he saw in the month of May. A lively discussion ensued, General Roget and General Deloye denying Lieutenant Brugère's statements.

General Roget asked Lieutenant Brugère if he was not the officer who had written M. Cavaignac, then Minister of War, a violent letter tendering his resignation and declaring it was a dishonor to serve in the French Army.

This declaration caused a scene, for Lieutenant Brugère, turning to General Roget, cried:

"I protest against General Roget's words. I affirm that I never said any such thing."

General Roget then backed down, saying:

"Well, that was the general sense of the letter."

A roar of disgust came from the audience at this apparent underhandedness upon the part of the general, and Lieutenant Brugère again emphatically declared General Roget was wrong.

General Deloye, to whom General Roget appealed, said he had been consulted by the Minister of War as to what ought to be done in connection with the letter, and witness read the report which he made on the subject to the President of the Republic, who, he added, immediately signed an order relegating Lieutenant Brugère to the Territorial Army.

After this Lieutenant Brugère again arose, and emphatically maintained that he made no statement in the sense indicated by General Roget, but had only alluded to some personalities, and had not mentioned the French Army. It would have been absurd to do so, he continued, since the French Army consists of all citizens over twenty years of age.

Maître Labori and Colonel Jouaust agreed that the letter should be obtained from the Ministry of War and read in court. Lieutenant Brugère expressed satisfaction at this step, while General Roget returned to his seat with less buoyancy than he left it.

The next witness, Captain Carvalho, a handsome young artillery officer, proved an excellent reinforcement for Dreyfus. He gave his evidence clearly and boldly, and emphatically declared that there were no special precautions to keep the mechanism of the "120-short" gun secret. He said the gun was frequently operated in the presence of non-artillery officers, who were told everything that they desired to know, including a description of the hydro-pneumatic brake. Moreover, he added that in April, 1894, the artillery officers had a description of the hydro-pneumatic brake given them.

Regarding the 1895 Firing Manual, witness said copies were obtainable in 1894 in all the regiments of the Army, and asserted that he had purchased a copy.

"Here," said Captain Carvalho, "is an actual copy of the manual, which I hand over to the court-martial."

M. Labori then had an animated discussion with Colonel Jouaust, who at first refused the counsel's request to read a letter which the latter had received on the evening of August 31st. After receiving a reluctant permission from the court, Labori read the letter, which proved to be from a spy named Corningue, stating that he had copied the Firing Manual in the room of Major Panizzardi, the Italian Military Attaché at Paris, in the presence of Colonel Schwartzkoppen, the German Military Attaché at Paris (referred to in the letter as A and B). Labori then said he was not certain whether this was the 1894 or 1895 manual, and begged the President to question Colonel Picquart on the subject.

Picquart said, in response, that he believed it was the 1895 manual, and that the copy was made in 1896 in Major Panizzardi's room in the presence of Major Panizzardi and another person. Colonel Picquart added that Major Lauth ought to know something about a certain mark on the manual. All the manuals at the Versailles garrison were ordered returned to headquarters in order to see which one was missing.

General Deloye admitted that he was not sure whether it was the 1894 or 1895 manual, and corroborated Colonel Picquart's statements.

Major Lauth expressed surprise at the fact that Colonel Picquart's recollections were so vague, and added that Picquart had relations with the spy, Corningue, who, he said, was a doubtful character.

Here M. Labori asked to what spy Major Lauth was able to give a good character, to which the major replied:

"Why, none." [Laughter.]

M. Labori then said that Major Lauth insinuated that Corningue was trying to levy blackmail. Was that his idea?

Colonel Jouaust refused to allow the question.

M. Labori then asked to be allowed to question Major Lauth further, but Colonel Jouaust refused. Counsel insisted, but Colonel Jouaust waved him down, whereupon M. Labori cried:

"You suppress all awkward questions." [Sensation.]

The Government Commissary, Major Carrière, said:

"I desire to point out that the defense is always asking to speak, while I am always refused permission to do so when I ask."

Colonel Jouaust, out of patience, retorted:

"I have heard enough. Be quiet. The incident is closed."

This cavalier treatment of the Government Commissary, who, however, made himself ridiculous whenever he opened his mouth, caused general laughter.

Addressing Colonel Picquart, M. Labori asked:

"When did you know that the Firing Manual was being copied?"

Colonel Picquart: "During the summer of 1896."

M. Labori having remarked that this was all he desired to ask at present, General Hippolyte Sebert, retired, of the marine artillery, deposed. He preceded his testimony by saying he did not think he ought to withhold the evidence he was able to give, as he felt it would contribute to the reparation of a judicial error.

The general then criticized the *bordereau* from a professional standpoint, pointing out that the writer must have been a low-classed man, negotiating directly with a correspondent on whose doles he was dependent. He said he was probably an officer, but certainly not an artillery officer, adding that this was proved by the employment of expressions an artilleryman could not have used.

General Sebert entered into long explanations of his statements, pertinently pointing out that an artillery officer would have known the interesting parts of the Firing Manual, and would not have written in the *bordereau,* "Take what interests you." The witness gave a number of instances showing the dense ignorance displayed in gunnery technicalities by the writer of the *bordereau,* and amid profound silence General Sebert declared that his study of the case had led him to the conviction that the *bordereau* could not have been written by an artillery officer or by an officer belonging to a special arm of the service who had passed through the Polytechnic School. [Excitement.]

General Sebert referred to the satisfaction he felt at knowing that the experts of the highest standing in handwriting had confirmed his opinion, and he dismissed M. Bertillon's assertions, saying that on examination he, the witness, had easily found proof of the worthlessness of that demonstration.

"It is painful for me," added General Sebert, "to express so severe an opinion on the man whose name is connected with the application of the anthropometric method, which has been of great service to our country. But French science cannot give its authority to lucubrations so pretentious as those M. Bertillon brought here. I reassert most emphatically that the *bordereau* was not written by an artillery officer or by an officer who passed through the Polytechnic School. I have been sustained in giving my evidence by my firm belief in the entire innocence of Dreyfus, and I am glad I have had strength enough to bring here the stone which I have to lay on the edifice of reparation, and conscientiously, while holding aloof from outside passions. This edifice is a work of appeasement and peace, which will restore the country to an era of concord and union." [Prolonged excitement.]

General Sebert also expressed his opinion of Valerio's evidence in support of M. Bertillon's system, saying that, in spite of the latter's talent, he had not succeeded in converting a false theory into a true one.

As soon as General Sebert had finished his testimony, M. Bertillon bounced up, and asked to be allowed to speak; but Colonel Jouaust quickly turned to the usher and said, "Bring in the next witness," whereupon M. Bertillon, extremely annoyed, returned to his seat.

Major Ducros then deposed that he commanded a field battery; that he knew Dreyfus and offered him certain information. But, he pointed out, Dreyfus never asked him a question, although he knew he (the witness) possessed much interesting information, especially particulars about the hydro-pneumatic brake.

General Mercier here intervened, and said that, at the time Major Ducros was speaking of, the Ducros field-piece had been rejected in favor of the Deport cannon, and, he said, Dreyfus therefore could have no object in procuring particulars of the Ducros gun.

Major Hartmann of the artillery was the next witness for the defense. He asked permission to refer to certain of the documents which were produced during the secret session of the court on August 31st, upon which, he said, he had reached important conclusions. But General Deloye objected, as it was contrary to the instructions of the Minister of War.

The major then asked the court to sit briefly *in camera*, and Colonel Jouaust promised to render a decision later.

More support for Dreyfus was forthcoming, however, in this deposition of Major Hartmann, since he expressed the opinion that the author of the *bordereau* did not know what he was writing about, as he spoke of the "120-short" gun when he meant the "120-long" gun.

The major led the court through a maze of technical details about artillery, until Colonel Jouaust asked him to refrain from technicalities as far as possible, evidently fearing that Hartmann might reveal secrets of the service. His evidence was directed entirely to show that Dreyfus was not the author of the *bordereau,* and that the artillery information mentioned in it was accessible to many officers of all arms in the Spring of 1894.

Proceeding, Major Hartmann testified on highly technical subjects, his evidence being the same as given before the Court of Cassation. He spoke in loud, energetic tones, and occupied the whole of the remainder of the session. The major's testimony was not concluded when the court adjourned.

So far as the depositions were concerned, Dreyfus certainly had every reason to be pleased with this day's proceedings.

September 2, 1899

There was a large attendance of generals at the Lycée at the opening of the session of September 2nd.

The interest centered in the testimony of Major Hartmann, of the artillery, which was interrupted by the adjournment of the court on September 1st, and was resumed at this session. The major, who had done great service for the defense, resumed his important deposition regarding artillery matters, and the bringing out of points and phraseology in the *bordereau* indicating that the writer could not be Dreyfus.

The witness wished to enter into the question of the Robin shell. But, on General Deloye's objecting to a statement on the subject in open court, Major Hartmann asked to be allowed to give it behind closed doors, saying it would only take him a few minutes to call attention to the point he had in mind.

The President of the Court decided to hear this part of the witness's testimony *in camera* at the end of the proceedings, or at the beginning of the session of September 4th.

In response to questions from Maître Labori, leading counsel for the defense, and M. Demange, Major Hartmann said any officer attending the Châlons camp would have obtained sufficient information to write notes on the covering of troops and Madagascar matters.

M. Labori then recalled General Mercier's attack on Captain Freystaetter, on the latter's declaration that the secret *dossier* communicated to the court of 1894 contained a document concerning a shell, for which General Mercier called the captain a liar. Major Hartmann affirmed that it was quite possible that particulars about a certain shell should have leaked out in 1894.

An interesting confrontation between General Deloye and Major Hartmann followed, the general declaring that he did not believe the major was keeping strictly to the truth. Deloye then proceeded to point to what he said were inaccuracies in Major Hartmann's testimony. He insisted that Dreyfus, in the course of conversations with artillery officers, could have secured information on the subjects mentioned in the *bordereau,* to which the major retorted that if any artillery officer had been questioned by Dreyfus he would already have come forward to say so as a matter of strict duty.

General Deloye, questioned by M. Labori and M. Demange, said the inventor of the Robin shell told him Dreyfus never asked him for particulars about his shell, except on a minor point. The general added he came as a technical witness to show Dreyfus could be guilty, adding that it was not his business to say whether he believed him innocent or guilty. He could only say that Dreyfus's contention that it was impossible for him to know certain matters referred to in the *bordereau* was untrue.

M. Labori asked General Deloye if he knew whether the documents which could have been betrayed by the traitor, especially by the writer of the *bordereau,* were important, whereupon the general turned to counsel and excitedly cried:

"Don't ask me! Don't ask me!"

These exclamations created a sensation in court, which was doubled when General Deloye added that there was sufficient in the *bordereau* to establish that the traitor knew the importance of the documents he was giving up. The witness added:

"When I read the *bordereau* I was dismayed."

Major Hartmann, in reply to General Deloye, reiterated that the author of the *bordereau* was ignorant of artillery matters.

"For," the major pointed out, "if he meant the '120' hydraulic brake, he gave particulars of what was long known, while if he meant the '120-short' he employed a wrong expression."

General Mercier reappeared in the witness box in an attempt to refute Major Hartmann's argument. He accounted for the use of the expression "hydraulic brake" in the *bordereau* by the fact that the Germans used the expression to designate similar brakes. Therefore, he added, it was natural that the correspondent of the Germans should employ the term.

General Deloye then said:

"I beg the court to allow me to say that in an army liable to find itself confronted by the enemy there is need of cohesion. Consequently, all the officers of France must march hand in hand, as brethren. I do not think it is good for it to be said that officers who have risen from the ranks should stop short at a certain point, and that individual merit should not count, and that there is a bar which cannot be passed. No! no! that is not satisfactory any more than it is true. Captain Valerio is an example. He has made himself, and a large number of others similarly able have filled the positions to which they have risen. Coming here as the representative of the Minister of War, I beg the court to allow me to say to one of our comrades who has risen from the ranks that these opinions are not ours. I think it was necessary to say so."

After a brief discussion between General Mercier, General Deloye, and Major Hartmann on the German expression used to designate hydraulic brake, the trio returned to their seats.

This ended the deposition of Major Hartmann, who certainly was a very valuable witness for the defense, although the effect of his testimony was somewhat weakened by General Deloye's theatrical statement in reply to M. Labori.

The next witness, M. Louis Havet, a member of the Institute, took up the *bordereau* from a grammatical point of view, declaring it to be his conviction, after studying closely the styles of Dreyfus and Esterhazy, that the latter wrote it. The witness entered into an interesting analysis of the phraseology of the *bordereau,* pointing out that certain phrases in it were met in Esterhazy's letters, but never in those of Dreyfus. He then traced the influence exercised on Esterhazy by his linguistic acquirements, notably traces of German construction.

The Government Commissary, Major Carrière, who was always blundering, asked M. Havet if he had been present at sessions of the court before he had testified.

M. Havet said "Yes," to which the major, with great severity, said:

"You have been guilty of a grave breach of judiciary discipline."

To this M. Havet quietly remarked:

"But I had not been summoned as a witness at the time I attended the sessions."

Major Carrière sat down, checkmated.

The letters exchanged between Colonel Picquart and General Gonse, at the time the colonel wanted a thorough investigation into the case, were then read, and M. Labori pointed out to General Gonse that these letters never alluded to the alleged confession of Dreyfus.

General Gonse replied that it was because he always advised Colonel Picquart not to mix up the Esterhazy and Dreyfus cases. Dreyfus, he added, had been condemned, and his case could not be reopened, but they were bound to see if there was not another traitor.

The general then made a bitter complaint of the fact that his letters had been communicated to M. Scheurer-Kestner, former Vice-President of the Senate.

Referring to this published correspondence, General Gonse exclaimed:

"When one procures the handwriting of a man one can get him hanged."
[Laughter.] General Gonse referred to a well-known saying of a French
judge, Laubardemont: "Give me four lines of a man's handwriting and
I'll have him hanged."

Continuing, General Gonse said:

"When a man intends to publish another's letters he asks what the
writer's meaning was. That is but fair. But, without doing so, Picquart
handed my letters to M. Scheurer-Kestner without my knowledge or consent. These letters have been published in a book which can be found at
every bookseller's, entitled *Gonse-Pilate.*"

M. Labori: Was not the *bordereau,* in conjunction with the *petit bleu,*
the basis of Picquart's belief in Esterhazy's guilt?

General Gonse: I said to Picquart: "Don't let us trouble about handwritings at present."

M. Labori: How could the Dreyfus and Esterhazy cases be separated,
when both were based on a common document?

General Gonse: Because at that time Dreyfus had been convicted, and
the *bordereau* was ascribed to him.

M. Labori: Was it not possible to reconsider an error?

General Gonse: There was nothing to prove to me that the *bordereau*
was written by Esterhazy.

M. Labori: Will General Gonse repeat what Colonel Picquart told
him concerning the conclusions of M. Bertillon?

General Gonse: I was not acquainted with M. Bertillon's conclusions,
but Picquart seems to exaggerate them.

At M. Labori's request, Colonel Picquart was recalled, and said:

"In a brief letter which I wrote to General Gonse in regard to M.
Bertillon's conclusions, I only referred to part of his observations, and
the best proof that I did not wish to exaggerate them is the fact that I
asked General Gonse to order a supplemental inquiry."

Colonel Jouaust: In what form did M. Bertillon communicate the result of his examination?

Colonel Picquart: Verbally, on two occasions. As regards General
Gonse's letters I handed them to a lawyer when I understood that I
was the object of abominable intrigues, and when I received from my
former subordinate, Henry, while in Tunis, a threatening letter, which
had been forwarded with the assent of Generals Gonse and de Boisdeffre. If this letter was published I cannot be held responsible for it.
[Excitement.]

General Gonse maintained that the Henry letter was written without
his assent and in reply to an insolent letter from Picquart. The latter, the
general added, saw machinations everywhere. He alleged that he was
sent to Tunis to be killed. The court could form its own conclusions.

Colonel Picquart remarked that he brought the secret *dossier* to General Gonse simultaneously with the *bordereau,* and that the general, consequently, was in a position to judge of the probabilities of the innocence of Dreyfus.

M. Labori asked if General Gonse knew of the plot hatched against Picquart, and if he knew that letters addressed to Picquart at Tunis were opened at the War Office? And the general admitted that a letter was opened in the Intelligence Department in November. He added that suspicious letters were always handed to him (General Gonse) by Lieutenant-Colonel Henry, so that he, the general, might report to the Minister of War on them.

M. Labori: Whom was the letter addressed to?

General Gonse: I do not know. No doubt to the chief of some department.

Colonel Picquart: It was addressed to me personally.

M. Labori: Does General Gonse know that the words in the letter in question were used for the purpose of fabricating a telegram intended to destroy the value of the *petit bleu?*

General Gonse admitted that the expressions seemed to him suspicious. If the letters were seized it was because they were addressed to Picquart as head of the department, and it was thought they might relate to official matters. He added that Picquart's letters were only opened when they looked suspicious.

Colonel Picquart retorted that it was curious his opened letters afterward reached him without a sign of having been tampered with.

Counsel then questioned General Gonse relative to the opening of the "Speranza" letter, and the general replied that this letter was not addressed to Picquart, but bore a curious address.

M. Labori: Why did General de Pellieux ascribe the letter to Colonel Picquart, whom he had never seen?

General Gonse: I do not know.

M. Labori pointed out that the first letter, which was genuine, was forwarded to Colonel Picquart after having been opened, while the "Speranza" letter was retained. The latter could therefore be regarded as the work of a forger.

Colonel Jouaust: You are entering into a discussion.

M. Labori (sharply): No, *Monsieur le Président;* by virtue of Article 319 of the Code, I merely say what I think in regard to the evidence.

General Gonse, replying further, dwelt upon the fact that it was necessary that the Intelligence Department should know the acts of Colonel Picquart, who had been removed on account of his conduct.

M. Labori: Does General Gonse think the Henry forgery was the result of a plot against Colonel Picquart?

General Gonse said he thought the forgery was "an unfortunate pro-ceeding." [Laughter.] He would have prevented it if he had been con-sulted. But he did not believe there was a plot against Picquart. Henry desired to have fresh proof against Dreyfus, "though fresh proof was not really required, as the diplomatic *dossier* contained ample proof."

M. Labori protested against such a statement, and asked which docu-ment of the *dossier* implicated Dreyfus.

Colonel Jouaust refused to allow the question, and counsel thereupon remarked that he reserved the right to form what conclusions he thought proper on this point.

Colonel Jouaust: Form as many conclusions as you like.

M. Labori next referred to the attempt to bribe Commissary Tomps and to erasures in the *petit bleu.*

General Gonse declared the *petit bleu* already had traces of erasure before it was first photographed.

This M. Labori vigorously denied, and asked that the evidence of the experts proving the contrary should be read.

Here General Roget reappeared on the scene, and, amid the keenest attention of all, described the forgery proceedings against Picquart as resulting from his (the witness's) discovery that erasures had been made in the *petit bleu.*

"It was General Zurlinden," Roget added, "who ordered Picquart to be prosecuted. I assume responsibility for all my own acts, but for my own acts alone. I am surprised that the defence should arraign me on this point."

M. Labori declared that he merely wished to show that the erasures could not be ascribed to Picquart, and that therefore they ought not to have formed the basis of a prosecution against him. Then counsel again asked the expert evidence on the subject be read, and Colonel Jou-aust promised it should be read during a future session.

Upon three occasions M. Demange asked General Gonse to explain why Picquart, on seeing the *petit bleu,* proposed to lay a trap for Ester-hazy, unless the *petit bleu* was addressed to Esterhazy. But counsel elicited no reply, until General Roget came to the rescue and said Pic-quart knew Esterhazy was coming to Paris in any case, and if he sent a decoy letter, Esterhazy would have appeared to come in response to it, whether he had done so in reality or not.

M. Labori declared this was untrue, and Picquart maintained that his conduct throughout was perfectly straightforward.

M. des Fonds-Lamothe, a former artillery officer, and now an engineer, was the next witness. He testified that he was a probationer simultaneously with Dreyfus. The witness said that in August, 1894, he borrowed the Firing Manual from Colonel Picquart and kept it as long as he liked.

"In 1894," M. des Fonds-Lamothe said, "Firing Manuals were given to whomever asked for them."

M. Demange: Can the witness, who was on the Headquarters Staff with Dreyfus, say whether, in 1894, he thought he would go to the maneuvers? [Excitement.]

M. Lamothe: I have only performed a conscientious act. I am convinced that not one probationer in 1894 could have believed he would go to the maneuvers.

M. des Fonds-Lamothe also stated that the probationers were informed by a circular dated May 15, 1894, that they would not attend the maneuvers. The object of antedating the *bordereau,* the witness added, was to make it a prior date to that of the circular. It had since been attempted to attain the same object by postdating the circular.

As to the postdating of the circular, witness said he did not doubt that different Ministers of War who had expressed opinions in the case were perfectly honest, but he thought they had made a mistake. [Excitement.]

The witness, who was a fellow probationer of Dreyfus, proved one of the strongest witnesses for the defense, as he brought out in support of his contention that Dreyfus could not have written the *bordereau* the following argument:

"If, as at first asserted, the *bordereau* was dated May, Dreyfus could not have written, 'I am going to the maneuvers,' because a circular was issued in May informing the probationers that they would not go to the maneuvers; while if the *bordereau* was written in April, as now asserted, Dreyfus could not have spoken of the Firing Manual, which was only printed at the end of May."

Not one of the generals found a reply to the last argument, which looked like a clincher, General de Boisdeffre alone declaring that, although it was true the circular mentioned was sent to the probationers, the latter knew that they could nevertheless go to the maneuvers if they made special application. Generals Mercier and Roget then went on the stage and confronted M. des Fonds-Lamothe, and a heated discussion ensued. General Roget asked when the witness had altered his conviction in favor of Dreyfus, and M. des Fonds-Lamothe replied:

"From the time of the publication of the proceedings before the Court of Cassation. I was expecting proof of my comrade's guilt, and I was thunderstruck when I saw the date of the *bordereau* had been altered."

General Roget asked if Fonds-Lamothe had not on several occasions expressed his belief in Dreyfus's guilt?

M. des Fonds-Lamothe admitted that possibly he had done so, before the publication of the proceedings before the Court of Cassation, but not at the time of the prisoner's arrest, for that was kept secret.

Asked the usual question, the prisoner reminded the court that in 1894, when Colonel du Paty de Clam had endeavored to make the date of the *bordereau* August, he had protested that he could not have written the sentence, "I am going to the maneuvers," since he would not be going on regimental duty until October, November, and December, and he dwelt upon the fact that at the time he handed M. Demange a note on the subject.

M. Demange corroborated the prisoner's testimony, and pointed out that the note mentioned by the prisoner had been added to the *dossier* by the Court of Cassation, while Dreyfus was still on Devil's Island, thus precluding all doubt as to its genuineness.

General Roget here interpellated that requests to go to the maneuvers were usually made verbally, so that it could not be proved whether Dreyfus had asked or had not asked to go to the maneuvers. The general, however, admitted that no inquiry had ever been made on this important point.

M. Demange created a stir by saying that it was most regrettable that no inquiry had been made by the War Office on a point of such importance.

General Roget was greatly excited during the foregoing scene, but M. des Fonds-Lamothe did not flinch. He retorted quickly to all the general's observations. The two men glared at one another, and once General Roget addressed M. des Fonds-Lamothe in such a bullying fashion that the audience hooted him.

M. des Fonds-Lamothe concluded with declaring that if the prosecution would follow up the pieces of evidence they would be absolutely convinced that Dreyfus did not write the *bordereau*.

The court briefly retired and afterward announced that it had been decided to hear the remainder of Major Hartmann's evidence *in camera* on September 4th.

The court then adjourned.

General de Galliffet Appeals to William II

"How does that concern me? I am not Kaiser of the French!"

Die Grosse Politik, *vol. 13, pp. 327–331. Translated by the editor.*

At the opening of the fifth week of the trial, M. Labori, Dreyfus's counselor, sent a telegram from Rennes to Emperor William II with the request—in the name of truth and justice—for permission for Colonel von Schwartzkoppen to appear as a witness before the court-martial. At the same time he sent another wire to King Humbert asking that Colonel Panizzardi be sent to Rennes for a similar purpose.

For William II the issue was of some consequence because it afforded him an opportunity to assume his favorite rôle as arbiter of the destinies of the world. On receipt of the telegram, however, he instructed a member of his suite to quote him as saying: "This is insolence, and it is, of course, impossible to comply with this request."

The French cabinet of Waldeck-Rousseau-Galliffet-Millerand, as a last step in a desperate situation, sent General de Galliffet, the Minister of War, into the battle. Taking advantage of an incident that had occurred during German maneuvers, Galliffet entered into an "unofficial" conversation with the German Military Attaché in Paris, Major Baron von Süsskind, "as man to man," in the hope that he would report it to the Emperor.

In the report, reprinted below from *Die Grosse Politik,* General de Galliffet expressed the hope that the Emperor would grant the request that Labori had made or at least to have von Schwartz-koppen make a complete deposition which could be used at Rennes. The shrewd French general attempted cunningly to work on the Kaiser's vanity. An old cavalry officer, de Galliffet knew that no amount of flattery, however exaggerated, would be rejected by the conceited Hohenzollern. William II, whose vanity was well known, was surrounded by sycophants and toadies and he was used to high-blown praise. General de Galliffet offered him stronger stuff in the task of making a favorable impression on the German monarch.

No. 3635

THE MILITARY ATTACHÉ IN PARIS, MAJOR BARON VON SÜSSKIND TO THE CHARGÉ D'AFFAIRES IN PARIS, VON BELOW-SCHLATAU

DISPATCH

No. 139   *Paris, September 6, 1899*

[*After discussing several questions*] . . . General de Galliffet requested that we speak for a moment outside our official capacities on a man-to-man basis.

General de Galliffet then stated how sympathetically he was drawn to His Majesty and how he regarded him with full trust.

His Majesty has shown his supreme care in easing the pain for France of her national calamity and humiliation in the years 1870–71.

Besides, all written and oral testimonies which revealed his interest in France, there were such actual facts as the release of officers arrested on grounds of espionage; the reception of French ships in Kiel; His Most Gracious Majesty's visit to the French training ship, *Iphigénie;* the welcome of officers and cadets on His Majesty's ship *Hohenzollern;* and the magnanimous and gracious intention of laying a wreath on French soil at the unveiling of the most recent monument on the battlefield of St. Privat.

He was convinced, continued the general, that His Majesty the Emperor would not reject his urgent request to allow full light to play on the truth. He, a simple soldier, appeals confidently to his most gracious generosity. He begs His Majesty to show his benevolence and not make the French Government responsible for the deplorable incidents at Rennes. A man like Mercier should be kicked like a mouse that desires to gnaw at one's boot; moreover, he should be punished with disdain.[1]

For His Majesty's reply to the lawyer Labori's request there are three possible courses of action:

1. Outright refusal.

    He requests urgently that this not be done.

2. Appearance of Colonel von Schwartzkoppen in Rennes.

    In this case he would guarantee Colonel von Schwartzkoppen's safety with his own head. But it should be understood that due to the excitement on all sides denunciations in the press and on the streets were to be feared, and the Government to a certain extent was powerless against them.

3. The third way would be for [Schwartzkoppen] to make a deposition in Germany in consonance with German legal codes.

He believes that His Majesty will reveal himself at the height of his great virtue in the interest of truth if he would order the procedure suggested in the last way, continued the general, and thereby contribute to the return of quiet and order in France.[2]

There would be an additional advantage for the mutual relations of both neighboring countries.

The opposing parties would at first raise up a furious cry, but that would soon be curtailed. The recognition of all Frenchmen of good will become a cornerstone for the further building of mutual good relations between our two countries.

---

[1] Apparently, the Kaiser was not satisfied with this punishment. He added a marginal notation at this point: "No, that is not enough!" (referring to the "kick") . "One has to crush such scum!" The Kaiser was careful to underline the word "crush."

[2] Marginal notation by the Kaiser: "How does that concern *me?* I am not Kaiser of the French! Besides, the court-martial does not want it."

If Dreyfus were to be set free, it would be necessary to repel the storm of the nationalists and the parties grouped around them. The Government would be strong enough to accomplish that. It would not avoid energetic means [3] and soon order would be restored.

On the other hand, if Dreyfus were to be found guilty again, it seemed to him that a revolution with all its unforeseen results was to be feared.[4]

The very existence of France is at stake.[5]

Certainly, His Supreme Majesty the Emperor, in the interest of the European balance of power, would not want this.[6]

Germany is so superior to France in trade and industry that in this matter she has nothing to fear from France.

Germany has a strong, recognized, dominating Army, but her weakest point (and one should forgive him this observation) is her fleet.[7]

Germany, indeed, has good relations with England. There are many examples of friendly exchanges. Intrinsically this has been due to royal family connections. However, this is regarded among most people today as of least importance for their existence.

Should for any reason a political clash come between Germany and England,[8] then the closeness of Germany and France would be an advantage.

General de Galliffet after this digression returned to the Dreyfus matter and said:

His request for the support of His Most Gracious Majesty for clarification of the truth bore no egotistic character. He had personally nothing more to gain. He undertook this difficult task for four reasons:

1. In order to restore the discipline of the Army; [9]

2. Under the stipulation that the Rennes court-martial is assured absolute independence.[10]

3. If at all possible to protect the judgment of the generals, who have been found wanting in this affair,[11] to put a halt to further attacks against the Army;

[3] The Kaiser: "Fort Chabrol! Nonsense!"

[4] The Kaiser: "Right."

[5] The Kaiser: "Yes."

[6] The Kaiser: "He should turn to the Tsar. Let Fredericks speak. Then the whole swindle would come to an end!"

[7] The Kaiser: "Right! But that will be corrected."

[8] The Kaiser: "In that case France would immediately go along with England. As at the Transvaal in 1896–97."

[9] The Kaiser: "A brilliant failure!"

[10] The Kaiser: "Instead of dismissing it!"

[11] The Kaiser: "Instead of dismissing them!"

4. To disappear again into the quiet of the background, once this task has been achieved.

General de Galliffet remarked that he was neither a Dreyfusard nor an anti-Dreyfusard. Personalities count nothing for him, only the truth.

I allowed myself to point out that the Military Attachés in Rennes had been most discredited, and it was to be feared that even correct statements by Colonel von Schwartzkoppen might be taken with doubt.

To that General Galliffet replied that, despite everything including insults that the opponents heaped on one another,[12] you can be certain that this suggested action would make a deep impression and would have the desired success.

The attitude toward Colonel von Schwartzkoppen was high enough among the right-thinking people of France.

In conclusion General de Galliffet said that he had avoided taking official steps in the matter.

Often in his life he has had unhoped for good fortune. He believes that in this sense an order by His Most Gracious Majesty for the appearance of the Prussian Military Attaché would be a highly fortunate arrangement, which he feels himself called upon to use, a matter which from his deepest inner being he lays at the feet of His Most Gracious Majesty.

FREIHERR VON SÜSSKIND

The Official *Reichsanzeiger* Note of September 8, 1899
"I declare in the most positive manner. . . ."

Reichsanzeiger, *September 8, 1899. Translated by the editor.*

William II was sarcastic in his marginal notes on the document from Paris, but evidently General de Galliffet's soldierly appeal made an impression on him. He gave orders that the official organ, the *Reichsanzeiger,* again publish the note of January 1898 stating that there never took place any relations between Dreyfus and the German Embassy in Paris.

M. Paléologue, the Foreign Office expert, read the note to the Rennes court-martial, but apparently it made no impression on the judges.

Berlin, September 8.—We are authorized to repeat herewith the declarations which the Imperial Government, while in loyalty observing

12 The Kaiser: "Need not necessarily take place."

the reserve demanded in internal matters of another country, has made regarding the French Captain Dreyfus.

For the preservation of his own dignity and the fulfillment of a duty to humanity, Prince von Münster von Derneburg, after receiving the orders of the Emperor, repeatedly made in December 1894 and in January 1895 to the Minister of Foreign Affairs, M. Hanotaux, the Minister-President M. Dupuy, and the President of the Republic M. Casimir-Périer, declarations to the effect that the Imperial Embassy in France never maintained, either directly or indirectly, any relations with Dreyfus.

The Secretary of State of the Foreign Office, Minister of State Count von Bülow, on January 24, 1898, made the following statement to the Budget Commission of the German *Reichstag:*

"I declare in the most positive manner that no relations or connections of any kind ever existed between the French ex-Captain Dreyfus, now on Devil's Island, and any German agents."

Reporting the Dreyfus Trial

"They saw their town almost taken possession of five weeks ago by a small army of foreigners and Jews."

New York Sun, *September 11, 1899.*

The court-martial at Rennes was in all probability the best-covered event in the history of journalism until that time. Some three hundred newspapermen assembled there from all parts of the world. On the opening day more than 650,000 words were transmitted over the six telegraph wires from Rennes to Paris and thence to every portion of the globe. The special problems met by reporters were described in this dispatch from H. R. Chamberlain, the correspondent of the New York *Sun* on September 11, 1899.

It is for the pleasure of writing something from Rennes which shall include nothing about Dreyfus and his cause that I am sending this letter. For five long weeks the three hundred newspaper men assembled here from all parts of the world where a public press exists have seen, heard, thought, dreamed, discussed, written—nothing but Dreyfus. Two or three times, while driving or cycling within a few miles of the Breton capital, I have come across intelligent, contented peasants who had never heard the name Dreyfus, and I envied and congratulated them. In an hour or two I shall leave Rennes, never, I hope, to return, but before I go I want to tell what a nice town it is and describe for them two or three odd incidents which have added a touch of comedy to the serious business of our mission here.

As for Rennes, most guidebooks tell us that it is the cleanest if not the healthiest city in Europe. One's eyesight tends to confirm the claim. They even skim the surface of the almost stagnant river in the center of the town every morning. One's nostrils suggest doubts on the subject, and one's experience of existence in so-called first-class hotels yields only cynical incredulity. I will not dwell upon the matter beyond remarking that scarcely any of those whose duties compelled them to remain in Rennes during the whole five weeks escaped one or more sharp attacks of illness.

As for the people of Rennes (always excepting two or three of the principal hotel keepers) their visitors have words only of grateful acknowledgment of kindness, courtesy, and most patient forbearance. American readers will not appreciate the significance of the latter phrase. Here is a provincial capital, outside the line of tourist travel, inhabited by a sturdy, honest, intensely religious but narrow-minded people. They saw their town almost taken possession of five weeks ago by a small army of foreigners and Jews. They hate each of these classes with the ignorant but accumulated hatred of generations. Moreover, they believed these invaders had come for the purpose of overthrowing a just judgment. Any other verdict than that given yesterday would have been an outrage upon justice in their ignorant eyes. And yet for five weeks the people of Rennes tolerated the presence of these unwelcome visitors, saw their streets, and cafés and public institutions almost monopolized by them, and said no word of insult, discourtesy, or resentment—except in their newspapers. I prefer to believe that the newspapers of Rennes, which in several instances heaped vile abuse and obscene invective, especially upon the correspondents of the foreign press, represent only the low, venal minds of their writers, who, alas, typify only too faithfully the degeneration of journalism in France.

It is not often that the professional side of a newspaper correspondent's work becomes a matter of public interest, but perhaps this unique experience here at Rennes is entitled to rank as an exception. No previous event in the world's history has called together a corps of chroniclers so representative in its scope. None, it should be remembered, came by invitation, as at the coronation of the Czar or the crowning of the little Queen of Holland. Even the Queen's Jubilee in London failed to draw such an international gathering of journalistic clans. Papers in Japan and even in Turkey sent correspondents to tell this story at Rennes. A paper which I had never heard of in Norway spent $100 a day to give its readers an account of the trial, and a single journal in Vienna expended more than $20,000 in telegraph tolls at "urgent" rates during the five weeks.

Every disposition to facilitate the work of the correspondents was shown by the authorities. We learned after a few days that each one of us had been quietly photographed, and full descriptions, with all that could be learned of our antecedents, had been sent to Paris in a special *dossier* by the omnipresent "agents of the State"; but nobody could object to this harmless and flattering attention. Neither could we find any fault with the assignment of places in the trial hall, which relegated the foreign correspondents to the seats most distant from the stage, where the testimony of many witnesses was inaudible. After all, the case to be heard was primarily a domestic French affair, and I doubt if in any other country on earth the same consideration would have been shown to foreign newspapermen, whose presence the great majority of Frenchmen regarded as an intrusion.

I explained in one of my earlier dispatches that each foreign correspondent received half a ticket to the *Lycée*. This was an immense concession from Colonel Jouaust's first dictum, which was: "Assign one ticket to each group of ten. That will enable each man to attend one session in ten, and it will be quite enough for him." Fortunately, the French military idea of journalistic needs did not prevail, and the committee of the *"Presse Judiciaire"* was able to induce the doughty president to take a more liberal view of the situation. Even the half-ticket regulation was modified to some extent, and each morning admission was granted to as many of the banished moiety of foreign correspondents as there remained empty seats after the ticket holders had entered. Finally the difficulty in hearing the evidence was partially overcome by securing reports of the testimony sheet by sheet from French reporters near the witness stand, and thus the actual proceedings in the courtroom were prepared for readers abroad.

The authorities of Rennes provided also a great hall with a special telegraph office, for the use of visiting correspondents. The *Bourse du Commerce* was transformed into a vast editorial room. One hundred and fifty writing tables, nailed to the floor to prevent noise and confusion, comfortable chairs, pens, ink, and paper, and courteous attendants were all at the disposal of French and foreign writers during the five weeks.

The problem of quick communication with the outside world was an ever-present difficulty from the first day of the trial until the last.

There were available six telegraph and four telephone wires from Rennes to Paris, two wires to Brest, the landing place of the French Cable Company's lines to America, and one wire to Havre, where the Commercial Company's cables touch. The best apparatus and most skilful operators in France were assembled at Rennes for the tremendous task of conveying the news of the trial to the four quarters of the world. Considering the facilities available, the result was probably the best accomplishment in telegraphy in this or any other country. On the first day more than 650,000 words were transmitted by telegraph alone. This quantity was exceeded on the day Labori was shot, and on other days it varied between the maximum and a minimum of 350,000 words.

It would be unfair, perhaps, to criticize the quality of the work in view of its overwhelming quantity. An operator who sends at highest speed long messages in any of half a dozen languages which he does not understand can hardly be blamed if the dispatches fail to arrive letter-perfect at their destination. I confess I groaned in anguish of spirit when copies of *The Sun* reached Rennes containing my dispatches sent during the early days of the trial. There was great improvement later—the French operator would probably be unkind enough to say this was due solely to my painstaking attempts to write a legible hand. When it is considered, however, that nearly one-half the matter sent over the wires from Rennes was written in English, German, Italian, Russian, Spanish, or Swedish, it must be admitted that the accomplishment of the Rennes telegraph corps was something stupendous.

There were some amusing incidents in connection with the sending of the news of the trial, and one or two will bear repeating. The correspondent of a London evening paper rushed to the telegraph office on the afternoon of the day Labori was shot, and handed in a dispatch of about nine hundred words. All correspondents had deposited in advance ample funds to cover the cost of telegrams in order to avoid the delay of frequent payments. The receiver, therefore, accepted the dispatch with the customary "*Merci, Monsieur.*" The sender happened to wait for a moment, and presently saw the telegraph clerk pick up his message, cross the room, climb on a chair, and carefully place the dispatch on top of a cabinet. The man returned to his seat, received a few more telegrams from the persons waiting at the window, checked them, gave them to a messenger to take to the operating room, got up again and carried a heavy ledger over to the cabinet and deposited it on top of the London man's dispatch. The correspondent was mystified, but did not interfere until the clerk had received a few more telegrams and had carried a few more miscellaneous articles across the room and piled them upon the cabinet. Then the Londoner remonstrated gently:

"Aren't you going to send my dispatch?"

"Your dispatch has been sent, *Monsieur*," was the calm reply.

"No, it hasn't. It's over there on top of that cabinet," insisted the correspondent.

The clerk looked at him as if he thought he had been bereft of his senses.

"Nothing of the kind. I sent your dispatch to the operating room as soon as you handed it to me," was the polite but firm reply.

The Englishman began to get angry, and in rather peremptory tones asked the clerk to verify his words by examining the top of the cabinet. The clerk was sure by this time that his interlocutor was crazy. He muttered something about these English, and sharply asked the insistent disturber to stand aside and not block the line at the window. The enraged journalist hurried off, and found a French *confrère* of influence, to whom he explained the situation. Together they returned to the telegraph office and sent for the chief. The case was laid before him. He went to the cabinet, lifted down a heap of things on top, and there at the bottom of all lay the dispatch. Then, naturally, the Londoner began to say things, but the chief interrupted him:

"Now, be reasonable, you mustn't be angry with this poor fellow. Have a little consideration of the circumstances. He has been in tears all day ever since he heard Labori had been shot. He doesn't know what he is doing. Really it isn't fair for you to be cross with him."

And what could the correspondent do after that explanation?

How to communicate the news of the court-martial's verdict most expeditiously to the waiting world has, of course, been the problem uppermost in every correspondent's mind for days past. Many schemes were devised for securing a few seconds' precedence, and some of them were sufficiently ingenious to deserve success, but in the end pure chance proved to be the controlling factor. This applies to the dispatches announcing the judgment filed by the correspondent here after the decision had been announced in court by Colonel Jouaust. These telegrams poured into the Rennes telegraph office in a perfect avalanche, and, as usually happens in times of such excitement, the order of dispatching did not follow the exact order of receipt. In fact, the last was sometimes first. Those of us who have had experience of similar confusion at presidential elections at Versailles and other occasions had prepared for this emergency. We wrote our dispatches in duplicate, filed one at the earliest possible moment, and waited to slip the other into the distracted clerk's hand at the moment when he handed over the swelling pile of telegrams for transmission. The chances were that the top or last message would be sent first.

It is probable, despite all the rush at Rennes, that the first news of the verdict reached New York via London. Some of us learned yesterday morning that the decision would be telephoned to the home office in Paris a few minutes before it was publicly announced in the courtroom at Rennes. As a matter of fact, at the moment when the decisive words were being read to the assembled audience in the Lycée, the news had been received at London, and had been transferred to the cable, which delivered it in New York three minutes late.

The fate of two plans of rival American correspondents for beating their fellows deserves to be recorded. They were not satisfied with conveying the news from the courtroom to the telegraph office—a distance of less than a quarter of a mile—by foot or bicycle; so they arranged systems of signals. In one case, a series of boys stationed at intervals along the route was to pass along the signal of "guilty" by holding the right hand high in the air, while both arms in that position would signify "innocent." The boys were carefully drilled, and the system worked perfectly until the fateful moment came. Then the first boy gave the signal properly, but the second lost his head. Instead of raising his hand he clapped both arms to his side and started pell-mell for the telegraph office. His employer saw him coming and ran to meet him, unable to imagine what had happened. The boy simply flung himself into the newspaperman's arms. Too much excited himself to think of any French, the correspondent shook the little wretch and shouted in English:

"What is it?"

Then the boy bethought himself. Up went his right hand high in the air. *"Coupable,"* he yelped, and trotted with his arm still up behind his employer the rest of the way to the telegraph office.

The other incident was no less tragic. Another series of boys were to wave red discs if the verdict was guilty, blue ones for the four-to-three verdict of dishonorable acquittal, and white for innocent. The correspondent who relied on this scheme made the fatal mistake of stationing a very small boy at the Lycée end of the line. A crowd of more than a hundred men and boys was waiting at the slot beneath a window through which the word was to come. All broke and ran at the same moment when the news was received, and the small boy with a red disc was simply knocked down and trampled on by the crowd before he could give the signal.

The Judgment at Rennes

"The majority agreed that there are extenuating circumstances. . . ."

Reported by The Associated Press, *September 9, 1899.*

On September 9, 1899, just as the court was about to retire, Dreyfus rose and spoke with deep emotion:

I affirm before my country and before the Army that I am innocent. My sole aim has been to save the honor of my name, the name borne by my children. I have suffered five years of the most awful torture. But, today, at last, I feel assured that I am about to attain my desire, through your loyalty and justice.

After the judges retired, the spectators settled down to await the verdict. After fifteen minutes had passed it became obvious that there would be no acquittal. The court deliberated for an hour and a half. On return of the judges, Colonel Jouaust read the decision. Dreyfus was not present, having left the hall, never to return, in accordance with the law.

Today, the 9th of September, 1899, the court-martial of the Tenth Legion Army Corps, deliberating behind closed doors, the president put the following question:

"Is Alfred Dreyfus, brevet captain Fourteenth Regiment of Artillery, probationer on the General Staff, guilty of having in 1894 entered into machinations or held relations with a foreign power, or one of its agents, to induce it to commit hostility or undertake war against France, or procure it the means therefor, by delivering the notes and documents mentioned in the document called the *bordereau,* according to the decision of the Court of Cassation of June 3, 1899?"

The votes were taken separately, beginning by the inferior grade and youngest in the last grade, the president giving his opinion last.

The court declares on the question, by a majority of five votes to two, "Yes," the accused is guilty.

The majority agreed that there are extenuating circumstances, in consequence of which and on the request of the commissary of the Government, the president put the question and received again the votes in the above-mentioned form.

As a result, the court condemns, by a majority of five votes to two, Alfred Dreyfus to the punishment of ten years' detention.

The judgment then ordered the Government Commissary to read the verdict immediately to the prisoner before an assembled guard. Dreyfus was to be notified that the law allowed a delay of twenty-four hours in which to lodge an appeal. The silence in the courtroom was broken by the rush of reporters to transmit the news by wire.

Two members of the court had voted for acquittal—de Bréon, an ardent Catholic who had spent many hours in prayer, and surprisingly, by President Jouaust, who had been rude and brusque to Dreyfus throughout the trial.

Dreyfus's reaction was despair. "Since when," he asked, "have there been 'extenuating circumstances' for treason?"

"The Fifth Act": Zola Denounces the Verdict

"Jesus was condemned but once."

L'Aurore, *September 10, 1899. Translated by* The Associated Press.

The announcement of the second verdict was greeted with enthusiasm by the anti-Dreyfus press. The offices of the *La Libre Parole, Le Soir,* and *Le Petit Journal* were brilliantly illuminated and decorated with flags. M. Drumont in the *La Libre Parole* described the court-martial as "a beautiful spectacle." "The judges are warriors," he wrote, "without fear and without reproach." Nothing could disturb them, neither outrages nor insulting flatteries. "This most flagrant of traitors has received his just reward."

This view was echoed by *Le Gaulois,* which congratulated the court on its "victory against the enemies of the Army and France." The *Croix* stated that the verdict confirmed France's military justice because "it was dealt without fear or favor, and without passion except such as was inspired with justice."

L'Éclair editorially reminded the country of President Loubet's declaration that he would bow before the judgment of the court-martial. "No organized society can live without respect for the decisions of justice." The *Courier du Soir* urged everyone to accept the verdict. It advised mercy because of the expiation that Dreyfus had already made. Only extremists would persist in the agitation against Dreyfus.

To Zola the verdict was a monstrous defiance of reason and justice. He straightway sent a powerful letter to *L'Aurore* denouncing the decision as a heinous outrage against humanity.

THE FIFTH ACT

I am in mortal fear. It is not anger, avenging indignation, the need to proclaim the crime and demand its punishment in the name of truth and justice that I feel now; it is terror, the sacred terror of the man who sees the impossible being realized, the rivers flowing back to their sources, the earth turning without the sun; and what I fear is the distress of our generous and noble France. My dread is the abyss into which she is falling.

We had fondly imagined that the Rennes court-martial was the fifth act of the terrible tragedy which we have been living for close upon two years past. All the dangerous stages seemed to us to have been passed. We thought we were approaching a *"dénoûment"* of pacification and concord. After the dreadful battle the victory of right became inevitable; the play must end happily, with the classic triumph of the innocent.

And we have been deceived! A new stage opens before us, and that the most unexpected and the most terrifying of all, still further darkening the drama, prolonging it and urging it toward an unknown termination, before which our very reason trembles and grows weak.

The Rennes trial was only the fourth act, and, great God! what will the fifth act be? What new tortures and sufferings will it bring? To what supreme expiation will it force our people? For is it not certain that the innocent cannot be twice condemned, and that such an ending would blot out the sun and arouse the nations?

Ah! that fourth act! that trial at Rennes! In what mortal agony did I not live through it, in that solitude where I had taken refuge in order to disappear from the scene like a good citizen desirous of giving no cause for passion and disorder! With what a tightening of the heart did I not await telegrams, letters, papers; and what revolt and what pain did their perusal not cause me! The days of that splendid month of August were blackened, and never have I felt the gloom and chill of mourning under skies so glorious.

Assuredly, for two years past, I have had my share of suffering. I have heard the mob shouting death at my heels. I have seen at my feet an ignoble mire of insult and menace. For eighteen months I tasted the despair of exile. Then there were my two trials—lamentable spectacles of villainy and iniquity.

But what are my trials in comparison with the trial at Rennes? Idyls, refreshing scenes where hope flowers.

We had been witness of monstrous things—the prosecution of Colonel

Picquart, the inquiry into the Criminal Chamber of the Court of Cassation, the *"loi de dessaisissement"* which resulted from it. But all that seems childish now. The inevitable progression has followed its course. The Rennes trial stands out above all like the abominable flower growing atop of all these heaped-up dunghills.

We have seen the most extraordinary collection of attempts against truth and justice—a band of witnesses directing the course of the trial, making their plans every night for the cowardly ambush of the morrow, pressing the charge, in place of the Public Prosecutor, with lies; terrorizing and insulting those who contradicted them, imposing with the insolence of their stripes and their plumes upon a tribunal knuckling down to this invasion of their chiefs, visibly annoyed at seeing them in criminal posture, acting in obedience to a peculiar mental process; a grotesque Public Prosecutor, who enlarges the bounds of imbecility and leaves to future historians a charge whose stupid and murderous emptiness will be an eternal cause of wonder; a man of such senile and obstinate cruelty that it seems to be irresponsible, born of a human animal not yet classed; a defense which it was at first endeavored to assassinate, which was afterward made to sit down every time it became troublesome, and which finally was refused permission to produce the decisive proof which it demanded, the only witnesses who know.

And this abomination lasted for a whole month, in face of the innocent —that piteous Dreyfus, the poor shreds of whose humanity would make the very stones weep. And his former comrades came and kicked him, and his former chiefs came and crushed him with their rank so as to save themselves from the galleys. And there was never a cry of pity, never a throb of generosity in those shameful souls!

And it is our sweet France that has given this spectacle to the world!

When the complete report of the Rennes trial is published there will exist no more execrable monument of human infamy. This is beyond all.

Never will a document of such wickedness have been furnished to history. Ignorance, folly, cruelty, falsehood, crime are displayed there with an impudence that will make future generations shudder. There are in that collection avowals of our baseness at which human nature will blush.

And it is this that makes me tremble, for in order that such a trial should have been possible in a nation, that a nation should lay itself open to the world for such a consultation upon its social and intellectual condition, it must be undergoing a terrible crisis.

Is it death that is approaching? And what bath of truth, of purity, of equity will save us from the poisonous mud in which we are agonizing?

As I wrote in my letter to the President of the Republic after the scandalous acquittal of Esterhazy, it is impossible for a court-martial to undo what a court-martial has done. That would be contrary to discipline, and the judgment of the Rennes court-martial—that judgment which in its Jesuitical embarrassment has not the courage to say yes or no—is the plain proof that military justice is powerless to be just, since it is not free, since it defies evidence almost to the point of again condemning an innocent man rather than cast doubt upon its own infallibility. Military justice is seen to be nothing more than a weapon of execution in the hands of the commander. Henceforward it can but be an expeditious form of justice in time of war—it must disappear in time of peace. The moment it showed itself incapable of equity, of simple logic, and of mere common sense it condemned itself.

Has thought been given to the atrocious situation in which we are made to stand among the civilized nations?

A first court-martial, deceived in its ignorance of the law and its want of skill in sifting evidence, condemns an innocent man. A second court-martial, which likewise was deceived by a most impudent conspiracy of lies and frauds, acquits a guilty man. A third court-martial, when light has been thrown on the matter, when the highest magistracy of the country consents to leave to it the glory of making reparation for an error, dares to deny the full daylight, and a second time finds the innocent guilty.

This is irreparable. The last crime has been committed. Jesus was condemned but once.

But let final ruin come, let France fall a prey to faction, let the country be aflame and perish in the embers, let the Army itself lose honor rather than confess that some members of it made a mistake, and that certain generals were liars and forgers. The ideal shall be crucified; the saber must remain king!

And so we find ourselves in this glorious condition before Europe, before the world! The whole world is convinced of the innocence of Dreyfus. If a doubt had remained in the minds of some far-away race the blinding glare of the Rennes trial would have carried the full light there. All the courts of the Powers that are our neighbors are well informed, know the documents, have proof of the worthlessness of three or four of our generals and of the shameful paralysis of our military justice.

A moral Sedan has been lost—a Sedan a hundredfold more disastrous than that other one where only blood was spilt.

And I repeat, what fills me with dread is that this defeat of our honor seems irreparable, for how are we to quash the judgments of three courts-martial? Where shall we find the heroism to confess our fault, to march onward with head uplifted proudly? Where is the government with courage to be a government of public safety? Where are the chambers that will understand and act before the inevitable final crash?

The worst of it all is that we have come to a reckoning day of glory. France desires to celebrate its century of labor, of science, of struggle for liberty, for truth and for justice. No century that has passed has been marked by more superb effort; this will be seen later on. And France has called together in her capital all the peoples of the earth to glorify her victory, liberty won, truth and justice promised to earth.

Thus, a few months hence the people will come; and what they will find will be the innocent twice condemned, truth trampled upon, justice assassinated. We have fallen beneath their contempt; and they will come and laugh at us in our very faces. They will drink our wines, they will kiss our maidservants, as people do in the low-class inn which is not above that sort of thing.

Is all this possible? Are we going to allow our Exhibition to be the foul, despised place where the whole world is willing to seek its pleasures only?

No! a thousand times no! We must have, and that at once, the fifth act of the monstrous tragedy, even if we have to lose our flesh and blood in the effort. We must have our honor restored before we salute the visiting people in a France healed and regenerated.

This fifth act haunts me, and I am ever recurring to it. I am working on it; I build it up in my imagination.

Has it been noticed that this Dreyfus Affair, this gigantic drama which moves the universe, seems to be staged by some sublime dramatist desirous of making it an incomparable masterpiece? I will not recall the extraordinary incidents that have stirred our souls. At every fresh act passion has swollen, horror has grown more intense. In this living piece it is Fate that has genius. Destiny is there, actuating the players, determining the incidents under the tempest it unchains; and assuredly it wants the masterpiece to be complete, and is preparing for us a fifth act—a superhuman act which will make France glorious once again and replace her in the forefront of the nations.

For you may be sure of this—it was Fate that decreed the supreme crime—the second condemnation of the innocent. The crime had to be committed for the sake of the tragic grandeur, the sovereign beauty, the expiation, perhaps, which will allow of the apotheosis, the final transformation scene.

And now that we have sounded the uttermost depths of horror, I await the fifth act, which will end the drama by delivering us, by restoring to us health and fresh youth.

I will now speak plainly of my fear. It has always been, as I have allowed it to be understood on several occasions, that the truth, the decisive, overwhelming proof should come to us from Germany. We must look the possibility of Germany bringing out the fifth act of the drama in a thunderclap squarely and courageously in the face.

Here is my confession.

Previous to my trial, in January, 1898, I learned with certainty that Esterhazy was the traitor; that he had supplied M. de Schwartzkoppen with a large number of documents; that many of these documents were in his handwriting, and that a complete collection of them was to be found in the War Office at Berlin.

From that time on I have, as a good Frenchman, been in constant dread. I thought with terror that Germany, our enemy of tomorrow, would perhaps slap us in the face with the proofs in its possession. Accordingly, with Labori, I decided to cite as witnesses the foreign military attachés. We were well aware we were not likely to bring them to the bar, but we desired to let the Government know we knew the truth, in the hope that it would take action.

No heed was taken. Mock was made of us. The weapon Germany has in her hands was left there, and matters remained unchanged up to the time of the Rennes trial.

On my return to France I hurried to see Labori. I insisted, with the energy of despair, on steps being taken to bring the matter before the Cabinet, to demonstrate the dreadful character of the situation, and to ask if the Government would not intervene, so as to obtain the documents for us. That was certainly a most delicate matter. Then there was that unfortunate Dreyfus to be saved, so that we were prepared to make every concession for fear of irritating public opinion, already at a high pitch of excitement. If the court-martial acquitted Dreyfus, it thereby deprived the documents of their nocuous virus; it shattered in the hands of Germany the weapon she might have used. The acquittal of Dreyfus meant the recognition of an error and its reparation.

My patriotic torment grew more intolerable when I felt that a court-martial was about to aggravate the danger by again condemning the innocent—the man whose innocence would one day be cried aloud by the publication of the documents in Berlin.

That is why I have never ceased to act, begging Labori to demand the documents, to cite M. de Schwartzkoppen, who alone can throw full light on the matter; and the day that Labori took advantage of the opportunity given him by the accusers bringing to the bar an unworthy foreigner, the day he arose and demanded that the court-martial hear the man from whom a single word would close the affair, he did his duty. His was the heroic voice that nothing can reduce to silence. His demand has survived the trial, and must inevitably reopen it and end it once for all by the only possible solution—the acquittal of the innocent.

The demand for the documents has been made. Their ultimate production is a certainty.

You see the awful, intolerable danger in which the president of the Rennes court-martial has put us by refusing to use his discretionary power to prevent the publication of the documents. Never was anything more brutal! Never was the door so wilfully shut upon the truth! And a third court-martial was added to the two others, in which the error was so blinding that the denial from Berlin would now condemn three iniquitous sentences.

The Ministry forgot that government is foresight. If it does not wish to leave to the good pleasure of Germany the fifth act, the *"dénoûment,"* before which every good Frenchman should tremble, it is the Government's duty to play this fifth act without delay in order to prevent its coming to us from Germany. The Government can procure the documents. Diplomacy has settled greater difficulties than this. Whenever it ventures to ask for the documents enumerated in the *bordereau* they will be given, and that will be the *"fait nouveau"* which will necessitate a second revision before the Court of Cassation, which will be this time, I hope, fully informed, and would quash the verdict *"sans renvoi"* in the plenitude of its sovereign majesty.

But if the Government still hesitates, the defenders of truth and justice will do what is necessary. Not one of us will desert his post. Invincible proof we shall finally end by obtaining.

On November 23d, we shall be at Versailles. My trial will recommence, inasmuch as it is to recommence in all its fulness. If, meanwhile, justice is not done we will again have to do it. My beloved, my valiant Labori, whose honor has but increased, will pronounce at Versailles the address which he was unable to pronounce at Rennes. And thus, as you see, nothing will be lost. He will merely have to tell the truth, without fear of injuring me, for I am ready to pay for it with my liberty and my blood. Before the Seine Assize Court I swore to the innocence of Dreyfus. I swear to it before the entire world, which now proclaims it with me; and I repeat, truth is on the march. Nothing will stop it. At Rennes it has just made a giant's stride.

I no longer have any fear except that I may see it arrive in a thunder-clap of the avenging Nemesis.   ÉMILE ZOLA

Zola's indignation was matched throughout the world. Journalists from every corner of the earth had witnessed the proceedings at Rennes and their reports had made it clear to most readers that Dreyfus was innocent. London reacted almost unanimously. *The Times* said: "We do not hesitate to pronounce it the grossest and most appalling prostitution of justice the world has witnessed in modern times. All the outrageous scandals which marked the course of the trial pale into insignificance beside the crowning scandal of the verdict." The *Daily Telegraph* observed: "This infamous judgment disgraces France, dishonors her Army, insults the Kaiser, and offends the best principles of humanity. There seems nothing left for France but a revolution and a war that will reduce her to the level of Spain." The *Daily Mail* remarked: "Rennes is France's moral Sedan."

In Berlin the verdict was called "one of the greatest judicial and political crimes of any age." According to the Cologne *Gazette,* "It is a cowardly verdict, in the barbarous spirit of the Middle Ages. By this crime the judges have imposed a line of demarcation between France and the rest of the world." Even in Russia, where there was a strong sense of anti-Semitism, the press described the judges as "criminals." In the United States, Congress was urged not to make any further appropriations for the Paris Exposition. In Chicago the head of an iron company said: "I have discharged all the Frenchmen in my employ, for one of them said that Dreyfus should be hanged. The judges violated every principle of law and justice."

Governor Theodore Roosevelt of New York Comments on the Judgment

"It was less Dreyfus on trial than those who tried him."

Reported by The Associated Press, *September 13, 1899.*

Among the thousands of comments made on the decision at Rennes was the following by Governor Theodore Roosevelt of the State of New York in a speech at Walton, New York.

Something recently happened which I want to speak about. I think it a rare thing for the whole nation to watch the trial of a single citizen of another nation. We have watched with indignation and regret the trial of Captain Dreyfus. It was less Dreyfus on trial than those who tried him. We should draw lessons from the trial. It was due in part to bitter religious prejudices of the French people. Those who have ever wavered from the doctrine of the separation of Church and State should ponder upon what has happened. Try to encourage every form of religious effort. Beware and do not ever oppose any man for any reason except worth or want of it. You cannot benefit one class by pulling another class down.

Judges of the Court of Cassation Assemble to Hear the Report in Favor of Revision, June 3, 1899 (Associated Press)

DREYFUS ABOARD THE "SFAX"

"My treatment on board the *Sfax* was that of an officer under arrest *de rigueur*. For one hour in the morning and one hour in the evening I was allowed to walk on deck; the rest of the time I was shut up in my cabin." (Associated Press)

THE "SFAX" ARRIVES AT PORT-HOULIGUEN DURING THE NIGHT OF JULY 1, 1899
"At nine o'clock the boat which was to take me to the steam launch was at the foot of the
Sfax's companionway. . . . The sea had become very rough, the wind blew a gale, the
rain fell heavily. The boat, tossed by the waves, was dancing by the ladder. I jumped for
it and struck upon the gunwhale, bruising myself rather severely. The boat pulled away."
(Associated Press)

THE LANDING AT PORT-HOULIGUEN

"The night was still black, the rain kept pouring down, but the sea was calmer.
I understood that we must be in port. At a quarter after two in the morning we
landed at a place which I afterward knew was Port-Houliguen." (*Graphic*, London,
September 14, 1899)

LAST STAGE OF THE JOURNEY TO RENNES

"At the station . . . we got into a train which, after two or three hours of travel,
arrived at another station, where we got out. There we found another carriage
waiting, and were conveyed swiftly to a city and into a courtyard. I got out, and
looking about me saw that I was in the military prison at Rennes. It was about
six o'clock in the morning." (*Graphic*, London, September 14, 1899)

COLONEL JOUAUST, PRESIDENT OF THE COURT-MARTIAL AT RENNES, 1899 (Homer Davenport, *New York Journal and Advertiser*)

DREYFUS ON HIS RETURN TO FRANCE FROM DEVIL'S ISLAND
Note his extreme emaciation and physical frailty. (*Graphic*, London, September 14, 1899)

DREYFUS LEAVING THE COURT FOR MILITARY PRISON
The passage of Dreyfus to and from court and prison was made between files of soldiers with their backs turned toward him, presumably to prevent any attempt at rescue but actually to express contempt for the "traitor." Dreyfus showed no outward feeling against these degrading marches. (*Graphic*, London, September 14, 1899)

DEFENSE COUNSEL: MAÎTRES DEMANGE AND LABORI AT THE RENNES COURT-MARTIAL (Homer Davenport, *New York Journal and Advertiser*)

DREYFUS BEFORE HIS JUDGES AT RENNES, 1899 (Gerschel, Paris)

THE SEVEN JUDGES AT THE RENNES COURT-MARTIAL

GENERAL MERCIER, CHIEF OF THE ANTI-DREYFUSARDS

GENERAL ROGET, ANOTHER ANTI-DREYFU-SARD

THE FRENCH GENERAL STAFF BESIEGED AT RENNES, AS SEEN BY "PUNCH," AUGUST 30, 1899

Roget and Zurlinden at the window at left; Cavaignac and Mercier squat on the floor; a tattered Esterhazy leans against the "Secret Dossier"; Boisdeffre clutches his shoulder at the door, with de Pellieux sprawled on the floor; du Paty de Clam stands arrogantly apart at the right.

Mme. Dreyfus with Friends (*Bibliothèque Nationale*)

MEMBERS OF THE AMERICAN PRESS AT THE RENNES TRIAL
Identifiable are (left to right, seated): Gaston Meyer, Warden, Middleton, and Crawford; standing behind Crawford is Fullerton (with beard). (Gerschel, Paris)

ON A PARISIAN STREET: READING ABOUT THE TRIAL (Associated Press)

THE STENOGRAPHIC SERVICE OF "LE FIGARO"

This large staff represented only one of the many Parisian newspapers. The demand for news was insatiable: the French public followed every detail of the trial. (Gerschel, Paris)

Outside the Rennes Courtroom

Newspaper and telegraph boys receive dispatches from inside the building through a specially guarded letter-box. (*Illustrated London News*, September 30, 1899)

THE ATTEMPT TO ASSASSINATE MAÎTRE LABORI, COUNSEL FOR DREYFUS: RENNES, AUGUST 14, 1899 (*La Vie Illustrée*, Paris)

DREYFUS GREETS HIS DEFENDERS (*Le Petit Journal*, July 16, 1899)

ENCOUNTER AT RENNES, AUGUST 24, 1899
In this remarkable courtroom scene, five central figures in the trial are talking at once. Colonel Jouaust, President of the court, is calling out "Silence!" In the center, three generals—Mercier, Billot, and Roget—are talking. Dreyfus gestures and speaks from his seat. Maître Labori, Dreyfus's counsel, stands at right. (Melton Prior, *Illustrated London News*, September 1899)

DREYFUS TO GENERAL MERCIER: "THAT IS WHAT YOU OUGHT TO SAY!" RENNES, AUGUST 12, 1899 (*Graphic*, London, August 19, 1899)

BERTILLON, EXPERT FOR THE PROSECUTION, DEMONSTRATES HIS "INFALLIBLE SYSTEM"
"With the gestures and the shrill pitched voice of a quack at a country fair, M. Bertillon produced every few minutes some fresh paper covered with incomprehensible hieroglyphics. He leans over the table to explain his mystifying diagrams. The spectators dissolved in laughter." (Associated Press)

Closing Scene of the Rennes Court-Martial, September 9, 1899 (*La Vie Illustrée,* Paris)

The Provost of the Gendarmes Reads Orders to the Police After the Verdict (*La Vie Illustrée,* Paris)

XI

Finale: Vindication and Rehabilitation

Both Dreyfus and his defenders were shocked by the verdict at Rennes. Ten days after his sentence, he was pardoned, but he announced that he would continue to seek amends for the shocking judicial wrong of which he was the victim.

On December 27, 1900, an Amnesty Law calling for an end to all suits and prosecutions in the case came into effect. Dreyfus protested again, saying that the amnesty struck him to the heart and insisting that it could benefit no one but General Mercier. In the Senate an ardent Republican asked: "Why don't you grant an amnesty to Esterhazy as well?"

In the meantime Dreyfus was resting to regain his health. Some of his most faithful friends, Labori, Clemenceau, and Picquart among them, reproached him mildly for his inaction. At length, on November 26, 1903, he asked the Minister of Justice for an appeal on the Rennes judgment. A month later the Committee on Appeal of the Ministry of Justice adopted a unanimous motion in favor of appeal.

Finally, after more than two years of consideration, the Court of Cassation set aside the Rennes judgment by a vote of 31 to 18. Several days later, on July 13, 1906, the Senate and Chamber of Deputies passed a bill reactivating Picquart with the rank of briga-dier-general and Dreyfus with the rank of major. On July 20, 1906, Dreyfus was made a Chevalier of the Legion of Honor and his stripes were restored in a moving ceremony at the *École Militaire*.

It had taken nearly twelve years from the arrival of the *bordereau* at the War Ministry to establish the innocence of an officer accused of the crime of treason.

The Minister of War Recommends Pardon

*"A higher political interest . . . suggests measures
of clemency or of oblivion."*

Text by The Associated Press, *in Harding,* Dreyfus: The Prisoner of Devil's
Island, *pp. 365–366.*

On the evening of his second condemnation Dreyfus signed an
appeal to the Appellate Court-Martial. Almost immediately the
Minister of War, General de Galliffet, sent a report to the President
of the Republic proposing that Dreyfus be "pardoned." He pointed
out that Dreyfus's health had deteriorated and was of a nature to
arouse anxiety. Moreover, there was "a higher political interest,"
and the Government should take steps "to efface all traces of a painful conflict." It was all for the welfare of France.

Monsieur le Président: On September 9th the court-martial of Rennes
condemned Dreyfus, by five votes against two, to ten years' detention,
and by a majority it granted extenuating circumstances. After appealing
to the Council of Revision Dreyfus withdrew his application. The verdict
has become definitive, and henceforth it partakes of the authority of
the law, before which everyone ought to bow. The highest function
of the Government is to enforce respect for the decisions of justice
without distinction and without reservation. Resolved to fulfill this
duty, it ought also to take into account what clemency and the public
interest counsel. The verdict of the court-martial itself, which admitted
extenuating circumstances, and the desire immediately expressed that
the sentence might be mitigated are so many indications that ought
to solicit attention. As the result of the judgment pronounced in 1894
Dreyfus has undergone five years' transportation. This judgment was
annulled on June 3, 1899, and a penalty less severe both in its nature
and its duration has been applied. If one deducts from the ten years'
detention the five years served on the *Île du Diable*—and it cannot be
otherwise—Dreyfus will have undergone five years of transportation,
and ought to undergo five years of detention. It has been suggested
whether it was not possible to assimilate transportation to solitary
confinement in a prison, and in that case he would have almost
completely purged his sentence. Legislation does not seem to permit this.
It follows, therefore, that Dreyfus ought to undergo a higher penalty
than that to which he has been actually condemned.

It results from information obtained that the health of the condemned
man has been seriously compromised, and that he could not, without the

greatest peril, bear a prolonged detention. Apart from considerations of a nature to arouse anxiety, others of a more general order tend to the same conclusions. A higher political interest—the necessity of calling up all their powers always exacted from governments after difficult crises and in regard to certain orders of facts—suggests measures of clemency or of oblivion. The Government would ill-respond to the desire of a country desirous of pacification if, by the acts which it behooves it to accomplish, whether on its own initiative or by a proposal to Parliament, it did not take steps to efface all traces of a painful conflict. It is for you, *Monsieur le Président*, by an act of supreme humanity, to give the first pledge of the work of pacification which public opinion demands, and which the welfare of the Republic dictates.

For these reasons I have the honor to propose for your signature the following decree.

GENERAL DE GALLIFFET
Minister of War

The decree in question was thus worded:

Article 1.—There is accorded to Alfred Dreyfus remission of the rest of the penalty of ten years of detention pronounced against him by decree of the court-martial of Rennes dated September 9, 1899, and also of military degradation.

Article 2.—The Minister of War is charged with the execution of the present decree.

General Order to the Army
"The incident is closed."

Text by The Associated Press, *in Harding,* Dreyfus: The Prisoner of Devil's Island, *pp. 366–367.*

At the same time General de Galliffet sent the following general order to the military governors of Paris and Lyons, as well as to the Army corps commanders.

To the Army:—The incident is closed. The military judges, the object of universal respect, have delivered their verdict in complete independence. We have, without any sort of reservation, bowed down before their decree. We shall likewise bow down before the act which a sentiment of profound pity has dictated to the President of the Republic. It is impossible that any question of reprisals of any sort whatever should henceforth arise. So I repeat, the incident is closed. I ask you, and if need be I should order you, to forget the past in order to think only of the future. With you, who are all my comrades, I cry heartily *"Vive l'armée!"* the Army which belongs to no party but only to France.

GALLIFFET

Dreyfus Accepts the Pardon

"It is nothing to me without honor."

Le Siècle, *Paris, September 21, 1899. Translated by the editor.*

At first Dreyfus greeted with hostility any idea of pardon. This was not what he wanted, and it was not justice. But Mathieu Dreyfus was insistent that it be accepted. Five years of terrible mental and physical suffering, he said, had taken their toll. On the one hand, he added, an important effect would result from a pardon immediately following a second unjust condemnation. On the other hand, an appeal was useless because of a question of law. Alfred, he said, had a duty toward his wife, children, and family. He must live and continue to work for complete exoneration.

After a long discussion, Dreyfus decided to withdraw his request for an appeal, whereupon the President of the Republic signed the pardon. The next day the newspapers of Paris published this declaration by Dreyfus.

The Government of the Republic restores me my liberty. It is nothing to me without honor. From this day forth I shall continue to seek the reparation of the judicial error of which I am still the victim. I wish that everyone in France should know by a final judgment that I am innocent. My heart will not be at rest until there is no longer a Frenchman who imputes to me the abominable crime which another has committed.

ALFRED DREYFUS

Efforts to Boycott the Paris Exposition of 1900

". . . it would be a gross injustice."

New York *Herald, September 15, 1899.*

The wave of indignation that swept throughout the world after the Rennes verdict was accompanied by a widespread movement to boycott the Paris Exposition as a protest against the decision. English newspapers were bombarded with letters from individuals and firms announcing their withdrawal from the coming Paris Exposition. In many parts of the United States steps toward a boycott were taken. Companies that had already made application for exhibit space temporarily ceased preparations for the event. Among those who cancelled their orders for space were the North El Paso and Northeastern Railway, which had planned a mineral exhibit, the Troy, New York, Paint and Color Works, and California Canneries of San Francisco.

The New York *Herald,* in an editorial dated September 15, 1899, opposed this effort to punish Frenchmen and injure France.

The newspapers are filled with threats of a sort of "holy alliance" against France and of boycotting the great Exposition of 1900. This would be more than a mistake; it would be a gross injustice. Foreigners are perfectly free to criticize the affairs of France, just as Frenchmen have a right to express their opinion on anything that takes place in no matter what country.

To criticize and condemn is one thing, but it is another and very different matter to interfere in the internal affairs of a country, as the would-be boycotters threaten to do. Anyone can think what he pleases about the Dreyfus case. Everybody is privileged to discuss the Rennes decision and to approve it or stigmatize it. But to go far beyond that by threatening to punish Frenchmen and injure France because of an unsatisfactory verdict by a court-martial for whose action neither France nor the French people are to blame is pushing matters to an extreme beyond all right, justice and reason.

"You cannot indict a people," said Edmund Burke. No more can you with any show of reason or justice boycott or indiscriminately condemn a nation or a people. Those who are so zealous in fomenting this absurd agitation must remember that they are striking as well at all those who have been battling in behalf of Dreyfus. To boycott the Exposition would be to boycott France, whose highest court annulled the condemnation of 1894 and may yet annul that of 1899, whose Government is known to have desired an acquittal, whose press in large measure has protested against the conviction, and many of whose people condemn the Rennes verdict.

It is these agencies in France—the government, the judiciary, the press and the people—that brought about revision, and it is these that are still desirous of attaining what they believe to be truth and justice.

The threatened boycott is, moreover, as foolish as it is unjust, since it would be as detrimental to the interests of the boycotters as to those of the boycotted.

The movement to boycott the Exposition is already losing ground in Germany. The proposed resolution by the Municipal Council that the city of Berlin should not send any special exhibit to Paris has been abandoned. The *Tageblatt* in an article on the subject reminded German exhibitors that by staying away from the great Exposition they would only be giving an advantage to their competitors.

The effort to get up a mass meeting in this city to boycott the exposition has been also abandoned by its advocates, as the prominent citizens they approached refused to participate on the ground that it was ill-advised.

Fortunately there is reason to expect that all ill-advised newspaper manifestations will pass away like a fit of bad humor, and that the Exposition of 1900 will have the great success it merits in view of the prodigious efforts it has called forth and the world-wide benefit it must prove. Both the United States and the German governments have refused to lend any official countenance to the foolishly-threatened boycott, and we trust their commendable example will be followed by every nation represented in the grand enterprise.

The First Interview After the Release of Dreyfus
"It is good to feel free, free, free!"

New York Herald, *September 22, 1899.*

The first interview with Dreyfus following his release was obtained by a reporter for *Le Figaro* of Paris. The enterprising newspaperman managed to follow Dreyfus when he left Rennes. Every precaution had been taken for Dreyfus to leave without inconvenience. At half-past two in the morning, M. Viguie, *directeur de la sûreté générale,* came to fetch Dreyfus in a carriage at the gate of the Manutention, from which they went to the station at Vern, some ten kilometers from Rennes. Here the reporter saw a bowed figure, dressed in black, making its way to a buffet at the station.

. . . In a moment we entered. Already the passengers are at the tables. In a small room at the further end Captain Dreyfus is seated eating. His brother draws near. He rises. His mouth opens in an affectionate smile, and the brothers meet with a long embrace, without speaking a word. No one but myself witnessed this scene, so touching in its melancholy sympathy.

Mathieu introduced me to his brother. Captain Dreyfus holds out his hand. I press it and speak of the profound joy which his freedom will give to so many beings to whom it will be like a personal deliverance. He wears a navy blue suit and over it a black overcoat, the collar of which gapes behind, and on his head a soft, black felt hat.

"It is in order not to be recognized," he says, smiling, "but it annoys me. I am not used to it, and I see nothing in it."

"Make haste," says his brother, "for we are going to start." He seats himself again obediently, and empties his cup of milk, for his stomach cannot bear anything else.

During this time M. Viguie has reserved seats in two compartments, for at present the service of surveillance is composed of three inspectors, chosen from among the best men of Hennion's brigade, who accompanied him to Rennes, and on whom falls the heavy responsibility of the long journey we are about to make.

Captain Dreyfus enters the sleeping-car compartment with M. Mathieu Dreyfus, M. Paul Valabregue, his nephew, and myself.

M. Viguie has just made his last suggestions, for he goes no further. Captain and Mathieu Dreyfus congratulate him on the skill and prudence he has displayed since their departure from Rennes, and the common wish is expressed that the rest of the journey may pass off equally well.

The train moves at two minutes of nine. I am seated facing Captain Dreyfus. I never remove my eyes from him for an instant. I am surprised at the effect he produces on me. I expected, whatever my sentiments might be as to his case, to find myself confronted by a being who awakened no sympathy. He has been described as a haughty and disagreeable person, with a harsh voice and wandering eyes. I had imagined him as hard, mistrustful, gloomy, if not bearing hate at least bitter; and I own that I was ready to forgive him all those things. I find before me a man with fine, regular features, with a calm and mild expression. He is pink of face, which would give him an expression of extreme youth if the top of his head were not absolutely bald, and if the hair on each side were not quite gray. This being is enfeebled by anemia, and what blood there is left in him flows toward the head, the last refuge of his prodigious vitality. His neck is thin, his hands are long and bony, and the knees are pointed like nails through the blue cloth of his trousers.

His chest is hollowed, his entire body is that of a vanquished being but for the energy of the mouth, the square jaw, and the will expressed in the look of his eyes. They are blue, charming and mild, limpid and clear. Far from shunning one's look, he fixes his eyes on you with assurance behind his eyeglasses, and his look is not that of a man of whom a monster of hypocrisy has been made, of whom one scoundrel has said that "he sweated treason."

The train rolls on toward Bordeaux. M. Mathieu Dreyfus looks at his brother with tender eyes.

"Well," he asks, "are you comfortable? You are not cold?"

"Oh, no! I am well covered up with my flannel vest, two wool shirts, my coat and overcoat. I am very well—and then you forget the freedom. It is good to feel free, free, free! Not to feel people everlasting round you spying each movement, each gesture. That, mind you, is the odious, insupportable thing. To be shut up one can bear, though it is painful after a long time; but the eye of that man whose hostile examination of the smallest movements of your body you have felt every minute for five years—oh! it is horrible!"

"Do not tire yourself too much," observed Mathieu, paternally. "You must be very tired."

"Let me alone," replied the captain, "I feel the want of speaking. Just think that I have not spoken for five years. Then I feel so well—no fatigue, no pain—excitement probably—and tomorrow I shall suffer for it, but today I mean to do what I please."

He smiles, with a fine and thin smile which is far from being one of gaiety, but which has rather the air of an unbending of the nerves of the mouth, which have so long been contracted.

Laugh? How could Captain Dreyfus ever laugh? His life, suddenly overwhelmed under the deluge of adversity and catastrophe, under the terrible chaos of misfortune, will always retain the crushing weight of sadness. His impoverished blood will never again course joyously through his cold veins, and between happiness and him will always intervene the black muslin of melancholy.

Already it sufficed to make sadness suddenly appear in his eyes that a name should be pronounced—that of General Mercier, mentioned by chance in the conversation.

"Mercier," I asked Dreyfus; "what impression did his depositions make upon you?"

Said he sharply: "He is a malicious man and a dishonest man, but I do not think he is conscious of the extent of the evil he has done. He is too intelligent for me to be able to say that he is unconscious, but if he is mentally conscious, he is morally unconscious. He is a man without moral sense."

The train rushes on through the fertile land of this admirable country of the Vendean Bocage. Captain Dreyfus looks at the country.

"How pretty this country is!" he says. "Look at that little village, those cocks, those hens, those fine trees, outlined by the mist! Think that during a year I have seen only the sky and sea, and during four years the sky only, a square of brilliant blue, metallic, hard, and always alike, without a cloud! And, when I came back to France, you know how it was—by night in the midst of a terrible storm, taken from a ship into a boat, from the boat into a carriage, thence into a wagon, to arrive at last at a prison at dawn. So these are the first trees I have seen."

The landscape unfolds itself. Here is a sparkling stream, bordered with poplars, a large wood, fresh and green, more pine spaces out on the slopes. An old woman is washing linen on the banks of a pond. White steeples and red steeples, golden ricks, ruins, a peaceful little village, which seems half in mourning with its white house points and slate roofs, sad meres full of reeds and faded water lilies, and, suddenly, wide barren spaces with a few meager pines and brambles growing between the rocks.

Captain Dreyfus looks at all these as if they were indeed something new to him. He devours them with his eyes.

"I should be as pleased as a child," he says, "to run about in those meadows and amuse myself with nothing. I am like a convalescent coming back to life."

Since the start he had never left off smoking.

"You smoke too much," said his brother.

"Let me smoke; let me talk. It is so long since."

We talk of the death of Scheurer-Kestner. He told us the infinite sorrow he had felt at the thought that he would never be able to thank him, that he would never see the man who had done so much for him, and to whom he owed his liberty. He seemed to dream for a moment. Then he said:

"What fine characters have displayed themselves in this Affair!"

"Have you written many letters since you returned?" I asked.

"None; I have not had time, but now I am going to write those that I ought to write. Think! I have received more than five thousand since my return to France, without counting those that my wife has received on her side—very humble testimonials, besides very high ones. Oh, it has done me good! Officers, even on active service, have written to me and signed their names. One of my comrades in promotion wrote me the simple words, 'Glad at your return; glad at your approaching rehabilitation.' That consoles me for many desertions and for the unexpected hostility of many of my comrades.

"Ah! What I suffered from those depositions in which they came spontaneously to say things which had no connection with the trial, but which they thought might injure me! And, mind you, I do not think it was out of malice against me—no, it was merely to please the chiefs. Ah! there are natures which conserve a very strange idea of duty. Instead of understanding by discipline obedience on the field of battle or in barracks, they extend it to the degradation of reason and moral liberty.

"For me, I never could bend myself to such discipline, and I never could have believed that it was possible for officers to do so."

"How do you explain this animosity against you since 1894 in the offices of the General Staff?"

"I think that the cause of it is rather complex. First, and above all, I was believed to be guilty. It could never have been suspected that they could have plunged so lightheartedly into error. Then there was anti-Semitism in a latent state. Lastly, my manner may perhaps have had something to do with it. Yes, it was rather curt, but only with my chiefs, for, of course, I strove to show as much consideration as possible to my inferiors. I scarcely associated with anyone, and when I entered the General Staff I had paid no visit to anyone. I contented myself with sending cards by my orderly to the chief and subchief of the General Staff and the chief and subchief of my office, and that was all.

"In my dealings with my chiefs I always retained my outspokenness and independence. If a plan or any piece of work seemed to me to be badly conceived, I did not hesitate to say so aloud, instead of considering myself obliged to approve everything in advance, as I saw done all around me, when it was a chief who spoke or acted.

"I know that people don't like that. Colonel Bertin-Mourot said something with deep meaning at Rennes, speaking of that admirable man, that hero, Colonel Picquart. It was felt that this officer did not walk behind the chiefs. That is their psychology and all their morality."

"Walk behind the chiefs as if it were in war or at the maneuvers?"

"Yes, certainly, but when it is a question of honor and duty is there any need to walk behind anyone? Has one not one's own conscience?"

The hour for luncheon was approaching. We reach La Roche-sur-Yonne. They brought us some well-stocked baskets, containing hard-boiled eggs, cold meat, two biscuits, some chocolate, white wine, mineral water, and two little flasks of cinchona and rum. All these were carefully packed in tiny boxes or wrapped up.

Mathieu wanted to prevent Alfred eating the meats. "You know quite well that Delbet forbade you."

"What does it matter for once? Tomorrow I will be good, but to-day is a holiday. Be easy; I feel so well. It is like a new life"—and Mathieu Dreyfus agrees to everything like a good-natured parent to a loved child whom he wishes to restore to health.

The conversation now rolled on everything at haphazard.

"And Esterhazy—what do you think of him?"

In quiet, measured accents, slightly doubtful, even like a savant propounding an hypothesis, he replied:

"I think he is a swindler, a *chevalier d'industrie,* who has swindled his country—it is not even his country—just as he swindled his cousin and his tradesmen, but without in the least realizing that he did so. He wanted money. That was the motive, for," he continued with animation, "for every crime there must be a motive.

"What could it have been in my case? No one ever saw me touch a card, so I was not a gambler. It was said that I had led a fast life. How can you explain, then, that I took the ninth place on leaving the college? Don't people know what arduous work these examinations mean? How can work be allied with debauch?

"General Mercier said that the search for a motive for a crime belonged to the domain of psychology, and that we were on the judicial domain. What does that mean? I was never in the law, but it seems to me that the first thing to be done when one suspects a criminal is to discover the motive for his crime. That is what I call sound sense."

He shrugged his shoulders, and his grave voice rose high in the silence of the stopped train. Then, lowering his voice, he repeated several times, accentuating each word, "Sound sense. Simple, sober sense."

The train started, and the captain went on:

"As to the theory of the court-martial upon the extenuating circumstances, it is just like this: Treason against his country is the greatest crime a human being can commit. A murderer, a thief may find some excuse for themselves; their crime is one against an individual. Treason is a crime against a collectivity. There are no extenuating circumstances. It is a monstrosity."

"What effect did the verdict have upon you?"

The voice was at once lowered, and sadly he said: "It was first of all intense anguish, then stupefaction, then very comforting when I learned that two officers had had the courage to declare me entirely innocent. I swear that those two brave officers were right."

In speaking Dreyfus uses two gestures. When he reasons his thumb and first finger touch, forming a circle. When he is impassioned or carried away his hand opens out with the fingers apart, as in the case of all sincere and frank persons.

His brother now questions him.

"What is exactly the climate over there?"

"Forty to fifty degrees [Centigrade = 104° to 122° Fahrenheit] by day, and never below twenty-five [77° F.] at night. That is the most terrible and most exhausting thing about it, for at a stretch one can bear heat provided one breathes a little fresh air from time to time; there— never."

"And you never knew anything of what was being done in France for you?" I asked.

"Never a word; not a single word. From time to time the rigors were redoubled. I know now that that coincided with the declarations of the Ministers of War. Every time one of them ascended the rostrum and declared that I had been justly and legally condemned, I felt the effects through the medium of my jailers. They cut off my food, or my reading, or my work, or my walk, or the sight of the sea, and, finally, moving about with the aid of the double *boucle*."

M. Mathieu Dreyfus regarded his brother with emotion.

"Is it not awful?" he said. "Happily, we knew nothing about it here, for our efforts would have been hampered thereby. If we had known that every step toward the truth brought him suffering, perhaps our ardor would have been diminished. But what pretext did your jailers give you?"

"None, and I did not ask for any. I did not wish to be beholden to those people in any way. Besides, I did not wish to discuss my sentence or its execution in any way, for to discuss it would have implied to recognize it."

These words were said with extraordinary firmness, almost with harshness.

"Yet one day," he went on, "the day when they put irons on my feet, I asked the reason of the barbarous treatment. They replied, 'Precautionary measure.' It was the day following that when a denial had been given of the bogus attempt to escape.

"Ah, I well remember that night. It was not nine o'clock. I was in bed, when I heard musketry fire and a great commotion all around me; I sat up in bed and cried, 'What is it? Who is there?' No one replied; my guard was silent. I did not stir, thanks to I know not what instinct. It was a good thing I did not, for I should have been instantly shot."

"And so you imagined that General de Boisdeffre was looking after your interests?"

"Yes. I see now that I was mistaken."

"Would you re-enter the Army if legally you had the right?"

"No; I will resign the very evening of my rehabilitation."

"In short, do you think it has been an error or a conspiracy?"

"I think that at the beginning, up to the time of the court-martial of 1894—that is to say, toward the end of this investigation—they believed—at least, the majority of the persons connected with it—that I was guilty, but at the court-martial it was different. I am certain that from that moment, as they felt they had made a mistake, they were afraid of being accused of carelessness, and they accumulated against me all kinds of machinations. The proof of this has been given by Captain Freystaetter.

"They have provided behind my back documents that they knew were false, in order to secure my condemnation. When Captain Freystaetter said this at Rennes, and uttered the words 'Panizzardi dispatch' in his calm tones, I shuddered in all my being. How could they do such a thing as that?"

In telling me this Captain Dreyfus's eyes opened wide with a frightened kind of stare, and he moved toward me as if the better to impress on me the horror that he felt.

I questioned him again:

"You speak in certain letters of your fear of madness. How, indeed, inactive as you were, ill in body and mind, without books and not knowing what your fate would be—how did you succeed in warding off insanity?"

"In 1896 and 1897, as I had resolved to live, I removed from my table the photographs of my wife and children, the sight of whom made me suffer and weakened me. I no longer wished to see them, and I ended by only regarding them as symbols without the human figure, the thought of which unnerved me too much. I did not want to weaken. When one has a duty it must be accomplished to the end, and I wanted to live for my wife and children. It was the same during the trial at Rennes. When I was in so much need of strength—well, I would not re-read my diary of Devil's Island, so as not to unnerve myself and to preserve my energy, for (and he repeated this several times) when one has resolved to do one's duty one must go on to the end."

His fist strikes the seat, giving emphasis to his words.

"Do you know," he continued, "what is most fatiguing in struggles like mine? It is a passive resistance. To have struggled like my brother for five years is indeed exhausting, but at least the effort leads to result. You move, go here and there, cry, but you act; while a passive resistance which mine had to be is more exhausting, and still more depressing because it exacts the effort of every minute in your life without resting a single minute. It is that, together with the lack of fresh air, which has exhausted me most."

"But you must have had terrible nightmares?"

"Oh, yes. I wrote them down in my diary afterward, but I could not recall them at present. When the guard heard me talking aloud in the night he would come to the foot of my bed to listen to my words, in order to report them next day in his report to the governor."

We were nearing Bordeaux. The captain once more looked out on the country.

"Oh, the beautiful vineyards!" he exclaimed, and continuing he said: "It is so sweet, so quieting. When evening falls just see what charm there is about those light mists encircling the trees."

"What are you going to do now, Captain?" I asked.

"To live alone with my wife and children henceforth. My children are my greatest joy on earth. The elder, it seems, remembers me. The girl was only a few months old in 1894, so I do not know her. I did not wish to see them at Rennes in order not to leave the sad impression of the prison on their young minds. One should not darken a child's imagination; but I am going to see them with great joy in two days' time. I want to bring them up myself, and in common with their mother to supervise their instruction and education, because I am opposed to boarding schools.

"When my children were small it was a holiday for me to talk with them, to form them from their earliest age. Unfortunately, events did not permit it, but I hope to catch up."

Bordeaux—Is the journey going to last thus to the end? Not quite.

Alas! the *Gironde* had received from Rennes a dispatch announcing that Captain Dreyfus had left for Nantes, and local men inferred therefrom that he was going to alight at Bordeaux.

Here they are indeed trying to recognize the captain, but we pass quickly through the crowd, and Mathieu Dreyfus alone is recognized. We at once enter the Hotel Terminus, which adjoins the station, and go upstairs for a wash. We are spotted. All the hotel knows about it straightway, as we can tell by the faces of the servants scrutinizing us. Still, we must dine and continue our route. We have the meal served in a salon, and dine with some gaiety under the curious eye of the head-waiter, who is flustered. The captain is in good spirits. He asks me point-blank:

"Do you wish to know my opinion on the *'affaire'*?" and as we all laugh over this outburst, he says to me, half serious, half gay:

"Well, the fact is, I do not yet understand how they could accuse me of such a crime."

The agents of the detective department send us word that they are in waiting. Our tickets are taken for Cette.

The station master is informed that we are going there to embark for Spain, and we hope he will spread the news, in order to lead the curious off the track. But all is in vain. A hundred people are stationed on the quay in front of the Hotel Terminus.

The detectives decide to have us go into the street and go on to the platform by a public entrance, which is now deserted. This is what we do, and the surprised crowd has barely time to see us shut ourselves in our compartments without being able to distinguish the object of its curiosity. Five minutes more we stay there. The crowd does not utter a single cry. What a sign of calmer days!

Then at thirty-eight minutes after seven o'clock the train starts without the shade of a murmur. Fifty yards away a railway employee cries, "Bravo!" while on the other side of the platform a voice cries, "Down with Dreyfus!"

Captain Dreyfus, who hears both cries, makes a reflection worthy of a mathematician that equals things up.

From now on it was known that the train had Captain Dreyfus on board, and calmly stretched out by the side of his brother Mathieu, in a sleeper, the blinds of which were drawn, the captain was trying to sleep for the first time as a free man.

The night passed off well, and when in the morning at five o'clock we saw the captain again, he seemed rested, content and happy, as on the night before, even happier at the approach of the final goal. I have not yet said that this goal was Carpentras, where the Valabregue family owns a beautiful place, well-situated and surrounded by other friendly families, and where Mathieu Dreyfus and Mme. Lucie Dreyfus had decided to shelter the captain directly he was liberated.

The day breaks. The sun rises amid purple clouds on the horizon. I go forward to say farewell to the captain, who is watching the marvelous spectacle through the carriage window. I had a few words from him as to the present state of his mind. He says to me:

"I have been the victim of ideas. I feel no bitterness. I nourish no hatred for those who have wronged me so deeply. I feel only pity for them. What we must know is that never again can such misfortune befall any man."

I ask him: "Are you aware of the intensity of feeling that your misfortune has aroused? You know that people hate you, but you know that there are many others whose hearts have bled for your sufferings."

"I cannot take it myself. I represent in the eyes of sensitive people part of the human suffering, but part only, and I understand perfectly that it is the kindness of my fellow beings which moved them at this symbol that I personify."

"Do you intend to live at Carpentras?"

"Yes, until my health is restored and I have completely rested. I would not go abroad as I was asked to do. The reception I might have had would have had the air of reprisals against the country, and I could not make up my mind."

We had not spoken of the pardon. It was time to do so.

"I did not ask for the pardon," he said, "but I accept it as an acknowledgment of my suffering and that of my wife, for we both need a little respite, but this pardon in no way affects my resolution to seek my rehabilitation. I will not know either insult or menace, but I will know no weakness—I mean mental weakness. Must not the soul dominate over the body?"

Avignon. The train stops. We all get off. In twenty paces we go out of the station. Two landaus are in waiting. A servant takes the luggage. The captain, M. Mathieu Dreyfus, and M. Paul Valabregue get into one carriage, the detective and inspector into the other.

We exchange a last shake of the hand through the window, and the historic procession quickly disappears around the great trees.

Carpentras is twenty kilometers from Avignon. This morning the prefect of Vaucluse telephoned to the mayor of Carpentras to inform him that Captain Dreyfus was within his walls, and to beg him to order police measures to be taken for his security and for keeping order.

The mayor replied that he was sure of the sentiments of the majority of the population in regard to the Valabregue family, and that he would be answerable for quiet and order.

"The Thunderer" Comments on the Release

". . . a plot as base and odious as any recorded in history. . . ."

The Times *(London), September 21, 1899.*

> Commenting on the pardon of Dreyfus, the London *Times,* true
> to its nickname "The Thunderer," denounced France for the "back-
> wardness of her jurisprudence" and "the weakness of her moral
> fibre." Justice was outraged, it said, when an innocent man had to
> slink away under the cover of a "pardon." The root of the mischief,
> contended *The Times,* lay "in the false education of the young in
> France."

The release of Alfred Dreyfus from his long and barbarous captivity
was accomplished yesterday, not as a public act of reparation, but as if it
were something of which the Government that "pardoned" him might
possibly be ashamed. In the early hours of the morning M. Dreyfus was
removed from his prison at Rennes, and, in company with his brother,
who has stood by him so faithfully all through this cruel ordeal, left for a
destination that is at present unknown. The persecution of an innocent
man—practically declared to be so by the inept judgment of the Rennes
court-martial and by the action of the chief of State—has thus been
exhibited, at last, to the world in its scandalous unrighteousness. It began
in illegal methods of procedure, adopted, as the inquiry at Rennes has
shown, to secure the conviction of the accused, and carried out by illegal
methods of physical and moral torture from which even medieval brutality might have recoiled. It is to be hoped, for the sake of France herself,
that the victim of a plot as base and odious as any recorded in history will
now have at least a chance of recovering a certain measure of health and
strength in retirement and seclusion. Whether or not M. Dreyfus will
proceed to an appeal before the Court of Cassation for the annulling of
the Rennes verdict we cannot say. The moral effect of that pitiable
decision has already been destroyed, not only by the force of public
opinion, but by the resolution of the French Government not to act
upon it. At the same time it is felt that justice is outraged when an
innocent man has to slink away under cover of a "pardon," while the
vile conspirators who did their best to send him back to Devil's Island
are even now swaggering about in their uniforms and their cassocks as if
they had the fortunes of France in their polluted hands.

France will bitterly regret the apathy with which she has treated the
most abominable of crimes, the systematic perversion of justice to secure
the ruin of an individual. She has displayed the backwardness of her

jurisprudence and the weakness of her moral fiber. In an interesting letter Sir Herbert Stephen points out that France is still in the stage out of which this country passed hundreds of years ago, when a trial was based, not on evidence, but on "compurgation." Unfortunately, the moral basis of compurgation, the truthful backing of a man by his honest neighbors, does not exist in a corrupt modern society.

The effect of what has been said and done at Rennes on the minds of independent foreigners is strikingly shown in a letter from M. Zakrevsky, a well-known Russian jurist and a member of the Imperial Senate, which is the High Court of the Empire. M. Zakrevsky has studied the proceedings at Rennes, and is appalled to see what they mean. The conclusion he draws from "this unheard-of spectacle" is that "modern French society has definitely fallen from the rank it occupied among civilized peoples. Where the sentiment of justice is atrophied by the intensity of political and religious passions grafted on to a monstrous national vanity passing itself off for patriotism, there is, I contend, no room left for the moral elements indispensable to a well-ordered form of society." Nor will M. Zakrevsky admit that only the five unjust judges of Rennes and their chiefs should be held responsible "for the iniquitous acts which have revolted the whole world." He dwells, not without force, on the lamentable want of moral courage displayed by the nation. "Take one instance amongst many. See how men who call themselves statesmen, who belong to the cream of society, like the Casimir-Périers, the Freycinets, when called upon to give evidence, to tell the whole truth, instead of throwing light upon important facts, are content to fence, or make oracular speeches. They think above all of themselves; their chief anxiety is not to depreciate their own value in the eyes of their great audience,—i.e., of the country which listens to them." Just as little does the Russian jurist mince his words concerning the motives which have led France to seek the alliance of his own country: "Unable in her vanity and thirst for prestige to recognize in her defeats of 1870–71 all that was irremediable and even just, protesting that she would never accept the Treaty of Frankfort as final, prating of her re-vindications, of her hopes, without venturing to strike a blow, France has gradually cut herself adrift in the helplessness of political disorder from the other Western nations, to which, with their great liberal traditions, the ties of centuries united her, and she has sunk amorously into the arms of Russia, of a country which represents and practices more than ever principles entirely opposed to those which France boasts of holding. From the Russian alliance she has inevitably and logically drifted into anti-Semitism, into anti-Protestantism, into oppression of the weak, into a recrudescence of brutal militarism, and, finally, into the Dreyfus Affair, crowned by the proceedings at Rennes."

No critics in this country or elsewhere have written anything so cruel and crushing as these and other even more uncomplimentary messages, for which we prefer to refer our readers to the French text. Yet it is plain that these views, so decidedly in unison with those of the great majority of Germans, Austrians, and Italians, as well as of Englishmen and Americans, are shared by Russians of every school. M. Zakrevsky is a Liberal; but a very eminent representative of old Russian ideas, M. Pobiedonostzeff, the Procurator of the Holy Synod, has come to the same conclusion about the Dreyfus case. He has said that "for all impartial observers the proceedings at Rennes proved the innocence of Captain Dreyfus," and has expressed his agreement with the contention of *The Times,* borne out by many independent testimonies, that the root of the mischief lies in the false education of the young in France. Even the most rabid anti-Dreyfusards will hardly contend, we suppose, that the Russians have also joined the great "cosmopolitan syndicate of treason."

Public Reaction to Dreyfus's Freedom

"There is some soul of goodness in things evil."

Quoted in Pierre Dreyfus, The Dreyfus Case, *trans. and ed. Donald C. McKay (Yale University Press, 1937), pp. 269–272. By permission of Curtis Brown, Ltd.*

The Rennes trial had a strong emotional impact upon people throughout the world, including celebrities. Among the vast correspondence after the Rennes trial were the two letters selected here, both written in English. The first was sent by the famed Australian soprano Nellie Melba to Mme. Dreyfus. The second was written by Mark Twain to his publisher recommending a procedure to restore Dreyfus's health and asking that Mr. Chatto and M. Zola convey the message to Mme. Dreyfus by translation or otherwise.

1

From Nellie Melba to Mme. Dreyfus

Hotel Ritz, September 23, 1899

Dear Madame:

I feel the impulse to address a few words to you to be quite irresistible. I am sharing with you so deeply the joy of the freedom of your beloved husband that I find my eyes continually filling with tears. For many months, nay years, I have followed your fortunes and his with the same intensity of emotion. This is needless to say—I have but shared the sympathetic interest of many millions. But I often wonder if any of the others shared the experience which I am about to relate to you. It was this: When in 1894 I read, with horror, the details of the degradation the thought came to me *What if he be innocent?* That thought came to stay—to remain in my mind with a strange insistence which grew into a positive, but purely instinctive belief, that a hideous blunder, or a hideous crime, had been committed. With a mind so possessed, you will well imagine, dear Madame, with what a passionate interest I have followed the later developments of your husband's case; have hoped and despaired with you, have wept and prayed with you. And now that an end is reached—an end which although legally unsatisfying, is rich with consolation in that you and your children have the beloved sufferer once more with you; that he is free to God's sky and air, and that in the hearts of the righteous and the womb of history, he is pure and great because of a martyrdom *nobly borne*—I ask you to accept the kiss of felicitation and to forgive me for unburdening to you my overcharged heart. I have said there are millions who feel as I do. One meets them everywhere; and their eyes will once more have been dim with tears as mine were this morning when I read an article describing the family group at Carpentras, in which was said "Every face is serene; in every eye at last a gleam of happiness; the mouths do not cease smiling" and again these quite simple, but how pregnant words "the children will be there tomorrow with their grandparents." When a great trouble comes to us in our lives we ask "Why was it sent?" You Madame need not ask that question. Your affliction was sent to prove the eternal truth of Shakespeare's words "There is some soul of goodness in things evil." The dew of a universal sympathy had not fallen upon the earth for very long. Human love seemed dead. It only slept! It awoke with a great cry at the spectacle of your husband's unmerited sufferings; his dauntless endurance; the tenacious persistency and titanic championship of truth of those friends whose self-sacrifice and heroism will never be blotted from the pages of history, and of your own unexampled devotion, patience and dignity; and it hovers reverently around you even now that your Beloved is at last at rest in the arms of unfathomable love.

> With many tender sentiments
> Believe me dear Madame
> Yours sincerely,
> NELLIE MELBA

2

FROM MARK TWAIN TO HIS PUBLISHER

Sanna, Sept. 24/99

DEAR MR. CHATTO,

Many people will write Madame Dreyfus and tell her of many sure ways to bring back health and strength to her husband. The good will that is at the back of the act saves it from being an unjustifiable intrusion. I wish to add myself to that list of unknown well-wishers, and ask you if you cannot, through M. Zola, get Madame Dreyfus to consider the idea of entrusting to Mr. Kellgreu (49, Eaton Square, S.W.) the restoration of Captain Dreyfus's health.

I have now spent twenty minutes every morning for the past ten weeks in Kellgreu's workroom (here) watching him perform upon his patients; experimenting with the treatment myself; observing the effects of the treatment upon my wife and two daughters; talking with the patients; asking questions of Kellgreu and his assistants—and making written notes (to the extent of 7,000 words); and as a result I am now satisfied that Kellgreu can cure any disease that any physician can cure, and that in many desperate cases he can restore health where no physician can do it, and where no physician will claim to be able to do it. He does not profess to do miracles, and the things he does are not miracles— they only seem so, until one has familiarized himself with the principles upon which his method is based; then they are recognizable as the logical and arbitrary outcome of natural laws, with no taint of miracle about them. He does not make extravagant promises, but he *makes* promises, and if the patient stays the allotted time, he makes the promise good. Years ago, when Nathaniel Rothschild of Vienna came to him after vainly submitting his shattered nervous system to the baths and specialists for years, he presently got tired and was going to leave, and Kellgreu said, "Then you will waste years again, and not get cured; if you stay here I will cure you; if you go uncured, it can bring an unmerited discredit upon my system, through the authority of your name; therefore, I say to you this, and it is worth considering: that if you go I will never touch your case again, for any money." Rothschild remained and was cured.

Then Rothschild said, "But now that I have been made well without medicines, I shall never be willing to have a doctor again, and what shall I do? I cannot cross Europe to come to you every time there is something the matter with me; since you will not leave London, you must give me one of your assistants."

It is what happens to Kellgreu—that kind of ill-luck: the rich man takes his pupils away (as Rothschild did) and leaves him shorthanded. Four or five members of the Rothschild family have been patients of Kellgreu—two London ones and a Frankfort one among the number— and if Madame Dreyfus should wish to apply to them for testimony, I will furnish you their names and addresses. Also, the London address of Mr. Cohen, whose daughter has been under treatment here these past ten weeks. Also the addresses of the other patients here if desired: they all want to testify—among them Miss Schuhmann (bad heart disease);

she is the daughter of *the* Schuhmann; among them also, Frau von Kopff of Bremen (bad heart disease) given up by the Berlin physicians 12 years ago, and set on her feet by Kellgreu, and kept in good condition ever since. He cannot *cure* her, but with two months treatment per year he enables her to climb mountains. I have climbed them with her. Also the address of an English clergyman whose daughter (dying of galloping consumption 9 years ago and given up by the physicians) Kellgreu saved, and she has been strong and well ever since. Also my wife can testify, and you know that she is not a flighty person, but has a thoughtful and well-balanced head. (She will edit this letter, and see that it has no exaggerations in it; the one I wrote last night she edited into the fire.)

Sincerely Yours
(Signed) S. L. CLEMENS

P.S. It was Frau von Kopff (mentioned above) who put this fortunate (as I regard it) idea into my head. Her heart, like the hearts of all the world, is with that wronged man and his heroic wife, and she came to me with the tears in her eyes and asked if there was no way to get this message to Madame Dreyfus. "She should know about Kellgreu," she said; "You know, twelve years ago he raised me from the dead." Those were her words. Do you know that old American friend of the German Emperor's and mine—Poultney Bigelow, 5 Oakley Street, Chelsea, and Reform Club? He can tell you what Kellgreu did for him when he was dying of dysentery and had been given up by the physicians; also, he can explain the Kellgreu system to you. The Prince of Wales wanted to call Kellgreu when he burst his knee in Rothschild's house—the doctors defeated it.

Truly Yours,
(Signed) MARK TWAIN

Cannot you and M. Zola get this conveyed to Madame Dreyfus, by translation or otherwise?

Consoling Words from Picquart and Clemenceau

". . . this terrible nightmare has finally come to an end."

Alfred Dreyfus, Souvenirs et correspondance, publiés par son fils *(Paris: Grossett, 1936), Appendix. Translated by the editor.*

Among the letters which Dreyfus received following his pardon were two of special importance to him, one from Picquart, his defender in the Army, and one from Clemenceau, his advocate in the press and courtroom.

1

FROM GEORGES PICQUART

Paris, October 20, 1899

MY DEAR DREYFUS:

I am happy, indeed, to learn that you are now with your family, and to realize that this terrible nightmare has finally come to an end.

Until that was done, it seemed to me that I was associated with your persecutors in a kind of complicity, and I could not rest until I saw you free.

There remains now only a formality, as you have been vindicated as no one ever was; you have been vindicated by the voice of the whole world.

Tous mes respects à Mme. Dreyfus et bien à vous.

G. PICQUART

2

FROM GEORGES CLEMENCEAU

Paris, October 15, 1899

Cher Monsieur:

Let me hasten to thank you warmly for your good letter. Fighting for you was simply to fight for France. The good people who have rallied to your cause have won in advance, no matter what happens to them, the most precious reward, in the feeling that they have performed their duty. May this work already begun be completed and may we deliver our unfortunate country from the insane men who confuse her and lead her to the brink of ruin.

You have taken a cruel share in this terrible drama. I do hope with all my heart that life will provide for you the compensations due to you. Your noble brother Mathieu and your admirable wife will help in this task. You are still quite young. Please work for those great ideals which, whatever may be said by the beasts, form the best part of the French nation.

Most cordially yours

G. CLEMENCEAU

Dreyfus Protests Against the Amnesty Bill, 1900

"*I beseech the Senate to leave intact my right to truth and justice.*"

Quoted in Pierre Dreyfus, The Dreyfus Case, *p. 146. By permission of Curtis Brown, Ltd.*

Shortly after Dreyfus was released, the Government introduced an Amnesty Bill, which was designed to extinguish all prosecutions and suits connected with the case. On December 2, 1899, Dreyfus sent a letter of protest to M. Clamageran, Chairman of the Amnesty Committee of the Senate. Early in March 1900 the Amnesty Committee was directed by the Government to accelerate the preparation of the bill. At this point Dreyfus wrote another letter of protest to the Chairman of the Committee.

Carpentras, March 8, 1900

In the presence of the bill which has just been laid before the Senate, it is my duty to renew the protest which I had the honor to direct to you last December, when the question of an amnesty was introduced.

The bill extinguishes prosecutions and suits, from which I had hoped revelations, perhaps confessions, would result. These would have enabled me to appeal to the Court of Cassation the unjust decision of which I have once again been the victim.

The bill thus deprives me of my most cherished hope, that of having my innocence legally proclaimed—innocence so evident and so manifest that the Government of the Republic made it a point of honor to prevent the execution of the judgment of September 9, 1899. Indeed it destroyed this judgment, upon the proposal of the Minister of War himself, on the very day following that on which it had been pronounced. I asked no pardon. The right of the innocent is justice, not clemency.

The liberty given me I prized above all, because I thought that it would facilitate my campaign for reparation of the shocking wrong of which I was the victim.

I will go so far, Mr. President, as to ask the eminent jurists of the Senate this question: if the amnesty is voted and the suits and prosecutions are extinguished, what legal means are left me to obtain an appeal?

The writers who have been proceeded against, and who are relying upon their trials to bring new facts to light, have protested in the name of that truth which is once more being suppressed.

I protest still more bitterly, in the name of justice, against a measure which leaves me disarmed in the face of iniquity.

No one wishes more ardently than I for peace, for the reconciliation of all good Frenchmen, for the end of the shocking virulence of which I was the first victim. The amnesty strikes me to the quick. It benefits only scoundrels who abused the good faith of the judges; who knowingly had an innocent man condemned through lies, perjury, and forgery; and who cast me into the abyss.

This amnesty will redound to the exclusive profit of General Mercier, the principal author of the crime of 1894, who, by a strange irony of fate, will be called upon, as a Senator, to vote in his own interest.

I beseech the Senate to leave intact my right to truth and justice.

Dreyfus's protest was seconded by Picquart and Zola among others. Picquart insisted upon the insufficiency of the charges against himself: "It would grant me an amnesty for an offense which I did not commit." He was determined not to be involved in the same bill with General Mercier and others of the General Staff. Zola spoke of the necessity of recalling the national conscience from the shadows into which it had been plunged. The discussion of the bill began in the Senate on June 1, 1900. Despite the efforts of several Senators, the bill was adopted by the Senate and in December by the Chamber of Deputies. The law closed to Dreyfus many avenues leading to an appeal of his case.

Dreyfus Appeals to the Prince of Monaco for Assistance
"Will not General von Schwartzkoppen now finally do his duty?"

Pierre Dreyfus, The Dreyfus Case, *pp. 163–164. By permission of Curtis Brown, Ltd.*

While the Chamber was discussing the Amnesty Bill, Dreyfus, who had never forgotten what had become the goal of his life, decided to seek help in convincing Schwartzkoppen to disclose the truth. On October 30, 1898, Prince Albert of Monaco had written a letter to Mme. Dreyfus in which he spoke of his admiration for her husband. "I have never ceased to defend Captain Dreyfus against acts of cowardice and stupidity. . . . I offer to you, whom I know only through your suffering, this token of my admiration, and I hope that your children will live to forget the cruel dream they have known as they grew. . . . Later they will learn to know their father's heart, revealed by a cry of distress unjustly suffered."

Encouraged by this friendly note, Dreyfus sent the following letter to the Prince of Monaco intimating that he would like to have assistance in convincing Schwartzkoppen to change his mind. There is no record of a reply by the Prince of Monaco. In any event it was fruitless: at this time Schwartzkoppen remained deaf to all entreaties.

Paris, December 7, 1900

On the occasion of my return to Paris, permit me to send you once again the expression of my appreciation and of my feeling of profound gratitude for the interest which you have taken in the cause of justice and truth.

Yours is a spirit too elevated not to make you sensible of how much sadness and pain there is still in my life.

To be sure, I have been given my liberty. I am with my family once again after so many years of terrible separation. I have found many friends united beneath the banner of truth and justice.

But I lived through five years of horrible torture only for my honor. I endured it all only that I might cleanse my name—the name which my children bear—of the shameful stain which has been placed upon it.

But the moral stigma of that injustice still remains, a situation as hateful for my children as for myself. I am insulted with impunity and my name is dragged in the mire, because legally I am a convict. I am the moral prisoner of this terrible situation; my hands are tied by it. It is improbable that the prosecutions and suits already begun will come to court, that testimony can then be taken by commissions of inquiry, and that new evidence will thus come to light which would enable me to request an appeal of my case. Hence the present situation may continue indefinitely.

Will not General von Schwartzkoppen now finally do his duty? Is it not time that he should tell the truth, the whole truth? Will not his conscience influence him to go to the French Embassy in Berlin, and there state the truth under oath?

For him who knows the truth, it is a duty not only before history, which will judge us all, but a duty to humanity, even more a duty to his conscience, to disclose that truth. It is for General von Schwartz-koppen to put his conscience at rest by making a deposition in the presence of the French Ambassador in Berlin, with supporting proofs of the crime committed by another, and among them the documents named in the *bordereau*. These will then enable me to resubmit my case on appeal to the Court of Cassation.

I hope that he who has the truth will finally accomplish the sacred duty which is incumbent upon him.

Zola's Tragic Death: Funeral Oration by Anatole France

". . . in him at one moment was set the conscience of mankind!"

Translated in Ernest A. Vizetelly, Émile Zola, Novelist and Reformer (London and New York: John Lane, 1904), pp. 520–522.

On the morning of September 29, 1902, Émile Zola was found dead in the bedroom of his Paris home. It was a terrible accident— the great novelist had been asphyxiated by the fumes from a defective flue. Mme. Zola, whose life had been spared, requested Dreyfus not to come to the funeral because she feared that his presence would give rise to hostile demonstrations. Dreyfus reluctantly gave his word, but Mme. Zola later changed her mind and asked him to attend.

Anatole France delivered an impassioned and eloquent oration at the grave. The speaker, who had testified for Zola at the latter's trial, placed special emphasis on Zola's role in the Dreyfus case.

Having to recall the struggle upon which Zola entered in the cause of truth and justice, is it possible for me to preserve silence respecting those who were bent on ruining the cause of an innocent man, those who felt that if he should be saved, they would be lost, and who with all the desperate audacity of fear therefore strove to overwhelm him? How can I remove them from your gaze, when I have to show you Zola rising, weak and unarmed, before them? Can I remain silent about their lies? That would mean silence as to his heroic rectitude. Can I remain silent about their crimes? That would mean silence as to his virtues. Can I remain silent about the outrages and slanders with which they pursued him? That would mean silence as to his reward and honors. Can I remain silent about their shame? That would mean silence as to his glory. No! I will speak out.

With the calmness and firmness which the spectacle of death imparts, I will recall the dim days when egotism and fear had their seats in the government councils. People were beginning to know something of the iniquity, but it was supported, defended, by such public and secret powers that the most resolute hesitated. Those whose duty it was to speak out, remained silent. Some of the best, who feared nothing personally, dreaded lest they should involve their party in frightful dangers. Led astray by monstrous lies, excited by odious declamation, the multitude of the people, believing they were betrayed, grew exasperated. . . . The darkness thickened. Sinister silence reigned. And it was then that Zola addressed to the President of the Republic that well-measured, yet terrible, letter which denounced falsity and collusion.

With what fury was he assailed by the criminals, by their interested defenders, by their involuntary accomplices, by coalitions of all the reactionary parties, by the deceived multitude, you know that full well. You saw innocently-minded people joining in all simplicity the hideous cortege of hireling brawlers. You heard the howls of rage and the cries of death which pursued him even into the *Palais de Justice* during that long trial when he was judged in voluntary ignorance, or false testimony, amid the clatter of swords. I see here some of those who then stood beside him, who shared his dangers. Let them say too with what firmness he endured it! Let them say if his robust kindliness, his manly pity, ever deserted him, if his constancy was for a moment shaken! In those abominable days more than one good citizen despaired of the salvation of the country, of the moral fortune of France. Not only were the Republicans defending the present régime terrified, but one of the most resolute enemies of the régime, an irreconcilable Socialist, exclaimed bitterly, "If present-day society be so corrupt as this, one will not even be able to found a new society on its fragments!" Indeed, justice, honor, common sense, all seemed lost.

But all was saved. Zola had not merely revealed a judicial error, he had denounced the conspiracy of all the forces of violence and oppression leagued together to slay social justice, Republicanism, freedom of thought in France. His courageous words awoke the country. The consequences of his deed are incalculable. They unroll themselves today in power and majesty, they spread out indefinitely, they have determined a movement of social equity which will not stop. A new order of things is arising, based on a better sense of justice, on a deeper knowledge of the rights of all.

Gentlemen, there is only one country in the world where such great things could have been accomplished. How beautiful is the genius of our Fatherland! How beautiful is that soul of France which in past centuries taught equity to Europe and the world! France is the land of ornate reason and kindly thoughts, the land of equitable magistrates and humane philosophers, the land of Turgot, of Montesquieu, of Voltaire, of Malesherbes. And Zola deserved well of the country by refusing to despair of justice in France. We must not pity him for having endured and suffered. Let us rather envy him! Set above the most prodigious heap of outrages ever raised by folly, ignorance, and malice, his glory attains to inaccessible heights. Let us envy him: he honored his country and the world by immense literary work and by a great deed. Let us envy him: his destiny and his heart gave him the grandest fate: in him at one moment was set the conscience of mankind!

André's Inquiry, 1903

". . . important documents favorable to the prisoner were not produced. . . ."

Quoted in Kayser, The Dreyfus Affair, p. 382.

On May 28, 1900, General de Galliffet resigned as Minister of War and was succeeded by General L. J. N. André, a zealous Republican. Approached directly by Dreyfus, André decided to undertake an inquiry on behalf of the Government. Hoping to find evidences of Dreyfus's guilt in the secret *dossier,* he was astonished to find documents favorable to Dreyfus. Assisted by Captain Targe, his aide-de-camp, he gathered a large amount of material and concluded his inquiry with a report to the Premier on October 19, 1903. Following is an excerpt from that report.

I am convinced that the Army should pledge its honor in order that the truth may finally emerge and that the uneasiness which has been aroused in so many consciences by the decision admitting extenuating circumstances in a case of high treason may at last be dispelled.

The Ministry for War intervened in the trial at Rennes by producing the so-called "secret" *dossier*. The Ministry had compiled this *dossier*. It was said before the judges and commented on by a general specially appointed by the Minister. It was, therefore, the work of the Ministry for War itself that was laid bare before the court. I have personally examined all the documents in our archives, some of which have been used in compiling the secret *dossier*. I have thus been able to ascertain that important documents favorable to the prisoner were not produced and that, on the other hand, certain documents in the *dossier* have been subjected either to material alterations or to erroneous comments which have distorted their meaning. Incorrect statements have been made to the court by officers and by the Government Commissary.

André then went on to give a systematic statement of the facts surrounding his conclusion. It was a full and objective report that was to be of some importance in the final disposition of the case.

Dreyfus's Request for an Appeal, 1903

"My condemnation . . . was . . . the product of forgeries and lies."

Alfred Dreyfus, Souvenirs et correspondance, *Appendix VI. Translated by the editor.*

On November 25, 1903, just five weeks after Minister of War André's report on the results of his inquiry, Dreyfus applied to M. Vallé, Keeper of the Seals, Minister of Justice, for a revision. He mentioned in particular the false evidence given by Eugene de Cernuschi, an Austrian refugee and witness for the prosecution, who appeared at the Rennes court-martial on September 6, 1899, toward the close of the proceedings. Heard *in camera,* Cernuschi, who claimed to be a retired Austrian officer descended from an ancient Serbian dynasty, stated that one of his friends in the Ministry for Foreign Affairs of a Central European state informed him that Dreyfus was a spy, and that his information had been confirmed by an officer on the General Staff "of another Central European state." In addition, he claimed to have seen a number of documents sent by Dreyfus. Taken by surprise, the defense lawyers investigated Cernuschi's background and found that he was a confidence man who had committed frauds throughout Europe, and that he was probably mentally deranged. Cernuschi, who was supposed to appear in court to repeat his accusations under oath, suddenly pleaded illness and refused to return to the trial. Dreyfus also mentioned new evidence concerning statements by Schwartzkoppen, Panizzardi, and Münster.

To the Keeper of the Seals, Minister of Justice, November 25, 1903

Monsieur le Ministre:

I have the honor to request of your Justice a review of the decision of the court-martial at Rennes, which, on September 9, 1899, by a majority of 5 votes to 2, found me guilty "with extenuating circumstances."

This verdict, inexplicable after the decision of the full bench of the Court of Cassation of June 3, 1899, was made on the basis of forged documents and perjury. New evidence shows that I was condemned for the second time though obviously innocent.

During the debates in the Chamber of Deputies on April 6 and 7, 1903, Deputy Jaurès proved that a bare-faced forgery had pressed on the conscience of several of the judges. This forgery is a document supposed to have been written by the German Kaiser, and it was said to have been used without the knowledge of the defense, which did not know of its existence.

On April 21, 1903, I had the honor to direct to the Minister of War, administrative head of the departments concerned with military matters, a request for an inquiry on the serious errors committed at my expense in the department under his direction.

The results of this inquiry, to which I cannot be refused access, have not yet been made known to me, but I have reason to believe that they positively justify the appeal which I am now asking.

The Minister of War, to whom my request will certainly be transmitted, will not fail to inform you of the results of the inquiry which he undertook in response to my request dated April 21, 1903.

In addition to the decisive results of this inquiry, a review is justified by the following points:

Perjury and Forgery

Perjury of Cernuschi: One Cernuschi, a new witness called to Rennes by agents of the prosecution, stated that he had learned from an Austrian Aulic Councilor [the Aulic Council directed the Austrian Army during the

Empire], Dr. Mosetig, that I was a spy in the employ of Germany. That this was false is demonstrated by an authentic statement of Dr. Mosetig, which I appended to my request for an inquiry on April 21, 1903.

In that request I stated to the Minister of War the important revelations of a certain Wessel concerning plots in which agents of the Intelligence Department and the perjured witnesses were embroiled. These revelations are confirmed by a memorandum by Wessel to his lawyer, Raimondo, sent along to Maître Mornard, and appended to this letter. In addition, they are also confirmed by a letter written by Mme. Wessel to M. Gabriel Monod, forwarded by the latter to the Minister of War.

Perjuries of Savignaud and Gribelin: Savignaud was a witness recruited by the prosecution to counteract the testimony of Lieutenant-Colonel Picquart, who had discovered the blunder made by the judges in 1894 and the machinations directed against me.

The Archivist Gribelin had been summoned to give evidence in a similar manner.

Savignaud's perjury is revealed by letters of M. Scheurer-Kestner and Maître Leblois. Gribelin has admitted his own perjury.

Forgeries: The secret *dossier* used against me contained documents that had been altered. In addition, those who used them must have known that they were false.

The document attributed to Kaiser Wilhelm the existence of which was explicitly recognized in a letter of M. Ferlet de Bourbonne, is a forgery. The letters sent by Dr. Dumas to Maître Mornard, and transmitted by my lawyer to the Ministry of War, show how this document was utilized at the Rennes trial.

New Evidence

Colonel von Schwartzkoppen and Colonel Panizzardi, who were, according to the prosecution, the Military Attachés to whom I was charged with giving secret documents, have both admitted that they never had any relations at all with me.

A letter from Colonel Chauvet of the Swiss Army to Professor Andrade, sent by M. Andrade to the Minister of Justice, Monis, subsequent to the Rennes trial, repeats the solemn statements of Herr von Schwartzkoppen.

Herr von Schwartzkoppen's words of honor that he never had any relations with me, either direct or indirect, was also made known to the prosecution, but they concealed it from my judges. The Minister of War has proofs of it in his records.

Also a letter from Count von Münster to M. Joseph Reinach contains the very same affirmations and showed for the first time that Colonel von Schwartzkoppen had admitted to his Ambassador that the man who brought him information was Esterhazy, and that their relations went all the way back to 1893. I am appending to this request this letter, which appeared in the *Temps* on April 25, 1903, and which the recipient was good enough to give to me.

Concerning Colonel Panizzardi, the telegram so often spoken about in the trial would have had a decisive effect on the minds of the judges, if the prosecution had not tried by illegal means to falsify it during the decoding. In addition, the Minister of War at that moment had documents concealed by my accusers and proving that the spy who was Colonel Panizzardi's informant continued his relations with the latter after I was arrested.

My condemnation, extracted with such difficulty from judges who gave expression to their doubts by admitting "extenuating circumstances," was, therefore, the product of forgeries and lies.

I ask for a revision of my trial for the sake of my children and for my own sake, and because I have never failed in any of my duties as a soldier and as a Frenchman.

Please accept, *Monsieur le Ministre,* this assurance of my deep respect.

The Keeper of the Seals, in response to this request, made an inquiry of his own, and then, supported by the unanimous recommendation of a commission appointed to consider the case, officially brought the matter to the attention of the Court of Cassation. The final vindication came on July 13, 1906, when the Senate and Chamber of Deputies passed bills reinstating and promoting Dreyfus and Picquart in their Army posts.

The Ceremony of Rehabilitation Described by Dreyfus

"My heart was beating as though it would break . . ."

Dreyfus's account: translated by the editor.

On July 20, 1906, in a military ceremony held on the grounds of the *École Militaire,* Dreyfus was rehabilitated. About twelve years earlier, on nearby ground, he had undergone the act of degradation while a mob shouted insults as he protested his innocence. Now, in a dignified and solemn ritual, his rank was restored and troops passed in review before him. His own account reveals how his mind was brought back to the past at this moment of triumph.

On the afternoon of July 20 (1906), my stripes were restored to me in a ceremony that took place in the courtyard of the Artillery quarters at the *École Militaire*. The setting of the *Cour Desjardins*, with its ancient grey walls, was unchanged since the time when I was a lieutenant in the mounted battery at the *École Militaire*. For this ceremony of rehabilitation they did not select the setting nearby, the great courtyard of the *École Militaire*, where about twelve years earlier the first horrible degradation had taken place. I had asked for this, because I was afraid that the emotion aroused by my memories would be greater than my strength, and that in the end it would conquer my courage.

At half-past one the troops that were to carry out the ceremony, two mounted batteries and two squadrons of the First Cuirassiers, took place in lines parallel to the three sides of the court. In command was Lieutenant-Colonel Gaillard-Bournazel of the First Cuirassiers. A blast of trumpets sounded at five minutes before two. General Gillain, Commander of the First Cavalry Division, an officer of military bearing and white moustache, entered the courtyard on foot and quickly passed before the troops. The silence was heavy and impressive. Amidst this silence my mind, bewildered, went back to memories of twelve years—the way the mob howled, the horrible ceremony, my stripes torn unjustly from my uniform, my sword broken and lying in pieces at my feet. . . . My heart was beating as though it would break, my blood surged to my temples, my forehead was bathed in perspiration. . . .

The command: *"Ouvrez le ban!"* awakened me from my painful dreaming and served to bring me back to the reality of the moment, the ritual of rehabilitation. General Gillain, with a nice flourish, drew his sword, and then presented the cross of Officer of the Legion of Honor to Major Targe. The act was completed with drum and bugle, which sounded immediately again to begin the ceremony for me. As General Gillain uttered the usual formula, his voice was shaken with emotion, and, as he pinned the decoration on me, he said in a gentle tone of voice: "Major Dreyfus, it gives me great pleasure to present this insignia to you. I know what fine memories the First Cavalry Division has had of you." He then embraced me warmly, and his eyes were moist.

Then the troops took up a position in close formation at the rear. The command "Forward march!" rang out. With the Lieutenant-Colonel at their head, and preceded by trumpets, the troops passed in review before General Gillain, Major Targe, and myself. The officers saluted with their sabers as they marched by. The brasses were distinct and clear on this joyful day.

The troops were gone. At once I was surrounded. There were cries of *"Vive Dreyfus!"* *"Non!"* I exclaimed: *"Vive la République, vive la vérité!"* Many eager hands reached toward me. I shook them warmly and embraced all my friends. The whole scene was so moving that I find it difficult to describe it in words. . . .

In his turn Anatole France came toward me, and said: "I am most happy and much moved. I just do not know how I can praise enough the constancy you have shown through so much trouble. Your constancy has allowed us to fulfill the work of justice and satisfaction, all crowned today in this solemn ceremony. Let me shake your hand and say no more."

I then embraced my son, my wife, and members of my family. These were happy greetings, indeed, from the ones I loved and for whom I had had the courage to live.

I sought out especially Colonel Picquart, who was there, and he shook my hand warmly. I told him of my deep gratitude, and repeated it to M. Badouin, who was there, too. But all this was a bit too much for me. I had a brief fainting spell brought on by a slight heart disturbance from which I suffered. As soon as I felt better, I drove off with Georges Bourdon, of *Le Figaro*, and my son.

What a splendid day of restitution this was for France and the Republic!

The "Last Days" of Esterhazy

"I have to work to pay my way."

Philadelphia Press, *February 17, 1908.*

Interviewers who came to see him in London found Esterhazy unrepentant and self-pitying. He attempted to give the impression that he was living his last days in extreme poverty. He emphasized that idea to a reporter for the Philadelphia *Press,* who interviewed him in 1908. Esterhazy lived on in exile for fifteen more years. He died in 1923. Above his grave in the village of Harpenden appears the name "Comte Jean de Voilement."

London, Feb. 16. Major Ferdinand Esterhazy, who, through false use of evidence, caused Captain Dreyfus five years of shame and imprisonment as a traitor to his country, has been found in an attic at 116 St. James Terrace, Warwick Ave., where he is dying, alone and in poverty.

Quite a recluse, and cut off from the world except for his own intimate circle of friends, he is now living under the title of Comte de Voilement.

He was found recently bundled up in an old armchair and clad in a well-worn light brown overcoat over the fire seeking to get warmth for his thin attenuated frame. The gray-bearded old man, with hair prematurely silvered and shoulders bowed, looks what he is—an outcast from society, whose only desire is to be left alone and to eke out his own life.

Answering an interviewer, he said:

"Have I a pension from the Brazilian Government? I wish that were true. I have not a penny beyond what I earn. I don't deny that I am Esterhazy. Why should I? The name I have now belongs to my family. In the old days the French Government used to open all the letters addressed to me as Esterhazy in London. So I assumed my present name.

"My memoirs? I would like to write them had I the time and the money. But I cannot stop my other work, or my income would stop. I have to work to pay my way."

It is interesting to note that the body of Zola, author of the famous letter "J'Accuse," which ultimately brought about Esterhazy's confession and Dreyfus's later vindication and reinstatement in the French Army, is about to be placed in the Panthéon.

Dreyfus Shot at the Tomb of Zola

"My blow was aimed less at Dreyfus than at Dreyfusism."

Philadelphia Ledger, *June 5, 1908.*

On June 4, 1908, a solemn act of homage was paid when, by order of the French Parliament, the ashes of Zola were transferred to the Panthéon, last resting place of the great men of France. It was a fitting tribute. "Men have been known," said Clemenceau on this occasion, "to oppose the most powerful of kings; but few have been known to oppose the mob, to stand face to face with the misguided multitude, excited to the worst excesses of fury; to challenge implacable rage, weaponless, and with folded arms: to dare, when a 'Yes' is demanded, to raise their heads and say 'No'!"

Dreyfus was present at the ceremony, despite the fierce campaign of hatred still being waged against him by royalists of the *Action Française*. What happened then was reported in detail in the Philadelphia *Ledger*.

Paris, June 4—Just at the close of the ceremonies attending the canonization of Émile Zola in the Panthéon today, when the President of France, the Premier and Ministers of State were taking their departure, Louis Anthehne Gregori, a military writer of note, fired two shots at Major Alfred Dreyfus, for whose liberty Zola had fought and won. Major Dreyfus was only slightly wounded in the forearm.

When the shots rang out there was intense excitement in fear that President Fallières had been assassinated, and the attempt on the life of Major Dreyfus created a profound impression. Soldiers speedily surrounded Gregori, and he was taken to jail, bruised and bleeding, with his clothes almost torn from his back.

The affair has created a tremendous impression in Paris, and the motive of the would-be assassin is the cause of much speculation. Gregori is no common fanatic, such as is carried away by the political passions of the moment, but he is a man of mature age, having been born in 1844, and was highly esteemed where he was known. His friends are at a loss to understand what induced him to commit such a foolhardy act, and many are disposed to question his statement that he simply shot as an individual in protest against the participation of the Army in the ceremonies attending the placing of the ashes of Zola in the Panthéon. . . .

Major Dreyfus was not seriously injured. A bullet entered his forearm, but did not injure the bone. At a late hour tonight the official statement was that his condition was favorable and that no complications are feared.

Gregori fired the first shot from behind Dreyfus, the ball penetrating the sleeve of his coat and burying itself in a flower pot at the base of the catafalque. When Dreyfus wheeled at the sound of the detonation he threw his left arm over his heart. The second shot was fired point-blank at his breast, the bullet entering the wrist and ranging upward. It was located this afternoon, but was not extracted.

Mathieu Dreyfus, brother of Major Dreyfus, who sprang forward to save him, chivalrously protected Gregori from the crowd which was raining blows with canes and umbrellas on the man, shouting, "It is not for us to punish. Let the law take its course."

Gregori made a statement to the police directly after his arrest, and during a second interrogatory tonight said: "I did not wish to kill Dreyfus. It is true that I aimed at him, but I only wanted to graze him. My object was to protest against the participation of the Army in the glorification of Zola and the rehabilitation of Dreyfus. My blow was aimed less at Dreyfus than at Dreyfusism."

Light from Germany: Schwartzkoppen Testifies Belatedly, 1930

"I was utterly amazed and indignant at these overtures!"

The Truth About Dreyfus, *from* The Schwartzkoppen Papers, *ed. Bernhard Schwertfeger (London and New York: Putnam, 1931), pp. 3–10. First published in Germany under the title:* Die Wahrheit über Dreyfus *(Berlin: Verlag für Kulturpolitik, 1930). By permission of G. P. Putnam Sons.*

Maximilian von Schwartzkoppen was said to be an honorable man. He was appalled by the tragedy, but he knew from the very beginning that Dreyfus was innocent. Had he spoken up in 1894, when he was repeatedly implored to confirm the guilt of Esterhazy, there would have been no Dreyfus case.

Schwartzkoppen was, indeed, an honorable man, but he was also a Military Attaché, and Military Attachés were a special breed with special duties and modes of behavior. They were expected to make themselves popular in the countries where they served, but never to forget the main purpose of their work—to keep their eyes and ears open and absorb every bit of military information they could obtain.

Schwartzkoppen came to Paris in 1891 and was there on duty when the Dreyfus case began. An able officer, he was well acquainted with every phase of the French Army system and regularly sent reports home to Berlin. His work brought him into contact with all kinds of characters, including traitors who were quite willing to sell military information. In this capacity he employed Esterhazy as a spy.

Once the case gathered momentum, Schwartzkoppen found it impossible to speak openly. He regarded his silence as officially imposed on him and he was distressed that he could not come forward in the cause of justice. His situation was extremely painful. "If I had been free to act as I would have wished, I certainly would have done so." But on examining things more closely, he decided not to mix in the matter because, in the given conditions, he would not have been believed anyway. "Moreover, diplomatic considerations opposed such an action." Schwartzkoppen felt that at the time the French Government "was in the process of taking the necessary measures to spread light and redress the injustice."

On November 15, 1897, at a time when Esterhazy was being denounced by Mathieu Dreyfus, Schwartzkoppen left his post and returned to Germany. In 1903 he wrote an account of his experiences in Paris in which he told the truth about Esterhazy, but it was not published at the time. In December 1916, while serving on the Russian front in World War I, he was gravely wounded. On his deathbed and in the presence of his wife, he proclaimed the innocence of Dreyfus. In 1930 his widow published his account under the title *Die Wahrheit über Dreyfus.*

Between three and four in the afternoon of July 20, 1894, the messenger in the military department of the German Embassy in Paris (Rue de Lille 78), August Burde, came in and told me that a Frenchman had come about his passport. This often happened; passports were then necessary for Alsace-Lorraine, and any French officer who wanted to go thither on leave had to have a permit from the *Statthalter's* (Governor's) office in Strassburg. Permits were often refused, and in those cases French officers would frequently come to the German Military Attaché to ask him to come to their assistance.

I told the messenger to let the caller come in, and in a few moments there entered a gentleman whom I recognized at once as a French officer in mufti. He seemed some 42 to 45 years old, and was of medium height and slightly built; he had drawn features, deep-set black eyes, a good head of greyish hair, and a strong moustache with streaks of grey in it. He had on a black overcoat, and was wearing the red stripe of the Legion of Honor in its buttonhole. As he came in he showed some embarrassment and nervousness; he looked gloomily round the room to make sure that I was alone.

I asked him what he wanted, and he represented himself to me as a French staff officer on active service, compelled by necessity to take a step which, he said, would make him contemptible in my eyes, but which he had carefully considered and had simply got to take, in order to save his wife and children from certain downfall and destruction. He had been unfortunate, had made unlucky speculations, and had been reduced to financial difficulties through his wife's illness. He had a small property near Châlons, and if he was to be able to keep this for his family he had got to get money in some way. He had tried every possible way to do this by straightforward and honorable means, but without success, and he had no recourse left but to offer his services to the German General Staff, in the hope that in this way he would before long be put in a position to meet his manifold obligations. He had given careful thought to it, and this was absolutely the only way out left to him; if it failed he must blow his brains out. The thought of his wife and children had kept him so far from doing this, although he could see perfectly well that it was really the right thing to do. He was in a very good position to render valuable service, as he had been for a considerable time in Algiers and was thoroughly familiar with military conditions there; he had also been stationed for a considerable time on the Italian frontier and had an exact knowledge of the frontier defenses; in 1881 and 1882 he had served in the Intelligence Department of the Ministry of War. He was a friend of Colonel Sandherr, Head of the Intelligence Department, and had been at school with President Casimir-Périer. He was also a friend of the Deputy Jules Roche, who had promised to make him an Assistant Chief of Staff if he, Roche, became Minister of War. At the moment he was on regimental service outside Paris, but he would soon be returning to Paris and would then resume his many connections with the Ministry of War. In a few days he would be attending important military exercises in camp at Châlons.

By way of evidence that he was already in possession of important information, he pulled out of his breast pocket a communication which he handed to me, asking me to read it.

I was utterly amazed and indignant at these overtures! A French staff officer on the active list unashamedly proposing to betray his country, and coolly asking a brother officer to arrange it for him!

I returned his document to him unread and told him that it was not for me to help an officer to swerve from the path of duty and honor; I could only advise him to abandon the idea, to go back and let me and himself forget the step which he had taken. He replied that he had given careful thought to the step he had taken, that he was well aware that in taking it he had brought himself down to the *canaille,* but that it was impossible for him now to turn back. If I rejected his offer he would try some other way of turning his knowledge to account, as by hook or by crook he must get money—and so on. I pointed out to him once more the enormity of his proposal and dismissed him, adding that in my position I was unable to entertain such suggestions. On that he took his leave, saying that he would return in a few days.

The day after this, July 21, I received a letter from this visitor, in which he wrote: "I am leaving very shortly on the journey I told you of" *—the journey to Châlons for firing practice. He added that owing to his family connections he could also give me important Russian news.

On July 22, 1894, I reported this meeting to the Intelligence Department in Berlin, and on July 26 I received instructions to negotiate further with the agent.

On July 27, in the evening, my visitor returned, coming unannounced into my office in the Embassy, and now introduced himself as Major Count Walsin-Esterhazy, commanding a battalion in the 74th Regiment of Infantry in Rouen. His wife was formerly a Mlle. de Nettancourt-Vaubecourt, and he was the owner of Dommartin, a country house near St. Ménéhould, in the Department of Marne. He was related to the families of Clermont-Tonnère and Banfrémont. In evidence of the accuracy of his statements he brought with him the Mobilization Instructions of the 74th Regiment, and he demanded a monthly remuneration of 2,000 francs. I tried once more to influence the Major and to show plainly to him the abominable nature of the thing he was doing. He insisted that he had reflected well on it, that he had had to do it, and that he would turn to some other quarter if I did not accept his offer.

In order to meet the desires of the Intelligence Department, I now proposed to the Major that he should get into direct touch with it, as I would have nothing to do with the business myself. He flatly rejected this suggestion, saying that business of this sort was only possible through

* *Je pars très prochainement pour le voyage dont je vous ai parlé.*

personal contact, and that to bring in any third party was dangerous. There was no danger whatever in having direct relations with me, as no one would think him capable of doing anything of this sort. He would only come to me at the Embassy, which could be done without attracting any notice, as so many people went in and out of the Embassy. I dismissed the Major telling him that I could not enter into his proposal and begged him once more to abandon his idea. He went, leaving behind the Mobilization Instructions and saying that he would take the book away shortly and would call on me again.

I felt it my duty to discuss the whole affair with the Head of the Intelligence Department or the Chief of Staff. I submitted this proposal and was informed that the Head of the Intelligence Department was on leave at Michelstadt, in the Odenwald, where I could meet him. I went there on August 3, 1894, and on the 4th I had the desired discussion with Major Müller, Head of the Intelligence Department. The upshot was that I was advised to enter into relations with this apparent source of very valuable information, if proof were forthcoming that communications of real value might be expected. Relations were, however, to be broken off at once the moment the reverse became evident. No definite monthly payment could be held out. The assessment of the value of the communications must be left to me.

With these instructions I returned to Paris on August 6; there I found a letter from Esterhazy, in which he gave me the following addresses: "Until August 10, Staff of the 3rd Artillery Brigade, in camp at Châlons; from the 10th to the 12th in the country, Château de Dommartin, par St. Ménéhould, Marne; after that, at my usual residence, which you will find in the *Annuaire*." *

On August 13 Esterhazy called on me again at my office in the Embassy, at 10 p.m. I repeated once more my unwillingness to enter into his proposal, pointed out to him the dangers which it involved for him and for me, gave him back the Mobilization Instructions, saying that they contained no information of importance to me, and advised him to break off the negotiations, as, I said, I was unable for my part to see any prospect of advantage from this very dangerous undertaking. Esterhazy tried once more to make plain to me that he was in a position to procure for me documents of the utmost importance, and that this was possible without any sort of risk for him and me, and said he could bring me the newly revised General Instructions for the Artillery on Mobilization. This document he brought on August 15. A rapid glance through this satisfied me of its value, and I felt bound to acquire this

---

* *Jusqu'au 10.8, état-major de la 3ième brigade d'artillerie, camp de Châlons; du 10 au 12 à la campagne, Château de Dommartin, par St.-Ménéhould, Marne; ensuite à ma résidence habituelle, que vous trouvez dans l'Annuaire.*

document for the General Staff, especially as I had several times been requested to procure detailed information as to the mobilization of the Artillery. Esterhazy received 1,000 francs [forty pounds] from me, and assured me of his intention to bring me further interesting information in a few days' time.

I had thus taken the critical step, well aware of the heavy responsibility which I was placing on my shoulders. I did it in the belief that I was bound so to act in the interest of my Army; but I was perfectly well aware that in doing so I was running the greatest danger of losing my position and that as a Prussian officer I might find myself in a very unpleasant situation!

Schwartzkoppen's Widow Sends Dreyfus a Copy of Her Husband's Memoirs

"I believe that I do this in the spirit of my husband . . ."

Quoted in Nicholas Halasz, Captain Dreyfus: The Story of a Mass Hysteria *(New York: Simon and Schuster, 1955), p. 267. By permission of Simon and Schuster.*

On June 1, 1930, Dreyfus received a letter from Hanover, Germany, signed by Louise von Schwartzkoppen, née Baronne von Wedel.

Much esteemed *Monsieur* Dreyfus: I am mailing you under separate cover the diary of my late husband, General of the Infantry Max von Schwartzkoppen, published by Colonel Schwertfeger, and called *The Truth About Dreyfus.*

I believe that I do this in the spirit of my husband whose wish has always been to testify in the monstrous trial of which you were the central figure and victim. For reasons that his memoirs clearly indicate, this was impossible for him to do.

Dreyfus Comments on Schwartzkoppen's Revelations

"Only it is deeply regrettable. . . ."

L'Oeuvre, *June 24, 1930. Translated by the editor.*

After reading Schwartzkoppen's memoirs and the reviews in the press, Dreyfus sent the following letter to the editor of *L'Oeuvre* on June 24, 1930.

With not a little excitement I have been reading the notebooks of Schwartzkoppen in *L'Oeuvre*. They have made me feel once more with excruciating intensity that physical moral pain which has not been lightened during the past years.

The notebooks are very arresting, and I am thankful to *L'Oeuvre* for publishing them. They substantiate irrefutably the facts that were brought out in the trial at the Court of Cassation and that led to the revision of 1906.

General von Schwartzkoppen has shown himself to be a man of honor, in that he revealed everything that he knew. Only it is deeply regrettable that he did not reveal it at a time when he knew that a violation of justice was being done.

The Death of Alfred Dreyfus, July 11, 1935

"It is understood that it was his wish to be buried with the same simplicity."

New York Herald-Tribune, *July 13, 1935.*

Following his rehabilitation, Captain Dreyfus was promoted to major and assigned to an artillery regiment in Vincennes. After two years of service he was retired into the reserves. He settled down to a quiet family life in an effort to throw off the effects of the privations on Devil's Island.

Dreyfus was in Switzerland in the summer of 1914 when he heard of the mobilization preceding the outbreak of World War I. He immediately returned to active service and served in the northern zones of the fortifications of Paris, as well as in two of the bloodiest battles of the war—Chemin des Dames and Verdun. In September 1918 he was promoted to lieutenant-colonel.

After the war he led a cloistered life. A rare venture into the limelight came when he accepted membership on a committee of French intellectuals who drew up a petition and forwarded it to officials in Massachusetts on behalf of Sacco and Vanzetti.

General Picquart became Minister of War in 1908 in Clemenceau's cabinet. On January 18, 1914, he fell from his horse and injured his skull. The injury did not seem to be serious. The next day he worked as usual, only to collapse and die at his desk in the afternoon.

Mathieu Dreyfus, broken-hearted by the death of his son in World War I, died in 1930.

Alfred Dreyfus, after a long illness, died quietly in bed on July 11, 1935.

Paris, July 13. Colonel Alfred Dreyfus, whose indictment in 1894 on a charge of espionage against France gave rise to the famous Dreyfus Affair and split France into two camps causing a violent conflict between Liberals and anti-Semites, died at 5 o'clock this afternoon at his home on a quiet Paris street. He was seventy-five years old.

Colonel Dreyfus had been in infirm health for many months. He died peacefully, surrounded by his family—Mme. Dreyfus, who never abandoned him during his long years of hardship including his servitude on Devil's Island, his son Pierre, and his daughter.

The date for the funeral has not yet been set, but only members of the family and the colonel's close relatives will be present.

Ever since 1906, when Colonel Dreyfus was rehabilitated by tribunal and public opinion, returned to the Army with higher rank and received the Legion of Honor, he had lived in retirement, avoiding all publicity. It is understood that it was his wish to be buried with the same simplicity.

Dreyfus was granted that last wish. The following brief report in *The New York Times,* July 17, 1935, described the funeral:

Paris, July 14. Lieutenant-Colonel Alfred Dreyfus was buried today, the national holiday of the Republic. The funeral of the leading figure of the famous spy case of forty-one years ago was strictly private, by his own wish. Only relatives attended the services, which took place in the Montparnasse Jewish cemetery. Colonel Dreyfus died on Friday at the age of seventy-five after a long illness.

THE LAST PHASE OF THE DREYFUS CASE
Justice takes Dreyfus into her chariot. (*Amsterdammer*)

THE FATE OF DU PATY DE CLAM
France: "A stone has been rolled off my heart now that this fellow has been swept out."
(*Nebelspalter,* Zürich)

"À Mort!"—1895—Dreyfus—"Vive!"—1899 (*Evening Post*, San Francisco)

TOWARD FREEDOM

Madame la République: "Welcome, *M. le Capitaine.* Let me hope that I may soon return you your sword." (*Punch,* London, June 21, 1899)

THE REHABILITATION CEREMONY, JULY 20, 1906 (*Bibliothèque Nationale*)

GREETINGS FOLLOWING THE CEREMONY OF REHABILITATION, JULY 20, 1906 (*Bibliothèque Nationale*)

DREYFUS IN WORLD WAR I
Dreyfus served with distinction in the battles
of Verdun and Chemin des Dames. In early
1918, in conformance with an order affecting
the age limit for officers, he was sent to the
rear. On September 5, 1918, he was promoted
to Lieutenant-Colonel. (*Bibliothèque Nationale*)

ALFRED AND LUCIE DREYFUS IN 1930 (Pierre Dreyfus, Paris)

DREYFUS IN 1934 AT THE AGE OF 75
He died on July 11, 1935. (*Bibliothèque Nationale*)

XII

The Dreyfus Case in History

Few cases in the history of espionage have received as much attention as that of Dreyfus. It has been a never-ending source of fascination for the public and for scholars. In the words of Marcel Thomas: "The drama of the individual crushed—without understanding why or how—by the indifferent wheels of a well-oiled machine that must be destroyed in order to be stopped, is doubtless not without relevance."

The Dreyfus Case—A Conspiracy?

The Dreyfus Affair was a kind of morality play, a drama having as its cast the entire French people. It stimulated an examination of the structure of French democracy. Was it fair that the rights of one lone individual should prevail over the security of all the people? What was the meaning of justice? What about national honor?

The case was critically important not only for France but for the entire world. In essence, it was a struggle between differing ideas about the rôle of the military in a modern democracy. It also revealed how secret files could be used unfairly against an unpopular Army officer. In addition, it showed the extent of anti-Semitism in French society.

Most impressive of all was the moral fervor of those men—Zola, Clemenceau, Picquart—who took it upon themselves to guard the good name of France. It was said that some opposed the most powerful of kings, but few have been able to face the mob crying for revenge. There was baseness in this case, but there was also heroism of an unusual kind. Intellectuals sensitive to the nature of honor in society came to the aid of the lonely Dreyfus on Devil's Island. Because of them a gross miscarriage of justice was finally corrected. But most of all they removed a stain from the good name of their country.

In itself, the Dreyfus case appeared to be but a small incident in history, but in reality it was a major event in the triumph of justice. The case had its martyrs, its crimes, its sad beauty. Now a part of history, it has become a legend in the annals of justice won against great odds.

Historians, journalists, history buffs, all have been fascinated by the ordeal of Dreyfus and its aftermath. The story has been interpreted in different ways by observers.

Hans Kohn saw the Dreyfus Affair as taking place against a background of antagonisms which divided France since the Revolution and which foreshadowed the critical tensions of the twentieth century. An increasing number of intellectuals explained the French Revolution and every other "evil" as the work of Freemasons, Protestants, and Jews. From there it was only a short step to the creation of a "great Jewish conspiracy" against France.

The Dreyfus case, Kohn pointed out, emerged in this framework. The issue at stake went far beyond the fate of the Jewish officer himself. It led to the most vigorous debate conducted anywhere about the nature of modern society, the claims of established authority and national interest against the rights of the individual, and the objectivity of justice. Against the position of national interest maintained by the Army, the Dreyfusards, originally fighting for objective truth and justice, were successful in rallying the anti-clerical, anti-militarist, and anti-monarchist sentiments of the French liberal tradition.

Added to this interpretation is that of J. Salwyn Schapiro, who sees the famous case in much the same light. Superficially, says Schapiro, the Dreyfus case was a detective story on a national scale, but it really marked an important epoch in the history of the Third French Republic. Royalism had been so discredited by the Boulanger fiasco that its influence in the public life of the nation rapidly declined. But the Army, sworn to defend the Republic, was officered by Royalists and members of the upper class. In the Army, reasons Schapiro, lay the one hope of the enemies of the Republic, who, at a propitious moment, were prepared to restore the monarchy. The outcome of the Dreyfus case asserted once again the supremacy of the civil power, and the Army was forced humbly to acknowledge its subordinate position in the Republic. As soon as the Army was republicanized, all hope for the restoration of the monarchy disappeared.

To Hannah Arendt, not the Dreyfus Case but the Affair in its entirety offers a forecast for the twentieth century and its special brand of totalitarianism. She sees the Dreyfus Affair, in its broader political aspects, as belonging to the twentieth century, while the Dreyfus *case* was quite typical of the nineteenth century. It is characteristic of that period, she believes, that a miscarriage of justice could arouse such political passions. The idea of equality before the law was so deeply entrenched in the conscience of the civilized world that a single miscarriage of justice could provoke indignation throughout the world.

In Arendt's view, the *dramatis personae* of the case might have stepped directly out of the pages of Balzac. She is not especially impressed with the figure of Dreyfus: she describes him as actually a *"parvenu,"* who continually boasted to his colleagues about his family fortune which he spent on women. She praises Picquart for his calm, clear-eyed, and slightly ironical honesty. To her the adventurer Esterhazy was so utterly bored by his bourgeois world that he attempted to find relief equally in heroism and knavery.

In its anti-Semitic aspects, Arendt sees the Dreyfus case as being a prelude to Nazism, a tendency played over the entire European stage. Anti-Semitism at the time was not a new phenomenon. What was new and surprising, says Arendt, was the organization of the mob and the hero-worship enjoyed by its leaders. The mob became the direct agent of a "concrete" French nationalism. Barrès, Maurras, and Daudet, apostles of French nationalism, despised the people but saw in the mob a living expression of virile and primitive strength. They were the philosophers of pessimism who delighted in doom—and whose ideas presented the first sign of the coming collapse of the European intelligentsia.

To Nicholas Halasz, author of a best-seller on the case, the Dreyfus case was the story of a "mass hysteria." It began, he says, as a morality play that was to achieve a grandeur unparalleled in the history of modern France and make France examine "in fire and in fear the bedrock upon which democracy is founded." It was a struggle between those who believed in the sanctity of the individual, a noble ideal, and those who as a practical matter opposed the sacrifice of the whole for the minutest part. "Is the moral vindication of one Frenchman worth jeopardizing the security of all Frenchmen?"

In facing that question, Halasz says, France, the nation of reason, went out of her mind. Those who had faith in the State and its Army went into paroxyms over any act that reflected on it. Those who protested against the infallibility of military courts were considered to be traitors. For a time the nation sided with a lie and declared it to be the only truth. The fact that the truth was discovered soon after the nation had accepted the lie made no difference—the lie had to be continued to be accepted.

Halasz uses the term "Dreyfusian revolution" to describe the unrest which from 1898 onward almost brought public and private life in France to a standstill. There were meetings, demonstrations, brawls, debates; families and friendships broke up forever; new human relations were formed. The life of the individual ceased to be of any consequence. He could be sacrificed without hesitation for the cause of truth and justice. Scores of duels were fought between former friends because of the Affair. There was a devastating battle of pamphlets. In this atmosphere "truth had a thorny path to travel."

To Jacques Kayser, a French newspaperman active in politics as secretary-general of the Radical-Socialist Party, the Affair was "an Army-Church conspiracy." Although it demonstrated the strength of anti-Semitism, the case in his view was something more than "the great Jewish conspiracy to deliver France to the enemy," but rather a most momentous political battle of the reactionary Right against the Republic.

Jacques Kayser on the Dreyfus Affair

"... the most momentous political battle ..."

Jacques Kayser, The Dreyfus Affair, *trans. Nora Bickley (New York: Covici-Friede, 1931), pp. 7–11. Reprinted by permission of Crown Publishers, Inc.*

The Dreyfus Affair is something more than a trial of exceptional character. Through its reactions on politics, both national and international, it constitutes an important chapter in the history of France.

Twenty-four years after the foundation of the Third Republic it let loose a flood of events which placed the new order for a moment in jeopardy; but by the final triumph of justice, which was the triumph of all who had the Republic truly at heart, that order was placed on a surer basis.

Child of defeat on the field of battle, the Third Republic enthroned itself on the ruins of the Empire, and reaped advantage from its unpopularity. But France as a whole was not yet ripe for republican ideas. The Republic was accepted by many as an arrangement merely transitional, and its infancy was passed in an atmosphere of latent hostility. Its enemies were in the majority, but the liquidation of the war of 1870, the events of the Commune, the necessities imposed by a drastic peace treaty, and the resolute effort of reconstruction drove political differences for the time being into the background.

If those who desired the restoration of the Empire were only a handful, there were vast numbers who desired the restoration of the monarchy. But they were divided on the question of who should be the future king of France, and their division was the Republic's opportunity.

Placed at the head of the executive, Thiers ruled as a republican; but it was his opinion that the Republic must be conservative or cease to be, and events seemed to justify him.

Indeed, when the popularly elected National Assembly was called upon to pass judgment on the new constitutional laws which were deemed necessary for France, and to decide on the form of government, there was a majority of one vote, and of one only, in favor of republicanism. In other words the Third French Republic, established under such conditions, was firmly bound in the chains which its origin and the compromise resulting from that first vote imposed on it, and had eventually to free itself from them.

The Republic was thus insecure. The clumsiness and violence of the President, Marshal MacMahon, who on 16th May 1877, attempted a sort of *coup d'état* against the Chamber of Deputies, were necessary to confirm it.

That bid for personal power fused the Republicans into unity and established the parliamentary régime which, by its system of direct representation, became the organ of the will of the people.

The Republic had tottered. Once victorious, it gathered strength and became the rallying point of the forces of France. The Republic was governed by republicans for republicans. Important legislative measures gave concrete expression to the desire and need of reform in every direction.

The Republic struck deep roots in the country. At every election the republican majority increased. The parties in opposition were crumbling. Since the death of the Prince Imperial the Bonapartists had been reduced to silence. The monarchists, divided among themselves and incapable of effective action, made but a show of interference. The Right was no longer led by the enemies of the régime but by those who asserted, as Thiers had done, that the Republic ought to remain conservative, and their influence, feeble in politics, was only effective in public life, among the middle classes, and in the world of finance. The Left, on the other hand, was active and of growing power in the country. It asserted its pretensions and its rights and proclaimed its faith in a Republic boldly radical.

Meanwhile the stability of France was subjected to influences and rivalries which put it in constant peril. A nationalist movement took shape, a protest against the policy of carrying out the Treaty of Versailles in 1871. The younger generation was ready for mischief. The League of Patriots, whose object was to foment the spirit of militarism and disseminate the cult of Vengeance, intensified its propaganda and worked up a dangerous agitation. General Boulanger, the Minister for War, by pandering to the passions of the chauvinists and playing the demagogue, gained no little popularity. An incident on the Franco-German frontier (the Schnaebele affair) made the situation more acute. The position of Boulanger, the "general of the *Revanche*," was strengthened by it, and demonstrations in his support were organized up and down a country seething with excitement.

In Parliament parties were in confusion. The Government, in despair, tried to discover a basis of agreement and tentatively initiated a policy of pacification. But a new crisis arose, the result of a scandal in which the son-in-law of the President of the Republic was implicated. It had to do with the sale of honors; the malcontents made the most of it; and it ended in the resignation of President Grévy.

"The Republic," it was said, "is the rule of nepotism and corruption." To the diatribes of the press was added the clamor of public meetings; and all the energy, skill, and integrity of the new republican leaders were needed to stand firm against this double attack, now consolidated into one, of the Nationalists and the Boulangists.

At last, however, it seemed that the Republic, which had gained strength at the new elections, was really on the point of inaugurating an era of peace and victorious prosperity. But a fresh scandal shook the régime to its foundations. This was the Panama affair, a case of corruption in which a large number of members of Parliament were involved and compromised. What a weapon this placed in the hands of those whose dream it was to destroy the Republic, and who accused the Government of complicity in dubious undertakings, may easily be imagined. But by now the new order had struck deep roots in the soil of the country, and this perilous ordeal served as a touchstone of the soundness of its institutions.

Nevertheless, this was a time of increasing social trouble. The first great strikes were coincident with the growth of the Socialist party which Jaurès was leading into battle. From the benches of Parliament and from the columns of the press the militants sent forth their rallying cry, and the swollen ranks of their effectives became a force in the Opposition.

Besides these concerted movements, the individual acts of anarchists spread terror through Paris. To draw attention to social injustice by shocking public opinion they multiplied their outrages, and devoted themselves to direct propaganda by deed. The assassination of the President of the Republic, Sadi-Carnot, was the culmination of their efforts, which were carried on to the accompaniment of the cry, "Society is rotten."

Thus at the beginning of 1894 the situation was fraught with trouble. The Republic was in being; it had gained strength. But morally it was compromised and the balance of parties was difficult to maintain. The Government could introduce no measure of reform which did not dissatisfy its supporters, and found itself driven to a policy of conflict. The union of republicans which had been formed in the hour of danger existed no longer. The Socialists, the vanguard of democracy, fought no longer for the Republic and were intent only on the defense of their own obvious class interests.

A reactionary nationalist movement was taking shape, directed at once outwards against the foreigner, and especially against Germany, and inwards against the Jew, represented as a profiteer and the agent of the foreigner, and the Socialist as the creator of disorder. The Army seemed to be the citadel of order. Its head, General Mercier, was obsessed by the transient glory of Boulanger and dreamed of popularity. The two great forces of resistance to democratic progress were the Church and the Army. They were in direct collusion. The generals and the bishops were leagued in their determination to thwart the work of republican action. They were in a communion of hatred against Liberalism and the Jews. Beneath their common preoccupations were manifest the unwearying efforts of the Jesuits, those implacable and irreconcilable enemies of modern and republican ideas.

With the Republicans at loggerheads and public opinion in a state of flux, troubled and at a loss, the Army and the clergy believed that the moment had come to launch a great offensive, hoping thereby to regain their grip on the country, which since 1870, and more especially since 1878, they had let slip from their control.

A case of treason gave them the opportunity which they sought; and the Dreyfus Affair was therefore no mere case for the Courts—"the great Jewish conspiracy to deliver France to the enemy"—but the most momentous political battle which the reactionary and clerical parties of the Right, in full panoply and at full strength and aided by all their technical resources have waged against the Republic.

Index

ABOUT THE AUTHOR

LOUIS L. SNYDER is professor of history at The City College and City University of New York, where he has taught since 1933. A graduate of St. John's College, Annapolis, Dr. Snyder studied at the University of Frankfurt-am-Main, Germany, where he received his Ph.D. in 1931. During this time he was a German-American Exchange Fellow and Alexander von Humboldt Foundation Fellow, appointed by the government of the Weimar Republic. He held the Schiff Fellowship in Political Science at Columbia University, 1931–1932. An Air Force officer during World War II, Dr. Snyder previously acted as a consultant for the Psychological Warfare Branch of the War Department. He received a Ford Foundation faculty fellowship in 1952, and in 1965 was awarded a Rockefeller Foundation grant for study in Amsterdam. In the summer of 1972 he was invited back to Germany by the Humboldt Foundation to visit 12 universities as its guest. He has written numerous books, including *The Meaning of Nationalism; Documents of German History; The Making of Modern Man: Western Civilization Since 1500; The Blood and Iron Chancellor: A Documentary-Biography of Otto von Bismarck;* and *Frederick the Great.* He is the general editor of Van Nostrand's Anvil paperbacks in history with 115 volumes in print.

The text of this book was set in Baskerville Lino-
type and printed by offset on P & S Special Book
manufactured by P. H. Glatfelter Co., Spring
Grove, Pa. Composed, printed and bound by
Quinn & Boden Company, Inc., Rahway, N.J.

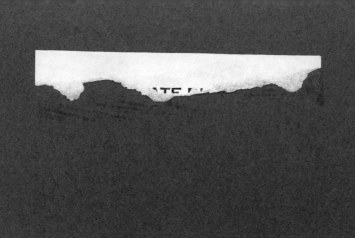